BUILDING CULTURE
IN EARLY QING YANGZHOU

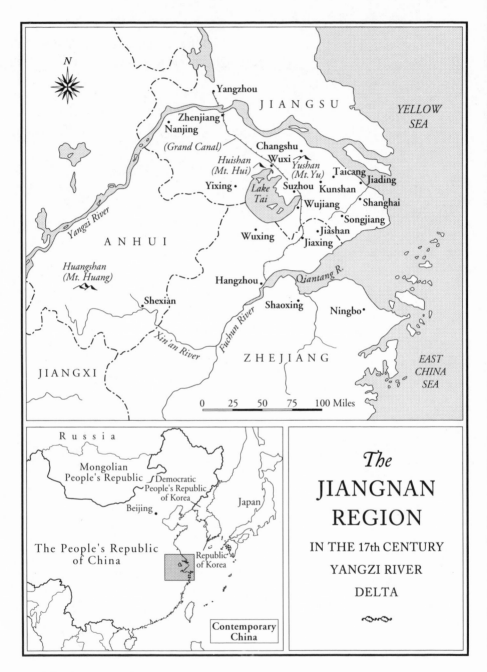

The Jiangnan region

The JIANGNAN REGION

IN THE 17th CENTURY

YANGZI RIVER

DELTA

Building Culture
in Early Qing Yangzhou

Tobie Meyer-Fong

STANFORD UNIVERSITY PRESS

STANFORD, CALIFORNIA 2003

Stanford University Press
Stanford, California

Page 13: Du Mu, "Getting Something Off My Mind," from *An Anthology of Chinese Literature: Beginnings to 1911,* by Stephen Owen, Editor & Translator, Copyright 1996 by Stephen Owen and The Council for Cultural Planning and Development of the Executive Yuan of the Republic of China. Used by permission of W. W. Norton & Company, Inc.

Publication of this book was partially underwritten by a grant from the Chiang Ching-kuo Foundation for International Scholarly Exchange (USA).

Library of Congress Cataloging-in-Publication Data

    Meyer-Fong, Tobie S. (Tobie Sarah)
        Building culture in early Qing Yangzhou / Tobie Meyer-Fong.
            p.   cm.
    Includes bibliographical references and index.
    ISBN 0-8047-4485-8 (alk. paper)
        1. Yangzhou (Jiangsu Sheng, China)—Civilization.   2. China—
    Civilization—1644–1912.   I. Title.
    DS797.56.Y374 M49   2003
    951'.136—dc21

                                                                    2002153634

Original Printing 2003

Last figure below indicates year of this printing:
12   11   10   09   08   07   06   05   04   03

Designed by Eleanor P. Mennick
Typeset by Integrated Composition Systems in 10/12.5 Sabon

For Hal and Van

Contents

List of Illustrations

Abbreviations

ECCP   Arthur Hummel. *Eminent Chinese of the Ch'ing Period.* Washington, D.C.: U.S. Government Printing Office, 1943.

LHYFZ   Xie Kaichong. *Lianghuai yanfa zhi.* Kangxi edition. Reprinted in Wu Xiangxiang, *Zhongguo shixue congshu.* Taipei: Xuesheng shuju, 1966.

WSZNP   Wang Shizhen. *Wang Shizhen nianpu fu Wang Shilu nianpu.* Beijing: Zhonghua shuju, 1992.

YZFZ, 1605   Yang Xun, ed. *Yangzhou fuzhi,* 1605.

YZFZ, 1664   Lei Yingyuan, ed. *Yangzhou fuzhi,* 1664. Reprinted in *Xijian Zhongguo difangzhi huikan,* vol. 13. Beijing: Zhongguo shudian, 1992.

YZFZ, 1675   Jin Zhen, ed. *Yangzhou fuzhi,* 1675.

YZFZ, 1733   Yin Huiyi, ed. *Yangzhou fuzhi,* 1733.

YZFZ, 1810   A-ke-dang-a and Yao Wentian, eds. *Yangzhou fuzhi,* 1810. Reprint, Taipei: Chengwen, 1974.

YZFZ, 1874   Yingjie, ed. *Xu Yangzhou fuzhi,* 1874.

YZHFL   Li Dou. *Yangzhou huafang lu.* Circa 1795. Reprint, Yangzhou: Guangling guji keyinshe, 1984.

Acknowledgments

This book, like the buildings and writings it takes as its subject matter, is the product of an extensive and supportive social network. It also carries within it memories of months spent sojourning away from home and days spent touring scenic sites with friends. These acknowledgments, like a travel essay or a stele, allow me to express my thanks publicly to the many people who contributed to its creation.

I continue to be grateful to two wonderful mentors, whose patience, generosity, wisdom, and humor made it possible for me to write this book. They showed me that learning could be about community and conversations, as well as Qing documents and graduate seminars. They also taught me (by example) that graduate students are a lifelong responsibility. Even retired, Harold Kahn has provided an extended warranty on my education far more comprehensive than any automobile company would dare to offer, and Lyman Van Slyke still generously shares wise words that work in all manner of situations. This book is dedicated to them.

I am grateful to Professor Jonathan Spence, who introduced me to Chinese history as an undergraduate, and to Albert Dien, James Ketelaar, Ellen Neskar, and P. J. Ivanhoe, who made invaluable contributions to my education at Stanford. I am also deeply grateful to the Chinese and Japanese language teachers at Yale, Stanford, Middlebury, and in Taiwan, whose instruction provided the fundamentals that made this book possible. They taught me to read in new languages and to think in new ways. The University Fellowship Program, the F.L.A.S. Program, the Mellon Foundation, and the Weter Foundation provided generous financial support during my years at Stanford.

Susan Naquin, Timothy Brook, and Jerry Dennerline read and commented on the manuscript, the latter two as readers for Stanford University Press. Nixi Cura, Angus Lockyer, Steven Miles, Jordan Sand, Elizabeth Morrison, Brian Platt, Roger Meyer, Michael Chang, and Robert DeCaroli critiqued various incarnations of individual chapters. Philip Kafalas has shared adventures in classical Chinese from Stanford to Washington, answering my many questions with humor and patience. Extra special thanks go to my classmate and friend Max K'o-wu Huang, who shared the Stanford experience and checked most of the prose translations, and to one-time Washington sojourner Anna Shields, who commented on several of the poetry translations. Reiko Shinno checked the transliteration of Japanese names and titles. With the help and insight of these careful readers and reviewers, there are far fewer mistakes in this book than there might have been. Responsibility for the remaining errors is mine exclusively.

Janet Theiss has been the best critic, friend, and partner in ideas that a historian could ask for, and the book reflects her incisive comments on practically every page. I am grateful to Dorothy Ko and Susan Mann for their inspiration, which kept me in Qing history, and to William T. Rowe for his comments, encouragement, and excellent collegiality. Jonathan Hay generously provided crucial suggestions in many very productive conversations. Qianshen Bai, Jonathan Chaves, Andrew Hsieh, Hajime Nakatani, Stephen Shutt, Lynn Struve, Ellen Widmer, and Judith Zeitlin offered guidance, asked and answered difficult questions, and supplied references. Antonia Finnane kindly shared her expert knowledge of Yangzhou and its socioeconomic history. Sheila Meyer rescued the photography and graphics from me, and David Hogge was the guardian angel for Asian language computing.

A grant from the American Council of Learned Societies / Chiang Ching-kuo Foundation funded six formative months at the Institute for Oriental Culture, Tokyo University. I would like to thank professors Hamashita Takeshi, Kishimoto Mio, and Oki Yasushi for making my stay in Tokyo a great intellectual adventure. Their advice and insights continue to shape my work. Professors Aoki Atsushi, Shiroyama (Sazanami) Tomoko, and Karasawa Yasuhiko generously shared their time and knowledge of Japanese sinology—often over good food and in unforgettable settings. Professor Ono Kazuko and her teacher, the late Shimada Kenji, introduced materials in Kyoto, most memorably the printing blocks from the *Pingshantang tuzhi* in the Kyoto University Library. Many thanks to the generous and ever-patient staff of the Tōyō bunka kenkyūjo library, as well as to the librarians at the Tōyō bunko, Naikaku bunko, Kyoto University, and Tokyo Metropolitan libraries.

A grant from the Committee for Scholarly Communication with China supported me during a year of research in Nanjing and Yangzhou. I would like to thank Professor Fan Jinmin of the Nanjing University History Department for guidance, and Zhou Tongke, who taught me to read poetry and proved that a literati aesthetic lives on in Nanjing. Ms. Shi Yang, a graduate student at Nanjing University, provided research assis-

tance, while Mary Buck Young provided excellent company. Bian Xiao-
xuan, Professor Emeritus of Literature at Nanjing University and Yangzhou native, generously offered learned comments on local culture, history, and sources. Jiang Yin of the Chinese Academy of Social Sciences in
Beijing, whom I met by marvelous coincidence in Yangzhou, introduced
me to the works of Zhang Chao and shared his own writings on Wang
Shizhen and Hou Fangyu. Numerous Yangzhou scholars contributed to
this project. In particular, I would like to thank Xue Feng, Zhu Jiang, Zhu
Zongzhou, Song Minli, and Zhao Weihang for their suggestions and for
sharing their infectious enthusiasm for Yangzhou history. I am deeply
grateful to He Qingxian and Shi Mei of the Nanjing University Library,
Division of Ancient Books, and to Ni Youchun and Zhang Linhua of the
Foreign Students' and Scholars' Reading Room at Nanjing University for
their advice, research suggestions, and friendship. I would also like to rec-
ognize the contributions of staff members at the Nanjing Library, the
Yangzhou Library, the Shanghai Library, the Palace Museum (Beijing), the
Beijing Library (Beihai Branch), and the Department of Painting and
Calligraphy at the Palace Museum in Taipei.

I am very grateful to Dr. Mi Chu Wiens and the staff of the Asian
Reading Room at the Library of Congress in Washington. It has been a
privilege and a pleasure to use the collection and the reading room on
a regular basis. I am also deeply indebted to the Sackler-Freer Gallery
Library at the Smithsonian Institution, which has been both a friendly
haven and an important resource. At Stanford University Press, I am
grateful to Janna Palliser, Judith Hibbard, Sumathi Raghavan, Sally
Serafim, Caroline Casey, and especially Muriel Bell, for nurturing the
manuscript through to publication. Thanks are also owed to the colleagues, classmates, students, and friends at (and around) Stanford,
George Mason, and Johns Hopkins universities who created social and
intellectual circles that made working, and playing, in California and in
the Metropolitan D.C. area a pleasure.

Most of all, though, I am grateful to an exceptionally involved and
supportive family—my sisters, Stephanie and Jessica Meyer; my parents,
Roger and Sheila Meyer; my parents-in-law, Chang-Ching and Yueh-Kam
Fong; and my husband, Ming-Yuen Meyer-Fong—for their unflagging
love and encouragement.

BUILDING CULTURE
IN EARLY QING YANGZHOU

1   *Rebuilding Yangzhou*

Seeing Yangzhou

    Yangzhou today is a city of ersatz memories of a time of splendor, the eighteenth century. Images of fabulously wealthy salt merchants, luxurious gardens, and touring emperors dominate our understanding of the city's past and have inspired recent efforts to reconstruct the city's tourist sites. Today, scholars and tourists alike are captivated by the glamorous world portrayed in the ubiquitous *Record of the Painted Boats of Yangzhou* (Yangzhou huafang lu), a late eighteenth-century account of the city's gardens, temples, restaurants, artists, and courtesans. Re-creations based on eighteenth-century models surround today's tourists: reproductions of eighteenth-century gardens line Slender West Lake; murals depicting scenes from the *Record of the Painted Boats of Yangzhou* adorn the walls of a memorial hall paying tribute to the renowned eighteenth-century eccentric painters, ostentatiously adorned tour boats ply the "Imperial Route" to Pingshan Hall; restaurants serve meals touted as "fit for the Qianlong emperor"; and a man costumed as the Qianlong emperor watches the annual dragon boat races from a barge, accompanied by a bevy of "palace ladies."

    As a glittering model for current commercial aspirations, the High Qing has overwhelmed the dynasty's rocky beginnings. Less glamorous, and too ambivalent to be marketable, the seventeenth-century legacy remains largely forgotten. The seventeenth century was a problematic period, complicated by the destructive event of conquest and the complex ambiguities of recovery. Although the moment of Yangzhou's fall to the Qing in 1645 remains a key event in the narrative of Chinese nationalism, the rest of the century remains largely overlooked. Today, few references to the late seventeenth century interrupt the tourists' eighteenth-century idyll. One exception comes to mind: a memorial that honors Shi Kefa

(d. 1645), the loyalist Grand Secretary whose stubborn refusal to admit the Qing army to the city led to the massacre of its inhabitants. Honored by the eighteenth-century emperor whose forebears sacked the city, Shi Kefa is celebrated today as a patriot, and retellings of his valiant last stand have incorporated the mythologizing rhetoric of revolutionary nationalism. The massacre at Yangzhou in 1645 is familiar to every schoolchild in China. But what happened in the city between the arrival of the Qing army and the golden age of the Qianlong period (1736–96) is unmentioned, and is thus familiar to no one.

Part of the problem is the lack of obvious sources detailing the city's late seventeenth-century transition from destruction to prosperity. Evidence exists, but is scattered in the local histories, enigmatically buried in the biographies of philanthropists, defeated generals, and chaste women—or in references to the reconstruction of famous buildings. Other sources, including poetry and literary essays, are not only scattered but difficult to read. These problems of sourcing have contributed to the relative neglect of late seventeenth-century Yangzhou, though they certainly are not insurmountable. In addition, the period in which Yangzhou recovered from the Qing conquest (from approximately 1645 to 1700) lies outside the purview of contemporary Western historiography of the Qing. Until recently, most research on the early Qing has concentrated either on the military and institutional aspects of the conquest or on the issue of loyalty to the Ming regime. Otherwise, American scholars, like their Chinese counterparts, have chosen to study the "High Qing" of the eighteenth century or (in an earlier generation) the disastrous years of the mid-nineteenth century.

This book is a study of a place, Yangzhou, as it was, and as it was imagined to have been, mostly during a period lasting from about 1645 to 1700. I do not intend it as a comprehensive exploration of urban society and institutions, nor as a definitive general history of the city. Instead, I intend to study the demarcation of space through personality, fame, and writing and the use of historical reference to describe and define contemporary elite identities. In it, I focus on the values associated with the physical construction and symbolic meanings of buildings during the decades that followed the Qing conquest. Thus, this project is about one kind of recovery, the reassembling in the latter half of the seventeenth century of the sites and sensibilities that were meant to mark the distinctiveness and resilience of an elite community. It is about place and memory, at a time when imagined architecture was more important than wood and walls. In a larger sense, it is a study of the effects of catastrophe on a society and the rapid cultural reactions that respond to rupture and loss. In a smaller sense, it is about the creation of a sense of connection among local elites, travelers, officials, and refugees in the city of Yangzhou during the tumultuous early decades of the Qing dynasty. It is thus a study of the self-conscious building and rebuilding of community and culture as expressed through the metaphor of physical reconstruction.

Despite my focus on buildings, this is not a work of architectural history. The buildings seen in Yangzhou today are not those of the early Qing but recent and imperfect reconstructions, and the physical descriptions of buildings found in seventeenth-century texts are inconsistent at best. Thus there is little evidence available for an exploration of these buildings as architectural artifacts. Instead, by examining the construction and use of four sites in Yangzhou, this study describes the performance of place, or the creation of a site through culturally informed actions, before an audience of contemporaries and an imagined posterity. Thus, I examine the ways elite men used these sites, the ways their writings shaped the reputations of these sites, the ways these sites (and texts) became building blocks of post-conquest culture, and the ways the sites and their uses reflect social and cultural change over time, and indeed the changing composition of the city's elite between the seventeenth and eighteenth centuries.[1] Each of the chapters that follow focuses on a site or building in the city: Red Bridge, the Tower of Literary Selection, Pingshan Hall, and Tianning Temple.

Each site has a distinctive historical legacy, and each is associated with a particular individual, either a renovator or a resident or a sponsor of leisure activities. In addition, each of these men represents a different constituency within the Yangzhou elite: a local official, a native son made good at court, a sojourning editor, and the emperor on tour, entertained by salt merchants. This configuration allows me to explore the relationship between place, memory, history, and social meaning. The men in my chapters themselves became part of the urban culture as they manipulated images of the city, its history, and its scenic sites in their own writings and as they in turn became the subjects of anecdotes about the city. Because elite men wrote prolifically about their leisure activities and social outings, I have been able to identify an extensive network of their friends and associates, in whose collected writings I have found materials on both the buildings and the city of Yangzhou. These writings seldom address the question of the city's reconstruction directly; indeed, they tell us little about its physical state. Instead, writers of the late seventeenth century used historically referenced symbols to describe how they *felt* about

the city and their world and how they related to their own and other social classes. By focusing on this sense of place, I am able to trace the cultural changes that accompanied the city's restoration, while at the same
time exploring questions of changing elite identity and social network
formation.

After the Qing conquest, the reconstruction of the city's famous sites
became a vehicle through which the literati elite presented themselves as
members of a single class. They did so by emphasizing what they had in
common, a heritage they claimed out of an historicized yet timeless past.
They wrote of an imagined Yangzhou, highlighting the role of widely recognized literary icons from the past, claiming a place for the city (and for
themselves) in an empire that they wanted to envision as unified and stable, even though it was not so until well into the 1680s. They drew upon
established images of the city in order to represent the past that they had
experienced and that they wished to commemorate. And they used the
city's scenery *(jing)* in order to express their feelings *(qing)*.[2] Thus, they
created the city out of a carefully chosen set of symbols that allowed them
to express or affect nostalgia for the late Ming while at the same time creating common ground for the reconstruction of literati society. Ironically
enough, these symbols and sites were subsequently adapted to very different purposes by the ascendant salt merchants during the eighteenth
century, and the sites were ultimately lost in the conflagration of the Taiping War in the nineteenth century.

In the aftermath of the Qing conquest, the renovation of famous buildings and historical sites in Yangzhou became an important activity for
both local and official elites. In addition, the sites themselves provided a
physical context for leisure touring *(you)*, a popular practice that facilitated the creation of an elite community lubricated by wine, tea, and the
exchange of poetry. Visiting famous sites allowed the literate to position
themselves in settings in which great men of the past had once stood, and
thus to celebrate the values represented by those great men. While these
practices had a long provenance in China, they took on new meaning
among elites whose self-image had been challenged by the increased social
mobility and factionalism of the late Ming and by the violence that
accompanied the dynastic collapse. Thus, self-referential and self-cele-
bratory activities were rephrased as serious efforts at rebirth, recovery,
and the reinvention of meaning.

The touring experience focused on a particularized set of sites, often
with historical or biographical associations, and often located in a defined
area outside the walls of an urban center. Such sites, known in Chinese as

mingsheng (literally, named or famous sights), possessed a literary heritage, often defined by association with a nationally known figure.[3] The set of privileged sites was not fixed, however. Particular historical figures commanded attention to sites associated with them, and fluctuations in the historical figure's reputation affected the popularity of the associated site. New destinations were also created through the intervention of famous (living) men. Prestige played an important role in touring practice. Elites used historical and cultural references to describe their touring as part of a social repertoire that distinguished them from other classes. Anyone could engage in "travel," but only someone with the requisite grasp of literature and history could truly "tour." Furthermore, during the early Qing, leisure touring allowed men of shared cultural commitments to overcome political differences born of the conquest and celebrate the cultural attainments that members of this group possessed in common.

Yangzhou in the late seventeenth century was a highly sociable place, and, according to the editors of the local gazetteer published in 1675, it was a place whose landscape was eminently suited to leisure touring.[4] Elite men gathered and wrote about their gatherings. They formed poetry clubs that included local residents, officials, refugees, and sojourners. These men played rhyming games while on boating parties on Baozhang Lake (also called Baozhang Canal, and later known as Shouxihu, or Slender West Lake) in the city's northwest suburbs. They toured the area around Red Bridge and climbed Shu Ridge to compose poetry at Pingshan Hall. They drank wine and saw the sites, and they recorded their activities in collections of anecdotes and essays. They made anthologies of their friends' writings and published their own casual comments on their friends' poems, letters, and essays as a public affirmation of their friendships. Some of these men demonstrated their loyalty to the Ming dynasty by refusing to serve in the new Qing government, while others went off to Beijing in search of appointment. Still others came to Yangzhou from Beijing in the service of the new regime. And yet political allegiances do not seem to have stood in the way of personal and literary friendships. Famous Ming loyalists mixed socially with equally famous supporters and servitors of the conquest regime. Their shared values and status were acted out against the backdrop of Yangzhou's famous sites.

I do not claim that any of these practices were unique to Yangzhou, although the city's destruction during the Qing conquest gave special resonance to physical and cultural (re)construction in the city. Many of these practices quite clearly occurred in other cities where early Qing elites gathered. The sites were different, but the sentiments were the same. Indeed, the men who wrote about Yangzhou sites were active not only in Yangzhou, but all over Jiangnan and in the capital, in their hometowns, in the cities where they sought refuge after the conquest, and in the cities where they served as officials in the Qing government. A closer examination of elite touring and renovation projects in Suzhou, Hangzhou, Nanjing, Beijing, or elsewhere would likely reveal similar phenomena, and even some of the same players. Mobility played a key role in elite self-definition during this period. These men traveled and sojourned, socialized and saw the sites—all the while writing about themselves and their friends. Their activities served to confirm and maintain their position in the social structure. This book explores the ways in which the images of urban sites contributed to the production of a trans-regional and trans-dynastic elite identity. Hence, leisure touring, travel, sojourning, and sociability figure prominently in this study.

Locating Yangzhou

In the early Qing, the walled city of Yangzhou was the administrative center of a sizable prefecture from which three departments (Taizhou, Tongzhou, and Gaoyou) and six counties (Jiangdu, Rugao, Yizheng, Taixing, Baoying, and Xinghua) were governed. The walled prefectural capital also served as the county seat for Jiangdu county and, after 1732, for the newly created Ganquan county. One department, Tongzhou, and the counties of Rugao and Taixing were removed from the prefecture in 1728.[5] The name Yangzhou itself is of ancient provenance, allegedly dating back to the age of China's mythic sage kings. However, the name did not always correlate with the geographic area subsequently occupied by Yangzhou prefecture and its eponymous walled prefectural seat. The association between the name "Yangzhou" and the region framed by the Huai River, the Yangzi, and the sea only became fixed during the Sui dynasty (581–618) with the creation of the Grand Canal. The Song dynasty poet and official Qin Guan (1049–1100) sought to clarify the various nominal and spatial incarnations of "Yangzhou" in his preface to *The Yangzhou Collection* (Yangzhou ji), a collection of poems about the district produced at the request of the local magistrate.[6] In this preface, Qin first identifies all of the places ever administered under the name Yangzhou, including the prehistoric state of Yangzhou, which extended across most of southeast China. He then focuses on the place that, during the Sui, became inextricably linked to the name Yangzhou, although it often was

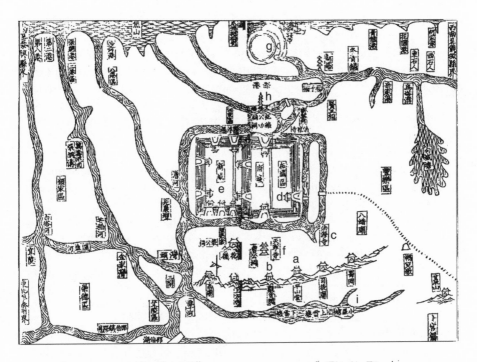

a. Pingshan Hall
b. Guanyin Pavilion
c. Ocean of the Law Temple (Fahai si)
d. Old City
e. New City

f. Tianning Temple
g. Guazhou Town
h. Wenfeng Pagoda
i. Thunder Pools (Leitang)

FIGURE I.I. Jiangdu and Ganquan counties, Yangzhou prefecture. Woodblock illustration. Source: *Yangzhou fuzhi*, 1733.

administered under other names. He suggests that this place, located several miles north of the Yangzi River and just west of the Grand Canal, represented the "real" Yangzhou, and he argues that poetry about other places called Yangzhou rightly had been excluded from the *Yangzhou Collection*. This conundrum evidently persisted into the Qing dynasty: the gazetteers prior to the Yongzheng edition (1733) include pre-Sui materials that Qin Guan would have rejected as relating to "nominal" rather than "real" Yangzhou.

In Qin's time the administrative unit and its urban seat were known principally as Guangling, and the name Yangzhou survived only as a cultural relic, an archaic (not administrative) designation for the region.

Qin Guan and the editor of the *Yangzhou Collection* resurrected the name Yangzhou. Thus, they invoked the region's heritage, while establishing themselves as cultural cognoscenti. Similarly (and ironically), seventeenth-century writers most often referred to the administrative unit that in their time was known as Yangzhou by the culturally resonant name of "Guangling," which had fallen out of administrative use after the Song.[7] It seems that in the early Qing, as in the Northern Song, writers favored older names for their ability to evoke the atmosphere of a place as a cultural, rather than functional or administrative, entity. Similarly, for example, Nanjing was generally referred to by its archaic names, Jinling and Baimen, in literary contexts during the early Qing, when the official name of the city was Jiangning.

The walled city of Qin Guan's time was located on the site of the Sui-Tang (581–907) city, though it was considerably reduced in scale.[8] Rectangular in shape, it was surrounded by walls 2,280 *zhang* (approximately five miles) in length. The city was crisscrossed by a canal running from north to south somewhat west of center and a major avenue running from east to west. The intersection of these two main thoroughfares created four districts, which to some extent also reflected functional distinctions. The northwest quadrant can be considered an administrative district, as it housed most of the government offices. Educational institutions were concentrated in the southwest sector, while military institutions and markets were located in the southeast. The northeast district housed shops and markets as well as several administrative offices.[9] On the south and east sides, the Grand Canal served as the city's moat. The city's eastern gate provided direct access to this important waterway, and thus shops and markets tended to be concentrated on the east side of the city. Seventeenth-century Yangzhou was smaller than the Song city, although the city was considerably larger than it had been in the early Ming.[10] And, as in the Song, the merchants, markets, and shops were concentrated in the eastern part of the city, the area most convenient to the Grand Canal.

Events during the Ming (1368–1644) left the city with a peculiar two-lobed configuration, divided by both an internal canal and a wall (which had once been a wall and its moat). The only access from one side of the city to the other was through the Greater and Lesser East Gates. Civil unrest in the years leading up to the Yuan (1260–1368) collapse had left Yangzhou in ruins and with a depleted population. In 1368, at the time of the Ming founding, only eighteen families remained in Yangzhou, and even with the arrival of refugees, there were still only about forty households.[11] In order to defend the city, and because the city's smaller popu-

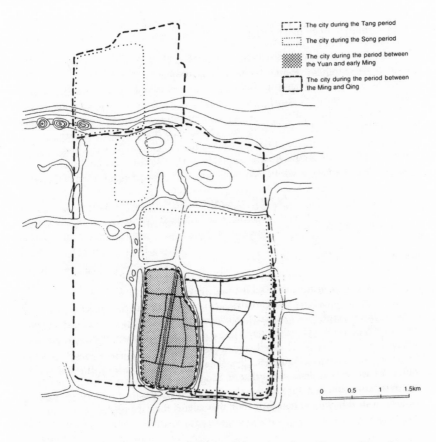

The city during the Tang period

The city during the Song period

The city during the period between the Yuan and early Ming

The city during the period between the Ming and Qing

0   0.5   1   1.5km

FIGURE 1.2. The changing morphology of Yangzhou from Tang to Qing. Source: Xu Yinong, *The Chinese City in Time and Space* (Honolulu: University of Hawaii Press, 2000), 68, fig. 3.8.

lation required less space, local officials decided to rebuild the city walls at some remove from the Grand Canal. Thus, the original Ming city, the "Old City," was packed into what had been the southwest corner of the Song city. As more merchants came to Yangzhou from Huizhou during the sixteenth century, they settled in the area between the city wall and the Grand Canal in order to practice their trade. When pirate attacks threatened this vital merchant community in 1556, local officials and merchants joined forces and built a wall to enclose the suburban neighborhood, thereby creating the "New City."[12]

Functional differences distinguishing the Old and New cities continued into the late seventeenth century, and indeed until the mid-nineteenth century. Early Qing residents and visitors experienced the Old City as an administrative and cultural center, housing the prefectural and county offices for Yangzhou prefecture and Jiangdu county as well as the county and prefectural schools. For the most part, this was a district for established gentry families, though there also were less prosperous residents who provided services and sold foodstuffs.[13] By contrast, the New City was the home of "rich and great merchants," who were said to "worship decadence."[14] The neighborhood also housed the office of the salt transport commission as well as the military barracks of the Green Standard Army stationed in the city. As the salt merchants prospered, the New City gained in importance relative to the Old City. With the extraordinary economic expansion that began in the early eighteenth century, the Old City was radically eclipsed by its more prosperous twin. Travelers more often opted to stay in the garden homes of merchant-patrons, elegant new residences were built, and fabulous shopping districts developed. Guidebooks to the city ignored the Old City almost completely, and its monuments and temples lost their appeal. During the late seventeenth century, however, the Old City still had its historic charm and scenic attractions, and many visitors to the city evidently chose to spend their time there. Furthermore, many of the major patrons of the period were officials living in the Old City. Naturally, their visitors sought lodgings in the Old City as well.

To some degree, Yangzhou's location shaped the imagery that developed around the city. The city's position at the intersection of China's two major navigable waterways—the Yangzi River and the Grand Canal—meant that the city periodically flourished as a major trading center, an entrepôt facilitating the movement of goods between north and south, and later as the preeminent regional hub in the monopoly salt trade.[15] At the same time, the city's location on the north bank of the Yangzi made it a strategically important crossroads between North and South China, leaving it vulnerable in times of conflict and division. Hence, as a result of its location and function, the city experienced periods of great prosperity and horrific destruction. It thus acquired a Janus-faced cultural legacy: at once the "City Prosperous" and the "City Destroyed." Over the centuries, writers and poets employed these motifs in depicting Yangzhou, despite the fact that the city receded into quiet insignificance for long stretches of its history. The rise and fall of the city became essential to its representation: the sudden reversal of fortune was in the nature of the place.[16] These standard motifs provided a vocabulary of cultural

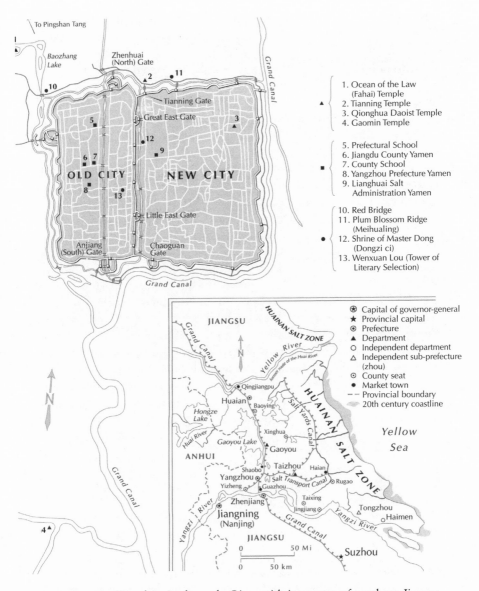

To Pingshan Tang
Baozhang Lake
Zhenhuai (North) Gate
Grand Canal
10
2
11
Tianning Gate
Great East Gate
5
3
12
9
6 7
OLD CITY
NEW CITY
8
13
Little East Gate
Anjiang (South) Gate
Chaoguan Gate
Grand Canal

1. Ocean of the Law (Fahai) Temple
2. Tianning Temple
3. Qionghua Daoist Temple
4. Gaomin Temple

5. Prefectural School
6. Jiangdu County Yamen
7. County School
8. Yangzhou Prefecture Yamen
9. Lianghuai Salt Administration Yamen

10. Red Bridge
11. Plum Blossom Ridge (Meihualing)
12. Shrine of Master Dong (Dongzi ci)
13. Wenxuan Lou (Tower of Literary Selection)

JIANGSU
Grand Canal
HUAINAN SALT ZONE
Yellow River
former route of the Huai River
Qingjiangpu
Huaian
Baoying
Hongze Lake
Salt Yards Canal
HUAINAN SALT ZONE
Huai River
Xinghua
Gaoyou Lake
Gaoyou
ANHUI
Shaobo
Taizhou
Haian
Yangzhou
Yizheng
Guazhou
Salt Transport Canal
Rugao
Zhenjiang
Taixing
Jingjiang
Tongzhou
Haimen
Jiangning (Nanjing)
Grand Canal
Yangzi River
JIANGSU
Suzhou
Yellow Sea

⊛ Capital of governor-general
★ Provincial capital
◉ Prefecture
▲ Department
○ Independent department
△ Independent sub-prefecture (zhou)
⊙ County seat
● Market town
-- Provincial boundary
〰 20th century coastline

0   50 Mi
0   50 km

4 ▲

Grand Canal

FIGURE 1.3. Yangzhou in the early Qing, with inset map of northern Jiangsu. Source: Jonathan Hay, *Shitao* (Cambridge: Cambridge University Press, 2001), 5.

meaning on which Yangzhou dwellers could (and still do) draw in order
to represent the city and its particularity. When one wrote about Yangzhou, one wrote either of a glorious city of moonlight and beautiful
women, populated by wealthy merchants and talented courtesans, or of
a city degraded by war, a smoldering ruin. These motifs were drawn from
history and from literature, and represented the cumulative cultural
legacy of many centuries of writers. The city was a palimpsest, but the
images inscribed tended to be redundant. During the early Qing, three
such images eclipsed all others.

Early Qing poets frequently used the name "Wucheng" ("Weed-
Covered City") to stand for Yangzhou in their writings about the city, and
indeed, this name came into increased use whenever the city was damaged
in war.[17] The term comes from a famous Six Dynasties rhapsody by the
poet Bao Zhao (414–66).[18] The poem, entitled "The Weed-Covered City"
(sometimes translated as "The Ruined Citadel") enjoyed wide circulation,
partly due to its inclusion in the then universally known anthology the
Wenxuan. The poem describes a prosperous urban center that had been
destroyed in a rebellion. In it, the poet juxtaposes images of the city's past
glory with references to its current ruin. The image of the weed-covered
city became a metaphor for the city in times of crisis and decline. Thus,
late seventeenth-century writers borrowed the name to stand for the city
as they knew it, once prosperous but now in ruins.[19]

The second image is historical and describes the city through the story
of the demise of a decadent ruler. The second Sui emperor, Yangdi, made
the city his southern capital and renamed it Jiangdu, or river capital,
thereby indicating the city's stature in the empire.[20] Indeed, it was the
third largest city in Sui China—only Chang'an and Luoyang were larger.
The emperor moved his court south, ordered the construction of his
famous pleasure palace, the Labyrinth, and, according to popular legend
and official accounts, forsook his royal responsibilities for a life of
pleasure and abandonment. The Song historian Sima Guang (1019–86)
writes:

When Yangdi went to Jiangdu [Yangzhou], his licentiousness increased further.
The palace there contained over one hundred apartments, each sumptuously
appointed and occupied by a beautiful woman. Every day, the order was given
for [the mistress of] a particular apartment to play the hostess. The prefect of
Jiangdu. . . . was in charge of providing wine and delicate foods. [The emperor]
together with Empress Xiao and the imperial concubine would proceed to conduct a banquet. Their drinking was incessant. The lesser concubines, numbering
over one thousand, were also frequently drunk.[21]

The emperor came to a bad end in Yangzhou—he was murdered by a subordinate in his Labyrinth. The city thus acquired an aura of decadent profligacy. The emperor and his Labyrinth became popular poetic tropes invoked to suggest the city's sensuous luxury, decadence, and resultant decline. Early Qing discourse manipulated this imagery to make an implicit comparison: just as Sui decadence presaged the emperor's murder and the city's decline, so late Ming profligacy prefigured the city's destruction in 1645. Nostalgic poetry on Sui sites thus suggested late Ming preoccupations.

The third image inscribed on this urban palimpsest was used by early Qing literati to represent themselves as well as the city. The Tang poet Du Mu (803–52) embodied a romantic lifestyle that they, inspired as they were by the late Ming cult of emotions, sought to emulate. By using Du Mu's language, they represented themselves as "fashionable personalities" (fengliu), and portrayed their city as the cosmopolitan pleasure ground seen in Du Mu's poems or in popular anecdotes and plays that took the poet as their subject. Du Mu filled his poems with descriptions of the city's romantic charms. His was a Yangzhou of pleasure boats and courtesans, moonlight and singing girls, a city of dreams and magical beauty. And his poems provide many of the images recycled across the centuries: the "blue mansions" of the entertainment quarters, the moonlight, the flutes, and the jade-white women. His poem "Getting Something Off My Mind" contributed to the city's romantic image. It reads:

> Footloose and lost on the rivers and lakes
> I went my way carrying wine,
> Chu women's waists, slender and fine
> Danced lightly on my palm.
> After ten long years I woke at last
> From a Yangzhou dream—
> I had won only fame for careless love
> In its blue mansions.[22]

Beginning shortly after Du Mu's death, the image of the poet enjoying himself with wine and women in the city's pleasure quarters was incorporated into popular fiction and drama under the name "Yangzhou dream."[23] This did not represent undiluted pleasure, however, for the notion of pleasure was inextricably linked to the notion of loss, even as prosperity seemingly inevitably led to decadence and decline. These pleasures are consistently portrayed as alienated from the present: the dreamer has awakened, and the lush Yangzhou dream has vanished. The literatus playing at being Du Mu in the early Qing presented himself as a romantic survivor grasping at memories. Yet many younger men, too young to have been adults in the bad last years of the Ming, adopted this persona for themselves as well. This pose suited the mood of their times, it was universally recognizable among the educated elite, and most important, it was inextricably linked to the city of Yangzhou in the popular imagination. When in Yangzhou, the early Qing poet recast himself as a Du Mu.

The City Destroyed

The image of the City Destroyed took on new significance during the mid-seventeenth century, when real-life experiences suddenly mirrored historical and poetic imagery. The city emerged from the flames more famous than ever, its image burnished even as the reality lay in ruins. Past images of rupture and loss were reinvoked for their explanatory power, even as real events confirmed the city's legendary capacity for annihilation and rebirth. And indeed, the particular violence unleashed on Yangzhou during the Qing conquest made the city itself an emblem of what had been lost in the conquest, a site upon which to enact what had been retained. Visitors to the city used analogy to remark on the city's demise, as sightseeing occasioned writings laden with reflections on the past. They fit Yangzhou's double reputation neatly into early Qing historical discourse on the causal relationship between late Ming decadence and the dynasty's destruction. The city, once of little significance to literati, became a place worthy of their attentions. In the aftermath of catastrophe, the mercantile and administrative center became a richly imagined space.

The remembered past and the historical past fused, as literati tourists drew upon a historically referenced set of symbols to comment on the contemporary state of affairs. The Sui emperor and his decadent court substituted for rulers of more recent memory. Red Bridge acquired the symbolic resonances of the romantic Twenty-four Bridge (Ershisi qiao) of the Tang dynasty. Buildings like Pingshan Hall, which had fallen into disrepair centuries earlier, were rebuilt after the conquest, a public statement of cultural renewal conveying a false sense of timeless continuity. Similarly, the legacy of Wenxuan lou, the Tower of Literary Selection, was significantly augmented—enhanced by a sham connection to an ancient and royal literary figure. Thus, sightseers and rebuilders alike asserted their position in lineages of cultural convention: they aligned themselves with admired cultural figures by positioning themselves quite literally in the same physical landscape. In the aftermath of the near total annihilation of the city, doing so represented an assertion of the immortality of those cultural lineages: politics were evanescent, but cultural meaning survived. By the Qianlong period (1736–96), historically referenced sightseeing and construction had largely been replaced by other, now more familiar, forms of tourism, spectacle, and conspicuous consumption. Literati musings on loss lost their meaning as the empire consolidated, and as the physical evidence of destruction was replaced by unprecedented mercantile wealth.

The destruction of Yangzhou was presaged by the fall of Beijing to bandits on April 24, 1644, when the forces of Li Zicheng entered the city. The next day, the last Ming emperor committed suicide on Coal Hill, behind the Forbidden City. Forty-two days later, after suffering defeat in battle at the hands of the former Ming general, Wu Sangui, and his new Qing masters, Li Zicheng sacked parts of his own capital and abandoned the city.[24] On June 6, 1644, the Qing army entered Beijing and formally declared their intention to rule China. News of the emperor's suicide rocked the empire. Armed militias formed in many of the major cities and towns of the Yangzi delta and the Huai River region. Local thugs also formed armed bands and, taking advantage of the confusion, preyed upon local officials and gentry households, who in turn organized servants and tenants into defensive units.[25] Armies and bandits and "protective militias" robbed, pillaged, and raped their way across Jiangnan province (modern Anhui and Jiangsu). Sometimes this social unrest had an ostensibly political focus, as when attacks were directed against the households of officials who had surrendered to Li Zicheng. In many cases, however, they were driven by the opportunity for looting and mayhem that the confused political situation afforded.[26] Often these local armed groups represented themselves as the loyal subjects of the last Ming emperor, whether or not they were in fact affiliated with the larger pro-Ming organizations and armies. Indeed, the pro-Ming armies were themselves unstable, for they included large numbers of bandits and other opportunists. Yangzhou's location was unfortunately strategic: the city lay in the path of several of these barely controlled armies. Moreover, the wealth of the local merchant population made the city an appealing target for armed organizations that relied on plunder to feed and pay their men.

Within two weeks of the Qing army's arrival in Beijing and in the midst of continued local turmoil, loyalist officials and soldiers based in the auxiliary Ming capital established a rump Ming government in Nanjing. After much debate, they chose the Prince of Fu, the profligate grandson of the last Ming emperor, to lead the Southern regime under the reign-name Hongguang. However, throughout its twelve-month existence, the Southern Court was riven by factionalism and intrigue, particularly among the highest-ranking officials and generals. In addition, conflict continued among the local militias and "loyalist" warlords, and the new regime offered little protection to the communities that supported it. To reward his military backers, the new emperor divided the territory ruled from Nanjing into four military fiefdoms, each led by a so-called guardian general.[27] These warlords, with their large armies and power-bases north of the Yangzi, were seen by the Southern Court as crucial to its defensive program, even as they committed outrages against the civilian populations they were supposed to protect. And again, Yangzhou lay in the middle of these competing armed forces, as well as between the Southern Court and its enemies at Beijing.

One guardian general, a former ally of Li Zicheng and defector to the Ming loyalist cause named Gao Jie, laid siege to the city of Yangzhou on June 2, 1644.[28] The city represented strategic benefits and enormous wealth to the warlord, if he could gain control over it. It also offered Gao a prestigious advantage relative to the other three guardian generals.[29] However, the local people were so frightened by their purported guardian that they refused to grant him entry to the city. Some rich residents sent their families away from the anxious city.[30] Those who remained were adamant that the warlord not be admitted. Zheng Yuanxun, the gentry envoy sent to parley with Gao Jie, advocated capitulation and was murdered by an irate mob upon his return to the city.[31] Upon hearing of Zheng's murder, Gao Jie reportedly was incensed and eager to avenge his death. The city suffered Gao Jie's siege for more than a month during the hot summer of 1644. Throughout this period, Gao's troops lived up to their fearsome reputation by raping and murdering civilians and pillaging the countryside, though they were unable to break through the city walls.[32] According to one source, the countryside was filled with the countless bodies of those killed by Gao Jie's soldiers.[33] The city temporarily was spared further suffering when the Ming loyalist grand secretary, Shi Kefa, finally persuaded Gao to remove his troops to the fortified river town of Guazhou, located several miles to the south. Shi Kefa then made Yangzhou his headquarters, the base from which he hoped to manage the contentious warlords, avoid the infighting at court, and defend the south from the rebels and Manchus. Still, despite Shi Kefa's steadying presence, the loyalist generals and their bandit armies continued to fight each other, showing more interest in personal gain than in the loyalist cause they purportedly espoused.

Shi Kefa saved Yangzhou from Gao Jie only to watch it devoured by the Qing army. Indeed, he bears much of the responsibility for the disastrous events of late May 1645, for it was his refusal to open the city gates that proved the immediate cause of the city's ruin. The city, under Shi Kefa's leadership, was the first to resist the Qing armies, and its people paid a terrible price as a lesson to the rest of the empire. Nearly a year after their conquest of Beijing, the Manchu rulers of the new Qing empire sought to consolidate their hold over South China and began a campaign against the rump Ming government at Nanjing. Yangzhou was the Southern Ming court's last line of defense north of the Yangzi River and the first city where the Qing army met sustained military resistance. Shi Kefa assembled a force of thirty thousand men inside the walled city, crowding them in among urban residents and refugees.[34] He rushed to reinforce the city's walls, installing gunnery platforms and foreign-style cannon on the ramparts.[35] His calls for additional forces went unheeded, however, for the armies of the guardian generals had surrendered to the Manchus. Indeed, the huge army that besieged the city in late May of 1645 included many of the same troops that had terrorized the local population during the previous year.[36]

On the rainy afternoon of May 20, 1645, after a seven-day siege, the Qing troops broke through the northwest corner of the city wall. The rape, fires, and carnage began at nightfall on the twentieth and lasted for six days. The 1675 gazetteer catalogues members of the city's examination elite who committed suicide when faced with the Qing army. A government student told his wife that "matters having reached this point, I will read the sage's books and retaining my honor I will die . . . " He jumped into a well while still reading the *Book of Changes*. Another government student killed himself in the Jiangdu county school next to the image of Confucius. One local degree holder hanged himself after drinking wine and writing a poem on a wall. His two younger brothers joined him in death. Others killed themselves alongside their wives. One member of the examination elite paid written tribute to the Ming emperor on a sheet of yellow paper, and then hanged himself. Additional men killed themselves by jumping into the Yangzi River, the canal, or the neighborhood well.[37] The gazetteer also contains a long list of women who killed themselves in response to the fall of the city and an essay paying tribute to the "Ten Exemplary Chastity Martyrs of the Sun Family," by the local scholar Wang Yan.[38] Wang's essay outlines the ways in which ten women of the Sun lineage killed themselves. Some jumped into wells, others hanged themselves, while still others slit their own throats. Wang continues his morbid catalogue, extending it to women from other households. We see the righteous dying in wells, in goldfish ponds, by hanging, by self-immolation, and by knife. Some of these women composed couplets or wished loved ones well before taking their lives, often committing suicide collectively in family groups.

A Jesuit missionary who lived in China at the time of the conquest, Martino Martini (1614–61), offered this account of the city's fall:

> The most rich and most noble city of Yangzhou experienced this force and at one point fought well against the Tartars . . . The honorable Shi was the most loyal to the emperor Hongguang. He was defending the city with the highly skilled force of the militia. Nevertheless, they were forced to give it up to the Manchus: all the soldiers and civilians were wiped out by the slaughter, all of the houses were destroyed. Soon the fetid cadavers created pestilence and putrefaction and so they all were piled on top of the houses which were burned in the entire city and in the suburbs.[39]

Martini's account was based on eyewitness accounts and contemporary documents. It is likely that he received information about the massacre from Catholic missionaries and parishioners residing in Yangzhou, as there had been a Catholic presence in the city from the late Ming. Martini himself was not a witness to the carnage, however, and his description of its totality appears overstated for the sake of dramatic effect. We know for instance that not every house was destroyed or every civilian killed. The gazetteers, for example, refer to heroic, filial, and chaste survivors.[40] Still, this passage provides a sense of the terrible scope of the disaster; the destruction must have *felt* absolute to those who experienced it. In addition, the passage gives us a sense of how these events were perceived and described in the seventeenth-century world beyond Yangzhou, and indeed beyond China.

The massacre at Yangzhou may seem familiar to many readers. One text has guaranteed its fame. A powerful account in diary form by an eyewitness named Wang Xiuchu, entitled "Yangzhou shiri ji" (An Account of Ten Days at Yangzhou), became a pivotal text of anti-Manchu, and indeed Chinese nationalistic, literature.[41] Suppressed during the High Qing, it was frequently republished in the decade prior to the 1911 revolution as an impetus for revolutionary action.[42] The "ten days' massacre" has become a symbol of Chinese suffering at the hands of foreigners; it is read backward through the lenses of 1911, and of Nanjing in 1937. These events are also familiar to Western students of Chinese history, due to the frequent translation and citation of Wang's account.[43] Ironically, Wang's account is credible precisely because it does not focus on the "inhumanity" of the Manchus, nor does it read as if it were manufactured in service of an early twentieth-century cause.[44] Wang Xiuchu describes the events of the six days of carnage followed by four days during which order was restored to the city. His account details the human cost of the conquest, portraying the dishonesty and greed of the soldiers and the terror and hunger they inflicted on the civilian population. He also describes the strategies employed by survivors like those in his own family: paying off soldiers, hiding in coffins and on rooftops, disguising themselves with coarse clothing and grime. However, while many sought shelter in hiding places, most were eventually found and killed. Two passages from Wang's account provide a sense of the events in Yangzhou in 1645. Wang describes the scene on the second day as follows:

Several dozen people were herded like sheep or goats. Any who lagged were flogged or killed outright. The women were bound together at the necks with a heavy rope—strung one to another like pearls. Stumbling with each step, they were covered with mud. Babies lay everywhere on the ground. The organs of those trampled like turf under horses' hooves or people's feet were smeared in the dirt, and the crying of those still alive filled the whole outdoors. Every gutter or pond that we passed was stacked with corpses . . . Their blood had flowed into the water, and the combination of green and red was producing a spectrum of colors. The canals, too, had been filled to level with dead bodies.[45]

The imagery is bleak yet vivid, filled with morbid descriptions of blood, filth, and death. Of the fifth day the disheartened author wrote:

Then fires started everywhere, and the thatched houses surrounding the He family graveyard easily caught fire and were soon engulfed in flames. Only one or two scattered houses were fortunate enough to escape the disaster. Those who had hidden themselves beneath the houses were forced to rush out from the heat of the fire, and as soon as they came out, in nine cases out of ten, they were put to death on the spot. On the other hand, those who had stayed in the houses—ranging from a few to even a hundred—were burned to death within the closely shuttered doors and no one could tell how many had died from the pile of charred bones that remained afterwards. At this moment, there was no place to hide, nor was it possible for anyone to hide, for if you were discovered you would die whether you had money [to pay the soldiers] or not. Dead or alive, one had no alternative other than lying among the dead by the roadside.[46]

The weather during those May days was rainy and overcast, preventing the fires from raging completely out of control.[47] Still, the human and material cost of the Qing assault was considerable. Wang Xiuchu claims that according to the cremation record more than 800,000 corpses were burned at Yangzhou. This figure has been contested in recent years, and indeed seems exaggerated, given that the total population of the Yangzhou region (including the much larger administrative area outside the city walls) was no more than one million. It seems fair to read it as a symbolic figure, an indicator of the unimaginable (and probably unknowable) number of people who died in the city during that period in May 1645.[48]

The Period of Recovery: 1645–1700

No single account of the physical reconstruction of the city survives, if indeed such an account ever was written. Generic conventions have relegated the processes of destruction and recovery to hidden corners of the gazetteer: they are buried in biographies and entries about particular buildings. There are no concrete, systematic assessments of the damage, nor are there reliable statistics. And if we cannot gauge the damage, how can we gauge the recovery? We are left with scattered images of finding, ransoming, returning, burying, and rebuilding. We see walls rebuilt, charitable projects organized, and monuments reconstructed, often along the lines of the late Ming city, but with some innovations. The city walls were renovated in 1647 according to the peculiar late Ming layout, retaining the division between the "old" and "new" cities, suggesting that the walls were not destroyed in 1645. By 1647, a dozen local men had taken and passed the metropolitan examination—an indication that some, at least, were willing to participate in the new Qing regime almost immediately after the conquest.[49] The first post-conquest gazetteer was published in 1664. Produced under pressure, it contained little original material, mostly replicating the last Ming edition. It was superseded a decade later in 1675 with a more elaborate, newly researched gazetteer that was filled with references to recent construction and fashionable poetry circles. A foundling home was built in 1655, perhaps to cope with the large number of infants left parentless by the conquest (though as the institution followed the event by a decade, the orphaned babies already would have been in their teens).[50] More likely it marked the city's recovery to the point that locals could afford philanthropy, rather than a direct response to the conquest. The city's residents not only developed philanthropic institutions but also built and restored structures of cultural and religious significance. The Tower of Literary Selection, included in the gazetteer as an "ancient relic" for centuries, was constructed as a "real" building in 1651, a symbol of cultural immortality amidst political turmoil.[51] Thirteen years later, Wang Maolin, a Hanlin Academician and Yangzhou native, together with the prefectural magistrate, organized the restoration of Pingshan Hall, an act symbolic of elite unity and the renewed fusion of local and national culture.

By contrast, the administrative buildings of the prefecture were not restored until somewhat later, when they were renovated and expanded under the leadership of the famous magistrate Shi Shilun, who served in the city from 1689 to 1693.[52] The delay is surprising, in that these buildings, like shrines, gazetteers, and schools, were "national" in character. Antonia Finnane speculates that this delay stemmed from a shortage of public funds, which led to the deferral of maintenance on urban infrastructure, and cites the delayed dredging of the city canal as further evidence.[53] It seems highly unlikely, however, that officials spent fifty years governing from decaying buildings, and indeed, one judge added a garden to his official residence during this period. Although a lack of public funds may have been one factor in the delayed overhaul of the city's administrative facilities, it is surely not the only one. If these buildings had in fact experienced total destruction, it seems likely that they would have been restored immediately. Quite possibly, administrative facilities may have been spared in the conquest, since the Qing rulers intended to put them to immediate use.[54] Furthermore, minor repairs surely occurred during the fifty years preceding Shi Shilun's massive renovation of the prefecture's administrative buildings. Such minor repairs would not have warranted coverage in the gazetteer. Indeed, evidence from the gazetteers suggests that national officials serving in the city did have access to funds and were actively involved in renovation projects, relying in particular on solicitations from leading officials in the salt and transport administrations and the landed elite.

The city's rebirth required the new Qing officials to carry out certain basic tasks. The population had to be induced to return, bodies had to be disposed of, those who had been carried off as captives had to be ransomed and brought back, and work and tax relief had to be provided. The local inhabitants had to be persuaded that the new regime intended to restore order, end banditry and warfare, and facilitate economic recovery. The former Ming official and renowned art collector Zhou Lianggong (1612–72) served as the first Lianghuai salt censor after the conquest. Zhou's gazetteer biography celebrates his role in these processes of reconstruction, return, and burial. It reads: "[Zhou Lianggong] soothed and pitied the exhausted and the wasted. On behalf of the people, he ransomed countless boys and girls who had been taken captive. White bones were piled like a mountain beyond Guangchu Gate and [he] arranged for a proper burial for them."[55] In addition, a contemporary detailed Zhou's critical role in the restoration of the salt administration, writing that

when Master Zhou took up his duty there, Guangling [Yangzhou]. . . .was still in ruins. [Salt] merchants had not yet regained their breath. The salt which had accumulated formed a salt wall. Merchants had fled and all the salt had been confiscated by the government. Master Zhou devised various plans to get these merchants back. He asked the government to return the wall of salt to the merchants. He arranged it so that all the unemployed got back their old jobs. He also asked the court to abolish the old system of levies on salt merchants and carried out his new system. As a result, a large number of merchants returned and the government revenue increased.[56]

Zhou and his fellow officials thus encouraged the local people to return to their homes and businesses. In this they received the support of the new Qing state, for the proceeds of Yangzhou's salt monopoly were viewed as an important source of tax revenues.[57] Agricultural lands, too, had to be returned to production after years of unrest. Bian Sanyuan, a native of Liaodong, served as prefectural magistrate from 1646.[58] The gazetteer praises him for his role in the restoration of the rural economy, stating: "At the time, things had just started to calm down, many of the people were out of work, so Sanyuan called together all of the displaced people and gradually they restored the fields."[59] This passage may also be a veiled description of the arrival of refugees on the land, replacing the large numbers killed in the conquest. Ordinary people also participated in philanthropic activities.[60] For example, in 1656 two natives of Gaoyou county organized efforts to raise abandoned children, provide caskets for the indigent, build rescue boats to save lives, and open dispensaries. They contributed large sums of money to support other construction projects. They renovated the county school, and they raised large sums of money to ransom local women who had been carried off as captives. One man was so keen on helping these former captives that he donated additional money to provide floors for their homes.[61]

Passing through on his way to Beijing in 1653, the historian and travel diarist Tan Qian commented that the city of moonlight had been ruined in the chaos of the preceding decade, and its beauty obliterated. Even so, he pointed to a more promising future. The city's placement in relation to the stars made it heaven's marketplace, and thus its earthly markets, too, should prosper easily, in ways that could not be matched by other places.[62] Still, despite concerted efforts to revive the local economy, the situation remained difficult for decades. While there is a common preconception that the Kangxi-Qianlong period constituted a "golden age" of prosperity, the first half of the Kangxi reign was marked by empirewide political instability and widespread poverty.[63] If Yangzhou's prosperity depended on both regional stability and the salt monopoly, as Antonia Finnane's work has demonstrated, neither of these preconditions was met in the early Kangxi reign. Real peace was achieved only after the suppression of the Three Feudatories Rebellion (1673–81), a revolt of three important Qing generals who controlled large areas in the southeast and southwest. Local farmers had difficulty meeting their tax assessments during the early Kangxi reign. Gaoyou county suffered alternating years of flooding and drought, and was frequently exempted from paying taxes from 1647 to 1685.[64] Jiangdu county received partial tax forgiveness during the late 1670s and early 1680s.[65] Yangzhou's salt merchants were far less affluent during the late seventeenth century than they became during the mid-eighteenth century.[66] They often were unable to meet their tax responsibilities, and did not begin making the lavish gifts to the state for which they became famous until 1717.[67] Even though the salt merchants sponsored major infrastructure projects including the dredging of transport canals, they found doing so a heavy burden. A representative of the merchants used the occasion of an early imperial tour to personally beseech the Kangxi emperor for the reimbursement of 80 percent of the merchants' contribution. The emperor complied, to the relief of the merchant community.[68]

Although salt merchants dominated the cultural world of eighteenth-century Yangzhou, they played a relatively minor role in the late seventeenth century. During this period of instability and economic difficulty, officials and men of letters organized social outings at the scenic sites of Yangzhou, composed poems, and alluded desperately to their common cultural heritage. They used scarce resources to construct or reconstruct famous sites, sponsoring banquets and picnics to create social and cultural meaning. A politically diverse group, they collected Ming relics, composed nostalgic poetry, and served the Qing—or refused to serve, but accepted the patronage of Qing officials. This was an age of permeable categories and fluid boundaries, an age of instability and creative potential. It was only later that these categories and identities were reinscribed as absolute loyalties and betrayals, and only later that "Qing Yangzhou" was irreversibly transformed into a city of merchants and those they patronized.

From the vantage point of the early Kangxi reign, the prosperous city of the eighteenth century could not yet be imagined. We are caught in a web of false expectations—the pose and pretensions of the seventeenth-century literati and our own anachronistic image of an urban economy dominated by decadent merchants. From today's vantage point, Qing Yangzhou is either the Yangzhou of the Ten Days Massacre of 1645 or the Yangzhou of the late eighteenth-century *Record of the Painted Boats of Yangzhou,* and as we have seen, the latter image has tended to dominate. The city is most often portrayed as an eternal city of gorgeous gardens and prosperous merchants. That image of the city is apocryphal, read backward through an accessible source and current scholarly obsessions with the commercial economy. As a result, many have assumed that Yangzhou has always been a city (and an urban culture) dominated by merchants as it was in the eighteenth century. However, merchants did not shape Yangzhou's culture in the late seventeenth century. There was an interim period when the merchants had not yet achieved the full measure of their influence, when a community of local and national figures tried to remake Yangzhou culture in their own image, marking the local landscape with their own values. Yangzhou has been typecast as a city of commerce, a city of decadence—a city of little interest to the literati elite. Nevertheless, a closer look reveals a community of men active in shaping the new, post-conquest culture both locally and nationally. During the late seventeenth century, Yangzhou was their world and their pleasure ground. If we look only to the obvious images, that world is lost to us.

2 *Personality and Meaning*

RED BRIDGE

Site and Sentiment

During the Kangxi period (1661–1722), the poet and writer Dong Yining, who was at least an occasional presence on the Yangzhou literary scene, commented on the ways in which places acquired significance through famous individuals:[1] "The fame of mountains and rivers is mostly due to outstanding people. Before Su Shi's excursion, the Red Cliff was just another stupid rock. Since Su Shi toured it, although the terraces are ruined and the pavilions are damaged, Red Cliff is still a famous mountain."[2] While visiting Red Cliff, Dong paid his respects to a portrait of the poet, who lived from 1037 to 1101, and read the poems by Su inscribed on the cliff. He even timed his visit to correspond to the season of Su's famous "Red Cliff Record." Clearly it was through Su's presence, and his creative legacy, that the place had significance for Dong Yining. As Craig Clunas has argued, the fame of a garden does not derive from "enduring intrinsic features of the site" but rather from literary and artistic representations of the property, and especially the reputation of the producer of those representations.[3] Although Clunas limits his discussion to gardens, his point can easily be applied to other famous sites. Fame and its transmission were crucial in determining whether or not a site was significant, and both required the continuous intervention of patrons either to create or to uphold the legacy of the place.[4] Indeed, when written by the appropriate person a prose record could legitimate even a humble wine shop, lending it prestige and respectability in the eyes of discerning tourists.[5]

The "outstanding people" referred to by Dong Yining were not necessarily figures from the ancient past, as he himself knew. If special weight was given to sites linked to historical figures like Su Shi and Ouyang Xiu (1007–1072), similar importance accrued to sites associated with contemporaries who were portrayed as analogous to their predecessors. Such an individual's power to consecrate a place derived from a potent combination of political and cultural authority, and, of course, consensus by the literati community that he possessed such talent and authority.[6] Even though the practices associated with the consecration of place and the characteristics of the consecrator remained relatively constant, the meanings and identities they engendered changed according to historical context. During the second half of the seventeenth century, the consecration and maintenance of famous sites enabled elites to articulate new social and cultural identities in reaction to the social flux and political crises of the late Ming and early Qing.

The association between officially sanctioned cultural figures and famous sites marked a reassertion of centralizing political values and a rejection of the social confusion of the late Ming, even as personalities left over from the pre-conquest generation retained their cultural weight. Dong Yining would have been well aware of these developments, for he was associated with a literary network involved in the cultural (re)construction of Yangzhou during the 1660s. That literary network at least nominally centered on Wang Shizhen, a young official from Shandong and an early Qing incarnation of the model cultural figure. Wang Shizhen's activities in Yangzhou gave new significance to a site, Red Bridge, and to the city itself, even as the bridge and the city enhanced the mythology that developed around Wang himself.

In this chapter, I examine the processes through which Red Bridge acquired a position in the pantheon of sites significant to China's transregional elite, Wang Shizhen became a model figure, and the city of Yangzhou gained new importance as a destination for literati and official travelers. The literary construction of city, site, and person converged in gatherings organized by Wang Shizhen at Red Bridge in 1662 and 1664. Wang Shizhen used these occasions in order to construct and define himself in the image of prominent cultural figures of the pre-conquest generation, who in turn used the bridge and its environs to reimagine the urban landscape of the late Ming. There are poignant and sometimes cynical ironies in these representations. The youthful embodiment of early Qing officialdom takes on the characteristics of a late Ming "outsider" to enhance his own literary prestige. A brightly painted bridge in Yangzhou's pleasure quarter becomes a mecca for literati gatherings. Ruined Yangzhou is reimagined as an avatar of the late Ming Jiangnan cities. The city, the site, and the person all served as building blocks in the construction of each other's identities, and the reputation of each was articulated in relation to the others.

City and Significance

The prominence of urban sites appears closely linked to the fortunes of the cities in which they were located. Sites and their celebrators were both source and symptom of the city's reputation and its position within the cultural hierarchy of places in late imperial China. A city's reputation was not fixed, but continually constructed and reconstructed in literature and through the depiction of local sites. Wealth was a less important precondition in this process, in this time and place, than a connection to famous men. An illusion of continuity was born of layers of historical and literary allusion. Set images of moonlight, willows, decadence, and destruction were recycled from the past, but to new purposes. In the early Qing, Red Bridge, a place with no literary heritage, acquired one. Cultural concerns and conventions that dated back at least to the Song shaped this new sense of place. Images of the city and its sites proliferated and changed in the aftermath of catastrophe and rupture. Yangzhou became prominent as a destination and as the subject of nostalgic writing. The city was recreated as a late Ming city in the post-Ming world, but with a difference: Yangzhou itself had not been a major cultural center in the Ming. The city had begun to emerge as a destination only in the late Ming, and even then, it was not yet what it would later become. Similarly, Red Bridge was built only in the last decade of Ming rule, and yet, in the early Qing, the bridge and its environs were reimagined as the embodiment of the late Ming Jiangnan spirit. The imaginary city was constructed on graveyard foundations, haunted by the ghosts of 1644 and 1645, even as the physical city was rebuilt on more prosperous grounds than ever before.

Although Yangzhou reached its economic zenith only in the eighteenth century, the city emerged as a cultural contender earlier, during the second half of the seventeenth-century, when the activities of a cohort of officials and literati made the city and particular places in the vicinity important. In this respect, Yangzhou followed a pattern set by other leading cities of Jiangnan during the middle and late Ming. As Suzhou emerged from a period of economic decline (which had resulted from the punishing tax policies of the early Ming) as the economic and cultural center of the empire during the mid-Ming, the city attracted a cohort of talented men whose activities imbued its scenic sites with particular significance. Word of their activities, and of the sites they frequented, circulated through their production of literary and artistic works. These scenic sites and gardens were then codified within the itinerary of famous places, one that increasingly featured scenic sites of contemporary, as well as historical, vintage. That Suzhou was a major publishing center and book market facilitated the spread of these images. In addition, mid-Ming Suzhou provided service personnel and a cultural model for other cities along the Yangzi River as Suzhou barkeepers, restaurateurs, and courtesans migrated elsewhere to make their fortunes, and elites and their imitators consumed more expensive and rarified images of the city.[7]

During the late seventeenth century, the presence of literary figures of national reputation similarly served as a catalyst to Yangzhou's social and cultural life. This contributed to the rapid emergence of the city as a major destination for literati and official travelers, and as a key node in the empire's hierarchy of cultural centers. The presence of well-known literary figures attracted others to the area. During the 1660s, Wang Shizhen's poetry parties drew literary friends and acquaintances from Nanjing and other Jiangnan cities. Yangzhou's new position among the cities of the realm did not go unremarked. By 1688, the city had become so attractive to the literary elite that Kong Shangren could comment: "Guangling [Yangzhou] serves as a giant inn for the gentlemen of the realm. Among all of those who have literary talent or artistic ability, there is none who does not live in Guangling [Yangzhou]. On the whole, it is like a shop with a hundred craftsmen [or officials]."[8] Yangzhou in the early Qing thus acquired a reputation as an appropriate destination for talented sojourners and travelers. These talented tourists and temporary residents participated in the reinvention of Yangzhou sights as part of a constellation of places significant to the highly mobile elites of this period. Moreover, these individuals consciously sought to identify places in the city with their favorite haunts in Jiangnan, positioning Yangzhou as a cultural center worthy of being placed alongside Nanjing and Suzhou.

In Nanjing, which ranked with Suzhou as the empire's major artistic and cultural center in the waning years of the Ming, the social and literary activities of famous men similarly contributed to the allure of the city. As Hongnam Kim has pointed out in her book on the seventeenth-century official and art patron Zhou Lianggong, "the confluence of such an array of notables in the city provided a catalyst to the social life of the city. Lavish banquets and poetry gatherings were common occurrences. Such activities were the talk of the town."[9] By the late Ming it had become common practice to tell stories about the parties and activities of famous people in their urban context.[10] From the 1630s, these activities in both Nanjing and Suzhou took on added political meaning, as many participants were affiliated with the Fushe, or Restoration Society, which was founded in 1629.[11] Not only were these parties and literary-political events often spoken of, they were also frequently written about. These writings, like those published in Suzhou, were often published in collections, both in small, ephemeral editions associated with particular gatherings and in the literary collections of the men involved.[12] Thus, through gossip and through the reading of contemporary writers, it was not difficult to discern who was socializing with whom, and which sites provided context for these meetings. In late Ming Suzhou and Nanjing, as in early Qing Yangzhou, networks of cultural luminaries played a leading role in the cultural mapping of major urban centers. The prestige and cachet of these cities derived at least in part from their social activities.

By contrast, Ming Yangzhou did not loom large in literati consciousness. Its fame was primarily as a booming marketplace, renowned for its trade in salt and women. After a period of relative isolation and economic stagnation in the early Ming, changes in the administration of the salt monopoly during the Chenghua (1465–87) and Hongzhi (1488–1505) reigns brought new wealth to Yangzhou, attracting a growing population of sojourning merchants. The Jiangdu county gazetteer from the Wanli period (1573–1619) traces this trajectory as follows:

In the beginning of this (Ming) dynasty, the people of Jiangdu [the constituent county of Yangzhou prefecture with its seat in the prefectural city] were simple in their tastes and attire. Their homes and clothing were not highly adorned, and they were diligent and hardworking. Even at times such as weddings and funerals they still retained their humble, pure, and simple ways . . . In recent times, however, merchants from all over the land have come here to set up businesses, and the wealth they generate enriches the people of the city. Those who have become rich then decorate their houses, acquire courtesans. . . . and in their eating and drinking and dress, they compete with kings . . . The women have nothing to do other than put on fancy makeup and compete over clever makeup and collecting gold and jade to decorate themselves. . . . and their gorgeousness and decadence are extreme. These were at first all members of merchant families. But then the profligate sons of ordinary families also rise up to compete and add to it. They drink and wander the streets with courtesans under their arms. If they don't have any money, they borrow it from rich men's mothers. Over time, these debts accumulate, and one day, it erupts into a fight that leads to the destruction of the household.[13]

The passage confirms that Yangzhou began to emerge as an economic center relatively late in the Ming dynasty. It further reveals that contemporaries were aware of the changes in the city's social milieu, and that some, at least in this official account of local customs, attempted to interpret them through an established discursive pattern. By equating prosperity and conspicuous consumption with immorality and decadence, and by attributing both to the influence of sojourning merchants and extravagant women, the anonymous author of this passage participates in a late Ming discourse on decadence, one frequently invoked to describe the economic rise and moral decline of urban Jiangnan.

Increased concern with leisure activities, beautification, and the creation of new scenic destinations also serve as indicators of the changing urban economy of Yangzhou during the late Ming, even as it reflected also the contemporary fad for leisure touring amid famous mountains. During the Wanli period, the prefectural magistrate launched several beautification projects, in one instance using earth removed from the newly dredged canals to create Plum Blossom Hill, which became a popular destination for picnics and parties.[14] The same magistrate also organized the rebuilding of Pingshan Hall, a site associated with the great literatus Ouyang Xiu, which had not been renovated since the Southern Song. Gazetteer evidence also suggests a marked increase in temple construction during the Wanli period.[15] Like the magisterially sponsored beautification efforts, temples and private gardens provided context for leisure activities. At the same time, the Wanli period was marked by the emergence of the city as a luxury market featuring restaurants, teahouses, and brothels, all modeled after those in Suzhou.[16] Indeed, the construction of leisure venues in Yangzhou seems to have begun in earnest during the Wanli period, in conjunction with growing commercialization and official patronage. These processes resumed, intensified, and accelerated in the early Qing as part of the post-conquest recovery. The cultural construction of the city as a destination for the national elite and the designation of important destinations within the city were both for the most part early Qing phenomena, as spatial, institutional, and economic factors determined the chronology of the city's transformation from Ming to Qing.

The gathering to view the rare yellow peonies and compose poetry at Zheng Yuanxun's Garden of Shadows and Reflections (Yingyuan) in 1640 can be seen as the precursor of the early Qing literary parties in Yangzhou.[17] After the gathering, the poems were submitted to the prominent poet and (then-retired) official Qian Qianyi (1582–1664) to be judged. Zheng awarded a prize to the winner—two golden goblets inscribed with the words, "Top Examinee of the Yellow Peonies." Zheng also arranged for the publication of the poems under the title "Jasper

Blossoms Collection" (Yaohua ji). Contemporary accounts state that the gathering was widely praised in the literary community. The combination of nationally famous participants, the publication of a volume of poetry associated with a particular event, and discussion of the event's success along both banks of the Yangzi, though typical of elite leisure in other late Ming cities, seems to have been a relative novelty for Yangzhou. In these respects, this event prefigures the literary gatherings of the early Qing. Indeed the garden, destroyed during the Manchu conquest and eventually reconstructed under a new name, became emblematic of the cultural world that had been lost—even as the literary salons of the early Qing surpassed it in both fame and influence.[18] Destruction itself appears to have been an important part of Yangzhou's appeal as a destination during the early Qing. Reflections on loss were part of what distinguished Wang Shizhen's gatherings from their late Ming equivalents.

In another context, Kong Shangren listed Yangzhou, along with Beijing, Nanjing, Suzhou, and Hangzhou, as one of the five great urban centers of the realm that merited a visit by all scholar-officials.[19] This was not the case in the late Ming, for despite the city's economic successes in the Wanli period, early seventeenth-century Yangzhou was known primarily as a city for the nouveaux riches and a marketplace dealing in concubines and courtesans. Although Wanli-era residents and officials may have aspired to build a Jiangnan city north of the river, or to revive the glories of the Tang, the city did not have the cachet of the great southern centers until several decades after the Qing conquest. It is particularly telling that Kong specifies "scholar-officials," for it was the presence of literary luminaries and talented officials that gave the city its aura of importance in the later seventeenth century and whose activities gave new meaning to its scenic sites. By contrast, in the mid-eighteenth century, the city became known for its wealthy merchants, the academies and cultural activities they sponsored, and their patronage of a new set of scenic sites ostensibly built in honor of the emperor's Southern Tour.

The late Ming efforts to develop Yangzhou as a destination were short-lived and relatively unpublicized outside of the local gazetteers. Ironically, it was only in the aftermath of disaster that scenic sites in Yangzhou became integral to elite itineraries, through the intervention of Qing official literary figures and their friends among the local *yimin* (Ming remnant subjects or loyalists), many of whom were famous for their poetic talent. This phenomenon was closely linked to the presence in the city of major figures associated both with the former Ming and the reigning Qing regimes whose prestige derived from both cultural and political achievements, whether through service or non-service to the regime. Thus, in post-1645 Yangzhou, one sees a curious dynamic between Qing insiders and *yimin* or commoner outsiders, or, from a local perspective, sojourning officials supporting and promoting the works of native or refugee residents. The city became a key place in the cultivation of a new post-Ming identity, which fused a stylized version of late Ming cultural habits with a new concern for official sanction. In the context of the early Qing, the central figure of the "cultured official" organized relations between the court and the locale, helping to define local cultural identity within a transregional and transdynastic elite class identity. Indeed, in the case of Yangzhou, many of the men most closely associated with the creation and organization of this post-Ming identity were outsiders, whether officials or sojourning literati. These men were conscious of both place and posterity as they wrote about their activities. Wang Shizhen, a young official from Shandong and an early Qing incarnation of the model "cultured official," provides an excellent example of this new dynamic, which embedded famous sites, late Ming cultural figures, and early Qing officials in a web of interwoven meanings, each enhancing the prestige of the others.

Identifying with Red Bridge

Red Bridge acquired its significance within the peculiar political and cultural context of post-conquest Yangzhou. The events of the conquest meant that cultural prestige at the local, and even the national, level, was drawn from two sources: the Qing state, and the fallen Ming. Wang Shizhen was emblematic of this duality, embracing both Qing official status and Ming literary values. Typically, cultural prestige had been bestowed through state authority via the civil service examinations. By the late Ming, however, the state system and its power to invest individuals with cultural authority had to a large extent broken down. The emperors reigned while competing factions engaged in a deadly power struggle. Men of talent pursued alternative avenues to cultural prestige. Many failed in the increasingly competitive examination system. Others abandoned the civil service after obtaining the lowest degree, which guaranteed them the benefits of elite status while avoiding the dangers associated with government service.[20] During the period of imperial consolidation, the Qing state attracted talented personnel, including men of the conquest generation (later termed "twice-serving officials") and those of the first generation to receive their degrees after 1644. Particularly after the Kangxi emperor began to rule in his own right in 1667, the state played an increasing role in the cultural life of the elite, conferring prestigious rewards and high office on men deemed talented in the field of culture.[21] Still, despite their official aspirations and state connections, many early Qing officials were strongly influenced by the cultural values of the late Ming, particularly as embodied by individual *yimin* whose talents gave them undeniable weight in the arena of cultural practice. Moreover, whether out of genuine nostalgia or as a kind of literary flourish, members of the Qing official community often affected an attitude of sorrow and longing in their writings, collected Ming stories and relics, and befriended members of the *yimin* community.

Discussion of *yimin* identity has traditionally been framed around the absolute question of loyalty to the fallen dynasty, but a closer look at the social world of Yangzhou in the 1660s reveals a more complex situation, and more frequent interaction among so-called loyalists and Qing officials than most previous scholarship has admitted. For some men, loyalty to the fallen dynasty provided a new justification for the late Ming option not to serve at court. For others, what is now called "loyalism" represented a cultural, rather than political, commitment. Still others continued quite literally to worship the relics of the Ming emperor, reenacting the symbolism of the loyal minister and deserving monarch. The epigrapher and seal carver Gu Ling, for example, regularly paid ritual respect to a sample of the Chongzhen emperor's calligraphy that he kept hidden at his home near Tiger Hill in Suzhou.[22] During the early Qing, the question of loyalty was in many circles subordinate to the question of talent (and of class), and many so-called loyalists in fact accepted the friendship and patronage of Qing officials, even of officials of the supposedly ignominious "twice-serving" variety. Our reading of the loyalty question has been overinfluenced by the values of the Qianlong era, when loyalty became a dominant value and the category of twice-serving official was invented, and by the anti-Manchu rhetoric of the late nineteenth and early twentieth century, when seventeenth-century officials were reviled as traitors to both "race" and nation.[23] From the vantage point of the 1660s, the range of options was far more nuanced than a simple trichotomy of "romantics," "stoics," and "martyrs" would allow.[24]

Literature provides one angle from which to approach the intersection of politics and cultural prestige during this period. For example, as Andrew Hsieh has pointed out in his article on the "unlikely" friendship between the "collaborator" Cao Rong and the "archetypal loyalist" Gu Yanwu, the two groups were not nearly as hostile as scholars have assumed.[25] Outside the political sphere, these men had alternative sources of identity that enabled them to form or maintain friendships across the political divide.[26] Indeed, my research suggests that interaction (rather than division) among these groups was a defining feature of seventeenth-century society, and that social class, with its attendant cultural symbols, figured prominently among the sources of literati identity. Literary friend-ships among talented officials and their non-serving counterparts brought elite cultural identity into sharper focus vis-à-vis other social groups. As we shall see, the presence of both communities was essential to the making of Yangzhou's reputation, and the luster of their names gave meaning to individual sites around the city. The poetry gatherings that represented the pinnacle of high culture in late seventeenth-century Yang-zhou afforded opportunities literally (or literarily) to act out what elites had in common in a confusing, unsettled time. The reemerging genre of song lyrics *(ci)* provided added opportunity for social and cultural engage-ment. Composing matched rhyme poems on social occasions functioned as a form of gift exchange, serving to reinforce relationships, which were then rendered public and tangible through the publication and cir-culation of small anthologies complete with commentary by other well-known friends and associates. Although this was long-established prac-tice among Chinese elites, it took on new significance in the context of the early Qing.[27] In fact, these men consciously drew upon these traditions in constructing their own identities. The combination of literary talents and men of high official position gave this circle considerable influence during this period, in the fields of both culture and power, but especially in the former. The venues in which particularly well-received lyrics were com-posed also became famous. As the writer You Tong (1618–1704) com-mented, "Where there is a place, there is a man; and where there is a man, there is a lyric."[28]

Wang Shizhen was just such a man. An exploration of the emergence of Red Bridge as a famous site and gathering place requires discussion of the "bridging" role played by Wang Shizhen, one of the first generation to take the Qing examinations. Wang socialized with talented poets cho-sen for their cultural weight, particularly those with close connections to the still-prestigious literary world of late Ming Nanjing. Indeed, while serving in Yangzhou during the 1660s, he regularly socialized with mem-bers of the *yimin* community both locally and while traveling. He offered these men patronage and friendship, and in return he benefited from their reflected cultural prestige and moral authority. The gatherings at Red Bridge that he sponsored included senior members of the Jiangnan *yimin* community, and as these gatherings centered around poetry composition, they offered the opportunity for shared experience, along with shared reflections on loss, leisure, transience, and memory (all of which were important themes in Red Bridge poetry). Thus, a discussion of the site and its consecration must include an exploration of the ways in which cultural and leisure practice provided common ground in a period of political dislocation and ambiguity. In socializing at Red Bridge, Wang Shizhen and his guests created a common class identity and a shared cultural heritage. Indeed, the leisure activities enacted at Red Bridge can be read as an assertion of what was held in common, a performance of shared values and cultural commitments distinguishing the in-group of male elites from the rest of society. In the early Qing, the bridge called Hongqiao, variously written with the homophonic logographs meaning "Red Bridge" and "Rainbow Bridge," in particular became part of the local pantheon of scenic sites and a key site for the cultivation of a new post-Ming identity. This came about through the attentions of the official Wang Shizhen and his network of friends and associates.[29]

A Man and His Bridge

There are no descriptions of Red Bridge that predate Wang Shizhen's arrival in Yangzhou, so inextricably is the site linked to the man. Later descriptions of the bridge invariably either allude to Wang Shizhen himself, or borrow images from his writings about the site. The reputation of the place thus derived from the reputation of the man, and its prestige increased along with his. At the same time, Wang Shizhen shaped his own reputation through the representation of his activities in Yangzhou, and at the bridge in particular. Anecdotes about his literary activities in Beijing suggest that while in the capital he interacted primarily with his fellow officials, when in Yangzhou, he composed poetry in the company of famous *yimin* at Red Bridge.[30] This may reflect conventions of place: Beijing was the center of official power where officials socialized with their fellows, while in the late seventeenth century, Yangzhou was reinvented as a city of late Ming memories. In Beijing, Wang was an official's official, or even the emperor's official.[31] In Yangzhou, he was an *yimin* by avocation. In co-opting the late Ming legacy by association, and in self-consciously patterning himself after other famous officials who had served and socialized in the city, Wang Shizhen enhanced his own stature in the local community. When writing biographies and anecdotes about Wang, others, too, used images of Wang among the romantics in Yangzhou to further increase his prestige.

Born in 1634, Wang Shizhen came from a wealthy and prominent Shandong family. He was only ten years old at the time of the Qing conquest, and his family seems to have weathered the transition rather uneventfully.[32] His paternal grandfather was a late Ming official, and two of his three older brothers held the highest degree.[33] Their mother was educated and seems to have taken an interest in her sons' aspirations, although their grandfather was said to have dominated the boys' education.[34] The eldest, Wang Shilu, and the youngest, Wang Shizhen, had a particularly close relationship, often traveling and composing poetry together. Wang Shizhen's advancement through the examination system was remarkably smooth. He passed the provincial examinations at the early age of eighteen *sui*, and passed the metropolitan examination four years later at the age of twenty-two. He took the palace examination at the age of twenty-five *sui* in 1658, placing in the second tier. Although in previous years those who placed in the second tier were granted positions as secretaries in the ministries in Beijing, the 1658 graduates in the second tier were assigned to positions in the provinces. Those who placed in the top ten of the second tier were made sub-prefectural magistrates, with the remainder granted posts as judges *(tuiguan)*.[35] As a result of this new job allocation policy, at the age of twenty-six Wang was assigned to serve as judge in Yangzhou in 1659, making him the third-ranking official in the prefecture, with the primary responsibility of supervising judicial proceedings.[36] He seems to have been loath to leave his active social life in the capital, as he spent most of 1659 in Beijing, where he lived at Ciren Temple attending parties and composing poetry.[37] At this time, he became acquainted with the prominent Suzhou native Wang Wan (1624–91), then serving as a secretary in the Board of Revenue, and the Hefei native Gong Dingzi (1616–73), who had arrived in Beijing to accept a position as an instructor at the National University, as well as Dong Yining, Zou Zhimo (jinshi 1658), and Peng Sunyu (1631–1700, j.s. 1659).[38]

During 1659, Wang Shizhen, his brother Wang Shilu, and Peng Sunyu published a small collection of their matched rhyme poems composed in Beijing.[39] Although both Wang Shizhen and Peng were relatively young and had received their degrees only recently, the publication of this volume attracted positive notice among their peers. In writing his own chronological biography, Wang considered the production of this anthology and his acquaintance with the above gentlemen among the major events of 1659 and worthy of special mention. However, as Wang's career was defined by his official and literary achievements, in compiling his autobiographical chronology, he quite naturally privileged events related to these two spheres in order to highlight the most familiar, and in his social world, the most important, aspects of his public persona. These months in Beijing were to prove formative, with *jinshi* classmates and patrons reappearing frequently in his social, literary, and official endeavors. Several of Wang's Beijing friends and contacts visited Yangzhou and participated in literary gatherings with him, and later with his brother Wang Shilu, and other members of his extended network there. They also appear regularly as preface writers and commentators in each other's literary collections and in various publication projects that came out of Yangzhou in the last decades of the seventeenth century such as Deng Hanyi's *Poetry Survey* (see Chapter 3) and Zhang Chao's *Collectanea for the Present Age* (Zhaodai congshu).

Wang's literary reputation predated both his arrival in the capital and his assignment to Yangzhou. Like most literary greats, he was said to have been a precocious child, composing his first poem at the age of eight *sui*.[40] His eldest brother Shilu, who was a member of a local poetry club, arranged for the publication of Shizhen's first poetry collection in 1648 when he was only fifteen *sui*. These poems were evidently much appreciated by members of the older generation, though again, we must take Wang Shizhen's own word for it.[41] A poetry party held at the Water's Surface Pavilion at Lake Ming in Ji'nan, the capital of Shandong, apparently contributed greatly to his national reputation. In 1657, at the age of twenty-four *sui*, Wang joined a group of gentlemen for a party. He later described this occasion in a preface, which is quoted in his chronological biography and reads as follows:

In the autumn of 1657, I visited Ji'nan. It was just before the provincial examinations so the gentlemen were gathered like clouds at Ming Lake. One day we met for a drinking party at Water's Surface Pavilion. Below the pavilion were about a dozen willow trees waving at the water's edge; in their gentle demeanor they resembled people. The leaves had started to turn a little bit yellow with the first dye of autumn's colors. From their posture, it seemed as if they would wave and then fall. I felt terribly sad, and composed four poems. At that time, several dozen men composed rhyming poems to match them. Three years later, when I arrived in Yangzhou, the four poems had already been around for a long time, and those north and south of the river who had rhymed to them were even more numerous. In this way, the "Autumn Willow Poems" were truly the talk of the world of talents.[42]

The poems became popular as they were recited and rhymed within the literary circles of the period. Even during the early Qing, analysis of these difficult and allusive poems centered on a possibly subversive subtext that nearly led to the banning of Wang's collected works during the Qianlong period.[43] These poems are (retrospectively) presented in Wang's biographies as marking his debut on the national literary scene and establishing his position as a leader of the literary establishment. However, the poems themselves were not the only factor contributing to his fame. His illustrious family background, with several generations of official positions, gave an aura of importance to his early literary compositions. Friends of his father, grandfather, and older brother paid special attention to him when he showed literary promise and guaranteed that his works were published and discussed.

The gathering at Water's Surface Pavilion and the "Autumn Willows Poems" may indeed have marked the moment at which Wang Shizhen was consecrated by his peers as a literary figure worthy of recognition. Certainly it is portrayed as an emblematic moment in the secondary and biographical literature.[44] Still, it was only after he acquired status through success at the Palace examinations that he gained sufficient legitimacy to bestow prestige upon other poets, artists, and even places. Indeed, as he became increasingly famous as both poet and official, Wang Shizhen's stature as a cultural critic and arbiter of literary taste grew, and his social presence and sanction were increasingly sought after.[45] He already enjoyed considerable literary prestige during his tenure in Yangzhou, as can be seen in the number of poetry collections he edited or wrote prefaces for and in the number of gatherings he sponsored or attended with other famous poets. His five years in Yangzhou were seen later as formative. For example, the epitaph by his friend and fellow poet-official Song Lao (1634–1713) states:

Yangzhou is located along the major transport routes. Boats and carts from the four corners of the realm gather here . . . He managed his tasks with skill and efficiency, and met with famous men for literary banquets without a day to rest. In the course of official business, he traveled to Nanjing and Suzhou. His poetry skill improved daily, and he began to use the sobriquet "Yuyang."[46]

The name Yuyang, which Wang chose upon seeing an island of that name at Lake Tai during one of his trips south of the river, was the one most closely associated with his role as a poet and critic. In this passage, Song Lao underscores the association between Wang's service in Yangzhou and the choice of his most famous sobriquet, thereby suggesting that his poetic identity was born during his tenure there.

Wang's fame as a poet drew attention to his actions as an official, and his talents (both literary and official) were portrayed together in literary and artistic descriptions of his achievements in Yangzhou. Inscriptions and colophons on a portrait of Wang Shizhen in his garden at Yangzhou painted by Dai Cang make Wang's dual identity as official and poet explicit. The painting shows a bearded but still very youthful Wang Shizhen seated on a rock holding a zither and wearing a recluse's cap. Two servants stand to the left, one filling a basin with water, the other scrubbing a wutong tree with a cloth. The zither alludes to the "Holding a Zither Pavilion" (Baoqin ting,) a pavilion in his garden in Yangzhou that he built as a retreat in his second year in the city. In another layer of allusion, the name of the pavilion refers to a painting by the Yuan artist Tang Di that Wang had received as a gift around the time that he completed his garden and by extension to a gathering in the garden with his friends and fellow officials, Cao Rong and Zhou Lianggong, when they viewed the painting and exclaimed over its authenticity.[47] The portrait of Wang Shizhen itself bears inscriptions by twenty-one of his contemporaries, with thirty-four additional colophons, all but twelve composed by Wang's peers. Many of the signatories are easily recognized as friends from his Yangzhou years, including a similar assortment of personalities (and indeed some of the same individuals) as attended the Red Bridge gatherings.[48] The inscriptions seem to gather around the figure of Wang Shizhen, the words serving as stand-ins for the men who composed them. They form, quite literally, a literary gathering of friends in his garden. Another portrait from this period, this one anonymous, shows Wang Shizhen, again with a recluse's hat, seated on a low chair and gazing at a vase of plum blossoms. The painting bears five inscriptions and forty-six colophons, all of them by friends and acquaintances from his Yangzhou years. Again, these constitute a similar spectrum of personalities, and again we see many of the same individuals as those represented on the other portrait—and at the Red Bridge gatherings. Indeed, we find many men discussed in this book: You Tong, Zong Yuanding, Peng Sunyu, Yu Huai, Mao Xiang, Du Jun, Yuan Yuling, Shi Runzhang, Lei Shijun, Song Wan, Wang Ji, Lin Gudu, Wang Maolin, Liu Tiren, Gong Xian, and Cheng Sui among others. Whether the painting was a farewell gift to Wang Shizhen, or something closer to an autograph book, it offers evidence of his role at the center of an important literary circle that served as a bridge between Qing officialdom and Jiangnan cultural figures. And many of the inscriptions, like the one written by You Tong, celebrate Wang as both an official and literary talent.

Indeed, achievement in his official capacity strengthened his reputation as a poet, and he was often represented as a contemporary Ouyang Xiu

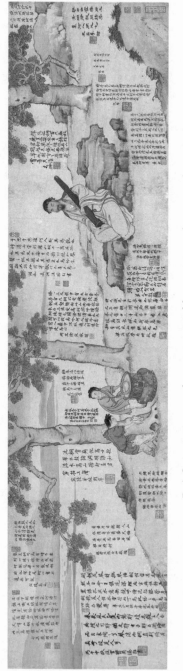

FIGURE 2.1. Dai Cang (seventeenth century), *Holding a Qin and Having the Wutong Tree Washed* (portrait of Wang Shizhen). Handscroll, ink and color on paper, 31.3 × 126 cm. Courtesy of Christie's Images.

or Su Shi, both great writers and officials who had served in Yangzhou. Specific episodes were chosen to represent the man as administrator, and indeed the same handful of episodes is recycled through various biographical retellings. Even the more recent secondary accounts of Wang Shizhen's activities in Yangzhou absorb and repeat biographical details from the official biographies and Wang's autobiographical chronology with no consideration of their narrative function.[49] Thus, the longer versions of Wang's biography present him in the context of challenging cases, towering over complainant and accused, delivering wise speeches, and resolving conflict; the shorter versions describe the same cases, but in a sketchier shorthand. In all accounts, Wang embodies the conventional characteristics of the upright official: he is shown to be energetic and devoted to his job—taking few breaks, working long into the night—as well as incorruptible, taking not even one copper coin in profit from his position.[50]

Close reading of the representative episodes reveals that an important element of these biographical accounts is Wang's resolution of difficult cases left over from the Qing conquest, his sympathy for the local people indirectly winning support for the new regime. The return to normality, although not overtly emphasized, was implicit in the type of events portrayed. In his many biographies, Wang is shown as a sensitive agent of the state, identifying pathways to consensus, freeing the innocent, and mediating between state and local interests. The specific administrative cases presented in the biographies appear only insofar as they reflect the virtues Wang was supposed to have brought to his official position. These cases show Wang manifesting generally desirable qualities like judiciousness, honesty, and frugality, as well as qualities particularly valuable during this period of imperial consolidation such as sympathy for the conquered population, lenience toward the innocent, and the ability to serve as a mediator between the Qing regime and its sometimes unwilling subjects. It should also be noted, however, that the biographies represent an officially sanctioned view of events, as they were written for inclusion in officially sanctioned texts like gazetteers and official histories. For these reasons, though the biographies state that Wang Shizhen resolved eighty-three major cases during his five-year tenure in Yangzhou, the details of the same two cases are juxtaposed in the various versions of Wang Shizhen's official biography and in the epitaph written by Song Lao.

The first of these cases is clearly linked to the political and military instability that continued to plague the Qing state during this period, and Wang Shizhen's solution suggests the triumph of moderation in handling dissent and sedition. During 1659, Zheng Chenggong (Coxinga)

(1624–62) gathered his forces for a major assault on the riverine cities of Jiangnan province. In early August, he succeeded in taking the Yangzi River port of Guazhou in Yangzhou prefecture, just a few miles south of the prefectural seat, seizing the city of Zhenjiang a week later. Although he succeeded in capturing numerous cities and towns further up the river in what is now Anhui, he was defeated in a battle for Nanjing in early September and eventually driven back to the Fujian coast. The Qing government became convinced that Zheng's military successes were due to the secret financial support of the people of the region. In order to frighten suspected contributors to the Ming revivalist cause, the court dispatched officials to Jiangnan to arrest and execute the so-called bandits and pirates. In 1661, the vice-ministers of Revenue and Punishments were sent to Nanjing to mete out punishments. The officials, in their zeal, arrested many innocent people and subjected them to torture. Wang Shizhen, with the support of his superiors, had the verdicts overturned and arranged for the release of those he found innocent, thus winning the gratitude and admiration of the local people.

The case of the unpaid salt taxes is the other "exemplary" case, and apparently its resolution hinged at least in part on the gratitude of local merchants for his role in the political case described above.[51] Between 1645 and 1660, the salt merchants of Yangzhou defaulted on the payment of salt taxes totaling approximately twenty thousand taels.[52] Evidently, many of the original merchants had died, and the previous prefectural judge had arrested the merchants' wives, children, extended families, and in-laws. According to his own account, Wang Shizhen felt sympathy for the merchants' families and sought permission from his supervisor to take up a collection in order to pay back the missing taxes. He gathered money from the local officials, including the salt commissioner, the transport commissioner, the prefectural magistrates, and the magistrates of all the subsidiary counties. He also collected money from the major merchant houses, which agreed to hand over the money, according to one source, because they honored and trusted Wang, on the basis of the reputation he had won through his mediation in the case of the so-called pirates and wrongful arrests.[53] In all, he managed to collect more than ten thousand taels of silver and persuaded the governor general of the province to forgive the rest.[54] This case shows Wang winning the trust of all concerned,

---

FIGURE 2.2. (Opposite) Anonymous (seventeenth century), *Portrait of Wang Shizhen*. Handscroll, ink and color on silk, 29.6 × 39 cm. Courtesy of Christie's Images.

including both officials and merchants. It further highlights the ways in which his sympathetic approach directly benefited both center and locale: he was able to collect more than half of the back taxes and win the sympathy of the Yangzhou merchant community. In contrast, the harsh methods of his predecessor only succeeded in enraging the local people and failed to recoup any of the lost taxes.

Mao Xiang, a famous *yimin* bon vivant with whom Wang Shizhen socialized during his Yangzhou years, commented about him:

It is true that Wang Shizhen is the model official of recent times. He is both humane and brilliant, hard working and sensitive, incorruptible and capable of caution. Yangzhou is a major metropolis between north and south, there are more than a million benighted merchants and people here . . . When Wang Shizhen arrived, he had a cure [for the people's] ills and used his wisdom and benevolence to guide them . . . He made judgments like a god. At that time, neither the clerks and runners nor the local bullies dared to do anything bad. How can we not call him humane and brilliant? Yangzhou is one of the most troublesome places in Jiangnan. The officials send the difficult cases down to the provincial commissions, who send them down to the local level. At early dawn, he sat in his hall. . . . surrounded by cases. . . . his responses flowed like a stream, ten or more clerks working until their wrists hurt. After several months, he had completed several thousand cases; this was an incredible, god-like feat. At night, he not only slept and ate, but also burned a giant candle and analyzed cases. . . . and in the time remaining he read the Classics and the writings of his contemporaries. He was a discerning critic and connoisseur.[55]

Continuing in this vein, Mao praises Wang Shizhen for his frugality, claiming that Wang was very careful in maintaining his household and had not wasted a single copper of local money. Mao then highlights Wang's literary achievements and notes their impact on the city's reputation, pointing out that during Wang's tenure in Yangzhou, his writings were transmitted all over the realm, and as a result, the number of visitors to Yangzhou's scenic sites was increasing by the day.[56] Mao concludes with a description of Wang Shizhen's leisure activities in Yangzhou, stating that he drank and composed poetry with his guests continuously, was always courteous and never entertained selfish thoughts.[57]

This juxtaposition of work and literary/social activities is common to many accounts of Wang Shizhen's life, and his years in Yangzhou in particular. For example, his friend the poet/official Wu Weiye (1609–72) commented, "When Wang Shizhen was in Yangzhou, he spent the mornings working on government business, and at night he met lyric poets."[58] In fact, his administrative tasks were generally presented as secondary to his literary activities. Even the section of his autobiographical chronology dealing with his Yangzhou years lists his social and literary activities before the administrative responsibilities that were said to have dominated his waking hours. Thus, though his official position lent stature to his literary activities, his primary identification (both in his own time and subsequently, by himself and by others) was as a member of an extensive literary and social network. This closely parallels the portrayal of cultural luminaries like Ouyang Xiu and Su Shi, who both served in Yangzhou during the Song. Identification with these former greats bolstered Wang Shizhen's reputation by representing him according to a familiar and widely accepted model. During the seventeenth century, Ouyang Xiu and Su Shi were seen as appropriate icons because they combined cultural authority and an official mandate. Indeed, Wang Shizhen liked to compare himself to Su Shi, both in his poetry production and administrative decisions. His peers also liked to make the same comparison. Song Lao writes: "When Wang Shizhen was chosen to serve as judge in Yangzhou, he did so with diligence and skill. There wasn't a day when he did not gather here for parties and excursions with the various gentlemen. It was like when Bo [Juyi] and Su [Shi] were officials in Hangzhou, the romantic spirit was unceasing."[59] Wang's eldest brother, Shilu, later commented that "even now, those who pass through Yangzhou talk about his previous actions, saying that they are like those of Ouyang Xiu and Su Shi, and do not merely recall Du Mu's [Yangzhou] dream."[60]

In a collection of random jottings compiled when Wang was in his early seventies, he compares his own abolition of the local new year's festivities in Yangzhou, an official celebration involving prostitutes and musicians, to Su Shi's cancellation of the Peony Festival during the Song official's period of service as magistrate in the same city.[61] He wrote:

It was formerly the custom in Yangzhou for the prefectural officials to welcome the spring at Hortensia Daoist Temple [Qionghua guan], and for the prostitutes to lead the way on horseback. The prefectural magistrate and the judge each had four, and the county magistrates and those lower in rank each had two. They held a banquet on their return. The prefectural clerks and runners took advantage of this as an occasion to profit through immorality. I told the magistrate to put a stop to this.[62]

The editors of the county gazetteer indicate the discontinuity in New Year's practice, although they do not credit Wang Shizhen, writing: "Officials formerly welcomed spring in the Eastern Suburbs. They had urban residents all build colorful pavilions and had musicians in bright clothes lead the way. They also had lotus-picking boats festooned with flowers and ribbons and filled with entertainment-quarter women. This has been forbidden because it stirred up the people, and the custom was changed to reverentially welcoming the clay ox and driver as is the normal custom."[63]

Wang Shizhen's friend, the local poet, painter, and plum blossom afi-cionado Zong Yuanding (1620–98), describes these earlier practices in his nostalgic, vivid, and almost ethnographically detailed poem, "Song to Welcome Spring in Guangling" (Guangling yingchun qu), which is in-cluded in the "Local Customs" section of the county gazetteer.[64] In the poem, Zong describes the enthusiastic crowds gathering at Hortensia Daoist Temple and beside the Great East Gate. Sichuan brocades hung from the tops of the pavilions, feasts were set out with exquisite and expensive decorations and goblets of wine. The parade of colorfully dressed courtesans, covered in real and gauze flowers, proceeded through the eastern suburbs, surrounded by the smell of incense and the sounds of shopkeepers hawking animal figurines made from ash and selling sea-sonal foods like bamboo shoots, celery, and special paper-thin New Year's cakes. The magistrate, dressed in purple silk, wore flowers in his hair and was accompanied by clerks on horseback and heavily made-up courte-sans. Shop-owners and brothel-keepers formed teams and sponsored lav-ishly decorated pavilions and boats for the holiday. Zong describes his pride in the splendor and prosperity of his hometown, and juxtaposes these images from his youth with more recent experiences of deprivation, writing: "How sad that for thirty years, we ate mud and trees at the Spring Festival."[65] He attributes this suffering to the greed of the clerks, though he adds that ordinary people, having now recovered from the seasons of want, find it hard to understand why their celebration has been reduced, especially now that some measure of prosperity has returned to the city. The transformation of New Year's festivities in Yangzhou was in fact part of a larger process through which the central government curtailed the involvement of official courtesans in local celebrations, required local administrative units to observe the New Year's festival with the "normal" custom of reverentially welcoming the clay ox and driver, and eventually abolished official courtesans altogether.[66] This heightened emphasis on the role of officials in organizing local practice marks a significant change, and may have derived from a Qing rejection of the social confusion of the late Ming. By abolishing what he considered to be lascivious New Year's customs that were an affront to official dignity, Wang Shizhen positioned himself as the representative of the state in the locale and as an arbiter of cultural norms like Su Shi, who had abolished the peony festival.

The connection among these three official luminaries was made tangi-ble during the Qianlong period, when Ouyang Xiu, Su Shi, and Wang

Shizhen were enshrined together in the "Shrine of the Three Worthies," which was located north of Tianning Temple. The site was marked with an inscription by the salt controller Lu Jianzeng (1690–1768), who often sought to represent himself relative to his fellow Shandong native Wang Shizhen.[67] The famous painter and calligrapher Zheng Xie (1693–1765), better known as Zheng Banqiao, wrote the poetic inscription, which reads: "Their traces fill the Jianghuai region, three men one rhythm / They loved talent as if it were life, different generations, one heart."[68] During Wang's lifetime, analogies drawn between him and the great Song figures both acknowledged and contributed to his cultural prestige in the community of his peers. By Zheng's time, such comparisons seemed beyond question, for they literally had been engraved in stone. In the nineteenth century, though, another Song figure, Han Qi, was added to the constellation "Three Worthies," and Wang Shizhen was enshrined separately on the grounds of the same building. The imaginative link between Ouyang Xiu and Su Shi, so powerful in Wang's own lifetime and in the Qianlong period when Wang was finally awarded posthumous honors, ultimately proved weak in the long term.

Like his predecessors Ouyang Xiu and Su Shi, Wang Shizhen was famous for sponsoring parties, and gatherings in beauty spots (including Red Bridge and the garden attached to his residence) seem to have occupied a considerable amount of his time. Leisure gatherings and administrative responsibility were not entirely separate enterprises, however. Parties were often convened in the context of official business, as the following quote from the local gazetteer suggests:

As part of their public duties, officials arrange straw mats of about 100 square [Chinese] feet. The flavor of rare delicacies from mountains and seas can be detected from far off. Performers act out operas or perform songs and dances or play musical instruments. Each presents his talent before the guests assembled in the hall. These matters are [made to seem] chance encounters, lest others object to their excessive grandeur. Similarly, when the literati or ordinary people prepare their own banquets, they also must arrange for musical and opera performances, and they burn lanterns all night, consuming all manner of delicacies and sweetmeats.[69]

Such banquets were an expected part of the official repertoire, and because of Yangzhou's location along transport routes, many visitors passed through the city and had to be entertained. According to an anecdote in the *Jin shishuo* ("Tales of the World" for Today), guests arrived to see Wang on a daily basis, and when he left the yamen, he would invite these guests to write poetry with him, the pure words flowing elegantly without end. The guests would watch in amazement and say, "Mr. Wang is truly a genius!"[70] Again, these comments reflect the social and performative aspect of poetry composition during this period and the degree to which social performance contributed to an individual's status and reputation. Anecdotes about these gatherings were transmitted orally and through published writings such as the *Jin shishuo,* thereby widening the person's circle of influence beyond a single city or a particular social network.

Travel, too, enhanced Wang's reputation and broadened his social contacts, and government business provided him with frequent opportunities to travel—especially in the Jiangnan area. He took advantage of these occasions to sightsee and socialize with poets and officials in this prosperous region, visiting Nanjing, Suzhou, Changzhou, and Zhenjiang. Such encounters contributed to his reputation, giving rise to tales of his cultured eccentricity and associating his name with famous people and local scenic sites. The poems he composed while traveling in Jiangnan were apparently published as individual anthologies during his Yangzhou years, affording him even more visibility.[71] His reputation was also enhanced through the retelling of anecdotes and the chanting or matching of his poetry by residents of cities like Nanjing. For example, in 1660 he went to Nanjing as an examination official. One dark night, he went out on the Yangzi in a small boat. Wang Zhuo's *Jin shishuo* tells it thus:

The boat reached Yanzi ji [a famous site along the Yangzi River in Nanjing] and Wang grew excited and wanted to disembark and climb up, but it was raining and there was new frost, the wind was soughing in the trees, the waves were ferocious, and the mountains and valleys seemed to call out to each other. His companions looked on in horror as he disembarked. Before he left, he inscribed several poems on the stone cliffs. He walked back to the boat casually and self-confidently. The next day, the poems were the talk of Nanjing, and in all several dozen men matched his rhyme.[72]

Similarly, when he visited Hanshan Temple in Suzhou, he was so overcome by the desire to leave an inscription that he again disembarked from a boat on a dark and rainy night in order to compose two poems on the temple door, and "everyone at the time thought this was crazy."[73] Odd behavior in the name of literary inspiration was a hallmark of late Ming culture; thus, by acting in this manner Wang Shizhen aligned himself with a slightly older generation of famous talents and literary romantics, who still enjoyed enormous cultural prestige in the early Qing. Characteristics like *fengliu* (romantic spirit or fashionable personality) and *fengya* (cultured elegance) were frequently invoked at the most stylish social gatherings, and again, these apparently carried over from the social world of late Ming elites. Wang's actions thus suggest the literary construction of an identity along the lines of the late Ming "romantics" or, as Odaira Keiichi puts it, a role acted out before the eyes of an appreciative audience, rather than the solitary actions of a poet.[74] Yet this identity must have meant something rather different when attached to a successful Qing official.

Service in the city of Yangzhou exposed the young northerner to urban Jiangnan. He traveled frequently to other cities in the region, becoming friendly with men associated with late Ming literary and political networks. These contacts, and his own literary talents, enabled him to develop a persona that was palatable to both official and *yimin* constituencies while strengthening ties between Yangzhou and cities south of the river. Interaction with *yimin* also contributed to his reputation as a talent and a connoisseur of talent. His travels also occasioned meetings with men who were not in government service and visits to places associated with the late Ming.[75] He invited Nanjing poets like Du Jun and Chen Yunheng to participate in his gatherings in Yangzhou. Wang offered these men his patronage and his sympathy, in many cases arranging for the publication and promotion of their writings. In such complex times, a promising young official could express sorrow for the passing of the former dynasty without hinting of hypocrisy. Essays written by Wang in the company of friends were at times suffused with nostalgia and longing for an age that he himself had never in fact experienced. A preface to a small collection of poems that he wrote with friends in Yizheng, one of the subsidiary counties of Yangzhou prefecture, for instance, is filled with allusions to lost sites associated with the Jin and Sui dynasties in Nanjing and Yangzhou. The sites define the sentiments expressed, evoking "distant dreams," desolation, separated friends, and lost splendor.[76] Here, he alludes to an itinerary of loss, the practice of touring ruined sites in order to reflect on past tragedy. He also underscores the power of friendship and poetry to overcome even the awful associations of haunted places.

The landscape resonated with images of the fallen Ming, with ruined traces from the Six Dynasties and the Sui triggering memories of desolate cities and scattered friends. By touring these sites with literary companions, one could transform these feelings into poetry and a sense of camaraderie. Similarly, by gathering with talented men of the former dynasty at Red Bridge, a new site symbolically linked to the entertainment quarters of Nanjing, Wang Shizhen could act out a cultural rapprochement, while at the same time contributing to his own reputation.

A Bridge and Its Man

Red Bridge had no literary legacy prior to the gatherings sponsored by Wang Shizhen. The 1664 Yangzhou gazetteer, published during Wang Shizhen's tenure in the city, lists only the name and location of the bridge in its section on bridges and fords. In fact, the only bridge listed with literary references is Twenty-Four Bridge (Ershishi qiao), made famous by the Tang poet Du Mu, which had long since ceased to exist.[77] By contrast, in a 1688 essay, Kong Shangren commented,

Along the city wall the rich and the powerful have built gardens and pavilions. Parallel to these is a stream, along which pleasure boats with flutes and drums pass constantly. At the turning point of the stream, a tall bridge hangs on high like a rainbow, thus it is called Rainbow Bridge. From the time of Wang Shizhen's parties here, they changed the characters of the name to the homophonic "Red Bridge," and the bridge became part of the cultural legacy [began to be transmitted].[78]

According to Kong, the bridge owed not just its significance but also its name to Wang Shizhen. In his eighteenth-century guidebook, Wang Yinggeng similarly asserts that Wang Shizhen and his gatherings were responsible for the bridge's reputation. Besides exaggerating the size of the gatherings (he called them "huge"), he concludes that awareness of the site was due to the popularity of Wang's "Seductive Spring" (yechun) poems, which he says were "chanted everywhere north and south of the Great River."[79] Li Dou underscores the bridge's central position in the city's cultural geography. In his introduction to the *Record of the Painted Boats of Yangzhou,* he describes the bridge as the focal point of the book's geographical structure, stating that "it all comes together at [Rainbow] Bridge."[80] He also highlights the link between the individual and the site by featuring the biographies of Wang Shizhen and his associates in the first of the two chapters named for the bridge.[81] The relationship between Wang Shizhen and Red Bridge is quite similar to that described by Dong Yining with reference to Su Shi and Red Cliff, except that in the case of Red Bridge, the site had become significant in the relatively recent past.

Built during the Chongzhen reign period (1628–44), Red Bridge was a relatively new addition to the Yangzhou landscape when Wang Shizhen arrived. It was located northwest of the Yangzhou city wall at the point where one of the city's canals opened into Baozhang Lake.[82] Physically, Red Bridge consisted of a graceful wooden span on pilings, allowing boats to pass underneath. Along the sides were railings covered with deep red lacquer, hence the name.[83] The bridge is featured prominently in the illustration of Pingshan Hall in the 1733 gazetteer. The illustration indicates that the span was not flat but consisted of two slanted segments leading up to a flat segment in the middle, mimicking the shape of an arched stone bridge. The midsection was bounded by two commemorative arches.[84] The illustration portrays the bridge as part of a scenic landscape replete with trees, bamboo, pavilions, small dwellings, and an occasional rice paddy. The bridge is positioned relative to the other famous sites of the northwest suburbs, which though unlabeled are symbolically marked and would have been clearly recognizable to contemporaries.[85] A corner of the city wall is visible next to Red Bridge, indicating its relative proximity to the city and underscoring its special position between the city and the suburban temples and famous sites.

Sometime after Wang Shizhen's departure, Wu Qi (1619–94) wrote brief introductions to the famous sites of Yangzhou to accompany a set of poems his friends had written on this subject.[86] The thirty-four sites commemorated by Wu and his friends include apocryphal, historic, and contemporary places. Most of the sites were of Sui, Tang, or Six Dynasties provenance, and the general mood of the introductions is nostalgic, even eulogistic. Only the descriptions of Small Gold Mountain and Red Bridge are presented with a brightly contemporary focus, and Wu describes these as the best tourist spots in the prefecture.[87] His description of Red Bridge combines historical and geographical information with fanciful literary imagery:

Red Bridge is located two *li* [two-thirds of a mile] northwest of the city wall. It was built during the Chongzhen reign by a geomancer in order to block the entrance to the lake. The bridge consists of cinnabar balustrades several *zhang* [a *zhang* equals ten Chinese feet] in height which cross the distance between the two banks. Saying it resembles a rainbow reclining on the waves or a red *jiao* dragon drinking the water is not enough to describe its charm. Moreover there is the fragrance of the lotuses and the beauty of the willows, and the villas and gardens lined up like fish scales and stretching for more than 10 *li* [3.3 miles]. Between spring and summer, abundant music and painted boats appear and disappear among them. Truly it is the most beautiful sight in the prefecture![88]

Wu uses vivid, if conventional, images to contextualize the bridge. The reference to the bridge resembling a reclining rainbow alludes to Wang Shizhen's 1662 "Red Bridge Excursion Record," and thus to the site's lineage of literary significance.[89] In describing the fragrance of the lotuses and the beauty of the willows, Wu draws upon stock metaphors from the demimonde: these plants are frequently used to stand for courtesans, and

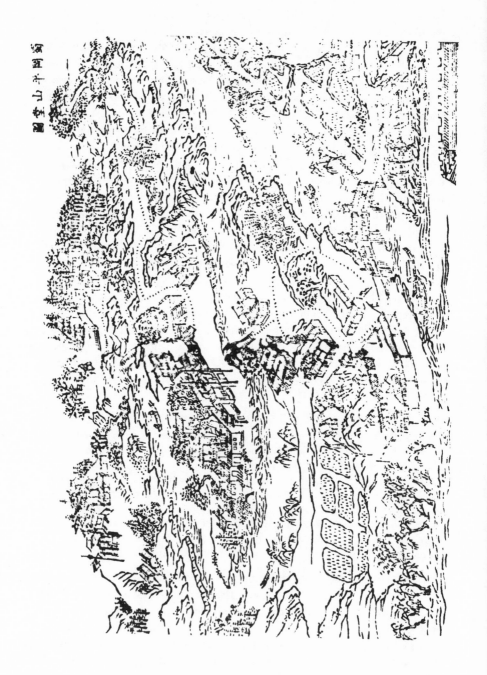

空中山門圖

fragrance and beauty represent their sensual attraction. The immobile luxury of villas and gardens symbolizes wealth and leisure; the mobile pleasures of boats and music suggest consumer entertainments. Wu's description presents the bridge as a site whose scenic beauty is defined by pleasure and its consumption. In this respect, the bridge had assimilated the attributes of the famed Twenty-Four Bridge of the Tang dynasty and had become an icon of urbanity and sensuality.

Red Bridge marked the boundary between the city and the expanding scenic district to the northwest. The canal leading to the bridge began near Lesser East Gate, ran along the wall between the Old City and the New, and passed beyond the city walls to the lake; thus it was formally called the Double Walls Canal (Chongchenghe).[90] Wine shops and houses lined the canal, and both the canal and the lake were popular pleasure boat venues, generating a festive atmosphere even in the early Qing.[91] Boaters exited the city through a sluice gate located between the Zhenhuai and Gongchen gates. This canal was popularly known as "Little Qinhuai," after the famous canal and pleasure quarter in Nanjing that it was said to resemble. Wang Yinggeng's eighteenth-century literary guide to Yangzhou's touring district makes this comparison explicit, quoting Zong Yuandu, who described the canal as follows: "From the wall between the two cities of Jiangdu, it connects to Baozhang Lake. It also serves as the northwest moat of the Old City wall. From Lesser East Gate northward, the two banks have residential buildings packed as close together as the teeth of a comb . . . Because the scenery resembles Nanjing, it has been given the name 'Little Qinhuai.'"[92] The name Little Qinhuai predates the eighteenth century, though probably not by more than a half century. It does not appear in the 1664 gazetteer's section on canals, though the canal itself existed at that time.[93] By the time the *Record of the Painted Boats of Yangzhou* was written in the late eighteenth century, the name Little Qinhuai primarily applied to the segment of the canal along the wall between the Old and New cities, although Li Dou points out that in Wang Shizhen's time, the length of the canal from the Lesser East Gate to Red Bridge was all known as Little Qinhuai.[94] The name appears to have come into vogue during the Shunzhi and early Kangxi periods, when poets used allusion to underscore an imaginative relationship between the two canals, and the two cities. The name "Qinhuai" nostalgically evoked the lost world of the Nanjing pleasure quarters, and its use appears closely related

FIGURE 2.3. (Opposite) Pingshan Hall and Red Bridge. Woodblock illustration. Source: *Yangzhou fuzhi*, 1733.

to the presence of a significant community of *yimin* in Yangzhou during
the second half of the seventeenth century. Men like Mao Xiang (1611–
93) had been active in Nanjing during the late Ming, and their names were
closely linked to the Southern Ming capital, especially to the Qinhuai district, where the examination halls and pleasure quarters were located.[95]
The Yangzhou canal thus became embedded in a poetics of loss and remembered pleasures associated with Nanjing.

   In the fifth poem of a ten-poem song cycle entitled "Little Qinhuai
Songs" (Xiao Qinhuai qu), Chen Weisong (1626–82) wrote:

> At the Sui palace gates, tangled grasses freeze
> Outside the walls of Jiankang, the vast waters flow
> Is it big Qinhuai or little Qinhuai? You should stop asking
> Crying for a thousand springs, it is always the same.[96]

Like most poems from this period, Chen's set of ten songs seems to have
been written on a particular social occasion and reflects the setting and
mood of that moment. These lines appear to have been written in 1665
at a gathering near the Little Qinhuai canal that was attended by Mao
Xiang and his son Mao Danshu, and indeed, this poem appears to be
addressed to Mao Xiang himself.[97] Although he was fifteen years younger
than Mao Xiang, Chen was a close friend of the famous bon vivant and
shared his reputation as a literary talent. At this time, neither man was in
the service of the Qing, although Chen's case was one of failure to pass
the examinations rather than ideological commitment. In this poem, Chen
uses familiar historical imagery to highlight the tragedies of two cities,
past and present. He aligns his poem with the *yuefu* tradition, a style often
used to convey a tone of simplicity and sincerity. The ruined Sui palace
is a frequent metonym for Yangzhou. The Liang capital at Jiankang, destroyed by the Sui in the sixth-century, was located to the south of the
later city of Nanjing, and its name was occasionally used by early Qing
poets to stand for the Southern Ming capital. The names of both sites
resonate with the sense of loss and destruction that suffused early Qing
poetry about Nanjing and Yangzhou. The parallel images of frozen
grasses and flowing waters further indicate ruin, and the sorrow of time
irrevocably past. The third line reiterates the connection between the two
cities and their traumatic histories, blurring the distinction between the
two canals—is it Nanjing, or is it Yangzhou? It is no longer worth asking.
This line, using the second-person pronoun *jun*, links the addressee,
unnamed but probably Mao Xiang, with both locales: the lost world of
his youth at Qinhuai in Nanjing, and Yangzhou, the capital of his home

prefecture, a city with its own recent ghosts. The final line effaces temporal and spatial difference: the sorrows of the millennia repeat and are ever the same in both places.

The mood of Chen's poetry cycle is one of melancholy reflection. The poems in his series on Little Qinhuai are carefully located in the Yangzhou landscape, mixing references evocative of the canal with images of loss, destruction, and alienation. This is also true of the poems written on the same occasion or at the same site (or both) by Mao Xiang and Mao Danshu. Several of these poems contain veiled allusions to the fall of the Ming, as does the second poem in Chen Weisong's cycle, which reads:

> After ten years, the feelings have yet to subside
> I again cross one of Yangzhou's bridges.
> In a small chair by a crooked fence, I recall past events
> My wounded heart and the setting sun, surrounded by willow
>   branches.[98]

Chen's second poem closely matches the rhyme of the corresponding poem in Mao Xiang's song sequence, as does each of his poems. In Chinese, the final characters of the first, second, and fourth lines are the same. Mao's poem reflects similar sentiments as well, reading:

> All sites cause the visitor to think of what is gone
> Following the stream outside the walls to Red Bridge
> No gorgeous views can sustain pleasures again
> The scenery at the Sui hunting grounds, only these willow
>   branches[99]

Mao Xiang's poem reminds us that landscape elements have the power to stir the visitor's memory, each place evoking a mood reminiscent of what has been lost. We follow him on a journey along the canal to Red Bridge, and yet he cannot find what he seeks there; the view alone cannot lighten his spirits with pleasing amusements. He closes with an image of a historical ruin, the Sui hunting park, now covered with willows. The references to willows in both poems draw upon a long tradition equating willows with courtesans (and with the city of Yangzhou, which was also called "The City of Willows"), highlighting another associative element in this landscape: its function as a pleasure quarter.[100]

The corresponding poems in each of the three song cycles (by Mao Xiang, Chen Weisong, and Mao Danshu) reprinted in Wang Yinggeng's book follow the rhyme scheme set by those in Mao Xiang's song cycle. Composing poems under such circumstances could, and often did, result in bland renderings of pretty scenery. And yet, as Mao Xiang's poem suggests, the landscape itself could trigger memories and impressions, providing the poet with a rich palette of emotional imagery. In turn, though these poems, too, were composed as entertainment in the context of a social gathering, the fame of the participants gave meaning to the place, and their association with the original Qinhuai in Nanjing gave meaning to "Little Qinhuai," both the name and the place. Finally, though many of the references in Mao Xiang and Chen Weisong's poetry cycles are to the historical past and indirectly to the Qing conquest, the eighth poem in each cycle centers on the person of Wang Shizhen, the recently transferred judge. Even after his departure, Wang's presence gave coherence to the extensive network of literary men in Yangzhou, and his peers agreed that his poetry had put Red Bridge on the city's cultural map. Even in the 1660s, a reference to the "Great Talent of Our Age," Wang Shizhen, was obligatory—for his presence gave meaning to the bridge, and the bridge, in turn, defined the area near the canal.[101]

Despite the rhetoric of loss and displacement associated with this area during the early Qing, it was not an isolated wilderness landscape but was in the process of becoming a bustling recreational area. The coexistence of loss and pleasure as the defining symbolic features of a site should not be surprising, for the two have long functioned as a binary trope in Chinese literature.[102] On the one hand, pleasure was not simply the locus for nostalgic fantasies about the former Ming but was also a very real aspect of the city's reconstruction. On the other, as the city was rebuilt, the contrast between new pleasure grounds and those that had been lost became an anchor for additional nostalgic imaginings and poetry, even among those with close ties to the Qing state. Evidence describing the physical reconstruction of "unofficial" Yangzhou is sadly insufficient, but it appears that facilities devoted to luxury and recreation were rebuilt relatively rapidly. References to courtesans at the Red Bridge gatherings of the early Kangxi period further suggest that the pleasure quarters near the bridge had been quickly restored.[103] In addition, at least three large pleasure boats plied the waters of Baozhang Lake during the Shunzhi era—suggestive, even though the number is small.[104] Boats and other forms of entertainment were closely linked in the imaginations of male consumers during the late imperial period. Indeed, the term "painted pleasure boats" functioned as a euphemism for the pleasure quarters of Jiangnan.[105] The boats, music, willow branches, and singing girls reinforced the association between this pleasure district and those of other southern cities, while at the same time reinforcing the imagery of loss with which these symbols were inevitably linked.

Like pleasure boats, wine shops seem to have been emblematic of the bridge and its environs. By the 1660s, there were already wine shops with colorful banners located in this area, purveying food and drink to the growing crowds of boaters.[106] Intimations of the bridge's "tawdry" public aspect are found in Wang Maolin's 1679 poem entitled "Qingming":

> Last year at Qingming I was at Tiger Hill
> To my annoyance the tower was blocked in by wind and rain
> We haven't had clear skies at Qingming in years
> All one can do is imagine that the touring is good
> The new love songs sung slightly off key
> The seductive ladies' new hairstyles piled high
> Thousands of dandies at Red Bridge
> Clap their hands in envy at brightly painted boats.[107]

Wang's poem expresses disappointment that the anticipated holiday revelry had not materialized, and he uses these foiled expectations to create an impression of what *should* occur at Red Bridge on such an occasion. In the opening line, he recalls the previous year at Tiger Hill in Suzhou, when bad weather prevented him from taking in the view from the famous pagoda. This sets up an analogy between the two sites, and the shift of venue to Yangzhou is revealed only in the seventh line. The colorful scene of fancy ladies with fashionable hairstyles, exuberantly dissonant music, and thousands of onlookers provides a glimpse of the Red Bridge area as an ordinary (not exalted) destination, and its popularity as a venue for holiday outings. This underscores the fact that Red Bridge was a site with significance for a wide range of visitors.

The Ganquan county gazetteer describes the bridge as follows: "Vermilion railings spanning the banks, green willows lining the dikes, and the wine shop banners furling and unfurling all make this the best place for leisure excursions."[108] The colors red and green, closely associated with leisure entertainment and the pleasure quarters, also appear frequently in descriptions of this site, whether with reference to the green willows and vermilion railings in the passage above, or to the clothing and boats of drunken tourists.[109] In describing their own entertainments, late seventeenth-century literati referred contemptuously to the presence of noisy revelers in pleasure boats. Such comments distinguished their entertainments from the similar activities of other social groups. The bridge and its environs thus functioned on several levels in literati social writings. It provided a context for reflection on personal and political loss, a venue for the appreciation of pleasures past and present, and finally an opportunity to distinguish themselves from their "social others" through both writing and practice. The bridge became one of the most popular poetry subjects in the prefecture, as indicated by the two and a half chapters devoted to it in Wang Yinggeng's eighteenth-century literary guide.[110] Once consecrated by association with Wang Shizhen and his extended social network, the bridge emerged as an important element in the Yangzhou landscape, offering a physical space in which subsequent officials could literally position themselves relative to their more famous predecessor.

The Gatherings at Red Bridge: Event and Meaning

The 1743 edition of the Ganquan county gazetteer entry on Red Bridge includes the following taken from the *Yuyang Shihua,* a collection of comments on poetry by Wang Shizhen written in 1710:

Wang Shizhen said: "I have had a banquet at Red Bridge with Yuan Yuling, Du Jun, and others. On that occasion I wrote an essay and three *ci* poems. The one that reads 'Green willows and city walls, this is Yangzhou' was one of them. Yuan Yuling was drunk and had the musicians play a Yuan style opera (nanqu) that he had written. On another occasion, I carried out the spring lustration ritual at Red Bridge with Lin Gudu, Sun Zhiwei, Zhang Zuwang, and others. The famous men of the time all used my twenty poems on the theme 'Seductive Spring' to rhyme with. When I left Yangzhou, I crossed Red Bridge. Many of those who saw and remembered turned this into a story of Yangzhou."[111]

Wang Shizhen frequently chose Red Bridge as a backdrop for his literary and social activities. Here he alludes to the two gatherings he felt were the most important, due to the literary works they inspired. The last line refers to his ceremonial departure from the city. That he left from the northwest via Red Bridge, rather than on the Grand Canal east of the city, underscores his affinity for the site, and seems born of a desire for a dramatic exit. We see here the flourish of an impressive ego, a man profoundly aware of his own importance and of his role in the creation and presentation of his own image. This sensibility is retrospective, written into existence years after his departure from Yangzhou. Here he portrays his activities in Yangzhou as crucial events, shaping his public persona and reputation.

This retrospective construction of significance obscures the actual events: we cannot know for certain who attended these gatherings—the lists vary and are incomplete. Nor do we know exactly what these men did at their gatherings, for the sources are burdened with the time-honored conventions for representing leisure or else were written many years after the occasions they commemorate. Errors by the annotator of Wang's chronological autobiography, Hui Dong (1697–1758), further confuse matters: was it the third month gathering or the sixth month in 1662 when Wang Shizhen wrote his essay and three ci poems with Yuan Yuling and the others? And if the two events were conflated by the annotator, can we trust him to know who was really present? The annotator evidently assumes that the men who composed matched-rhyme poems to the three ci poems composed by Wang Shizhen were present at the spring gathering. But since the poems were actually composed at the summer gathering, how can we know who was present in the spring? Li Dou also confused the same events, probably basing his discussion on the annotations.[112] These mistakes indicate the degree to which the image of the spring gatherings overwhelmed subsequent representations of Wang Shizhen's activities at the bridge.[113] In the end, the particulars are irrelevant: Wang Shizhen is remembered, and clearly wished to be remembered, for his spring gatherings at Red Bridge in 1662 and 1664.

The spring lustration festival that occasioned Wang Shizhen's Red Bridge gatherings historically was a day on which people went to the water's edge to cast off evil influences. Later it became an occasion for drinking, singing, and poetry composition. During earlier dynasties, people of all social classes practiced this custom, but over the centuries it was increasingly associated with the official elite. Both the date and associated activities were inevitably and imaginatively linked to the most famous spring gathering, that sponsored by the renowned calligrapher Wang Xizhi at the Orchid Pavilion (Lanting) in Zhejiang in 353 C.E. On that occasion, Wang Xizhi and his friends floated wine cups down a stream and composed poetry, and the calligrapher later wrote a preface for his friends' poems. This became one of the most esteemed works of calligraphy in the artistic canon, and, as Stephen Owen points out, it remains the "classic statement on parties."[114]

The last couplet in the "Seductive Spring" series written by Wang Shizhen in 1664 makes explicit the analogy between the gathering at Red Bridge and the gathering at the Orchid Pavilion. It reads: "Remember well the year 1664 when we commoners drank / Bamboo West Pavilion became the Orchid Pavilion."[115] References to the gathering at the Orchid Pavilion abound in writings about poetry parties and scenic sites in seventeenth-century Yangzhou. This is, perhaps, due to a perceived continuity of feelings with those expressed by the Six Dynasties calligrapher: a sense of time passing, the loveliness of the scenery, and the transient pleasure of friendship. Another more tenuous spatial connection linked Wang Xizhi's gathering and the gatherings of fourteen Southern Song loyalist poets in 1279 to mourn the desecration of the Song imperial tombs by a Tibetan lama in 1278.[116] Five sets of song lyrics were composed during five meetings held to mark the tragic event, all of which allude symbolically to the remains of the emperors, empresses, and their consorts. Materials related to these events were published for the first time in the early Qing, and the poems were edited by Zhu Yizun, himself a fellow *ci* poet and associate of Wang Shizhen.[117] It is not inconceivable that late seventeenth-century allusions to the Orchid Pavilion carried a subtext relating early Qing political concerns with those of their Yuan predecessors.

Wang Shizhen's essay "An Excursion to Red Bridge" was written in the summer of 1662, and by 1666, it had been inscribed on a stone tablet installed in the Ocean of the Law Temple, which, as the essay itself indicates, was one of several stopping places on the conventional tourist itinerary.[118] In this essay, Wang describes Red Bridge in the context of an abstracted season and a specific day, as part of a general itinerary and as a particular site. The description is thus simultaneously intimate and distancing, the reader is both a vicarious participant in the event described and a "recumbent" tourist following an impersonal itinerary. The essay historicizes Wang Shizhen's party through allusions to the distant past, while at the same time describing a deeply satisfying present-day experience. There is a note of ambivalence. The site triggers an emotional response, but one that lies ambiguously between joy and sorrow. He also suggests an emotional continuity between past and present, wondering at how similar his sentiments are to those of distant, Six Dynasties period forebears. The essay reads as follows:

Beyond Zhenhuai Gate, following the stream as it winds its way northward, the varied shapes of the sloping shore are lush with bamboo and trees, and the shining stream looks like a silver belt. Many people have used the water to make gardens; the pavilions and dikes are mysterious and bright, truly capturing the beauty of the four seasons. We took a small boat and followed the canal to the northwest. Where the row of trees ended there was a lovely bridge, which seemed like a rainbow that had come down to drink from the flowing waters, or like a beautiful woman looking at her reflection in a bright mirror. This is the so-called "Red Bridge." When leisure tourists ascend Pingshan Hall [note: in 1662 it was still a ruin on the grounds of a Buddhist temple], they reach the Ocean of the Law temple first, leave their boats there and continue by land. This route passes below Red Bridge. The bridge is surrounded by houses, and during the sixth and seventh months, the lotuses planted on the dikes bloom in abundance and the fragrance can be smelled for miles. The green wine shop banners and white boats seem interwoven like cloth. Truly this is an excellent outing! On the several occasions that

I have come north of the city wall, I have always had to cross Red Bridge, and so I feel glad whenever I see it. When I climb the bridge and look around, I always feel an ambiguous need to sigh. It is a feeling between sorrow and joy, and I cannot fathom its cause. I remember Wang [Xizhi] and Xie [An]'s ancient words at Yancheng [ca. 4th century], and I think of how Master Jing and Master Yan shed tears at Cow Mountain [5th century]. I recall the past today, and wonder at how similar it is to the present. In the summer of 1662 on the day of the full moon, Yuan Yuling, Du Jun, and Chen Yunheng spontaneously took a boat; we drank wine and were extremely happy. I wrote two poems, and the gentlemen all rhymed their poems to mine. Then we took old songs and rhymed according to them. Yuan Yuling went even further and wrote an essay, which I also did. Alas! Why must beautiful music be written at middle age? The pure music of the scenery transforms itself into beautiful [poetic] lines. I seldom have the chance to meet with these gentlemen; indeed, a good gathering is never easily encountered. Perhaps because of our meeting here the fame of Red Bridge will be considered worth passing on to subsequent generations, thereby increasing the ambiguous need to sigh of those in the future who cherish the past and grieve for it as I do today. But this cannot yet be known.[119]

The closing lines highlight the connection between the reputations of men and places and mirror the closing lines of the Orchid Pavilion Preface.[120] This meeting of friends, he implies, might make Red Bridge a gathering place for future generations.

In this essay, Wang Shizhen adopts the time-honored persona of Wang Xizhi at the Orchid Pavilion, though perhaps with greater ambivalence about the sensibility of future generations. While a Qing official's self-representation as a recluse might seem ironic, the pose was quite popular in elite circles at that time. This identification was not just literary: Wang and his peers had their portraits painted with the symbolic attributes of great recluses. For example, in 1700, Yu Zhiding (b. 1647) painted Wang Shizhen, by then the head of the Board of Punishments in Beijing, as the famous Six Dynasties poet and recluse Tao Yuanming releasing a silver pheasant, in a pun for "release to leisure" or "release from official service."[121] The painting shows Wang Shizhen seated on a low wooden couch in his garden, wearing the hat of a recluse and holding a string-bound volume in one hand, the other hand resting lightly on his forearm. His servant has just released the pheasant from a bamboo cage, and turns back to inform Wang of the bird's departure, even as Wang stares out of the picture-space to meet the eyes of the viewer. The artist's inscription makes the link between Wang Shizhen and Tao Yuanming explicit.[122] As Richard Vinograd indicates, this portrait, like several other paintings of Wang Shizhen by Yu Zhiding, conveys a "tone of escapism within an elaborately staged anecdotal set piece."[123] He adds that Yu Zhiding provided

FIGURE 2.4. Yu Zhiding, *Wang Shizhen Releasing a Silver Pheasant*. Handscroll, 26.1 × 110.7 cm; on silk. Courtesy of the Palace Museum, Beijing.

his "clientele of scholars and officials with consoling visualization of their ideal identities" and "made claims of value and status for the sitter in a cultural and often literary role."[124] As we have seen above, Yu Zhiding's sitters engaged in similar cultural projects on their own, using their writings and leisure outings to position themselves as analogues of great men of the past. The use of Wang Xizhi's Orchid Pavilion Preface as a model similarly makes Wang Shizhen's Red Bridge essay a staged anecdotal piece, rendered in words rather than pictures.

By adopting the guise of Wang Xizhi in his Red Bridge essay, Wang Shizhen suggests that poetry composition among friends could provide release from the despair associated with reflections on the past and its relics, transforming those feelings into a more generalized reflection on the evanescence of all things. Such reflections on the passing of time seem particularly appropriate given Wang's choice of companions for the outings to Red Bridge that he and later compilers chose to immortalize in essays and poetry. The three men mentioned by name in the excursion essay enjoyed considerable cultural prestige in their own time, and it is not surprising that Wang sought to emphasize his contact with them. One was an official and a writer, and the other two were poets whose later fame was in part due to their refusal to serve. The first, Yuan Yuling (1592–1674), was a Suzhou native and a late Ming government student. The local elite of Suzhou asked Yuan to write their notice of surrender to the Qing forces, and in 1645, he became the magistrate of Jingzhou. His principal area of cultural achievement was as a composer of operas, the most famous of which is the Romance of the Western Tower, although his reputation seems to have diminished subsequently.[125] By contrast, Du Jun and Chen Yunheng have both been celebrated over the centuries as loyalists, and their works are frequently anthologized in collections of works by Ming *yimin*. Both maintained residences in Nanjing and periodically traveled to Yangzhou to socialize with friends and fellow poets there.

Chen Yunheng was a native of Jianchang, Jiangxi province. His father was a well-known writer, who committed suicide upon hearing the news of the Chongzhen emperor's suicide.[126] Due to his talent as a poet, Chen Yunheng was able to establish contact with the most famous writers of the late Ming. He fled his hometown as a result of the chaos that erupted during the late Ming, eventually settling in Nanjing, where he lived in poverty for many years. While he was living in Nanjing, famous men, especially *ci* poets, sought to make his acquaintance.[127] Chen was an integral part of a community of poets who rejected government service under the Qing. Wang Shizhen seems to have taken special interest in these poets, offering them money and assistance, as well as inviting them to his poetry gatherings.

Similarly, Du Jun came from an official family in Hubei, and in his youth he prepared for the examinations. During the 1639 provincial examinations, he was deemed an "honorable failure," for being the best among those who did not pass. He tried again three years later but again failed. Instead of pursuing an official career, he embarked on a journey to visit the famous mountains of the realm, a stylish alternative in the final decades of the Ming. After the conquest, he settled in Nanjing, where he wrote books and poetry and tried to avoid the attentions of those who wished to pay their respects and obtain writings from him. He took on the role of the authentic romantic, rejecting wealth and power in favor of poetry and social eccentricity. An epitaph by the well-known essayist Fang Bao (1668–1749) describes Du's behavior as follows: "He was elegant, but did not wish to be famous for his poetry, so he was uniquely respected by his peers . . . Nanjing is the crown of the four quarters, and a major intersection for travelers. The rich and famous seeking famous poets all wished to call upon him, but he didn't always comply. Even if someone was famous or a high official, he would not necessarily receive him . . ."[128]

According to Fang's account, Du Jun was willing to go to great lengths to avoid undesirable visitors and would keep even those with appointments waiting on a bench outside his house. Du Jun's biography in the "Hermits" section of his hometown gazetteer emphasizes his lofty purity, ideals, and literary talent. The biography continues, stating, "All of the elders of Jiangnan, whether they chose to serve or stay at home, all competed to pay their respects to him. Finally he moved to an isolated corner of the city, to the west of Jiming Hill. This was good for the quality and purity of his writings. He struggled against poverty, and refused to serve."[129] These efforts at isolation seem to have only contributed to Du Jun's prestige. There are many anecdotes that reveal Du Jun's aversion to wealth while demonstrating his talent as a poet. All of them are set in Yangzhou and involve lantern boats, prize money, and Du's poetic prowess.[130] In fact, these tales seem to be versions of the same story, with the number of mythic elements growing with each retelling and as the distance from actual events increased. A portrait of Du Jun by his contemporary and fellow Nanjing resident, Zhang Feng, shows the poet seated in a chair overshadowed by a pine tree, a conventional symbol of resilience and lofty ideals, visually underscoring the values ascribed to him by his biographers.[131]

Wang Shizhen, who eagerly cultivated and publicized his contact with

FIGURE 2.5. Zhang Feng (active 1636–62), *Portrait of Du Yuhuang [Du Jun]*, Qing dynasty, seventeenth century, hanging scroll; ink and color on paper, 134.6 × 50.2 cm. S. M. Nickerson Fund, 1952.251. Courtesy of the Art Institute of Chicago.

the elusive senior poet, wrote that "Du Jun lived as a sojourner in Nan-jing. He was extremely poor. On several occasions he visited Yangzhou. In 1664, on the seventh day of the first month, it was snowing hard, and I had nothing to do, so I decided to visit him. We engaged in pure con-versation for the whole day."[132] In his poetry criticism and random jot-tings, Wang Shizhen relates anecdotes about Du Jun, comments favorably on the older poet's writing, and shares Du Jun's comments on both of their poetry. In writing his account of the gathering at Red Bridge, Wang Shizhen sought to identify himself with famous men of talent of an older generation. He further publicized these relationships by arranging for the publication of the *ci* poems composed at the gathering under the titles *Yisheng chuji* and *Hongqiao changhe ji*.[133] The former collection con-sisted of *ci*, and at least by the eighteenth century had been given the occa-sional title "Recalling the Past at Red Bridge," ironic given that Red Bridge itself was of quite recent provenance.[134] The internal imagery, however, is very much in the "recalling the past" mode. Red Bridge pro-vides a contemporary vantage point from which to view spaces once occu-pied by the Sui palaces and tombs. The first of Wang's lyrics contains the line "Green willows and city walls, this is Yangzhou," one of the most commonly quoted lines of Yangzhou poetry even today.[135] According to the annotations later added to Wang's autobiography, Wang himself chose the rhyme, and several others, "from Du Jun down," composed matching poems, again underscoring Du's stature relative to the other guests. The account continues, stating that the poems were transmitted north and south of the Yangzi River and that a painting was commis-sioned to commemorate the event, and "as a result, most of those who visited Yangzhou looked for Red Bridge."[136]

Wang Shizhen held a second lustration festival gathering at Red Bridge two years later. The activities undertaken at the second gathering were probably similar to those at the first, although no description survives. Its reputation rests instead on the renown of the host and his guests, and the recitation and imitation of the poems they composed. On this occasion, Wang Shizhen wrote twenty *jueju* couplets entitled "Seductive Spring," and his guests composed harmonizing poems. They formed a poetry club, which they called the "Seductive Spring Poetry Club," after the title of the *jueju* series that Wang led them in composing. Again, the most honored guests were poets of the late Ming. These included Lin Gudu, Zhang Wangsun, Sun Zhiwei, and possibly Du Jun.[137] Internal evidence from the "Seductive Spring" poems indicates that Cheng Sui, Sun Mo, Xu Cheng-xuan, and Xu Chengjia were also present.[138]

Lin Gudu was the most senior guest at this gathering. Lin was a native of Fuqing, but in the late Ming he moved to Nanjing with his brother in order to meet the famous poets of his generation. He counted the great Ming aesthetes Cao Xuequan and Zhong Xing among his close friends and literary influences. After the Ming collapse, he continued to reside in Nanjing, though in more humble accommodations. Lin was said to have been extremely poor and is described as having lived in a humble, rustic house where he played the zither and wrote songs to achieve happiness.[139] The use of terms virtually identical to those used to describe Chen Yun-heng's circumstances suggests that there were set conventions for describing late Ming literary figures who continued to live in Nanjing after the dynasty's fall. Due to his literary reputation, he attracted the patronage of officials like Zhou Lianggong and Wang Shizhen.[140] On the occasion of the second spring gathering at Red Bridge, Wang served as the older man's walking stick, thereby honoring the senior poet and reflecting that honor onto himself.[141] In the "Seductive Spring" poems, he also flatter-ingly compared Lin to an immortal exiled from heaven and equated him with the former worthies.[142] Wang Shizhen's patronage of Lin extended well beyond party invitations, as can be seen in his letter to Cheng Kun-lun, which reads:

Mr Lin is eighty-three this year, and his literary works are much respected . . . At the time of our last meeting, he showed me all of his writings, which he had hid-den away at Breast Mountain [Rushan, near Nanjing]. These poems, written between 1604 and the present, have not been published. Lin is extremely poor and cannot afford to seek publication, and were his poems published we fear they will be lost among the ephemera. People nowadays are brazen and inexperienced, their learning consists of worthless noise, and they publish reams of writings and dis-tribute them all over the city. Whereas this old man who has been famous for sev-enty years cannot even transmit one word to posterity. Isn't it a shame? My inten-tion is to first edit his recent works, then to ask those who like to do good works to sponsor a volume each . . .[143]

Others among the guests had similar reputations. Zhang Wangsun, though less well known than Lin Gudu and Du Jun, also has been con-sidered an *yimin*.[144] Like the more senior guests, Sun Zhiwei (1620–87), who was only fourteen years older than Wang Shizhen, had been a gov-ernment student during the late Ming, and in the 1660s he was still described as a "loyal" subject of the Ming.[145] When Li Zicheng's forces attacked his hometown in Shaanxi in the 1640s, he helped organize the young men of his district into a militia. When the town fell, he fled and became a successful merchant in Yangzhou.[146] After accumulating considerable wealth, he abandoned trade and became quite well known for poetry.[147] When Wang came to serve in the city, he called on Sun. The two became friends and often socialized together. Sun Mo, called a "cultivated person living in retirement" in the "Seductive Spring" poems, was a connoisseur and poetry collector living in Yangzhou. In his funeral address, Wang Shizhen characterizes Sun Mo as follows:

Wuyan [Sun Mo] and I knew each other for twenty years, so I know what kind of person he was. In general, he was honest and not opportunistic; he esteemed moral duty and avoided vainglory. Casting off his wife and child was to him as removing his sandals, but his love for literature and friends was no different from the way hunger and thirst are to eating and drinking. So Wuyan, though he was an old and impoverished commoner, was known throughout the realm. Wuyan's hometown is below the thirty-six peaks of Huangshan, though he lived in Guangling [Yangzhou] and did not return home. Natives of Xin'an [Huizhou] residing in Guangling are rich and engage in conspicuous consumption, whereas Wuyan alone was a poor, humble man. He lived in the marketplace on a crooked alleyway with a hidden gate. However, famous people from all over the realm who passed through Yangzhou stopped their boats and looked for Sun's household, trying to pay a visit.[148]

Once more we have a poor, eccentric poet, talented, and fond of socializing. These characteristics seem to have been integral to the image of the late Ming urban recluse living in the early Qing city, for they purportedly were shared by most of Wang Shizhen's guests. In organizing his second gathering at Red Bridge, Wang seems to have chosen his guests on the basis of their cultural standing. He presented himself as the official sponsor and patron of these late Ming talents. His political position gave him the stature to host such gatherings, and the social and cultural prestige of his guests added further luster to his reputation.

On this occasion, Wang Shizhen composed a series of twenty *jueju* entitled "Seductive Spring." The series as a whole consists of a cluster of disparate images, some historical, others contemporary. Each poem is like an album leaf portraying a single dimension of the larger symbolic or emotional landscape. As a composite, the poems draw upon imagery associated with the bridge and the city, ranging from sensuous images of flowers and trees to reflections on the past and descriptions of individual participants in the events of the day. In keeping with the suggestive title, Wang Shizhen begins his series with five poems that feminize and eroticize the Yangzhou landscape. The east wind, flowering fruit trees, birds, and butterflies are conventionally represented as (and represent) beautiful women. The first is typical and reads, "This year the East wind has been a playful tease / blowing sunshine and making rain as it sends in the spring / The plums along the river fell like red snow in one night / then the tantalizing peach blossoms opened in profusion."[149]

The next three poems recall past events: in the first two, the poet mourns the destruction of the Sui palaces, and in the third he borrows the persona of Su Shi to regret the passing of Ouyang Xiu. In the ninth poem, the subject shifts to the day's gathering: "When the East Wind and flowers come to the River City / And vendors already hawk their sweet confections / We'll think of each other on other days and never can forget / The five years I spent Qingming below Pingshan Hall."[150] The tenth and eleventh poems also describe the atmosphere of this particular day, referring to the fame of the guests, the nearby temples, the flowering crabapple trees, and the feelings of melancholy inspired by drinking in this setting. In the twelfth poem, Wang praises his guest of honor, Lin Gudu, by comparing him to an immortal, and in the thirteenth, he alludes to the year when "the cannons forced down the walls." Poems fourteen and fifteen refer to the other invited guests, and sixteen and seventeen highlight the restorative power of poetry and friendship. By referring to his guests in the poem series, Wang binds together the day, the guests, and the poems—event, personality, and cultural legacy. The eighteenth poem is another landscape verse, whereas number nineteen refers to the "Autumn Willow" poems that Wang Shizhen composed at Ming Lake in Shandong, and which a guest apparently had praised. The final poem creates an analogy between the day's events and those at the Orchid Pavilion.

The alternately bright and dark images seen in these poems became part of the set of poetic conventions used to portray gatherings in this area of the city. Pleasure and loss coexisted. Writing about the charms of today, Wang Shizhen invoked the melancholy of yesterday. The nostalgic literati pose gradually diminished in importance, however, as the city was inundated by an influx of merchant wealth in the eighteenth century. By the early Qianlong period, poetry was all about pleasure and all about today. Invocations of "Seductive Spring" became literal and physical, as Wang Shizhen's words were incorporated into a landscape created for the delectation of the increasingly visible merchants and their imperial guest.

Red Bridge Revisited

The "Seductive Spring" poems became wildly popular, and they were widely imitated and chanted. As a result, the phrase "seductive spring" entered the poetic lexicon and became an established theme in the local repertoire of landscape poetry.[151] Furthermore, Wang Shizhen's parties had a significant impact on the naming and depiction of the local landscape, and, even after his departure, association with Wang continued to be invoked as a measure of local poets' worth. In developing scenic sites and gardens, names linked to the gatherings came into increasing use. During the Kangxi period, a teahouse adopted the name "Seductive Spring Club," after the poetry club founded by Wang Shizhen and his friends.[152] The inscription for this teahouse was written by Kong Shangren, who himself adopted the persona assumed earlier by Wang Shizhen. The property was later incorporated into a private garden, but it retained the name, if not the function, of the teahouse.[153] Even now, the name Seductive Spring Club continues to be used by a restaurant specializing in local snacks, and there is a small park near the Xiyuan Hotel called "Seductive Spring Garden."[154] One of the lake views constructed in 1765 was known as "Green Willows, City Walls," after the line in another of Wang Shizhen's poems composed at Red Bridge in the summer of 1662.[155] A view called "Lustration Ritual at Red Bridge" was added to the garden on the site of Wang Shizhen's gatherings, a site later used for the same purpose by his emulators Kong Shangren and Lu Jianzeng. According to Li Dou, this view was one of the twenty-four represented in the set of ivory gaming tiles used in drinking games during the Qianlong period. The garden also contained a pavilion called "Lustration Ritual Pavilion."[156] The Qianlong emperor composed several poems to commemorate his visit to this garden during his Southern Tours, and renamed it "Leaning Rainbow Garden." A picture appears in the commemorative volumes combining woodblock illustrations of sites in Yangzhou with imperial poetry, several versions of which were published at court. Wang Shizhen's lustration festival gatherings were thus commemorated through naming, poetic imitation, and leisure practice. Officials serving in the prefecture represented themselves as Wang Shizhen, gathering at the site near Red Bridge in order to highlight their connection with the local community and its literary heritage. Though not a local by birth or residence, Wang Shizhen was assimilated into the local landscape, to be invoked in the formal setting of leisure as status performance.

By the late 1660s, touring northwest of the city wall had become enough of a cliché to be the subject of caricature. Lei Shijun, a local writer with a reputation as something of a wag, offered the following vision of an expedition to Red Bridge:

Chen Shixiang of Tongzhou was living temporarily outside the north gate of the prefectural city. Wu Ershi, along with Sun Jinli, Wang Yan, and Sun Mo, set out by boat to pay a call on Chen Shixiang. I chanced upon them and went along for

FIGURE 2.6. Leaning Rainbow Garden (Yihong yuan). Woodblock illustration. Source: *Guangling mingsheng tu*. Court edition, Qianlong period.

the ride. It was a rainy day. Ershi said, "Red Bridge is a famous site, so we should stop there for an excursion too." Ershi knew Sun Jinli and I [would go], and if we went, then Wang Yan would come, too; his feet must follow along, and we would have to sit together. He said, "Let's invite him." Sun Jinli said, "It's raining, even if you invite him, he won't come. Let's just go. Just going and coming back, that is the reason for this outing." So we launched the boat and left through the sluice gate. The pure wine was then poured, excellent victuals were laid out. . . . The rain fell heavier. Only the boat was [stowed] under the willows and dikes. We didn't even get there, but had to turn back. Sun Jinli and I were both drunk. Jinli clambered up the bank and slipped, injuring his rear end. He returned and drank even more, and was unaware of his injury. I vomited off the side of the boat, and was unaware of his fall. The true gentleman says that a rainy day excursion is in the category of obsession. We were drunk on the occasion of our rainy day excursion. Jinli did not realize his injury, I did not realize he had fallen. This is in the category of madness. So I have recorded it.[157]

This 1667 essay exaggerates, distorts, and deflates the highly self-conscious excursion essays composed by Lei Shijun's peers, though the emphasis on drunken madness and authenticity is also reminiscent of the late Ming interest in obsession and eccentricity. An outing during which the guests not only fail to reach the famous site but end up drunk and injured, without any poetic achievements, contrasts neatly with the images that developed around Wang Shizhen and his friends. The contrast is particularly apropos (even if it is not necessarily intentional), since one of the men named here, Sun Mo, also had participated in Wang Shizhen's second lustration gathering. In addition, Lei Shijun himself knew and corresponded with Wang Shizhen.[158]

Over a decade later, in the late 1680s, the irrigation official and sixty-fourth generation descendant of Confucius Kong Shangren (1648–1718) came to the city. He took the practice of gathering with poets in the northwest suburbs, and Wang Shizhen's legacy, very seriously. As Richard Strassberg has pointed out in his literary biography of Kong, Wang Shizhen provided a model for Kong's social identity as a successful official, talented poet, and fellow Shandong native.[159] Like Wang, Kong used his poetic talents and patronage to attract members of the *yimin* community, and he socialized with many who had earlier formed part of Wang Shizhen's circle.[160] Indeed, by alluding to Wang's presence in the city, Kong highlighted his own interest in socializing with the late Ming–influenced cultural elites resident in the area. Shortly after his arrival in the city, Kong composed the following poem:

> It is right that Wang Shizhen was an official in Yangzhou
> A later incarnation of Du Mu's romantic fun
> At Bridge Twenty-Four they've added more wine shops
> Below the thirteen brothels the poetry recitation is famous
> No willows at rest in the painted boats of yore
> Again at gauze windows the same oriole songs
> Then, too, the able poet who wrote of the Weed-Covered City
> And the fine lines on "misted blossoms" give rise to much
>   feeling.[161]

Here, Kong praises the poets of Yangzhou, starting with Wang Shizhen, a comparison picked up by his contemporaries and by later biographers.[162] For example, Huang Yun, who was one of three local poets to compile and comment on the poems in Kong Shangren's *Huhai ji* (Lakes and Seas Collection), wrote of this poem: "Unlimited romance! This poem is extremely good. After Du Mu, we again had Wang Shizhen, Kong Shangren!"[163] The second commentator, Deng Hanyi, used this opportunity to repeat an anecdote about Wang Shizhen, stating that when Wang left Yangzhou for Beijing, he had his friend Cheng Sui make him a seal that said "Wang Yangzhou."[164] This, too, underscores the connection between Wang and the city, and by analogy between Kong Shangren and Wang Shizhen. In his response to the earliest of Kong's many poems on Red Bridge, the third commentator, Zong Yuanding, who had earlier painted a scene of Red Bridge and sent it to Wang Shizhen in Beijing, wrote: "These three or four images are truly pictures of Red Bridge. Wang Shizhen's essay and Kong Shangren's poem will be immortal together."[165] The identification of Kong with Wang, and thus by analogy with Ouyang and Su, is a subtext in the commentary on the *Huhai ji*.[166] The connection between Kong Shangren and Wang Shizhen was not just inscribed in words but was also acted out in deeds. In 1688, Kong Shangren quite consciously imitated Wang Shizhen and organized twenty-four of his friends for a gathering at Red Bridge on the third day of the third month.[167] The essay he composed on this occasion focuses on the pleasant weather, the joys of touring, and the enjoyment of shared pleasures as reflections of a prosperous age, and although the commentator emphasizes its resemblance to Wang Xizhi's preface, the resemblance is mostly functional— both essays were written as poetry prefaces.[168]

In writing his own interpretation of the "Seductive Spring" theme, Kong skillfully juxtaposed images of the city of pleasure and the city destroyed.[169] His poem, written at Red Bridge in 1686, reads in part as follows:

> Red Bridge spans the green waves
> Its spirit forever seductive
> Wine shops open beside the bridge
> Bamboo fences divide the flower gardens.
> Two points of Jiangnan Mountains
> Were truly spat out from the treetops.
> Whenever anyone crosses the bridge
> Seeing the mountains they are moved by a sense of history
> The pleasure boats emerge from the flute songs
> The weeping willow branches emerge from mist and rain
> Guiding my shoes on a seductive excursion
> Walking upon broken wastes and burial grounds.[170]

The contrast between pleasure grounds and grave sites, present and past, gave meaning to Red Bridge and highlighted the continuity between Kong's generation and the one that preceded it. Sensitivity to the concerns of his elders enabled Kong to enter more fully into the most prestigious social circle in Yangzhou, a network whose worth was measured in cultural attainment rather than monetary wealth. During the early Qing,

Wang Shizhen and Kong Shangren, and indeed Red Bridge itself, were portrayed (and in the case of the men, portrayed themselves) as occupying a liminal space between pleasure and loss, present and past.

A generation later, the meaning of Wang Shizhen as a symbol had changed somewhat. Poetry gatherings at Red Bridge (now known as Rainbow Bridge) no longer evoked the atmosphere of the late Ming city reimagined. The salt controller Lu Jianzeng also sought to model his social identity after Wang Shizhen, and he often undertook endeavors that heightened his identification with Wang. For example, he published for the first time the collection of poems by his friends that Wang had edited, and, like Wang, he was said to have met with poets daily, holding gatherings in his yamen and in the northwest suburbs. These were said by his peers to be the best literary gatherings in Jiangnan, though others made fun of his efforts at cultural performance. According to Li Dou, Lu presided over the construction of numerous new scenic sites in Yangzhou, including the twenty-four vistas built in 1765.[171] Lu believed in the grand gesture, and he emulated his fellow provincial Wang Shizhen with great enthusiasm and on an unprecedented scale. On the third day of the third month in 1757, he held a lustration festival gathering at Rainbow Bridge and wrote four seven-character regulated verse poems. More than seven thousand people matched his rhymes, and he edited the poems into a three hundred-juan book. This extraordinary event is described in the same terms as Wang Shizhen's gatherings. However, the intimacy has been effaced, leaving only pose and artifice. By the time Lu's cohort gathered in Yangzhou, the city was no longer a city for nostalgic poets. It was a place in which vast merchant wealth from the salt trade could purchase prestigious artifacts—or friendship with scholars and painters—through the act of patronage. And yet, the fame of Red Bridge, of Wang Shizhen, and of his gatherings there remained potent symbols, though the symbolism, and the city, had changed.

3 Anthologies, Monuments, and the Invented Past

THE TOWER OF LITERARY SELECTION

A History of Misnomer?

As we have seen in the previous chapter, literati and officials seeking to bolster local or personal prestige could self-consciously manipulate the cultural legacies of famous sites, utilizing these sites in their strategies of self-interested or civic aggrandizement. Such manipulation could take the form of inventive cultural patronage, as significance accrued to new places through unprecedented literary intervention, as in the case of Red Bridge. Or it could revive a site's reputation by invoking earlier accretions of cultural meaning associated with the place through physical construction and literary reference, as we shall see in Chapter 4 in the case of Pingshan Hall. Community consensus regarding the origins and cultural significance of these sites made these processes of local and personal aggrandizement relatively straightforward, and indeed gave these sites utility as symbols supporting a variety of local and national agendas. Such consensus was, however, neither guaranteed nor permanent, as even extensively documented sites could fall out of fashion and repair. Moreover, present-day concerns could lead residents and local officials to create or embellish famous places by manufacturing both physical structures and their supporting narratives. In such cases, the very invented quality of a building's heritage could become an element in its symbolic function, as patrons either accepted the falsified past for their own purposes or positioned themselves as arbiters of authenticity by revealing the "truth" about local history.[1] This chapter explores shifts in the patronage and function of a "fake" historical site as a window onto changing intellectual, cultural, and political priorities.

During the early Qing, residents of Yangzhou sponsored the construction of a famous site, the Wenxuan lou, or Tower of Literary Selection, to honor Xiao Tong (501–531), the editor of the *Wenxuan,* one of China's most famous literary anthologies. The early Qing builders located their tower on the grounds of a Buddhist temple, the Jingzhong si (Manifest Loyalty temple), in the Old City, not far from the Little East Gate. There was historical, or at least literary, precedent for their actions. A building called the Wenxuan Lane Tower (Wenxuan xiang lou) had existed in the Sui-Tang period, though with somewhat different associations and implications from those invoked in the Qing. An imaginative lineage linking Yangzhou's tower to the compilation of the *Wenxuan,* and to the princely editor, first emerged in the Song. A single line in a rhapsody, and a somewhat later Song geography text, asserted that the Tower of Literary Selection had been the residence of Xiao Tong, although this explanation does not seem to have described an extant landmark. Indeed, even many of the builders' contemporaries in the early Qing questioned whether the famous editor had ever visited the city, even as they invoked the invented legacy in their own poetry.

As the purported Yangzhou home of a historical figure who in fact had never lived in Yangzhou, the tower acquired fame through poetic allusion, as well as through physical construction. Perhaps this was a case, as the 1664 gazetteer implies, in which the cultural authority of a man was used to lend weight to a place under false pretenses.[2] In the 1670s, the invented cultural legacy of this new site acquired further weight through reenactment. Deng Hanyi, a then well-known poet and literary tastemaker from nearby Taizhou, lived in the tower while editing a collection of contemporary poetry. By taking this site as his temporary residence, he alluded to the lingering power of cultural convention, situating his self-consciously present-day project in relation to the site's supposed past. Moreover, his collection itself took on some of the attributes of the site in which it was compiled: it commemorated, and provided context for, the literary and social values of the editor's peers. The tower, and indeed the anthology, in its early Qing incarnation, served as a locus for the celebration and reinvention of cultural identity in the aftermath of rupture, destruction, and loss. Truly, the tower was an "ancient relic" whose invented past was constructed, embellished, and invoked in service to the present.

By the mid-eighteenth century, displaced by more stylish lakeside destinations and stripped of its historical pretensions, the tower lost its position in local touring and literary itineraries, and, perhaps as a result, it is totally absent from today's tourist circuit, which emphasizes the city's eighteenth century splendors alongside monuments to earlier exemplars of international contact.[3] During the nineteenth century, the name Tower of Literary Selection enjoyed a brief revival when a locally born and nationally famous official, Ruan Yuan (1764–1849), rejected the tower's false legacy, replacing it with a more persuasive narrative and a new physical structure located on his family's property.[4] He thus symbolically, even literally, took possession of the tower, in the process establishing his position as a rightful arbiter of historical accuracy and local identity. Moreover, Ruan Yuan, too, was involved in anthology production. He sponsored and participated in the editing of several literary collections, including the *Heroic Spirits of the Huaihai Region* (Huaihai yingling ji), which included only poems by Yangzhou natives. Here we see a shift in emphasis from the transregional to the local, both in the use of the site and in the editorial principles of the anthology.

This chapter traces the history of the Tower of Literary Selection from its construction in 1651 through Ruan Yuan's efforts to rectify and appropriate its legacy in the early nineteenth century. The first sections of this chapter explore the tower's symbolic, literary, religious, and residential functions during the early Qing and the ways in which the construction of the tower and its embellished legacy contributed to Yangzhou's recovery from the Qing conquest. Next I examine Deng Hanyi's anthology project and the ways in which it reflected and drew upon the site's symbolic function, particularly in relation to the preservation and propagation of a transregional, transdynastic cultural identity for China's literati elite. Then I will explain the Wenxuan Tower's fall from prominence in the eighteenth century and the censorship of Deng Hanyi's anthology, both of which resulted from the emergence of new, Beijing-centered definitions of cultural value. I conclude with a discussion of Ruan Yuan's activities in Yangzhou and the role they played in the creation and validation of a local native-place identity, particularly in relation to the emerging Yangzhou school of classical exegesis. Throughout the chapter, I explore the relationship between the Tower of Literary Selection, the practice of assembling anthologies, and prevailing cultural and intellectual discourses.

Constructing: The Tower as an "Ancient Relic"

Every edition of the Yangzhou gazetteer from the early Qing contains an entry for the Tower of Literary Selection, or Wenxuan lou, built in 1651 within the old section of the walled city on the grounds of a temple that, according to local legend, stood on the site of an ancient tower. The newly built tower had several competing, but not contradictory, functions. It was at once a recently built "ancient relic" *(guji);* part of a Buddhist temple complex occupied and restored by monks; a shrine to the Song patriot Yue Fei (1103–42); a shrine to Wenchang, the Daoist god of literature and patron of examination candidates; and a hostel for literati sojourners. The tower purportedly honored a monumental compilation project, marking the site where its princely editor, Xiao Tong, had lived and worked. However, the Resplendent Crown Prince of the Liang dynasty (Zhaoming taizi), as Xiao Tong was known after his premature death, never lived in Yangzhou. He lived in the capital at Jiankang, just south of modern Nanjing, surrounded by a coterie of talented poets and scholars.[5] Still, many of those who publicized the new building in poetry and local histories claimed, or at least implied, that the prince had lived in Yangzhou. Such assertions were not unique to promoters of Yangzhou, however. As the 1664 gazetteer points out, Xiangyang, too, had a Wenxuan Tower, and Zhenjiang and Changshu had Reading Terraces, which also were said to be sites where Xiao Tong prepared his anthology.[6] The 1664 gazetteer editor asks rhetorically: "Since Xiao Tong died young, how could he have traversed Wu and Chu [southeast and central China]?"[7] And indeed, as David Knechtges suggests, the claims to reflected glory made by cities other than the Liang capital at Jiankang were utterly spurious.[8]

Why then would local boosters champion the idea that the *Wenxuan* had been compiled in their city? First, interest in the *Wenxuan* had been revived in the late Ming, with several new works of *Wenxuan* scholarship published in the late sixteenth and early seventeenth centuries. This trend continued into the early Qing, with prominent scholars engaged in textual study of the collection.[9] In addition, anthology making was a popular pastime in the early Qing, with editors creating massive compilations of their friends' poetry, letters, and short prose. These men recognized Prince Xiao Tong as the progenitor of the genre in which they were working, and they praised the *Wenxuan* as the most renowned prototype for their own compilation projects.[10] It is not surprising that renewed attention to the book was accompanied by construction on the site. Interest in particular literary works and specific historical figures inspired several construction projects in Yangzhou during the early Qing. Such projects addressed the spiritual and "touristic" needs of the literati, often functioning as shrines and recreational spaces, while at the same time celebrating solidarity with earlier literary heroes. Finally, the "reconstruction" of the tower enabled local residents and officials to develop a symbol of transregional cultural significance for their locale.

Clearly, local elites in many cities desired the cachet of an association with the prestigious *Wenxuan,* even if the connection was of admittedly questionable authenticity. Buildings like the Wenxuan Tower affirmed their participation in the cultural heritage that included the *Wenxuan.* Additionally, the tower may be another example of the kind of blurring of geographical boundaries that we saw in Chapter 2. Again we have the insistent substitution of Yangzhou for Nanjing, perhaps in a conscious evocation of the former Ming capital. Even as the poetics of Nanjing memories became embedded in Yangzhou spaces, those Yangzhou spaces also were repositioned as the setting for Nanjing events. Although the tower celebrated transcendent cultural values, it may also, at least on an unspoken level, have commemorated the lost dynasty. Such ambivalent (or multivalent) symbols were exceedingly useful in the reintegration of communities across the dynastic divide.

The 1685 gazetteer uses literary evidence, or its absence, to both assert and hedge a connection between the Yangzhou site and the *Wenxuan* project. Although it cites the same several texts as the late Ming gazetteers, it also adds new material and information, including an important reference to the tower's recent renovation. As in the earlier gazetteers, discussion of the tower opens with a quote from a Tang collection of writings about the Sui dynasty, which states that "the Sui emperor once visited the Wenxuan Tower of Prince Xiao Tong. Before the carriages reached the tower, he ordered several palace ladies to climb the tower to welcome him."[11] Even though this statement underscores the link between the site and the historical figures to whom it ostensibly owed its reputation, the gazetteer then states: "Early texts contain no indication that the Wenxuan Tower of Prince Xiao Tong was in Yangzhou. Only the Yangzhou Rhapsody [Yangzhou fu] by Wang Guan of the Song dynasty locates the Wenxuan Tower in Yangzhou. It contains a line which reads: 'The Prince has departed, the Tower of Literary Selection is left empty.'"[12] The account continues: "Legend has it that the Temple of Manifest Loyalty (Jingzhong si) north of Taiping Bridge occupies [the tower's] former site."[13] The gazetteer points out that the site's connection with Xiao Tong hinged on a single Song dynasty reference from a nostalgic rhapsody by Wang Guan.[14] The Song dynasty geographical compilation *Fangyu shenglan* (Famous Sites of the Realm), edited by Zhu Mu, mentions Wang Guan's rhapsody when describing the Wenxuan Tower among Yangzhou's famous cultural landmarks.[15] The types of sources cited in this cryptic and formulaic entry suggest that at least in the Southern Song, the tower was likely a literary construction and not a physical monument. Given these antecedents, and their own tendency to privilege poetic reference in defining famous sites, the early Qing gazetteer editors must have felt justified including the reference to Sui Yangdi's visit to the Tower of Literary Selection, even if they understood that the link between the site and the prince was tenuous at best. Their reference to the Sui emperor's visit was probably understood as strengthening the bond between the site and the prince. Everyone knew that the Sui emperor not only had visited Yangzhou, but also had died a decadent death in the city, surrounded by singing girls in his marvelous Labyrinth.

By conflating the Sui emperor's presence in the tower in the former Liang capital, Jiankang, with his presence in Yangzhou, his own Southern capital, the gazetteer writers may have thought to reinforce the weak association between Yangzhou and the Liang prince. It is also possible that just such a spatial conflation inspired the line in Wang Guan's *Yangzhou Rhapsody* (Yangzhou fu), the Song dynasty *locus classicus* of the myth. In any case, textual reference, not physical presence, was the main criterion for inclusion in the "Ancient Relics" section of the gazetteer. Even a spurious reference could be used to make a place meaningful. As Stephen Owen has pointed out, "minor, dubious, and even fictitious events have, through strong texts, become a real past, which historians labor in vain to undo . . . The historian's austere truth is often ignored if it endangers the past that a culture has enshrined. A good story, the legend of a person, or the image of a city, will outlive the facts."[16] The survival of a "good story" may also be predicated on the fiction's persuasive power in the present, a persuasive power inextricably linked to prevailing standards of utility and relevance. In this case, the narrative webs linking Yangzhou to Nanjing and the decadent Sui to the fallen Ming were already part of early Qing cultural discourse in Yangzhou, and thus the story of the tower had currency, if not incontestable credibility, at that particular moment. When the *Wenxuan* myth ceased to be useful (or compelling) in the eighteenth century, the facts overtook the fiction, and the site faded from view.

Even with myth on their side, some local writers sought further justification for the tower's name. The editors of the 1685 gazetteer conclude their discussion of the tower's history by quoting the *Comprehensive Gazetteer of the Ming:* "'Cao Xian was a native of Jiangdu [Yangzhou]. He served the Sui as director of the Palace Library. He used the *Wenxuan* to teach his students and disciples . . . His residence was called Wenxuan

Lane Tower.' And so the Wenxuan Tower in Yangzhou was named for Cao Xian's residence."[17] This explanation provides an alternative lineage for the building, one still linked, if more obliquely, to the *Wenxuan*. In this version of the story, the building in Yangzhou was the earliest center of scholarship about the *Wenxuan*, not the actual place of its compilation. The Manifest Loyalty Temple by this account occupied the site of the *Wenxuan* scholar Cao Xian's residence, not the site of Prince Xiao Tong's studio. The anthology, through the school of study it inspired, still accounted for the building's reputation, and the question of its authenticity was elided through a subtle change in the story's emphasis. By dropping the word "lane" from the building's former name, the architects of the site's legacy were left with the more resonant name of the prince's tower. The site thus maintained a double identity in the gazetteer: as mythic site of the *Wenxuan*'s creation, and as the birthplace of *Wenxuan* scholarship. When Ruan Yuan revised the narrative in the nineteenth century, he drew upon this second thread, emphasizing the tower's significance as the fountainhead of *Wenxuan* scholarship, rather than of the *Wenxuan* itself.

Descriptions of the new tower and its dimensions differ from one gazetteer edition to another, again suggesting that literary, rather than physical, knowledge took precedence in depictions of famous sites during this period.[18] According to the 1664 gazetteer, the project was begun under the supervision of the temple monk Huijue, with supplies and money collected from among the officials and residents of the prefecture.[19] This gazetteer describes the building as "magnificent and brilliant, a grand view," and adds that scholars and officials contributed money to have an inscription engraved in stone on the wall below. Such stone stelae were, as we have seen elsewhere, the conventional mark of elite patronage of famous sites. Li Songyang, the salt monopoly official who had helped facilitate the city's economic recovery in the immediate aftermath of the Qing conquest, wrote the commemorative stele, an act of literary patronage that signals a connection between the tower's construction and the processes of physical recovery that took place in the first decades of the new dynasty.[20]

The building functioned as a shrine to Lord Wenchang, the god of literature and patron of examination hopefuls, and served as a shrine to Prince Xiao Tong through sacrifices to his portrait. This pattern of worship indicates support for the return to normal bureaucratic processes, an affirmation of (Jiangnan) elite cultural values, and possibly an effort on the part of the temple monk Huijue to attract more generous patronage.[21] An essay by Wang Youding (fl. 1598–1662), a writer and calligrapher who took up residence in Yangzhou after the fall of the Ming, links the building's legacy to the words and deeds of Prince Xiao Tong through the lineage of *Wenxuan* scholarship based at Yangzhou.[22] Thus, without overtly locating Xiao Tong's anthology project in Yangzhou, Wang Youding claims the prince's legacy for this site. He adds that the offerings of grain and chickens that marked the building's construction further strengthened the bond between the site and Xiao Tong. The tower thus became the spiritual residence of the Resplendent Crown Prince, ritually reinforcing earlier assertions of his actual presence there.

Men interested in reviving Yangzhou traditions and constructing Yangzhou monuments thus endeavored to link the city to the *Wenxuan,* a renowned multi-generic anthology, thought by them to embody the best that the early Chinese literary canon had to offer. In addition, because the *Wenxuan* was created in the highly social context of Prince Xiao Tong's literary circle, the tower also had special resonance for literati clubs. A history of the Fushe (Restoration Society), an important late Ming point of reference for early Qing literary circles, begins with a catalogue of important literati organizations and gatherings through the dynasties. The original text included a reference to the men associated with the Wenxuan tower, along with mention of the Seven Sages of the Bamboo Grove and the famous gathering at the Orchid Pavilion, all of which were classic examples of literary fellowship.[23] Men involved in the construction of the tower were contemporaries of the Restoration Society's founders and thus well aware of these associations. To educated elites of the early Qing, the tower represented immortal literary achievement and the sociability of cultural production, both of which were issues of deep concern to them, as we shall see in the discussion of *Poetry Survey* (Shiguan) below. In this monument to Prince Xiao Tong of Liang we can see an appeal to "universal" literary ideals: a shared past of literary greatness and a man who defined cultural values by anthology. Why else would a new Tower of Literary Selection have been built in Yangzhou at this juncture— only six years after the Qing conquest? The perception that the *Wenxuan* represented eternal and empire-wide cultural values seems obvious: the tower thus was conceived as an architectural symbol of what was True and what was Ours.[24] However, its local roots were weak. As even those who celebrated the building and inscribed the tower in the local histories among the city's authentic ancient traces were aware: The prince had never come to Yangzhou. The tower's Yangzhou heritage was falsified. Alternate sources of legitimacy then were sought to bolster the site's reputation. These included poems, rituals, and reenactment.

Rhyming: The Tower as Poetry Subject

The tower and its contrived history figured prominently in late seventeenth-century poetry about the city of Yangzhou and its sites, at a time when poetry written and exchanged played an especially crucial role in the articulation of literati social networks. As poetry subjects, famous sites similarly supported the formation, maintenance, and legitimation of these social networks, contextualizing these social connections through references to shared cultural priorities and a shared past—whether historical or experienced. In organizing and introducing his friends' poems on the famous sites of Yangzhou, Wu Qi (1619–94) gave pride of place to the Tower of Literary Selection, positioning the tower as the starting point of an imaginary itinerary that referenced ruins, dreams, and historical fictions.[25] Most of the famous places on Wu's list had their origins in the Han, Six Dynasties, or Sui periods, and most were no longer standing, although several, including the Wenxuan Tower, had been built or reconstructed within his lifetime. His description of the tower reads as follows:

Located in the Wenxuan [Literary Selection] Lane, near the Lesser East Gate in the prefectural [Old] city, on the site of today's Manifest Loyalty Temple. It was said to be the place where the Brilliant Prince Xiao Tong of Liang compiled the *Wenxuan*. Sui Yangdi frequently visited this building and watched the palace ladies lean on the balustrades with the wind blowing through their rainbow-colored skirts. That it was destroyed through his sensuality is even more profound. The temples of the Liang [dynasty], too, have been burned to ashes. Only the place where Prince Xiao Tong read still exists among us. And the product of his hard work . . . still circulates after myriad generations.[26]

Here, Wu highlights two elements in the tower's legacy of particular interest to his peers. First, he points to its association with Crown Prince Xiao Tong. Second, he links the structure to the decadent life of the Sui emperor Yangdi, adding fanciful new details to the account contained in the *Daye shiyi ji* cited in the gazetteer. The references to the rainbow-skirts of the ladies, the Sui emperor's "frequent visits," and the building's destruction due to decadence appear to be borrowed from accounts of the emperor's famous Labyrinth (Milou), long a staple of Yangzhou lore. These familiar images of the Sui presence in Yangzhou further serve to cement the connection between the city and the tower. By emphasizing the association between this site, decadence, and the collapse of dynasties, Wu Qi also relates the tower to the dominant poetic motifs of his own time. Finally, he confirms the link between the immortal legacy of Prince Xiao

Tong, his anthology, and the tower, all of which survived sensuality, loss, fire, and dynastic change.

By choosing poetic imagery over historical accuracy, Wu Qi creatively reconfigures the city's past to conform to the literary and emotional needs of his contemporaries. Ultimately, Wu seems to be telling us, it is not important whether or not the tower was in Yangzhou or whether or not it really housed the Crown Prince of Liang. These questions of presence and placement address a superficial physical truth. To local adherents, the myth addressed a higher cultural truth and affirmed the city's position within a transregional framework. Thus even after destruction, dynastic change, and myriad generations, Wu claims, what survived was great literature—immortal and universally recognized. To Wu, the ashes of the Liang imperial temples symbolize the evanescence of political power. By contrast, he points out, the tower and the anthology were both immortal monuments to a past era and its culture. In his brief preface, the tower becomes a monument to culture, literature, and loss transcended.[27] And the anthology it celebrated was also an undying monument to that culture.

During the first decades of the Qing, China's literary elite produced virtually unprecedented collections of contemporary writings, reflecting a profound interest in their own generation and its experiences as reflected in their literary output.[28] These collections replicated in print the social networks that connected the empire's urban centers. The Yangzhou gazetteers published in 1675 and 1685 shared in this obsession with contemporary cultural artifacts, featuring noticeably enlarged sections highlighting recent poetry in various genres. Indeed, later writers criticized the 1675 edition of the Yangzhou gazetteer for this excessive attention to literature, and especially to poetry, perhaps reflecting the very changes in cultural priorities addressed in this chapter. The editors of the gazetteer used the writings of their friends and associates to bestow a literary legacy on local sites through the very public vehicle of the prefectural gazetteer. This literary legacy was not locked in the past but, especially in the case of newly constructed or reconstructed sites, was often created or augmented by the famous (living) men of recent times. The gazetteer editors explained that descriptions of famous places in the "Ancient Relics" (guji) section would be accompanied by works of poetry by the famous visitors and touring officials who flocked to the region.[29] For the entry on the Tower of Literary Selection as "ancient relic," both the 1675 and 1685 editions of the prefectural gazetteer include poems by three men who were prominent in local literary circles: Wang Shizhen, Zong Guan, and Peng

Gui.[30] Moreover, all three were socially connected to the five poets who served as nonofficial editorial consultants on the 1685 gazetteer project.[31] As we shall see, those who wrote poems on famous sites did not always express themselves in such portentous tones, and some of them tweak the tower's problematic provenance. Still, by recasting buildings as sites of memory and culture, they participated in the formation and maintenance of communal identity, both locally and transregionally.

Wang Shizhen's poetic evocation of the tower should be interpreted as a boost to the prestige of the new building, a seal of approval bestowed by a leading connoisseur. His poem entitled "Embracing the Past at Wenxuan Tower" overlooks questions of authenticity and appears, at least on the surface, to take the legend at its word. He follows the conventions of the "Embracing the Past" mode, reflecting on the passage of time and his own ostensibly bereaved circumstances. The poem reads as follows:

> Wherever one climbs twilight sorrows arise
> The Age of the Xiao Liang seems so far away
> My heart mourns over words in the treasured book's poems
> My tears wet the Resplendent Prince's riverside tower
> The romantic men of Paradise Garden have departed
> At the gates of the Weed-Covered City the grasses first wither
> In the locked and silent monument the bequeathed book is
>   here
> Incense fires and temple bells face the sunset stream.[32]

The reference to Paradise Garden, a garden on the palace grounds at Jiankang during the Liang dynasty, may be Wang's way of pointing obliquely to his knowledge of the "true" location of the Wenxuan Tower. The parallel reference to the "Weed-Covered City" returns us to Yangzhou, thereby creating a doubling effect in which Nanjing and Yangzhou, and the two cities' twin towers, are simultaneously identical and distinct. This poem bolsters the reputation of the site with a nod to the site's falsified legacy, by drawing upon the weight of Wang Shizhen's own reputation in the Yangzhou poetry community.

Zong Guan resided in the prefectural city of Yangzhou, though technically he was a native of Xinghua, one of the constituent counties of Yangzhou prefecture. He qualified as an "honorable failure" in the 1642 provincial examinations, and thus received some recognition for his efforts, even though he did not succeed in passing the examination.[33] His examination career seems to have been cut short temporarily by the fall of the Ming dynasty in 1644, and, according to the gazetteer biography, he turned instead to a life of literary creation and study. He accepted the status of government student under the Qing in 1654, however, and subsequently participated in the editing of the *Jiangnan Provincial Gazetteer* beginning in 1683.[34] This project attracted many Jiangnan literary talents of the conquest generation, including Deng Hanyi, Deng's friend and fellow Taizhou native Huang Yun, the Huizhou poet and painter Mei Qing, and Zong Guan's more famous cousin Zong Yuanding, all of whom actively participated in Yangzhou poetry clubs and literary-social circles.[35] Zong Guan later served as an official in the local schools of Guichi in 1686, and in the same position in Changshu.[36] The gazetteer biography of Zong Guan notes that Wang Shizhen loved and appreciated his poems.[37] This is another indication of Wang Shizhen's lasting prestige as an arbiter of literary taste in Yangzhou. Even after he left the city, the reputations of local writers were often linked with, and subordinate to, Wang's reputation. Zong's role in the commemoration of the renewal of Pingshan Hall in 1674, and his appearance at parties sponsored by members of Yangzhou's political and cultural elite, reflects his own prestige in the local or provincial community.

In his poem, Zong Guan does not bother to disguise the apocryphal origins of the tower. Instead, his poem exposes the false pretenses behind the tower's popularity. The untitled poem reads as follows:

> A noble house fancifully inscribed "Wenxuan Tower"
> What business does that palace have in Yangzhou?
> Tourists don't have to bother praising Cao Xian
> Mourning the past and grieving for the present are one kind
>   of sorrow.[38]

Here, Zong interweaves the two accounts of the tower's history to create a single poem. He belittles the fanciful yarn about the prince and questions the relevance of the site to the city. Even so, the second couplet offers an explanation that exculpates the tourists who fail to recognize Cao Xian, the true source of the site's prestige. To Zong Guan, "embracing the past" was a legitimate emotional exercise, even if the past embraced by the poet was known to be fake. Although the palace would ordinarily have no business in Yangzhou, recent history justified transposing it into the local landscape. Thus, at the same time Zong Guan mocks the site's fanciful link to the historical past, his poem legitimates the site as a vehicle for mournful "embracing the past" poetry like Wang Shizhen's.

The third poem included in the entry for the Tower of Literary Selection in the "Ancient Relics" section of the gazetteer is by Peng Gui (b. 1632), a prolific writer from Liyang who lived in Yangzhou during the 1670s and possibly at other times as well. While living in Yangzhou, Peng participated in the *ci* poetry salons that were a mainstay of leisure society in the city. He worked as a private secretary and also served as an editorial consultant for the 1675 gazetteer, in which his own poems are prominently featured alongside entries on famous sites including the shrine honoring the southern Ming official Shi Kefa. Peng compiled his collection of lyric verse, the *Churong ji,* attended parties, and commented on the writings of his friends. According to the Liyang county gazetteer, Peng Gui was friendly with many of the major talents of the time, and during his lifetime wrote no fewer than ten thousand poems.[39] His poem on the Tower of Literary Selection combines elements of Wang Shizhen's poem with a hint of resigned skepticism. The poem begins with an empty tower facing the setting sun, thus alluding to Wang Guan's Song-dynasty Yangzhou rhapsody. He touches upon the romantic spirit of the Liang prince, the tradition of *Wenxuan* scholarship, and the anthology's role in preserving the literature of the Six Dynasties period. He then refers to the function of the *Wenxuan* as a textbook used to introduce children to the literary canon.[40] Like Zong, he introduces the explanation of the tower's origins. And, similarly, he suggests that visitors were so preoccupied with the spurious that they overlooked the real.

Most other poems on the Tower of Literary Selection reflect the singular preoccupation with the Prince of Liang described disdainfully by Peng Gui and Zong Guan. These poems mark the emergence of a set of historically referenced conventions for seeing and describing the tower in verse. The literature chapter of the 1685 gazetteer features six such poems, which contrast neatly with the poems discussed above. With one exception (a poem by Zou Zhimo), these six poems were all written by relatively little-known writers of Jiangnan origin, three of whom were natives of Yangzhou prefecture.[41] All of them either celebrate Prince Xiao Tong and portray the building as the physical embodiment of his literary achievements or follow the thematic model of Wang Shizhen's "embracing the past" poem. The latter poems evoke a bleak, sorrowful mood, portraying tearful scholars carrying out mourning rituals amid the tangled grasses. One Yangzhou native, Zong Xuezeng (quite likely a relative of Zong Guan and Zong Yuanding, as the surname is unusual), transposes objects from the Liang capital onto the Yangzhou landscape, moving relics of the Six Dynasties to the "weed-covered city" of ruined Yangzhou. His poem, "Embracing the Past at Wenxuan Tower," reads:

> The relics of the Six Dynasties are in the Weed-Covered City
> Remaining ruins desolate beneath the tangled grasses
> Clouds surrounding the empty tower are only Buddhist
>   incense

A wind blows against the steep railing amid the sound of bells
A thousand years separate us from the days of the Xiao Liang
The mourning rites begin again this evening
Does the Prince's treasured book still survive today?
Falling flowers and calling birds duplicate my feelings.[42]

Again, the poet uses historical images to represent himself within the landscape, even though in this case the historical setting was located many miles across the river to the south.[43] The book and its legacy, the Prince in the Tower, are read into the Yangzhou landscape as metaphors for cultural renewal. Poetic conventions have displaced geographical and historical accuracy. The physical site disappears behind the more evocative myths of its invented past.

Patronage: The Tower and the Temples

Like Pingshan Hall, the Tower of Literary Selection stood on the grounds of a Buddhist temple. And again like Pingshan Hall, as a monument to cultural values deemed transcendent and universal, the tower appears temporarily to have overshadowed the Buddhist monastery whose land it shared. In early Qing texts, the history of the temple is often framed in relation to the "history" of the tower, although the space occupied by the tower was defined by the temple precinct. By the eighteenth century, however, the tower's importance had greatly diminished, and today, despite a brief revival of the tower during the early twentieth century, only the temple remains. Moreover, during the early Qing, the tower proved more successful at attracting prestigious patrons than the temple itself. The tower's attractiveness to members of the city's literary elite may, in fact, have been what motivated the monk Huijue to use it rather than the temple in his initial efforts to raise funds for renovation projects. As a shrine to both Xiao Tong and Wenchang, the tower had an obvious connection to, and thus greater appeal for, the city's cultural elite. Indeed, the Temple of Manifest Loyalty (Jingzhong si) appears to have had difficulty attracting major financial and literary sponsors during this period, and ultimately was restored through the intervention of a salt merchant philanthropist. Furthermore, the temple appears to have lacked the poetic and cultural aura that took shape around the Tower of Literary Selection, or indeed around Pingshan Hall and Red Bridge. The repair of the temple, unlike these other sites, can be viewed as a relatively minor event, an act of charity performed without reference to empire-wide concerns, although the act of temple patronage itself should be read as part of larger trends in philanthropy at the local level. If temple patronage in general can teach us about something other than religious faith, then the renovation of the Temple of Manifest Loyalty in particular can provide insights into the motives and priorities of Yangzhou's gentry and mercantile elite.[44]

The first evidence of a temple on the Yangzhou site later associated with the Tower of Literary Selection and the Temple of Manifest Loyalty comes from the Southern Song period, when a temple in Yangzhou, evidently identified with the Jizhao Cloister, was given the name Gongde Cloister in 1164. At this time, the temple was rededicated to the Song patriot Yue Fei, who notably fought a battle in Yangzhou prefecture in 1131 and was, even his own lifetime, celebrated in shrines constructed in his honor in villages around the prefecture. Although the Song general did not formally enter the state-sponsored religious pantheon until the Ming dynasty, some commemorative temples, like the one at Yangzhou, were founded much earlier, either during or very shortly after the period of active conflict between the Song and Jin armies in the area.[45] Two other Southern Song generals, Wei Jun and Wang Fang, who died trying to keep the Jin armies from crossing the Yangzi River near Yangzhou in 1161, also were enshrined there during the Xianchun reign (1265–75) of the Southern Song.[46] Their enshrinement apparently led to the renaming of the temple to reflect its honorific function: celebrating the memory of Song loyalty martyrs who had died adamant in their opposition to the Jin. Thus, the temple came to be called the Temple of Manifest Loyalty.[47]

The 1810 gazetteer underscores the eclectic nature of this complex by listing it under the double name of Literary Selection Tower–Manifest Loyalty Teaching Temple (Wenlou Jingzhong jiaosi).[48] "Jiao" (teaching) is one of the three designations for Buddhist temples imposed by the first Ming emperor as part of his efforts to exert control over Buddhism, the other two being "Chan" (meditational) and "Jiang" (preaching). A "teaching temple" was supposed to be for monks who studied the sutras, and the use of this term suggests that the temple was in active use at the time of the early Ming adjustment in terminology. Typically, the gazetteer locates the temple, first by indicating the temple's spatial position relative to the prefectural yamen to its northwest and then by tracing its history back to the Six Dynasties period. The editors introduce the legend of Prince Xiao Tong and the Wenxuan Tower and then describe the tower's conversion to a Buddhist monastery called the Jizhao Cloister (Jizhao yuan) by a monk in the sixth century. This element of the story is consistent with the account of the Sui emperor's visit to the Tower of Literary Selection, who was also said to have listened to a monk lecture on Buddhism while there with his palace ladies.[49] But again, the claim is fictitious, as the temple in question was located in Jiankang (Nanjing), and not in Yangzhou. The pre-Song history of this temple, if indeed it has a pre-Song history, is obscured by the efforts of later gazetteer writers and poets to construct a historical legacy linking the temple to the *Wenxuan* and its royal editor.

According to Timothy Brook, patronage of Buddhist temples by members of the local gentry surged during the last century of the Ming. He sees this trend as continuing into the first decades of the Qing, and describes it in relation to a growing concern for community affairs and a reorientation away from the state.[50] Brook suggests that the Buddhist temple occupied a complex position in relation to both the imperial state and local society. He shows that temples occupied a special place in the gentry imagination and were supposed to represent a sphere of activity removed from an official realm that was, especially in the last decades of the Ming, increasingly tainted by factional fighting and corruption. In part, this association between religious institutions and gentry interests occurred because temples were distinctly local institutions by the late imperial period, since there was no empire-wide network of Buddhist temples, and China's gentry elites were increasingly inclined to see the locale as their proper sphere of activity. Temples thus emerged as the object of patronage firmly situated within the local community, the site of status performance aimed at a local, not national, audience.[51] Famous cultural sites, termed "ancient relics," functioned differently, perhaps especially in the early Qing. Unlike temples, these sites functioned as nodes in the self-consciously transregional reconstruction of elite values. As we shall see, the narrative that justified the tower's existence interwove local and national threads, whereas the patronage networks that invested in the temple's restoration and maintenance were firmly tied to the local community, especially the community of sojourning salt merchants.

An exploration of patronage in post-conquest Yangzhou, and at this temple in particular, suggests a subtle shift in the balance of power between the center and the locale, and moreover provides evidence of a status hierarchy among the objects of patronage, at least as represented in the sources covering acts of patronage. Acts of conspicuous literati patronage and renovation took place on sites that celebrated shared aspects of China's cultural heritage and symbolized the reintegration of elite social networks against a transregional backdrop. These acts were presented in stelae and gazetteers as events of considerable prestige and great symbolic importance. Famous historical sites, including the most prominent Buddhist temples of the region, became the object of intensifying patronage activity among elites, especially during the Kangxi period. Increasingly, patronage was portrayed as an arena for accommodation with the state, or as the articulation of an agenda shared by both local elites and the center. The most prominent religious patron in Yangzhou after 1684 was, after all, the emperor himself, as he bestowed inscriptions, sutras, rosaries, and Buddhist images on many of the city's temples. Even then, despite efforts to enhance and broaden its appeal, and despite the compelling presence of the Tower of Literary Selection, the Temple of Manifest Loyalty itself remained firmly embedded in local merchant patronage networks and the focus of purely local concerns.[52] The temple was overlooked by the Kangxi emperor, who neglected to give it even a small token of his favor during the period of his Southern Tours.

An essay commemorating the 1674 renovation of the temple is appended to the 1810 gazetteer entry. The essay is by Sang Zhi, a Yangzhou native active in the 1670s and 1680s who became a government student in 1686. Sang Zhi was respected as a calligrapher, seal-carver, painter, and essayist. These skills literally gave Sang his place in the history books, though his reputation, like that of Zong Guan, seems to have been primarily as a local talent.[53] His writings were already difficult to find in the early nineteenth century, when Ruan Yuan (1764–1849) compiled a collection of miscellaneous notes on his hometown and its poets.[54] Again, like Zong Guan, Sang Zhi appears to have participated in cultural activities organized by men of national reputation resident in the area. He painted illustrations of selected lines from Wang Shizhen's poems and presented them to him, thereby earning Wang's praise.[55] Here, too, Wang makes an appearance as the outside arbiter of a local artist's worth—perhaps a sign of the increased role officials played in assigning local value. Sang also attended parties sponsored by Kong Shangren, including an excursion to Plum Blossom Ridge on the Double Ninth day festival that was attended by Deng Hanyi, Wu Qi, and Zong Yuanding.[56] He and six other local artists presented Kong Shangren with a painting entitled "Returning to Court" on the occasion of his departure from the Yangzhou region. Thus, he seems to have been part of a select group of local cultural figures chosen for participation in outings by more famous outsiders.[57]

The reputations of men like Sang Zhi were measured primarily in terms of cultural achievement. Although these men were often mistakenly categorized as "loyalists" (yimin), in the patriotic discourse of twentieth-century Chinese scholarship, they cannot all in fact be considered "political outsiders." As in the case of Sang Zhi, their local prominence was enhanced by their connection to nationally recognized officials such as Wang Shizhen or Kong Shangren, complicating our reading of their political stance. During the post-conquest period, such local literati played an active role in promoting the reconstruction of historical sites in their prefecture, often with the material support of Qing officials. They were solicited as the authors of commemorative essays and stelae when weightier national figures were unavailable, unaffordable, or unwilling. They also wrote inscriptions and commemorative essays for projects when a mixed group of national and local figures was required, as in the case of Zong Guan's essay commemorating the 1674 renovation of Pingshan Hall. It is not clear whether Sang Zhi's essay on the Temple of Manifest Loyalty was the only one written to honor the occasion, or whether it was simply the only one included in the gazetteer. It seems likely, however, that the work of the most prominent essayist would be chosen for preservation in the gazetteer. That Sang Zhi appears to have been the most prominent essayist to write on the renovation of the temple suggests that the project lacked either the prestige or the monetary resources to attract a more famous literary patron. Indeed, in 1674, the year in which the restoration commemorated in the essay took place, the city had many visitors and residents more prominent than Sang, and other projects more celebrated than the restoration of this temple.[58] That the essay was written by Sang Zhi thus underscores the limited audience for this project and indeed highlights the relatively narrow significance of the temple's renovation.

Sang Zhi retells the story of the temple in a direct and concrete style, without invoking symbolically charged vocabulary or resorting to literary embellishment. He states simply that this temple is the site of the Resplendent Crown Prince of Liang's Wenxuan Tower and traces the history of the site based on that assumption. Like the poets cited above, Sang validates the legend by incorporating it into his own literary efforts: moreover, he inscribes it for display on the site for posterity. A native son, he may have had a vested interest in affirming the significance of his hometown's monuments, although he does so in a relatively detached tone. His discussion of Yue Fei and the two generals is similarly clinical. He notes the temple's physical parameters, commenting that at the front there was a main hall with a larger tower standing at the rear. Sang suggests that the temple and the tower functioned separately as objects of patronage. According to Sang, as the temple prospered, the tower fell into decline, although he does not specify when these events took place, or indeed whether the tower in question was called the Tower of Literary Selection. The salt controller and former Yangzhou magistrate Cui Hua restored the tower in 1651 but did not extend his largess to the temple's main hall.[59] The monk Huijue, who had organized the construction of the tower in 1651, collected money for three years to renovate the temple but to no avail. Sang attributes the monk's initial failure to collect money to the "isolated" location of the temple—surprising, since the temple was located in the heart of the Old City, not far from the prefectural yamen. He adds that the earthquake that rocked the region in the summer of 1673 badly damaged the temple. And so, a year later, a local man called Min Yutian persuaded his father to donate a sum of money to help with the repairs.

Sang Zhi's inscription identifies these two men only by their style names, providing no indication of their occupation, personal names, or native place. However, the generous father who "loosened his pursestrings" in support of the project can be identified as Min Shizhang (*zi* Xiangnan, b. 1607), a merchant and the subject of an essay on philanthropy written by the well-known literatus (and sometime hired pen) Wei Xi.[60] In this essay, Wei describes the older Min as an extraordinarily generous benefactor, renowned as one of the most important local philanthropists in Yangzhou. He also identifies the source of Min Shizhang's wealth: he had worked in the salt trade until he accumulated enough money to feed his family and to indulge his love of lavish good deeds. Min was the first benefactor of the Yangzhou foundling home in 1655 and paid for medicines during the epidemics that infected the city in 1660, 1662, and 1674. Moreover, during the early 1670s, he provided food for those afflicted by catastrophic floods, repaired the poorhouse, and helped endow a system of rescue boats.[61] Clearly, Min was an admired and central figure in local philanthropic circles, which, in the early Qing, seem to have centered on the salt merchants, whose philanthropic activities are carefully detailed in the relevant sections of the Lianghuai salt monopoly gazetteers of the Kangxi and Qianlong periods. Min's role as the major patron of this project underscores its communal roots and its remove from the concerns of the literati patrons who fixated on symbolically charged sites like Pingshan Hall and the Tower of Literary Selection.

Based on the 1810 gazetteer alone, one might assume that the temple had been neglected during the Ming dynasty and had revived, possibly as a center for the celebration of loyalty (or loyalism), in the first half-century of Qing rule.[62] However, as the 1664 gazetteer makes clear, the Temple of Manifest Loyalty was repaired at least twice during the Ming.

Indeed, it was during the Ming dynasty that the Song martyr Yue Fei achieved his apotheosis and was transformed into a Daoist deity and at the same time became the empire's leading symbol of political loyalty.[63] The symbolism of this shrine to three Song loyalty martyrs might seem to have factored into the decision to restore this site in the early Qing, when loyalty to native regimes took on new significance, especially in cities like Yangzhou, where civilian martyrs to the Ming cause had been so numerous. However, although it is tempting to read the early Qing renovations of this temple as locally sponsored attempts to commemorate the city's sacrifices in the name of loyalty to the lost Ming cause, there is little hard evidence to support this conclusion. Despite its obvious links to loyalist values through Yue Fei and others who struggled against the Jin, and despite the historical and genetic linkages between the Jin and the Qing, the Temple of Manifest Loyalty does not seem to have functioned as a site of resistance to Qing rule. It is possible, however, that evidence of such activities may have been lost or suppressed. Still, loyalty and resistance were not necessarily synonymous. Beginning at least in the early eighteenth century, official (Qing) patronage of loyalty shrines became an important expression of political centralization and legitimacy. Indeed, as we will see below, a nearby temple similarly dedicated to Manifest Loyalty received the generous attention of Cao Yin, an imperial bondservant serving in the salt administration in Yangzhou.

The renovation of this second site dedicated to and named for Manifest Loyalty appears symptomatic of a growing official interest in supporting certain (controlled) expressions of political loyalty (regardless of their dynastic object). The Manifest Loyalty Shrine-Temple, or Jingzhong miao, was located east of Sanyuan Lane and northwest of the teaching temple in a similar neighborhood of the Old City. This shrine-temple was devoted to the memory of the same two martyred Song generals, Wei Jun and Wang Fang, that were enshrined in the Manifest Loyalty Temple. These two generals, who died trying (unsuccessfully) to prevent the Jin from capturing the nearby town of Guazhou, and thus from securing the gateway to Jiangnan, were said to have appeared to the first Ming emperor, Zhu Yuanzhang, in a dream. The Ming emperor subsequently ordered the construction of shrines in their memory.[64] Patronage of the shrine-temple, imaginatively linked to both political loyalty as a value and to the Ming founder as the rightful object and arbiter of that loyalty, epitomized Qing efforts to lay claim to the Ming legacy beginning in the 1680s and 1690s. The Kangxi emperor personally carried out rituals honoring Zhu Yuanzhang, the Ming founder, at his tomb in Nanjing in 1684, repeating these rites on all but one of his successive Southern Tours.[65] By patronizing sites associated with the first Ming emperor, the Kangxi emperor upheld the principle of loyalty to the Ming but displaced the object of that loyalty temporally, from the late Ming to the early Ming. These rituals enabled the Kangxi emperor to position himself as the legitimate heir to the centralizing political values associated with the first Ming emperor, while insinuating that the later Ming emperors had lost the right to rule by falling away from those same values.[66] Although acts of imperial patronage could be carried out by the emperor himself, as when he bestowed gifts and calligraphy on Jiangnan temples or performed rituals in person at Xiaoling, they could also be delegated to a select number of trusted officials, like Cao Yin.

The renovation of the Manifest Loyalty Shrine-Temple attracted the patronage of a highly connected official sponsor, Cao Yin. In addition, Zhu Yizun (1629–1709), a nationally renowned writer, former participant in the Ming history project, and close friend and colleague of Cao Yin, composed the stele at Cao's request.[67] The participation of both Cao and Zhu reveals that the renovation occurred between 1704 and 1708, since Cao Yin served as Lianghuai salt censor in the alternating years of 1704, 1706, 1708, and 1710, and Zhu Yizun died in 1709. Cao Yin, who also served as Textile Commissioner at Nanjing, was part of the innermost circle of officials during the Kangxi reign. He was active in promoting the court's agenda in Yangzhou and elsewhere in Jiangnan during the early eighteenth century. He hosted the Kangxi emperor during his Southern Tours and had the honor of serving as the emperor's proxy in the rituals honoring the Ming founder at Xiaoling during the fourth tour in 1703.

The involvement of a uniquely well-placed official like Cao Yin in the renovation of the Manifest Loyalty Shrine-Temple should be interpreted in the context of the Kangxi emperor's efforts to consolidate his legitimacy relative to the Ming legacy, and the court's growing involvement in the accommodative processes already at work in the locale. As an official, Cao Yin was expected to play a role in the local community through conspicuous displays of benevolence, such as repairs to schools and temples or donations to local infrastructure projects.[68] Certainly the restoration of the shrine-temple can be read as an act of Confucian philanthropy. However, this particular official's direct personal ties to the emperor also bound his actions more firmly to the court, even as they strengthened existing links between Yangzhou and Beijing. According to Zhu Yizun's commemorative essay, Cao Yin issued orders to restore the shrine-temple, which had fallen into disrepair after a long period during which it had not been maintained. Zhu quotes Cao Yin's orders as follows: "The gods and spirits within these precincts are those to whom my people make sacrifices. And so the old ceremonies for Manifest Loyalty must be practiced and cannot be neglected."[69]

Although one wonders who and what Cao, a Han bondservant in a Manchu Banner, meant when he said "my people," his participation in this project clearly placed it in a much larger political context, and in front of a much larger audience. Almost exactly a century later, in 1807, when Ruan Yuan explored the site of the shrine-temple and searched for Zhu's inscription, the shrine-temple was in shambles, the images broken, and the stele missing—again, perhaps, signaling shifts in the political and ideological landscape.[70] Still, in the early eighteenth century, the participation of well-known figures like Cao and Zhu in the restoration of the shrine-temple contrasted neatly with the local sponsorship and commemoration of the Jingzhong Temple and suggests the emergence of heightened official sanction for loyalty as embodied in monuments or shrines. Although we lack concrete evidence for this, it may indicate the temporary displacement of an unofficial, locally favored site, by an officially endorsed and endowed site. Certainly the restoration of the shrine-temple was one symptom of the court's intrusion into locally centered processes of accommodation to Qing rule, an intrusion made first and most obviously manifest in the Southern Tours, which literally brought the emperor into the locale.

Living (in) the Legacy: Residential Reenactment

Like many temples in late imperial China, the Tower of Literary Selection also functioned as a hostel for traveling and sojourning literati. The tower's location in the heart of one of the wealthiest neighborhoods in the Old City made it a convenient and desirable lodging place for visitors and short-term residents. Indeed, during the early Qing, this neighborhood, not far from the Lesser East Gate and thus accessible to the markets of the New City, had a reputation as Yangzhou's premier residential district for gentry households.[71] The district also may have had smaller markets of its own, which would have provided goods and services to visitors as well as to permanent residents.[72] Compared to the New City, which from its founding in the Ming was recognized as a merchant district, this was a quiet and orderly area shaped by the administrative and cosmological considerations of its official function. The streets ran at right angles, the city walls were neatly square. By contrast, the New City was an unplanned maze of winding streets and twisting alleys.[73] Although many of the temples and shrines located in the Old City and the New City, as well as several temples in the suburbs, were known to offer comfortable lodgings to travelers, one can easily imagine that a quiet spot inside the city wall would have been an appealing choice. Moreover, the tower stood in close proximity to the administrative offices of both Jiangdu county and Yangzhou prefecture. Thus it was a particularly convenient lodging place for those visiting with local officials or those who benefited from their patronage. In addition, the Zhenhuai Gate on the north side of the Old City provided access to the scenic area northwest of the city. Visitors lodging in the Old City could rent boats at the Lesser East Gate located just behind the tower and travel on the Little Qinhuai Canal along the east side of the wall between the Old and New cities. They could then exit the city through the sluice gate, traveling on to Red Bridge, Baozhang Lake, and the Ocean of the Law Temple. This route seems to have been the most popular sightseeing itinerary, and Chen Yunheng and Wang Shizhen began their excursion to Red Bridge in just this way.

But the Tower of Literary Selection was more than just a convenient place for literati tourists interested in seeing the scenic sites of Yangzhou. It had the added cachet of its contrived connection to the Resplendent Crown Prince and his renowned anthology. This fanciful history acquired a literal dimension when, within a decade of its construction, the tower became the site of residential reenactment as poetry collectors eager to establish the legitimacy of their projects began to use the tower as a temporary home. By living in the tower, they linked their collections of contemporary poetry with the universally appreciated *Wenxuan,* even as many of these editors used their prefaces to link their works to the Confucian *Poetry Classic* (Shijing). Moreover, these compilations of early Qing poetry edited by early Qing poets themselves replicated the functions of restored famous sites by providing a metaphorical gathering place for the writers of the time. These collections also may have provided a venue for maintaining in an alternative guise the connections forged in the context of late Ming political and social clubs like the Fushe, even as the editing of the *Wenxuan* itself served as a prototype for late Ming (and thus early Qing) literati sociability.[74]

Interestingly, Wang Shizhen himself may have conceived of the practice of selecting literature in the Tower of Literary Selection, since the first well-publicized case of an editor residing in the tower took place under his patronage. In 1662, Wang Shizhen brought Chen Yunheng to Yangzhou, where, as we saw in Chapter 2, he attended the lustration festival gathering at Red Bridge. Wang arranged for Chen to stay in the Tower of Literary Selection, and while there Chen worked on two anthologies of early Qing poetry, the *Shiwei chuji* and the *Guoya chuji*. In a collection of his random jottings, Wang Shizhen indicates that he was the impoverished senior poet's patron, providing Chen's food and paying for his accommodations at the Wenxuan Tower during his extended visits to Yangzhou, which were in part intended to facilitate Chen's work on the two anthologies.[75] Indeed, Wang's own preface to the *Guoya chuji* was written and dated in the tower, emphatically linking the site to the project, and, at least obliquely, linking both to Wang himself.[76] Certainly, as we have seen elsewhere, the young official Wang Shizhen made active use of the reputations of senior (Ming) poets and the famous sites of Yangzhou to amplify his own prestige. Moreover, association with Wang Shizhen continued to enhance the stature of the sites and practices with which he was connected. Other references to his sponsorship of the project and the poet survive, indicating that these acts were well known to his peers, particularly those residing in the Yangzhou-Nanjing area. Moreover, Wang Shizhen's investment in poetry compilation, and indeed his own anthology-making activities, could not have helped but foster the early Qing fad for anthologies of contemporary poetry, and, perhaps, the use of the tower as a site for anthology compilation.[77]

The link between the act of editing an anthology and the hallowed site associated with that editing is made even more explicit in Yu Zhou's preface to Chen's *Guoya chuji*, which uses references to the Wenxuan tower(s) as a framing device designed to celebrate the achievements of Chen Yunheng. He characterizes Chen's work in relation to the accomplishments of great anthologists of the past, and in particular refers to the stature of Xiao Tong as the foremost practitioner of poetry compilation after Confucius. He explains that in some respects Chen Yunheng may even have surpassed Xiao Tong, given the troubled times in which he lived and his personal poverty. He writes,

Xiao Tong was a scion of the ruling house, what could he not accomplish? Wherever he traveled he could build a house to live in [this perhaps accounting for the proliferation of Wenxuan Towers cited in Yu's opening sentence], and in the time he had left from reading, he could enjoy pleasure outings. Although Chen Yunheng was born into a rich family, he has recently fallen into poverty and moreover he is often ill. Wherever his travels take him, whether it be Nanjing, Hangzhou, or Yangzhou, he carries a bundle of poems and essays and a bundle of bedding, and he lives in temples or commoners' houses . . .[78]

By staying in one of the (supposed) residences of the traveling prince, the impoverished Chen was shown to have taken up the mantle of the earlier editor. Thus, Xiao Tong's legacy and achievements were adapted to suit the circumstances of a figure emblematic of the post-conquest world, the impoverished *yimin* poet. The association between site and practice lived by Chen Yunheng, and affirmed by Wang Shizhen, appears to have lasted at least into the next decade. During the 1670s, the poet, editor, and publisher Deng Hanyi made use of the tower's location and reputation as he compiled a massive anthology of contemporary poetry by his friends and associates, the *Poetry Survey* (Shiguan). The first volume was completed in 1672, and the second and third volumes were published in 1678 and 1689 respectively. Positioning himself in relation to a lineage of cultural convention, albeit an obviously fabricated one, embodied by the tower, he sought to reconstruct a positive generational identity for himself and all of his peers, even as he sought to make sense of potentially divisive political realities.

On a practical level, the tower appears to have provided an environment conducive to conversations about poetry and anthology creation, perhaps facilitating the imaginative reenactment of the sociability associated with Xiao Tong's *Wenxuan*. Indeed, while living in the tower, Deng Hanyi had many visitors who came to discuss Deng's compilation projects and their own. For example, in his preface to a collection of the then fashionable lyric poems *(ci)* edited by the poetry collector Sun Mo, Deng Hanyi states, "I stayed for a long time in the Wenxuan Tower. At that time, Sun Mo used to visit me there often. Whenever he published a collection of lyrics by our friends, we would discuss it together, always sighing over the excellence of a phrase or correcting mistaken characters."[79] Deng Hanyi's friend Kong Shangren evidently also visited the tower, although his visit took place after Deng Hanyi had already moved elsewhere.[80] One of the poems in Kong Shangren's poetry cycle on the famous sites of Yangzhou describes the Tower of Literary Selection and its status as a monument to the cultural values embodied in the *Wenxuan*. Deng Hanyi's published comment on Kong's poem refers to the tower's function as a hostel and reads as follows: "When I edited the *Poetry Survey,* I lodged upstairs in this building. Many guests came to see me. Who says that pen and ink have no power?"[81] Deng does not refer directly to the contents of Kong's poem but rather uses the poem to reflect on his own period of residence in the tower and the relationship between his own literary project and the famous site.

The social aspect of Deng Hanyi's life in the tower is evident in another poem in Kong's literary collection, this one written in 1688 and entitled "On Visiting the Shrine of Master Dong in Jiangdu [Yangzhou] While Deng Hanyi Was Editing Volume Three of the *Poetry Survey*." Though he arrived too late to visit Deng Hanyi at the Tower of Literary Selection, Kong Shangren clearly knew that his friend had stayed there in the past. He begins the poem by juxtaposing the Tower of Literary Selection, where Deng Hanyi edited Volume Two of the *Poetry Survey,* with the Shrine of Master Dong, where he edited Volume Three. He creates an equivalence between the two sites, using the standard poetic vocabulary for describing ruins and winter to suffuse both sites with a bleak, archaic mood. Kong contrasts these desolate exterior images with a cozy interior space suffused with friendship and warmth. He recalls how late at night, he and Deng warded off the cold by drinking tea while they selected poems by Shandong men for the collection.[82] Clearly, Deng's days (and nights) in Yangzhou were social; his editing tasks were far from solitary. Kong Shangren's poem portrays these "historic" buildings as sites for both sojourning and socializing. And indeed, these two activities were often linked. Interludes away from home often provided men with opportunities to expand their social networks, and encounters with friends and acquaintances in temples and inns were poetic motifs of ancient provenance.

Deng Hanyi prepared the first volume of the *Poetry Survey* at his home in Taizhou. For the second and third volumes, he moved to the prefectural city, where he temporarily resided on the grounds of two monuments. He thus positioned himself at the administrative center of his home prefecture, an increasingly important node in the empire's social and transportation networks. Perhaps even more significantly, he located himself in physical spaces linked to historical figures universally recognized as embodying shared cultural values, positioning himself and his project in relation to an untroubled and affirming past. He could have chosen to lodge in any of the numerous temples offering temporary accommodations. But he chose sites with grand canonical associations. Li Yesi (1622–80) of Zhejiang invoked this symbolism in a letter to Deng Hanyi, writing: "I hear that you have taken up (lofty) residence in the Wenxuan Tower and continue its rites [e.g., anthologizing] across the vast expanse of time."[83]

Unlike the Tower of Literary Selection, the Shrine of Master Dong where Deng edited his third volume was located in the New City. However, it too stood in convenient proximity to one of the gates connecting the Old City to the New. It also had the prestige of being a named site associated with a famous former inhabitant. The shrine was the ritual home of the renowned Han Confucian Dong Zhongshu (ca. 179–104 B.C.E.), who had served for a time in Yangzhou.[84] Early Qing accounts portray Dong as the defender of Confucian thought, promoting the works of the sage after the Qin emperor's notorious book burning. Descriptions of the shrine emphasize the resilience of culture and celebrate the ability of ideas and books to transcend adversity, a theme with obvious contemporary resonance for Yangzhou residents who had experienced the fires of 1645. According to local legend, Dong Zhongshu's actual residence occupied the exact site of the Lianghuai salt controller's office, where there was a well called "Dong's Well" after the Han Confucian. During the Ming dynasty, rituals honoring the Han Confucian were carried out in a shrine located just behind the yamen. By the time Deng Hanyi took up residence in the shrine, it had been moved to a new location. The new Shrine of Master Dong was located in North Willow Lane, a residential neighborhood located just southwest of the Lianghuai salt controller's office, where it had been rebuilt with money from the salt tax during the late Ming.[85] Like the tower, the shrine had the advantage of proximity to other well-known residents. For example, Deng's good friend and sometime colleague, Sun Zhiwei rented a house next to the shrine during this period.[86]

Perhaps Deng's choice was merely a matter of convenience: both sites were well located within the city walls, offering Deng ready access to the comforts of urban living and to residents with similar tastes and talents interested in participating in his editing endeavors. Or, as seems more likely, Deng himself sensed the symbolic possibilities: a literary monument created in a physical monument, an anthology produced in Anthology Tower, a new *Wenxuan* for his own times. As we shall see, Deng Hanyi conceived his poetry anthology as a monument to the poets of his age, reflecting and celebrating the distinctive character of his own generation and its values, suggesting that he too saw the parallels between what he sought to do in print and what others had done in wood and brick. The next section will explore the ways in which Deng Hanyi's collection itself functioned as a monument to the values and attributes most treasured by the mobile, networked, and urbane elites that produced the poems it contained and whose achievements it commemorated. However, the *Poetry Survey* was to prove a less than enduring monument to the complex and ambivalent conquest generation, as it was suppressed a century later. The Tower of Literary Selection, too, lost its relevance in an age more interested in historical accuracy than in impressions of cultural truth.

Gathering: Editor and Anthology

From the beginning, Deng Hanyi conceived of his anthology as a monument to his generation, a celebration of their distinctive character, and a reflection of their values, describing the first volume as "truly the book of an age."[87] In certain respects, this literary monument was analogous to the physical monuments built in Chinese cities during the early Qing, including the Tower of Literary Selection. Like a physical monument, the anthology served as a gathering place for the editor's friends and associates and formed a context in which political differences could be transcended, or at least overlooked. Like the physical monuments constructed in Yangzhou during the early Qing, the anthology celebrated cultural values that were simultaneously and emphatically transregional and transdynastic, values that were, moreover, closely linked to prevailing ideas about poetry. Again, like a monument, the anthology required the involvement of patrons to support its construction and finance its preservation. In order to understand the relationship between the anthology-as-monument and the cultural sensibilities that shaped its creation and determined its destiny, we must also examine the events and experiences that defined Deng Hanyi's character and sensibilities more generally, and his generational identity in particular. Deng, emblematic of the post-Ming *fengliu* (fashionable personality), was at least as typical of his generation as the more often studied "loyalists" and "twice-serving officials," providing a useful counter-example to those who would like to read the conquest in morally absolute terms. Deng Hanyi's experiences, and his ideas about "literary selection," carried out in part in the Tower of Literary Selection, provide an entry point into the world of early Qing literary elites, their cultural values, and their literary and leisure practice.

Born in 1617, Deng Hanyi was a native of Taizhou subprefecture, one of the administrative units governed from Yangzhou. He also spent many years living in Suzhou, and some seventeenth-century sources describe him as a Suzhou resident and Taizhou native.[88] During the 1630s and 1640s, Suzhou was a major educational and publishing center, and the focus of literati cultural and social aspirations. Deng Hanyi would have found the city a veritable magnet for talented, ambitious, and politically motivated young men like himself. New activist literary and political networks like the Fushe flourished in this environment during the late Ming, giving added cohesion to elite society and enhancing elite self-identity.[89] Here, poetic and political goals converged, as literary revival reflected social change and political objectives took root in literary organizations. Social activities, cultural production, and political networking coalesced in groups of men organized around common interests and activities. The social and literary practices associated with the Fushe underlay the formation of poetry clubs and the assembling of poetry anthologies during the early Qing, though perhaps with a less explicitly political purpose.

Even if Deng Hanyi did not formally join the Fushe, and we have no record of his having done so, we know that he participated in the group's activities.[90] During the spring of 1642, Deng Hanyi attended a party at Tiger Hill that was sponsored and attended by members of the Fushe.[91] The gathering was hosted by Yangzhou native Zheng Yuanxun (j.s. 1643, d. 1644), the owner of the Garden of Shadows and Reflections, and Li Wen, the leader of a Songjiang-based subsidiary of the Restoration Society. Other guests included such young luminaries as Fang Yizhi (d. 1671?), Gong Dingzi, Cao Rong, Du Jun, Yu Huai, and Mao Xiang.[92] Among the men in attendance at the Tiger Hill gathering, several maintained lasting relationships with Deng Hanyi. These friendships lasted beyond the conquest and continued into the next generation: Deng continued to socialize with the sons of Mao Xiang and Du Jun, even after the two older men had died. Again the longevity of these relationships is a testament to the tensile strength of friendship: though strained by distance and the political turmoil at mid-century, these relationships endured. Moreover, the Fushe organization itself seems to have provided a model for Deng Hanyi's post-conquest interactions, and perhaps even for his anthology, the *Poetry Survey*, which constituted in new form the transregional networks behind clubs like the Fushe. Several of his friends, including those who participated in Fushe activities, later also compiled anthologies of recent poetry by their friends and associates. Deng Hanyi's Fushe contacts had a significant impact on his social and literary practice—especially his ideas about anthologies, friendship, and publishing, ideas clearly manifested in his large-scale anthology project, the *Poetry Survey*.

Deng Hanyi did not hold any official position under the Ming. Like many of his generation, he seems to have rejected the examination life in favor of other options afforded by literary talent and good connections. Though references to the poverty of many of his literary companions abound, he does not seem to have suffered from economic hardship even after the conquest. At the same time, the conquest seems to have triggered a dramatic increase in literati mobility, and Deng Hanyi, who was twenty-eight when the Qing forces crossed into Jiangnan, partook of this strange mixture of displacement and wanderlust.

By his own report, he spent the years following 1645 on the road. He traveled "tens of thousands of *li* by cart and by boat," reaching Henan, Hebei, Hunan, and Guangdong, and especially visiting the "graveyards"

of Henan and Shanxi.[93] While in Beijing during the early 1650s, he socialized with Chen Zuoming and Han Shi, who were in the process of editing one of the earliest collections of Qing poetry, the *Guomen ji*, a project
that might well have contributed to Deng's own later interest in anthology-making.[94] He went to Zhejiang with his friend from Taizhou, Huang
Yun, in 1654, and while there, both studied with the loyalist and Ming
historian Zha Jizuo (1601–76).[95] In 1656, Deng Hanyi traveled to Guangdong with Gong Dingzi, probably as a member of his secretarial staff.[96]
He also spent time in Nanjing socializing and, years later, working on the
provincial gazetteer. In 1670, he lived for a time at the home of his friend
Mao Xiang in Rugao. His travels suggest restlessness and a sense of discomfort, both at home and on the road, as he, like many of his peers,
searched for old friends and tried to make a living in a changed world.
One of Deng Hanyi's friends compared these feelings of discomfort to
insomnia, writing that

> It is as if one were lying down in order to pursue a bed. The bed is there and one
> is already in it. But perhaps one cannot sleep in it. So you toss in it and you turn
> in it, you flip from one side to the other . . . The point of being alive is to pursue
> peace and serenity. You already have it, but perhaps you haven't really got it. The
> most suitable place for a gentleman is in his hometown where the fields and gar-
> dens are familiar. Living outside one has friends and landscapes that one has
> known longer than those at home. Tired of home, one expresses a desire to leave.
> Having wandered outside for a long time, one expresses a desire to go home . . .
> We live in troubled times. Those living at home have been shocked by the military
> catastrophe and have left home with their families. Those living outside have
> rushed toward the beacon fires and, with their wives, sought to return home . . .
> This is in the category of tossing and turning and flipping and flopping.[97]

Despite the complex feelings that motivated men like Deng Hanyi to take
to the road, the actual experience was not necessarily unpleasant. While
traveling, Deng Hanyi met many of his fellow poets and acquired a reputation as a perceptive poetry critic. Aspiring writers began to present
him with their poetry in exchange for comments and advice. The poems
he collected in this way served as the core of the first *Poetry Survey*
collection, his literary monument to the experiences and values of his
generation.[98]

   During the first decades of the Qing, Deng Hanyi also participated
actively in the literary and social activities of Yangzhou, though he lived
in the city only sporadically. Friends described him as a leader of the city's
increasingly stylish literary scene and recorded his presence at numerous
parties and excursions in the city. By their own account, Deng Hanyi and

his friends played an important role in the revival of *ci* poetry, a movement with strong regional and contemporary associations.[99] The "lyric
poetry boom" of the early Qing appears to have been another literary by-
product of the transregional elite culture that formed in Suzhou, Hangzhou, Yangzhou, Beijing, and Nanjing both before and especially after the
Qing conquest.[100] Indeed, at least one contemporary enthusiastically portrayed Yangzhou as the epicenter of the lyric craze, writing that "Weiyang
[Yangzhou] is gorgeous, and so it is the place for lyric poetry."[101] Prominent visitors and residents composed lyrics, and many collections were
produced and published in Yangzhou during this period. Deng Hanyi's
lyrics and commentaries appear in several such collections.

As we saw in Chapter 2, poetry parties provided context for encounters between men of divergent political experiences. Gatherings of more
than ten men for political purposes were prohibited during this period, at
least in theory, and the lines between sociability and politics remained
ambiguous, due to the legacy of late Ming literary-political clubs.[102] Still,
large literary parties, outings, and clubs seem to have been quite prevalent in Yangzhou even under this prohibition, and such activities feature
prominently in poetry collections of the period. Deng Hanyi attended a
gathering of forty-six people at Red Bridge in 1666, and he met monthly
for poetry and drink with those in attendance who remained in Yangzhou
after the initial gathering. Members of this club constituted a diverse
group including provincial officials, local officials, and members of the
local and regional literary elite. Their contacts were extended through
travel and postal correspondence, and their fates reflected the varied political commitments and occupations of men who participated in Yangzhou
social networks during the 1660s and 1670s. According to the group's
record-keeper, Sun Jinli, one member returned to Nanjing to live in retirement, one traveled to the capital, one served as a magistrate, and another
died, broken-hearted about the fall of the Ming.[103] Collections of contemporary poetry, like the *Poetry Survey,* served as a printed monument
to these transregional, and often explicitly transdynastic, social and literary communities.

This project became central to Deng's public persona as a poet, critic,
and friend to the famous. It also functioned as a vehicle for the enhance-
ment of his friendship network. In the pages of his anthology, he cultivated an image of himself as a gregarious, but morally serious, poetry
critic and publisher, simultaneously setting high standards for inclusion
and commenting chattily about the poets whose work he includes. Although this image was to some extent based on the Ming precedent of the

cultural raconteur, it made use of a distinctly early Qing medium, the anthology of contemporary writings. Through his anthology, Deng Hanyi constructed a nonofficial public identity similar to that of urban men of letters who situated themselves outside the examination system during the late Ming. This persona was the embodiment of the late Ming values of authenticity, spontaneity, and sociability, and it continued to enjoy great currency in the first decades of the Qing. It was, for example, used to great effect by the early Qing official Wang Shizhen, as we saw in Chapter 2. As something shared, recognized, and explicitly nonpolitical, the familiar image of the "fashionable personality" or *fengliu* provided one of the building blocks for early Qing cultural and social reconstruction. Editors like Deng Hanyi positioned themselves at the center of extensive communities of contemporary writers, consciously adopting this familiar role to establish a place for themselves in new social and political circumstances.[104]

Like his late Ming predecessors, including Chen Jiru and Feng Menglong, Deng Hanyi produced private editions under his own imprint. He published his books, including the three volumes of the *Poetry Survey* and several works of literary criticism, under the name of his residence, the Shenmotang, literally the "Careful with Ink" Studio. These printing projects seem to have been carried out in Yangzhou, as the *Poetry Survey* appears on a list of locally published books included in the 1733 gazetteer.[105] However, Deng appears to have been less market-oriented than late Ming publishers like Chen Jiru who were famous for their commercial productions. Indeed, the *Poetry Survey* series does not seem to have been profitable, for by his own account, Deng had to solicit monetary contributions from officials in order to publish all three of the collections. Still, the *Poetry Survey* circulated widely in the cities of Jiangnan. In a flattering letter to Deng Hanyi, Li Yesi, a native of Yin County, Zhejiang, praises the collection for having an impact around the empire from the time of its publication. At the same time, Li complains that the book was unavailable in his own "isolated" hometown near Ningbo.[106]

The persona of the *fengliu* was derived from two sources: the books he edited and published and the men with whom he socialized.[107] During the early Qing, these two sources were closely intertwined: the books edited by the *fengliu* figure often contained the writings of the men with whom he socialized, reproducing in print the self-consciously transregional social networks of the editor. Deng Hanyi had an extraordinary social network, the outlines of which survive in his comments on poems in the *Poetry Survey*. Even though the context for these publishing activities was often clearly urban, and more often specifically "Jiangnan," men like

Deng Hanyi conceived of both their social networks and their collections of poetry as explicitly transregional and explicitly contemporary. The list of contributors to the *Poetry Survey* includes men from every province, though the Jiangnan core is obviously overrepresented.[108]

Early Qing anthologies of early Qing poetry were material manifestations of early Qing social networks. Although face-to-face gatherings played an important role in these projects, contact across distance carried out through letters was also crucial. Like many of his peers, Deng Hanyi actively corresponded with friends and associates all over China, and he sought to include writings from around the empire in his anthology. Indeed, many of the poems that appear in the *Poetry Survey* were said to have been collected by mail. References to postal communications became virtually *de rigueur* in the editorial principles *(fanli)* section of early Qing anthologies, as editors sought to underscore the breadth, accessibility, and contemporary focus of their projects. Even the prefectural gazetteer published in 1675 mentions that the editors received submissions of poetry by mail.[109] Such references also may in fact represent a show of enthusiasm for the restoration of long-deteriorated infrastructure and the resumption of transregional connections that accompanied the consolidation of Qing rule. Attention to the contemporary character of these collections, as well as an almost obsessive emphasis on their simultaneously transregional and personal nature, was a hallmark of early Qing literary anthologies and, more broadly, of the social networks that the books recorded and celebrated. The chatty style of the editorial comments replicate in print the sociable aspect of these literati communities. Collections like the *Poetry Survey* commemorated a generation's shared experiences and affinities—events associated with the conquest—and a love for contemporary poetry. Even as the newly rebuilt Tower of Literary Selection honored a shared cultural heritage rooted in poetry and literati sociability, the *Poetry Survey* also celebrated these same core values and contributed to the reintegration of the broader community.

Deng Hanyi gave his collection the formal title *Tianxia mingjia shiguan* (Poetry Survey of the Famous Writers of the Realm). The full title suggests a transregional approach; indeed the editorial principles indicate that he sought to include poets from all over the empire, although in fact writers from Jiangnan and Zhejiang predominate. In addition, by involving a broad cross-section of literary and official elites—ranging from Ming-inspired suicides, militant loyalists, quiet bystanders, talented women, cultured monks, and a full spectrum of figures in between—Deng Hanyi contributed to the construction of a new, post-conquest sensibility, a

transdynastic sensibility that simultaneously—and, I argue, very consciously—drew upon images and personalities representing the Ming past
and a Qing future. Moreover, he (somewhat disingenuously) indicates
that his collection is not arranged hierarchically. Instead, he claims that
the poems are printed in the order they were received. The biographies of
his male contributors do not refer to official titles, positions, examination
performance, parentage, or other markers of social status and achievement. He states explicitly in the fanli: "I do not distinguish between my
peers who serve and those who live in retirement. Those whose poems
reached me were selected for inclusion. Those with whom I had long-
standing friendships, but whose writings are hard to find, I also included."[110] Deng thus gestures toward the reconstitution of a community
rooted in cultural achievement, thereby effacing divisive distinctions
between those who served the new dynasty and those who did not. His
anthology embodied the shared values of his peers, manifesting in print
their vision of a universal (elite) culture shared through social networks,
transmitted via a living cohort spread out across the empire. Anthologies
like the *Shiguan* and buildings like the Wenxuan Tower, thus, shared a
function as sites of imagined continuity with the past, realized (or compiled) in the present, and ultimately pointing toward future reconciliation.

Although his social network included many Qing officials, Deng Hanyi
himself refrained from taking the examinations until 1679, when he took
the special boxue hongci examination as a commoner. His political position prior to the examination appears to have been neutral, particularly
compared to close associates like his teacher Zha Jizuo (a once-militant
loyalist) and Gong Dingzi (a thrice-serving official). He seems to have
been invited to take the boxue hongci examination on account of his im-
peccable connections, for he was close to some of the most famous official
and cultural figures of the period, and perhaps because of his own stature
as a poet, editor, and poetry critic. Deng's biographers portray the examination as the most important event of his career, even though he failed
the actual examination—not surprising since official position generally
dominated biographical writing, and this was Deng's only brush with
official sanction. The prefaces to his poetry collection, dated 1672, 1678,
and 1689, also reflect his growing acceptance of Qing rule, culminating
with his participation in the boxue hongci examination. He describes the
excitement of participation in the examination and the productive convergence of great writers in the capital. Moreover, he depicts the examination as a mark of imperial magnanimity and a herald of the new
regime's legitimacy.

Deng Hanyi lived for a decade after his trip to Beijing for the examination, continuing his compilation work in Yangzhou until just prior to
his death in 1689 at the age of seventy-three *sui*. The third collection in
the *Poetry Survey* was in fact published posthumously in 1689, with help
from Deng's friend and editorial associate Zhang Chao. The *Hezheng lu,*
a collection of biographies linked to the boxue hongci examination, contains the following description of Deng Hanyi's final years:

> He had thoroughly penetrated the classics, histories, and the words of the "hun-
> dred philosophers." He especially excelled at poetry criticism and was a leader in
> elegant poetry circles. After returning from the examination, he did as he liked
> with his leisure, composing poems and drinking wine. He also took a small boat
> to the prefectural seat [Yangzhou] and took up residence in Master Dong's Shrine.
> The carriages and horses of those who sought his instruction crowded his lane.
> He organized the poems of recent celebrities into the *Poetry Survey,* which con-
> sisted of four collections [sic—this was a standard mistake by the eighteenth cen-
> tury]. He cut out false genres and pursued elegant tone with all his might. Those
> who discussed poetry in the realm all honored him. On occasion, he composed
> matching rhymes with Wu Weiye and Gong Dingzi . . . Wang Shizhen also praised
> one of his poems . . .[111]

Here the author presents Deng as a serious scholar in retirement, using
his talents to enjoy himself and to improve the writings of his peers. By
using the clichéd image of a lane packed with admirers, the author underscores Deng's stature and popularity. Importantly, the author also places
Deng Hanyi in the company of the leading poets and critics of his age,
thereby conferring added prestige upon his subject. An account by the
nineteenth-century Yangzhou scholar Ruan Yuan, similarly emphasizes
the high esteem in which Deng was held by his peers, claiming that those
seeking his advice crowded the marketplace near the Shrine of Master
Dong.[112] In another context, Ruan Yuan states that "Deng Hanyi of
Taizhou selected poems by early Qing poets for the *Poetry Survey* in
14 juan. He also selected women's poetry for the *Shiguan bieji* in two
juan."[113] All of Deng Hanyi's biographers mention the *Poetry Survey* as
his major literary achievement, though some later critics described the
collection in less flattering terms. For example, the Qianlong emperor's
sometime favorite poetry critic Shen Deqian (1673–1769) states that
"while the *Poetry Survey* is no more than social poetry exchanged among
friends, it is still worthy of selection by later people."[114] This assessment
reflects changes in the standards for evaluating poetry collections and,
indeed, a changed attitude toward the cultural values of the early Qing
literary elite. By the end of the eighteenth century, copies of early Qing

poetry anthologies, including the *Poetry Survey*, were hard to come by, as Ruan Yuan and his peers observed. These carefully constructed literary monuments to the conquest generation proved as evanescent as the men and values they commemorated.

Forgetting: The Impermanence of Monuments

In the eighteenth century and subsequently, with the rise of political and moral systems that demanded absolute loyalty from even deceased subjects, Deng Hanyi and his book were seen as too ambivalent to be tolerated. Along with the book he edited, which was banned during the Qianlong period, Deng Hanyi fell into obscurity almost a century after his death. His public persona, like his anthology, or indeed, like the Wenxuan Tower in which he compiled the second volume, lost its meaning outside the early Qing historical and cultural context. Xia Quan, the nineteenth-century Taizhou native who attempted to compile a new collection of Deng Hanyi's writings, noted that due to the strict banning of books during the Qianlong period, Deng Hanyi's private library, and many of his personal writings, had been burned. Moreover, when Xia Quan asked Deng's family to see if any of the books had survived, they found that the few remaining books had been ruined by insects and mice, and so they burned those as well.[115] Although the gnawing of vermin no doubt contributed to the loss of Deng Hanyi's writings, the initial destruction, which took place as part of the mid-Qing crackdown on subversive writings, was clearly the more significant.

The censorship of seditious texts marked the second stage in the compilation of the imperial library collection, the *Siku quanshu*. Indeed, although not included in the library itself, the *Poetry Survey* had the dubious distinction of being noted in both the *Siku quanshu* annotated catalogue and in the indices of books banned in conjunction with the *Siku* project.[116] Evidently, the *Poetry Survey*'s poetic content initially met with the approval of the compilers of the *Siku* as they embarked on their work in the mid-1770s, and the book thus received notice in the annotated catalogue. However, as increasing numbers of early Qing writers fell into disfavor for their supposedly questionable conduct or slanderous words, those responsible for the censorship of seditious texts ordered that problematic parts of the *Poetry Survey* be destroyed. In particular, the inclusion of several authors whom the censors deemed to be particularly seditious justified its suppression. The suppression of the *Poetry Survey* corresponds to the emperor's 1776 edict on books to be preserved, changed, or destroyed, the relevant passage of which reads: "If among the anthologies and prose of various authors, there occur the productions of Qian Qianyi, Qu Dajun, and their ilk, they should be eliminated, but the balance of the original may remain. It is not necessary to make all suffer because one or two miscreants are included."[117] The official entry on the *Poetry Survey* contained in the *Jinshu zongmu* (Index of Books to Be Banned) reads as follows:

I have inspected the *Poetry Survey*. It was edited by Deng Hanyi of Taizhou. It is a selection of poems by all the poets of the early Qing. In all, it contains the work of more than five hundred men. With the exception of those poems which ought to be burned because they are by Qian Qianyi, Qu Dajun, and Jin Bao, and those selections which contain incendiary language, it is not necessary that the rest be destroyed.[118]

Those initially involved in the suppression of suspicious works of literature clearly did not intend the total destruction of the *Poetry Survey* but rather sought to eliminate materials by authors that the state deemed "dangerous" or "subversive." In so doing, they followed the rules for handling anthologies established by the *Siku* commission. These rules called for the careful labeling of the relevant passages for extraction and burning, and the removal of those passages from the original printing boards.[119] Physical evidence of a partial suppression of the *Poetry Survey* can be seen in a Qianlong period edition of the *Shiguan chuji* held in the Nanjing library. In this version, all references to questionable figures, such as Qian Qianyi and Jin Bao, are blacked out, having been planed off of the original woodblocks.

At some point, however, probably in the late 1770s, the policy calling for the partial censorship of the *Poetry Survey* became a mandate for the destruction of the entire collection. Writing during the 1790s, Ruan Yuan commented that because the *Poetry Survey* contained those authors who were banned, a decree was enacted calling for it to be burned.[120] Apparently, the suppression of the *Poetry Survey* was carried out by local officials eager to implement imperial policy more effectively than was required by the central government. After all, they evidently reasoned, if a partial ban was good, a total ban might be even better.

As Kent Guy points out in *The Emperor's Four Treasuries*, there was no uniform procedure according to which particular books were suppressed. Instead, the procedure involved gentry and officials at several levels. First, local book collectors chosen from among the gentry would submit materials to provincial authorities for evaluation. Then, provincial officials would submit books determined to have seditious potential to Beijing. Once officials in Beijing made the final determination, provincial governors were supposed to search out the printing blocks and send them, along with copies of the books, to Beijing for destruction.[121] Due to lack of coordination between these local and national groups, standards for implementation and punishment varied widely from province to province, and even from locale to locale.[122] At the local level, censorship was carried out by local elites and could be manipulated by local leaders for their own purposes. The process became a witch hunt reminiscent of the 1768 soul-stealing scare described by Philip Kuhn, as provincial officials were rewarded for searching out large numbers of seditious materials and local elites turned the search to their own ends.[123] Someone, somewhere, perhaps in Taizhou, decided that the *Poetry Survey* contained enough seditious material to justify total suppression. The collection was burned, along with many of Deng Hanyi's other writings. Of course, "total suppression" did not mean that every single copy of the book was condemned to the flames. Censorship was enforced unevenly in practice, and the success of such bans depended largely, if not entirely, on the zeal of local officials in prosecuting such cases. Still, the mid-eighteenth-century suppression severely limited the number of copies, especially complete copies, that survived into the twentieth century. Kanda Kiichiro, a Japanese scholar of Chinese literature, noted in 1922 that though the *Poetry Survey* was probably the most important early Qing poetry anthology, it was extremely rare. He stated that he did not know anyone with a complete set; even the Naikaku Bunko (Imperial Collection, Tokyo) had only the first two parts, and he himself had only the first and third.[124] He speculated that the anthology was probably equally rare in China, and, indeed, complete sets do seem hard to come by.[125]

In a sense, the *Poetry Survey* fell victim to its own inclusiveness and also to a change in literary-political values. Its contents seemed innocuous enough in the late seventeenth century, when the conquest provided a mournful context for nostalgic poems by members of the literate class regardless of their political affiliations. Even the writings of Qing officials were touched with tragic memories. These expressions provided catharsis for those who had experienced the conquest, and they became conventionalized as characteristic literary tropes of the times through poetry games of matched rhymes and paired images. Social and literary networks crossed political boundaries, as we have seen, with the poems of "hermits" and those of committed officials appearing side by side. These men socialized together, drinking and composing poetry, using leisure, poetry, and publishing to recreate the appearance of a unified elite class. The late

Ming cultural repertoire, with its emphasis on creativity, authentic emotion, and sociability, provided building blocks for these efforts at a time when political turmoil made room for a somewhat more open cultural arena. This was a world of pose and pretensions acted out through poetry and leisure excursions. The poetic imagination, and also the historical imagination, played important roles in these elite activities, as these men sought to reimagine a shared cultural heritage. An anthology of poetry memorialized the social networks and aspirations of these men while also providing them with yet another forum for shared literary and cultural production. And a building with a fake history allowed them to imagine a cultural heritage for a city of merchants and thereby appropriate the urban space for their own purposes.

A century later, such expressions and ambiguous identities appeared ominous. Even though the political world tolerated confusion that could be manipulated by both emperor and bureaucracy, it brooked no ambiguity in the world of letters. Individuals long dead were suddenly categorized according to rigid standards of loyalty and uprightness. New orthodoxies crept into ordinary life as well as court life. Perceived anti-Manchu innuendo could lead to the suppression of a work of literature. The categories invoked in the eighteenth century seem especially ill-suited applied to men of the seventeenth century, with their flexible and poetic public personae. Yet they were forced by historians and critics into the Procrustean bed of the Qianlong emperor's literary and political standards. The much praised *fengliu* personality of the seventeenth century lost its cachet in the eighteenth. Deng Hanyi, whose surviving writings appear relatively apolitical, was found guilty by association for his inclusion of men retroactively deemed problematic, like Qian Qianyi and Jin Bao, in his anthology. And the product of his pleasant labor in the Tower of Literary Selection was condemned to the flames.

The tower where Deng Hanyi labored was also forgotten in the eighteenth century. Poetry and myth could no longer sustain its reputation, and it fell out of fashion as newer, more marvelous scenic sites were created in the Yangzhou suburbs. Perhaps the apocryphal tale of the prince's presence in Yangzhou lost its resonance after real emperors visited and, through their presence, transformed the city. The merchants and evidential scholars who made eighteenth-century Yangzhou famous appear to have favored the novelty of gardens and "prospects" that were constructed, at least ostensibly, in honor of the touring Qianlong emperor and his entourage. Indeed, the eighteenth-century city was increasingly in thrall to the values and projects centered in the court at Beijing. The eighteenth-century commercial economy was irrevocably bound to imperial favor through the salt monopoly. New buildings increasingly reflected northern influences, as did the city's celebrated Weiyang cuisine. Indeed, the increasingly fashionable evidential scholarship, too, had its links to the court through the *Siku quanshu* project. And, like the new gardens that dominated Yangzhou's eighteenth-century landscape, the *Siku* anthology was itself a physical monument: a monument to the new, less forgiving cultural world of the eighteenth century.

Authenticating and Appropriating

During the nineteenth century, a new Wenxuan Tower was built in Yangzhou, giving the name a new structure, a new location, and a new explanation. Located on the grounds of the great nineteenth-century scholar-official Ruan Yuan's family temple, this new construction represented the triumph of evidential research over local myth, and the search for, and promotion of, an "honest" or authentic local heritage based on, and affirmed by, scholarly research. This new "Sui Tower of Literary Selection," as it was called, revised the narrative supporting the tower's presence in Yangzhou, emphasizing links to academic traditions admired by "Yangzhou school" advocates of pre-Song scholarly traditions. At the same time, as an act of conspicuous individual patronage, this new structure inscribed Ruan Yuan's lineage into the urban landscape, even as it signaled the family's rise to national prominence through his academic success. Moreover, the construction of this new tower was part of a larger process through which Ruan Yuan sought quite literally to make a mark on his hometown landscape, rendering the local personal through acts of architectural, scholarly, and charitable patronage. As a young man in his thirties and forties, Ruan Yuan was an enthusiastic promoter of Yangzhou's cultural heritage, committed to both meticulous scholarship and the preservation of temples and tombs. He appeared bent on simultaneously augmenting his family's presence in the region while renewing and organizing the prefecture's literary and historical past. In addition to reconstructing local monuments, he also compiled anthologies of works by local writers and encouraged his friends, relatives, and other associates to publish their writings about the city. The editor of the 1810 gazetteer describes Ruan Yuan's publishing projects as an important new source of more accurate information about the prefecture.[126] The glittering image of eighteenth-century Yangzhou familiar today is the creation of Ruan Yuan and his close associates, who actively promoted the city through works like the *Guangling shishi* (Poems and Events of Yangzhou), the *Yangzhou huafang lu* (Record of the Painted Boats of Yangzhou), and the *Hanjiang Sanbaiyin* (Three Hundred Rhymes of Hanjiang [Yangzhou]).[127]

Formally a native of Yizheng county, Ruan Yuan was born in 1764 at his family's home in Yangzhou.[128] The family had moved to Yangzhou from Huai'an (Northern Jiangsu) during the late Ming, and later established a refuge at Gongdao Bridge in the suburbs near North Lake to escape Gao Jie's siege of the city in 1644. They also acquired property in the vicinity of the Thunder Pools north of the city, which in Ruan Yuan's time became the site of the family's tombs. Ruan Yuan's grandfather was an assistant regional commander in Hunan during the Kangxi reign, and he served in the mid-eighteenth-century campaigns against the Miao people in Southwest China. His father chose not to pursue an official career, instead working in the salt business with his mother's relatives and engaging in philanthropic activities.[129] Ruan Yuan spent his early childhood in the city of Yangzhou. His mother taught him to read when he was a boy of five *sui*. When he was six, she sent him to live with an aunt whose husband worked as a teacher. There, he was first exposed to the classics, and he began to recite and write poetry by the time he was eight.[130] He then transferred to the school of a well-known local Confucian, who introduced him to the study of the *Wenxuan*. Ruan Yuan passed the provincial examinations at the age of twenty-three *sui*, and went to Beijing, where he passed the metropolitan and palace examinations and was appointed to the Hanlin Academy in 1789, at the youthful age of twenty-six.[131]

During his extraordinarily long and successful career, Ruan Yuan served as an education official in Zhejiang and Shandong, as governor of Zhejiang and Jiangxi, and as governor-general of Guangdong and Guangxi. He worked as a compiler in the Hanlin Academy and was promoted to a position as tutor to the heir apparent. He also held positions in the Board of Revenue and the Board of War. He catalogued the imperial painting collection and served as Grand Secretary, retiring with the title "Grand Guardian of the Heir Apparent" in 1838. His scholarly writings cover an enormous range of topics, including epigraphy, classics, history, poetry, bibliography, art, astronomy, and mathematics. Upon his death, at the age of eighty-five, the emperor honored him with a commemorative biography and tomb inscription as well as the posthumous honorific of "Wenda."

Through scholarly, philanthropic, and patronage activities in his native place, especially during the years from 1798 to 1821, Ruan Yuan helped define a distinctly local Yangzhou identity for his contemporaries, especially for members of the local elite. By putting the full weight of his prestige as a scholar and an official behind local editing and construction projects, he contributed to the creation of an ideal elite identity that was firmly rooted in the local community—an ideal that he promoted and exported through his official position and through his sponsorship of similar activities in the locales in which he served. In addition, by patronizing particular types of local projects, and by consciously constructing a local heritage for the particular type of scholarship he most valued, he emphasized the local roots of elite identity both at home in Yangzhou, and again in the locales where he served. His "rectification" of the myth supporting the Wenxuan Tower is typical of his activities in Yangzhou. The project demonstrates his commitment to a specific type of scholarly and intellectual method, to his family's reputation, and to the reputation of his hometown. Ruan Yuan did not conceive of the Wenxuan Tower in terms of myth and poetry, nor did he articulate its position within a system of transcendent or transregional values. Instead, his priorities were patently local, even genealogical, in orientation, despite, or perhaps because of, his service elsewhere. He sought to identify correct antecedents for his own scholarly practice, articulating them in patterns that resembled lineages, rather than the networks more familiar to his late seventeenth-century predecessors.

Ruan Yuan's involvement with the Tower of Literary Selection began in 1804, when, as a very young and already very successful official, he purchased land in the Old City of Yangzhou, just north of the seventeenth-century Tower of Literary Selection. Acting at his father's request, he hired workers, purchased materials, and built a temple honoring his ancestors, who had recently been recognized by the emperor in connection with Ruan Yuan's own achievements. He endowed the temple with paddy land, ritual implements, and ritual clothing, and erected a wooden stele tracing the family's history, paying special attention to their several centuries of residence in Yangzhou prefecture.[132] In 1805, Ruan Yuan, again acting in accordance with his father's wishes, built a clan school on a piece of land immediately west of the family temple. He erected a stele on the site, naming it the "Sui Tower of Literary Selection," referring specifically to the Sui-dynasty beginnings of *Wenxuan* scholarship, which he had traced back to a Yangzhou native named Cao Xian who lived in the neighborhood, and whose house, the Wenxuan (Lane) Tower, evidently was the "real" and "original" Tower of Literary Selection in Yangzhou. Ruan

Yuan's new building functioned as a clan school, a shrine to Cao Xian and other Yangzhou natives who made early contributions to *Wenxuan* scholarship, a guest house, and his own personal library. In an essay describing the new Sui Tower of Literary Selection, he is careful to distinguish his building project from the earlier Tower of Literary Selection in Yangzhou. The essay corrects, through evidential research, the earlier tower's false legacy, replacing it with a narrative that he saw as both more persuasive and more relevant to his own purposes. He asserts that the former tower incorrectly honored Xiao Tong, who had never visited Yangzhou (more poetically: the outside source of meaning is invalid—the famous hero who allegedly brought the light of culture to Yangzhou—never even came). Still, he argues that Yangzhou is in fact entitled to celebrate a link to the *Wenxuan*, because, as "those who investigate ancient matters" have learned, the city was the home of *Wenxuan scholarship* (or Wenxuanxue), because the Sui-dynasty progenitors of this important field of knowledge and scholarship were in fact *natives* of the city. He uses evidence from the Tang histories to trace the intellectual lineage of *Wenxuan* studies, strongly emphasizing the native-place connection he shared with the men who originated this field of study, while at the same time firmly linking the field of study to the Yangzhou locale.

In the same essay, he also highlights the importance of *Wenxuan* scholarship to contemporary *kaozheng* scholarship (also called evidential research), and particularly, to a branch of evidential scholarship that is now known as the "Yangzhou school." On the basis of a thorough investigation, he is able to "prove" the existence of a genealogy of *Wenxuan* scholarship carried out by seven Yangzhou men in Yangzhou prefecture. Moreover, he links the practice of this type of scholarship with his own contemporary scholarly interests by highlighting the earlier *Wenxuan* scholars' success in the areas of epigraphy and ancient style prose, both of which were key elements in evidential research. He writes, "I say that ancient people, ancient-style prose, philology, and *ci* and *fu* (types of poems prominently featured in the *Wenxuan*) have one source and flow together," again, using a selective local past to validate current practice. He also highlights the attraction that *Wenxuan* scholarship had for him (personally) beginning at an early age. Throughout the essay, and indeed elsewhere in his writings, Ruan Yuan demonstrates linkages between the *Wenxuan* scholars of the past, the evidential scholars of the present, and Yangzhou prefecture, positioning himself as the rightful arbiter of historical accuracy and the rightful heir to the *Wenxuan* legacy.

He further publicizes his appropriation and personalization of the site's legacy by using the tower's name as one of his own style names, and by using collector's seals inscribed "Wenxuan Tower," "Sui Wenxuan Tower," and "Resident of the Wenxuan Tower in Cao Xian of the Sui's Old Neighborhood in Yangzhou," during the years following the tower's construction.[133] He also used publishing and scholarly activities to publicize his connection to the site and its scholarly legacy. In 1807, he purchased an important and very rare Southern Song edition of the *Wenxuan*, whose provenance he traces in a preface. Not only did he retain the book for his own use, but he also collated the text, reprinted it, and gave copies to other scholars. In the preface to his new edition of the *Wenxuan*, he describes his family's residential proximity to the Wenxuan Tower Lane and his construction of a new Tower of Literary Selection near his family temple.[134] In addition to publishing a new edition of the *Wenxuan* based on the Song edition he stored in the tower, he also published an important collectanea *(congshu)* under the tower's name and used the tower's name for one of his several publishing operations. In addition, a collection of Ruan Yuan's poems with explanatory notes published in the Jiaqing period bears the title *Poems from the Wenxuan Tower* (Wenxuanlou shicun), and he published a collectanea including his own writings, as well as works by his friends and relatives, serially between 1790 and 1840 under the title *Wenxuanlou congshu*.[135] In an inscription on the Sui Tower of Literary Selection, Ruan Yuan includes a poem that begins with references to the buildings and scholars linking the neighborhood to *Wenxuan* studies. The second half of the poem takes possession of the site for the Ruan family, and highlights its new function with references differentiating it from the earlier (false) Tower.[136] He publicly and repeatedly rejects the poetic link between the tower and Prince Xiao Tong, writing (in several places) that historical references to the Wenxuan Tower in Yangzhou have *nothing* to do with the prince, an assertion that gets picked up by other nineteenth-century writers, particularly when they refer to Ruan Yuan's new tower.[137]

Indeed, in Ruan Yuan's collected writings, we see persistent efforts to connect himself and his family to the locale, and to evidential scholarship. As essays in his collected writings reveal, he was frequently involved in efforts to restore, reconstruct, or rediscover famous historical sites in the prefecture. For example, he describes his efforts to find and rehabilitate the Sui emperor's tomb, which was formerly located near Thunder Pool, in the vicinity of the Ruan family graves, as follows:

The Jiajing *Weiyangzhi* map shows a grave stele north of Thunder Pool bearing the four characters "Sui Yangdi ling" [Tomb of Sui Yangdi]. This was not very long ago and should not have been lost. So I asked people in the city, but no one knew about it. In 1807, I lived near there and coincidentally asked an old farmer of North Village where the old site was. The old farmer said "the tomb is still there, the local people call it Emperor's Grave Mound, it is 3 *li* due north of here." So I followed his directions and went to the base of the tumulus. It occupies 4–5 *mu* . . . The tomb itself is 7–8 *chi* in height, 2–3 *mu* around. The old farmer said that below the earth there is a tunnel and an iron door facing northwest; when he was young he dug there and saw it. For my part, I sat below the tomb and called villagers to bring dirt, and for each *shi* weight of dirt, I paid one copper cash. In only a few days, we accumulated 8,000 *shi* of dirt and planted 150 pines and the tomb was grand again. I had the magistrate Yi Bingshou [Moqing] write a stele in clerical script, which we erected upon its completion.[138]

Here, as in the case of the Wenxuan Tower, the monument Ruan restores is located in close proximity to sites of personal or familial significance, in this case, the Ruan family tombs at Thunder Pool. Moreover, we see Ruan relying on textual evidence to correct or rediscover lost symbols of the prefecture's history. Here, however, we also see the introduction of a new motif: Ruan's use of local informants, especially villagers, as a source of historical information. This motif is repeated in Ruan Yuan's account of his efforts to rediscover and restore the Dragon King Temple, also in the vicinity of Thunder Pool. In this case, Ruan is confused because his family's tombs are located in Dragon King Temple Village, and yet there is no Dragon King Temple in the area. With the help of an old farmer, Ruan finds the temple's stele, restores it, and makes a rubbing of it. By studying the stele, he gains access to information of local significance unavailable through the official history books. With further research, Ruan is able to recover the whole story about the Dragon King Temple, and, by doing so, he recreates the rituals honoring the Dragon King. With these accounts, Ruan Yuan affirms the importance of local history, especially when retrieved through on-site investigations, and, even more especially, through investigations involving the study of stone stelae, that is, epigraphy.

In a series of essays produced during the early nineteenth century, including the ones just cited, we see Ruan Yuan investigating, rectifying, and reconstructing local monuments, and, at the same time, affirming his personal place among them. Moreover, in his preface to the *Record of the Painted Boats of Yangzhou*, he praises Li Dou for his application of similar methods, writing that "[Li Dou] worked on this for twenty years, examining the gazetteers and stelae, interviewing elderly residents, and inquiring of boatmen and shopkeepers. What he has made is somewhere between the elegant and the base, deeply according with the form of ancient books. I received and read it, admiring its strong points . . ."[139]

Thus, Ruan Yuan uses, and encourages others to use, an engagement with architectural sites to "correct" or "rectify" local history. In the process, he identifies sources in the local past that validate contemporary practice. That these sources are explicitly local to Yangzhou, and that they must be proven and explicated through the methods associated with evidential scholarship, is a marked departure from the emphasis on poetry, myth, and transregional networks that had prevailed in the seventeenth century.

Ruan Yuan also involved himself in philanthropic projects benefiting his fellow Yangzhou natives, even when he was away from the city. For example, on New Year's eve in 1814, he received a letter from the abbot who supervised his family tombs at Thunder Pool reporting that the dry field farmers of the prefecture were starving. Ruan Yuan responded by donating the funds to provide rice gruel to the hungry, and he also donated money to help bury those who died in the famine. Here, even while helping to resolve a general crisis in his home prefecture, he still frames the discussion spatially in relation to his family's tombs at Thunder Pool and the Buddhist priest he had engaged to supervise the site. He also helped underwrite the renovation of the Yangzhou *huiguan* (native-place association) in Beijing, paying for the construction of new buildings and providing money to cover the costs of landscaping the property. He planted several hundred stalks of bamboo and thus was able to invoke a Tang dynasty nickname for Yangzhou, "West of Bamboo," in naming the pavilion at the *huiguan,* which he called "Little West of Bamboo Pavilion." He also planted flowering fruit trees to evoke the spirit of a famous Tang poem on the spring season, thereby alluding to the springtime of Yangzhou's ancient prosperity. He thus underscores an emerging identification of "native son" with leadership in philanthropy, an association that had specifically local antecedents. Yangzhou had been an early center of organized local philanthropy in the seventeenth century, with institutions like orphanages and soup kitchens sponsored mainly by sojourning salt merchants. The city also played an important role in the mid-eighteenth century bureaucratization of community welfare organizations, as leading officials who served locally, like Chen Hongmou, began to encourage the replication of these institutions elsewhere.[140]

Like his seventeenth-century predecessors, Ruan Yuan too was involved in anthology production. He sponsored and participated in the editing of several literary collections, including the *Heroic Spirits of the Huaihai Region* (Huaihai yingling ji), published in 1798, which expressly included only poems by deceased Yangzhou natives active in the Qing dynasty. Here again we see a shift in emphasis from the transregional to the local in the editorial principles of an anthology, even as we saw such a shift in the reinvention of a building. According to the preface, the collection celebrates the achievements of local poets, especially those who combined literary talent with moral worth, like the righteous officials, filial sons, famous Confucians, talented gentlemen, extraordinary personalities, and exemplary women who, according to Ruan Yuan, were especially abundant in Yangzhou. He writes, "My reason for recording this collection is not to dare to take the poems of the gentlemen of my hometown and measure them or select them based on literary standards, nor is it a plot to enhance my reputation by relying on dead poets."[141] Instead, he proclaims that he embarked on this project for the noble purpose of gathering poems together for the convenience of later researchers. He points out that in recent years, the number of writers has increased, yet the number of people involved in editing anthologies has decreased, and that many worthwhile writings have been scattered. He emphasizes the native-place angle by signing his preface *"xiangren"* or native son, again highlighting his personal connection to the collection and the prefecture. He provides biographies of each of the poets included in the collection. Those who achieved official rank, attracted official or imperial notice, or were particularly virtuous, chaste, or filial are given lengthy biographical notices. These notices include excerpts from gazetteer biographies and other published sources, using tomb inscriptions and formal obituaries wherever possible. This practice makes Ruan Yuan's editorial voice less direct, less personal, more formal, and more textually mediated than that of the editor of the *Poetry Survey*, Deng Hanyi, whose collection is filled with lively anecdotal commentaries and marginal remarks, and whose purposely spare biographies explicitly exclude all references to official status. Again, the emphasis seems to be on genealogy and an evidential approach to the past, rather than on contemporary connections and a mythic view of the past.

The collection *The Heroic Spirits of the Huaihai Region* contains poems by approximately three thousand Qing writers representing the twelve districts that had been part of Yangzhou during the Qing. Administrative changes meant that not all of these districts were still part of Yangzhou prefecture in Ruan Yuan's lifetime. Ruan Yuan notes: "All of the poets included here are already deceased. Rare poems and old collections are either borrowed from friends or from their descendants or pulled from published anthologies. Each one has a short biography recording his deeds in the prefecture."[142] In contrast to Deng Hanyi, who conceived of his *Poetry Survey* as a monument to his own generation and underscored his personal connection to those poets whose works he included, Ruan Yuan uses the *Heroic Spirits of the Huaihai Region* to commemorate the achievements of the "dead poets" of Yangzhou, constructing a genealogy of literary achievements in his native place. Indeed, poems by outsiders *(waishengren)* are included only if the poets either lived in and were active in Yangzhou their whole lives or had formally adopted Yangzhou native-place registration.[143] Famous sojourners such as Wang Shizhen, Lu Jianzeng, and the Ma brothers were not included, even though they had made major contributions to local culture. Ruan anticipates that these poets might require a collection of their own in the future.[144]

The *Heroic Spirits of the Huaihai Region* consists of ten collections, which are named using the stems and branches system. The first five collections include poems, as noted previously, by dead Yangzhou men. The sixth consists of poems by (46) Yangzhou women, and the seventh is reserved for poems by (approximately 15) respectable monks. The remaining three are left blank in anticipation of future additions. The last *juan* of the fifth collection is extraordinary and suggests the rationale for the entire project. It is devoted exclusively to Ruan Yuan's relatives, the men of his patriline (that is, those surnamed Ruan) first, listed under the subheading "Poems by the Ruans of North Lake [a suburb of Yangzhou]." Each poet is listed with the honorific meaning "the late" or "deceased," and, in most cases, their biographies describe their family connection to Ruan Yuan himself. The next section bears the subheading "Poems by the Jiangs of She County (Anhui)," who are Ruan Yuan's male relatives through his grandmother and his wife (who were related to each other). The final section carries the subheading, "Poems by the Lins of Xishan (Fujian)"—in other words, Ruan Yuan's male relatives through his mother, whose surname was Lin. This chapter thus revolves around Ruan Yuan himself. Poets originally from outside Yangzhou are included by virtue of their familial connection to Ruan Yuan, a connection which domesticates them and renders them local. Again, family connections, local identity, and shared native place are conflated by Ruan Yuan for purposes linked to the formation of a local elite identity based on a genealogy of native-place connections. Moreover, Ruan Yuan's ideas about the local sources of elite identity may have spread through the involvement of large numbers of fellow Yangzhou natives in the research and editing process. Certainly Ruan Yuan's name appears as the sponsor, patron, or preface author of most works about Yangzhou history and culture published in the last years of the eighteenth century and the first decades of the nineteenth century. In addition, he sponsored projects that investigated, organized, rectified, and developed local sources of elite identity in the regions where he served. For example, he founded academies, organized libraries, published works cataloguing stele inscriptions, and generally promoted his vision of local elite education and service in Shandong, Zhejiang, Guangdong, and elsewhere.

Ruan Yuan's vision of Yangzhou was first undermined by the city's economic problems, and then destroyed in the Taiping War (1850–64). Writing in 1834, Ruan famously commented on the city's decline in a pair of epigrams *(ba)* for the *Record of the Painted Boats of Yangzhou,* observing that the city had lost much of its glitter during his decades of service elsewhere. He blames the city's decline on the diminishing fortunes of the salt merchants, who by 1834 had "mostly closed out their businesses and scattered," adding that as a result of this exodus, "the old schools and scholars have mostly succumbed to poverty, and the servants and clerks and peddlers can no longer make a living."[145] He also notes the impact of recent natural disasters, especially the flooding of the Yangzi and the Huai.

After Ruan Yuan's death, the Taiping War wreaked further havoc on the city of Yangzhou. The city first was occupied by the rebels in 1853, and it suffered further damage in 1856 and 1858. In the aftermath of that disaster, many forgotten cultural forms, including *huaigu* (reflections on the past) poetry, began to reappear. Even as writers consciously paralleled the cultural outpourings of early Qing survivors, Ruan Yuan's scholarly and civic achievements served as another reference point, as survivors sought to make sense of their badly damaged world. By the late nineteenth century, the original Tower of Literary Selection and the Temple of Manifest Loyalty appear to have vanished from the local landscape, eradicated like many, if not most, of Yangzhou's landmarks by the cataclysm of the Taiping War. The post-rebellion gazetteer confuses the Manifest Loyalty Shrine-Temple with the Teaching Temple. With hundreds of pages listing dead residents and chastity martyrs, the editors certainly had more pressing concerns.[146] Ruan Yuan's Sui Wenxuan Tower remained standing, as did the family shrine in the city, but his family home in the suburbs at Gongdao Bridge was the site of horrific fighting and much loss of life in 1858.[147] Though the substance of Ruan Yuan's celebration of local culture and local institutions had been lost in the disaster, texts and sites associated with his legacy were redrawn or rewritten in the form of maps, paintings, anecdotes, and reminiscences. The ruined gardens described by Ruan Yuan's friend Li Dou in the *Record of the Painted Boats of Yangzhou* were even resurrected in the form of a board game, which retraced ruined itineraries as nostalgic entertainment.[148]

An album entitled "Illustrations of Master Ruan Wenda's Illustrious

Deeds, Ten Scenes" (Ruan Wenda Gong yishi shi jing), painted in the late nineteenth century, features ten sites associated with Ruan Yuan's achievements. Eight of the scenes depict buildings and vistas associated with Ruan's activities in Yangzhou. Specifically, they are the buildings that were the subject of his renovation and rectification efforts in the early nineteenth century. Among them, we find the family residences, tombs, and temples—at Thunder Pool, North Lake, and in the Old City. We see the gingko trees and the Tower of Literary Selection at the family temple in the Old City, the Dragon King stele at Thunder Pool, and the willows near the thatched hut at North Lake. The remaining scenes depict a gathering of scholars at West Lake, Hangzhou, during Ruan Yuan's tenure as an education official in Zhejiang, and a posthumous shrine honoring Ruan Yuan, also located in Hangzhou. The artist, Wang Jun (b. 1816), was a native of Yizhen who specialized in landscape and flower paintings, and like Ruan Yuan was also interested in epigraphy and collected seals by contemporary carvers.[149] He shared Ruan Yuan's native-place priorities, and he is perhaps best known as the editor of the *Yangzhou huayuan lu* (A Record of the Painters of Yangzhou), a collection of biographies celebrating local artistic achievements during the Qing, which he completed in 1883 at the age of sixty-eight.[150] The function of these biographies is explicitly commemorative. Wang Jun frames his collection in relation to the disastrous events of the Taiping War, positioning it as an effort to rescue the painters of his native place from oblivion.

The album, which also was commissioned in 1883, posthumously celebrates Ruan Yuan's achievements and also appears to be part of a larger response to the Taiping catastrophe. Certainly other works from the post-Taiping period invoke Ruan Yuan as a touchstone of local identity.[151] In the inscription on the last leaf in the album, which depicts the commemorative shrine in Hangzhou, the artist explains that he selected "those sites mentioned in the record by Ruan Yuan's students that could be represented." He refers here to the chronological biography *(nianpu)* assembled by Ruan Yuan's students under the title *Leitang'an zhu diziji*, or the *Disciples' Record of the Master of Leitang Cloister*. Each leaf bears an inscription explaining the significance of the site it portrays, in several cases incorporating textual excerpts from the chronological biography, often in Ruan Yuan's own words. The album thus can be read as a set of illustrations to this chronological biography. The events and sites chosen for inclusion mostly date from the early Jiaqing period, the period of Ruan Yuan's most intense engagement with the rectification and reinvention of his hometown. Thus they seem to evoke the local values and idealized times Ruan Yuan had come to represent. Stylistically, the understated outlines, despite the architectural subject matter, and the quiet shades of gray, blue, peach, and pale green combine to create a nostalgic mood. The most explicit reference to the destructive events of the intervening years appears on the leaf depicting the gingko tree on the grounds of Ruan Yuan's family temple. The inscription describes how Ruan Yuan had planted two gingko trees on the temple grounds, adding that "in 1853, when the Taiping rebels occupied the city, the temple and the trees both survived in good condition." The artist then cites a line from a Du Fu poem, the words of which, he claims, show that the survival of these relics from Ruan Yuan's time was nothing short of miraculous.

The second leaf in the album depicts the Wenxuan Tower, shown as a two-story structure surrounded by trees and Lake Tai rocks. A window on the second floor opens onto a room containing a table covered with books. Three men stand in the garden, evidently engaged in a conversation. The inscription emphatically underscores Ruan Yuan's rejection of the false Wenxuan Tower. It reads as follows:

The Wenxuan Tower of the Resplendent Crown Prince is not in Yangzhou. In fact, Yangzhou has only the tower where Cao Xian and Li Shan wrote their commentaries on the *Wenxuan* and that is all. Master Wenda thus had a tower constructed west of his family temple in Wenxuan Tower Lane in which he stored his books and paintings. He also commissioned an Iron Smelting Pavilion, and the prefectural magistrate Yi Bingshou [Moqing] wrote the couplet for the inscription.

The painting affirms Ruan Yuan's vision of the Tower of Literary Selection, linking the site to a lineage of Yangzhou natives famous for their scholarly practices, which were, not coincidentally, shown to be the antecedents of Ruan Yuan's own favored methods. Moreover, the album leaf places the tower in a larger landscape of buildings and scenes significant for their connection to Ruan himself and to his family, and to the by-then-lost world of scholars and salt merchants. In this context, the tower becomes an emblem, a surviving remnant of Yangzhou's ruined past, an object of nostalgic reflection in its own right. Today, however, Ruan Yuan's tower has vanished completely from the local landscape, though an inscription marks the former site of his family temple. The Sui Wenxuan Tower is no longer even an object of nostalgia. Still, in a peculiar return to older myths, a Tower of Literary Selection on the grounds of the old Temple of Manifest Loyalty was rebuilt or renovated at the turn of the twentieth century, and it is mentioned in guidebooks and essays from the Republican period. Today, this tower, too, has disappeared. Damaged during the Cultural Revolution and subsequently destroyed in a fire in

FIGURE 3.1. *The Tower of Literary Selection* (Wenxuan lou). From Wang Jun, "Ruan Wenda yishi shijing," album of ten landscapes, ink and color on paper (27.3 × 33 cm). Private collection (Katherine Wetzel photo).

1992, the Tower of Literary Selection, with its echoes of an older tradition, has been replaced by a blandly named "Tower for Storing Sutras."[152] Today's tourist will find no Tower of Literary Selection in Yangzhou. It again has lost its physical form, and thus, in this more literal age, it is largely forgotten.

The practices seen in this chapter—restoring famous sites and compiling literary anthologies—were not unique to a particular period, but their meanings shifted to reflect new intellectual trends and new ways of thinking about the relationship between the locale and the realm. During the early Qing, both the compilation of anthologies and the construction of sites commemorating former worthies were part of the construction of elite values and were aimed at the knitting together of elite identities that had been challenged by the chaotic politics of the late Ming and by the Qing conquest. During the late seventeenth century, Yangzhou literary and official elites spoke of themselves and their activities through an idiom of poetry and myth, and to them local significance derived from transcendent values that originated outside the locale. By the early nineteenth century, these practices seem to have become more closely linked to elite identities defined by (or within) the local context. This locally based form of elite identity played an increasingly important role over the course of the nineteenth century, as has been demonstrated in the work of Mary Rankin and Philip Kuhn.[153] In his discussion of localism and loyalism in Jiangyin, Frederic Wakeman alerts us to the strengthening of communal identities over the course of the dynasty, marking key shifts in the imputed locus of loyalist sentiment in the Qianlong reign and the early nineteenth century.[154] Similarly, in both the seventeenth and nineteenth centuries the manifestations of elite identity appear relatively constant in practice: the construction of monuments and the compilation of anthologies. However, the content and orientation of those identities reveal a striking contrast. In the seventeenth century, these projects used poetry and legend that drew meaning from sources outside the locale to create a lineage of cultural convention that transcended the local context, ultimately fitting the locale into a transregional and transdynastic network of individuals and values they shared and held to be universal. By contrast, Ruan Yuan used historical research to overturn myth and to identify local sources for local identity, in the process celebrating his "brand" of evidential scholarship and anchoring himself and his peers firmly in their local context. In other words, for Ruan Yuan and his peers local places were important because they were local, and local elites derived their identity from local stories and local sources. The Tower of Literary Selection was a site built in the late seventeenth century on a wobbly foundation of invented traditions and transregional aspirations. Even though it went largely forgotten in the eighteenth century in the frenzy of construction surrounding the Qianlong emperor's Southern Tours, its legacy was rectified and reinvented by Ruan Yuan in celebration of local scholarly traditions after the spectacle of the tours had begun to fade.

4 Re-Creation and Recreation

PINGSHAN HALL

Siting the Hall

The preceding chapter examined the Tower of Literary Selection in relation to an invented tradition regarding its origins. By creating imaginative links between the tower and a famous historical figure, early Qing writers articulated an elite identity that derived its significance from what they saw as timeless and universal values that transcended more recent conflicts. These practices were, however, historically contingent and specific to the early Qing moment, as we saw in the rectification of this myth by the early nineteenth-century evidential scholar and official Ruan Yuan. In the late seventeenth century, poetry, anthologies, and myth provided fertile ground for the nurturing and reintegration of social networks and communities left over from before the conquest. Like the construction of the Tower of Literary Selection in 1651, the renovation of Pingshan Hall, the event at the heart of this chapter, provided an occasion for local leaders to enact reconciliation and reintegration. Moreover, after three decades of Qing rule, the processes of accommodation to Qing rule discussed in the previous chapters were already well under way, and the gestures affirming shared literary and political values represented by the renovation seem in this case almost routine.

In the case of Pingshan Hall, unlike that of the Tower of Literary Selection, the symbolic apparatus surrounding the renovation derived its power from history or, rather, from the idealized image of a historical figure who really did serve in this locale. The renowned Song official Ouyang Xiu (1007–72) functioned as the ideal symbol of local identity within a national context, and as the embodiment of a shared cultural heritage held in common by all educated elites. In this way, his function parallels that of Wang Shizhen and Xiao Tong in relation to Red Bridge and the Tower of Literary Selection. The initiator of the renovation project, Wang Maolin (1639–88), who was both a native son and an official and poet of national reputation, made active use of Ouyang Xiu's reputation to garner support for his project from the prefectural magistrate and other patrons, as well as to bolster his own reputation and social status. He also explicitly described the renovation of scenic sites as an important element in the administrative reintegration of the empire. However, even as landed and official elites saw the renovation of the hall as an event of major significance to their community and depicted it as an expression of shared values and political integration, there was a strong tension between the site's symbolic value for elites and its position at the center of the city's most popular touring itinerary, a route shared by the local elite with sight-seers (and pilgrims) of all social classes. Moreover, despite their protes-tations of universality and timelessness, the ideas about the site embraced by early Qing elites were themselves quite transitory. By the early eigh-teenth century, the meaning of the site was increasingly represented in relation to the presence of the touring emperor.

Pingshan Hall is located five *li* (about 1.66 miles) northwest of where the Yangzhou city wall once stood. It occupies Shu Ridge, the highest point in a landscape that was acclaimed for its scenery, despite the absence of conventionally favored mountains. The hall offers a commanding view of the surrounding terrain, including the mountains south of the Yangzi River, which were portrayed as "spread out in an arc below the eaves, as if they could be grasped."[1] Indeed, the hall was named "Level Mountain Hall" for this appearance of being "level with the mountains" in the dis-tance. As we have seen, however, the key elements in the Yangzhou land-scape were manmade and transitory, not natural or immutable. In gazet-teer terms, Yangzhou's fame lay in its "ancient relics" rather than its "mountains and rivers." Thus, the buildings and their histories "made" the heights scenic, and not vice versa. And both the buildings and their histories were symbolically charged structures sited in changing cultural contexts, as well as in the natural landscape.

Pingshan Hall was not a constant physical presence in the Yangzhou landscape, and we should not be misled by seventeenth-century writers' frequent reference to its six-hundred-year legacy. The legacy that they invoked was literary rather than material: from the vantage point of 1674, the hall's reputation, and not always the hall itself, had survived for more than six centuries. Moreover, as we have seen, the conventions and rhet-oric associated with famous sites were no more immutable than the sites themselves, expressing instead the priorities and values of those who built, renovated, and promoted individual sites at a given historical moment. Caught in a pattern of rise and decline defined by factors as diverse as wars of dynastic conquest, economic fluctuations, and changing elite values, Pingshan Hall appears to have been in a state of disrepair through at least half of its history. Originally built in 1048 by Ouyang Xiu during his tenure as Yangzhou magistrate, the hall derived its importance primarily from its association with this great Song literary and political figure. As Shen Gua (1031–95) wrote, "Later those people who came here for pleasure came mainly because of Ouyang Xiu and not because of the buildings and pavilions. As a result of this, the name Pingshan Hall became famous throughout the realm."[2] Ouyang Xiu's reputation as an elegant aesthete and his use of the hall as a backdrop for social and leisure activities made him an ideal role model for those who sought to stake out a similar social and cultural position. Furthermore, his service as local magistrate and his national reputation made him an ideal symbol of the city's position within the realm. Restorations of the hall thus coincided with assertions of elite identity within a transregional framework.

Pingshan Hall was restored periodically during the Song; once destroyed during the Yuan conquest, it does not seem to have been rebuilt again until the late Ming.[3] The Qing gazetteers and literary guidebooks are curiously coy about this long period of decline, suggesting that the renovations for the two dynasties "cannot reliably be determined"; nor, they add, did Yuan and early Ming writers produce much poetry about this site.[4] Given that commemorative essays from the various Song renovations have survived, conferring immortality upon those who renovated the hall by linking their names with that of the renowned Song literatus and official, we can surmise that Yuan and early Ming elites lacked either the resources or the interest necessary to restore it. An essay commemorating the Wanli era (1573–1619) renovation written by Zhao Hongji suggests that the late-Ming restoration was inspired both by a resurgence of interest in the values represented by the former magistrate Ouyang Xiu and the fortuitous correspondence of the Wanli-period magistrate's style name, Pingshan, with the name of the building.[5] In addition, even beyond Yangzhou, the late Ming was marked by elite investment in the construction and renovation of gardens, scenic sites, and monasteries.[6] The renovation of Pingshan Hall during the Wanli period might well have been part of this construction boom. Indeed, as we have seen in earlier chapters, several magistrate-sponsored beautification projects were undertaken in areas of Yangzhou, including Plum Blossom Ridge and the northwest suburbs, during the administration of this same magistrate, suggesting that forces other than nominal correspondence were at work.[7]

The hall was damaged between the late Wanli period and the early
Qing, possibly during the tumultuous period of the Qing conquest. The
damage was much regretted by local scholars and officials.[8] The famous
writer (and later official) Zhu Yizun recalled a visit to the site prior to the
renovation, describing it as so overgrown that he could not determine
where the broken walls had once stood.[9] Zhu's account may be somewhat
exaggerated, however, given the gazetteer's claim that the hall had been
incorporated into a monastery at Daming Temple. Other authors similarly describe the hall as being beyond restoration, beyond recovery,
or absent. These contradictory accounts of a single physical space during
a single period raise questions about the representation of place—
suggesting that rhetorical conventions took precedence over descriptive
accuracy. These rhetorical conventions interfere with our ability to visualize the hall: we cannot know *what* Qing visitors saw when they toured
the site, because the texts tell us only *how* they saw it. The sources con-
cur, however, that the site, including whatever survived of the hall, was
occupied by Buddhist monks during the first year of the Kangxi reign.
Early Qing writers suggest that the encroachment of Buddhist monks was
the most lamentable fact in the hall's recent history, displacing or eliding
the events of the conquest. Indeed, the renovation of the hall generally
was portrayed as the heroic rescue of the site from monks and yokels,
rather than restoration after disaster.[10] The last line of the 1664 gazetteer
entry for Pingshan Hall reflects this sentiment and reads: "In recent times,
it has unfortunately been taken over by monks who are using it as the
main hall of their temple. It would be commendable if someone fond of
scenic sites were to soon restore it."[11] Ten years later, the hall would be
restored at the behest of Wang Maolin, a compiler in the Hanlin Academy
and an active participant in literary and leisure activities both in his home
town of Yangzhou and in the capital.

The "fondness for scenic sites" alluded to in the gazetteer had a deeper
meaning consistent with the values and sociocultural interests of the educated elite. Timothy Brook has highlighted the role of places and things
in the formation and performance of class identity among late Ming elites,
writing:

Gentry society was constituted by the social interactions of those individuals
(known for their successful performance on examinations) and their families.
Gentry society availed itself of a great variety of means to provide contexts for
that interaction. Things were useful in this regard. Through clothing, one presented oneself to others; through antiques and paintings, one joined with peers in
the refined experience of connoisseurship; through gifts, one mutually established
or reaffirmed status. Public institutions were similarly useful. By building a school

or a hillside pavilion, one made choices of architectural style that signalled good taste to those trained to appreciate it; by furnishing a setting for drinking parties or poetry soirees in a garden teahouse or at a monastery, one designed a space that expressed a relationship to one's social equals. All such social interactions required money . . . But money alone and inert was not enough. Without the interactions that things and institutions made possible, the investments in them could not have been converted into public status.[12]

Similarly, in the early Qing, Pingshan Hall as site and the activities related to its renovation afforded both the context and the occasion for elites to act out the social relationships, cultural ideologies, and political dilemmas of a particular period and place. It also afforded the opportunity for Yangzhou residents and boosters to claim the place in Jiangnan that they craved. Descriptions of the hall and related landscape elements were deployed in order to underscore Yangzhou's position among the great cultural centers of Jiangnan, despite its actual location on the north bank of the Yangzi River. Zong Guan, in his essay commemorating the 1674 renovation of Pingshan Hall, comments that ". . . .Yangzhou has no mountains of its own, so all of the mountains of Jiangnan are its mountains."[13] Declarations about shared mountains highlighted connections between Yangzhou and the cultural centers of Suzhou, Hangzhou, and Nanjing, as did comparisons between Pingshan Hall and scenic sites like Tiger Hill in Suzhou and West Lake in Hangzhou, or shared place names and invented histories like those we saw in chapters 2 and 3.[14]

Pingshan Hall stood, when it stood, on the central of the three peaks of Shu Ridge, an earthen rise described as winding around the dikes and hills from the northwest. Early sources hypothesized that the ridge itself was an extension of a mountain range in Sichuan (the ancient state of Shu), although this theory was given diminishing credence during the Qing, when sources making extravagant claims for the ridge were quoted largely for their ancient provenance rather than for their geological accuracy.[15] A more recent source describes Shu Ridge as a loess ridge extending from west to east, rising between ten and twenty meters above the Yangzi flood plain.[16] The cultural geography of early Qing Yangzhou, as recorded in the gazetteers and invoked in poetry, was centered on the heights around and including Shu Ridge. Because the ridge offered strategic advantages during periods of military activity, the earliest fortresses and walled cities in this region were built on the heights. This strategic position gave the ridge a lineage of military and historical associations dating back to the Spring and Autumn Period (722–481 B.C.E.). Indeed, the potent combination of physical elevation and historical resonance made this area an integral element in early Qing touring itineraries, even before the sites in this area were fully restored and subsequently expanded. Legacies were attributed to these particular physical environments, and those meanings themselves changed over time, as buildings were replaced, were allowed to decay, vanished, and were recorded in or omitted from the local gazetteers. Finally, in the eighteenth century, new sites were developed, with reference not to the distant past, but to the court and its Southern Tours.

Although it was lofty relative only to the flat plains along the river, Shu Ridge was one of the few local sites that afforded an inspiring view. The view, and the ridge's proximity to the prefectural city, contributed to Pingshan Hall's preeminence in touring itineraries, as well as to its reputation as a prestigious burial site.[17] The practice of ascending the heights to view the surrounding scenery is one of ancient provenance, associated with meditation on the past, spirit journeys, and encounters with immortals. During the late Ming and early Qing, artists and writers frequently portrayed actual or imagined social gatherings with reference to this practice of ascending the heights. This practice had a seasonal component, as it was customary to climb hills on the ninth day of the ninth month and on the seventh or fifteenth day of the first month. Such gatherings could be represented as part of a "calendar" of activities in the leaves of an album, or in the annual cycle of local customs described in the gazetteers.[18] This cycle of seasonal events provided regular opportunities for gatherings and excursions—and thus poetry composition—as can be seen clearly in the frequent mention of holiday dates in poetry titles. It was, for example, also customary for the people of Yangzhou prefecture to "quit the marketplace and climb up to Shugang in the Western suburbs" during the days before and after the Qingming Festival. Even though this holiday was associated with the sweeping of ancestral graves in other parts of China, evidently it occasioned festive excursions to the scenic sites in Yangzhou, and grave sweeping took place in the autumn.[19] The highest point in the landscape thus enjoyed a privileged place in both leisure itineraries and burial practices. Commanding views certainly contributed to the hall's popularity as a destination for both the living and the dead.

The hall's location contributed to its renown in other ways. The area northwest of the Yangzhou city wall was especially rich in sites of scenic, historical, or literary significance and thus was a popular destination for leisure excursions. Jonathan Hay has termed this type of area a "leisure zone," a sub-urban area devoted at least in part to a leisure culture featuring temples, pleasure boats, restaurants, tea houses, wine shops, and courtesans.[20] In Yangzhou, this leisure zone extended from the canal north of the city wall to Pingshan Hall, and these boundaries are frequently alluded to in the contemporary literature.[21] Zhao Zhibi, the author of the *Illustrated Gazetteer of Pingshan Hall*, pointed out that though he began his book with Pingshan Hall, he later expanded its scope to include the lake, and from the lake he further expanded it to include the gardens and other architectural elements in the area. What this suggests is that by the mid-eighteenth century, when his book was published, Pingshan Hall served as both anchor and metonym for a larger leisure zone, an area that included all of the scenic sites on the ridge, Baozhang Lake, and the various gardens, pavilions, shrines, and temples northwest of the city.[22]

During the late seventeenth century, the leisure zone recovered and expanded. Even though a Wanli period painted map of Yangzhou depicts many temples and canals in this area, indicating that it had similar functions in the late Ming, increased growth in this area appears to date from the early Qing.[23] In 1674, when Pingshan Hall was renovated, this area already boasted several temples and numerous private gardens along the canals and on the ridge. According to one contemporary account, by 1664 there were more than one hundred private gardens along the canals outside the city walls, the most spectacular of which played host to gatherings of famous residents and visitors.[24] This account suggests that the basic elements of a "leisure zone" were already in place northwest of the city ten years prior to the renovation of Pingshan Hall in 1674. Pleasure boats could be rented, musical troupes and portrait painters could be hired, and the physical environment conducive to a culture of play was already under construction. In addition, whereas the Guanyin Pavilion on Shu Ridge was still in ruins, the Ocean of the Law Temple (Fahai si, later called Lianxing si), a popular stopping point en route to Pingshan Hall, had been improved during the Shunzhi reign when a local man built a pagoda beside it, and it was restored again in 1675.[25] Although still limited, the economic recovery had progressed sufficiently by this time to permit garden and temple construction and a thriving leisure culture.

Such leisure zones were associated with all the major cities of the Lower Yangzi Delta, and, as Jonathan Hay points out, images of Qinhuai in Nanjing, West Lake in Hangzhou, and Tiger Hill in Suzhou stood for those cities in popular and elite imaginations.[26] As Kong Shangren observed in 1689, there was a special category of famous sites conveniently located near major roads and waterways. Kong claims that the sentiments evoked by visiting these sites differed, but he points out that each of these was associated with a Jiangnan city, and that they were all popular destinations for tourists and travelers. He includes in this category Pingshan

Hall, Tiger Hill (Suzhou), West Lake (Hangzhou), Jinshan (Zhenjiang), and Huishan (Wuxi).[27] A brief examination of Yuan Hongdao's (1568–1610) essay on Tiger Hill written during the late Ming suggests points of similarity: "Tiger Hill is perhaps seven or eight li [2–3 miles] outside the city walls [of Suzhou]. The hill itself is lacking in precipitous cliffs or deep ravines, but simply because of its proximity to the city, not a day goes by without flutes, drums, and fancy boats clustering there. On any moonlit night, flowery morning, or snowy evening, visitors come and go like threads of some great tapestry."[28] Both Tiger Hill and Pingshan Hall were located within a few miles of the respective city walls, close enough for an afternoon excursion. Neither site offered striking scenery; instead, each provided a venue for social outings featuring pleasure boats and musical entertainments. Each was located on the physical perimeter of an urban center and was intimately connected to the practice of urban social life. The development of such leisure zones appears to have been driven by commercial prosperity, with Tiger Hill emerging as a scenic site as Suzhou flourished in the mid- to late Ming and Pingshan Hall reaching its zenith in the eighteenth century. This process can be traced through the dates of publication of major guides or gazetteers for these scenic sites.[29]

Shu Ridge and the canals that surrounded it were appreciated for scenery that lent itself to pleasures like boating and ascending the heights, for their association with the rich and powerful who built gardens there, and for echoes of an ancient past invoked in nostalgic poetry. In its early Qing guise, as the site of numerous excursions and gatherings, the leisure zone was the material embodiment of growing urban prosperity and elite leisure culture. Thus, its development paralleled the rise in Yangzhou of a social class with resources to invest in the construction of gardens and an interest in promoting the cultural reputation of their (in many cases adoptive) hometown. By participating in its construction, individuals demonstrated their position in the social class able to re-create the social, cultural, and physical landscape of Yangzhou. According to Timothy Brook, elite participation in monastic patronage was inscribed literally and publicly onto the projects that they funded through the use of stelae and plaques. Similarly, involvement in the leisure zone, through construction projects or participation in literary parties, was also highly public. Even when stelae were not raised, accounts were published in gazetteers and literary collections. Social and cultural claims on famous destinations were not constant, however. The official and landed elite patrons of garden construction, poetry parties, and renovation projects of the late seventeenth century were eventually replaced by even wealthier salt merchants in the eighteenth century. These merchant patrons brought the

Yangzhou cultural milieu into closer alignment with the interests of the throne—on which they depended for their mercantile privileges within the imperial salt monopoly. In contrast, during the 1650s and 1660s the scenic zone served as the locus for nostalgic expression, as the site of a poetics of loss and remembrance. In spite of the rebuilding that was already under way, images of nostalgia, loss, and ruin dominated references to Yangzhou's northwestern suburbs during the first decades of the Qing. The reconstruction of Pingshan Hall in 1674 seems to have occurred at a symbolic crossroads, perhaps representing the moment at which a vibrant and pleasure-oriented present overtook and displaced the mournful images of the past.

Ruminations on a Ruined Landscape

Poetry from the Shunzhi and early Kangxi reigns suggests a preoccupation with the vacant locations of former scenic sites, and with the long-abandoned ruins of Sui Yangdi's (r. 605–618) palaces and estates, also located in this area. Historic sites, which were termed "Ancient Relics" and recorded in the gazetteers and in literature of various genres, were part of the city's cultural and social heritage, rather than its physical geography. Thus, materially present or not, they reflected the priorities of leading local figures and enjoyed immortality in memory, if not in actuality.[30] Unlike the ruins of Athens and Rome, contemplated as ruins by European Grand Tourists in the eighteenth and nineteenth centuries, Chinese historic sites were either physically, often creatively, restored or allowed to disappear completely. This difference seems, at least in part, to be due to the primacy of wood in construction in China, for wooden structures needed to be conscientiously maintained, repaired, and replaced. A large building was not expected to last more than fifty or sixty years, even if it was well maintained.[31] A Song-period essay on the renovation of Pingshan Hall indicates that the hall had to be completely overhauled within twenty years of Ouyang Xiu's departure.[32]

Despite the transience of architectural elements, the physical space remained significant, even as it was transformed through reconstruction or loss. Indeed, even though the virtues associated with the building and its first patron were described as if they were immutable, its physical rise and decline became a trope even during the Song.[33] Themes of destruction and reconstruction figure prominently in the essays honoring the restoration of Pingshan Hall from the Song, late Ming, and Qing, perhaps because of their function as commemorative essays. As Susan Naquin has pointed out in her work on Beijing temples, this genre conventionally emphasized the difficulty of renovation, alluding to "damage wrought by the passage of time" and the "painful" experience of viewing the dilapidated structure.[34] At the same time, writing fifteen years after the renovation, Kong Shangren describes Pingshan Hall as the only one of several famous sites that by its nature inspired a sense of melancholy associated with reflections on the past.[35] He makes the further claim that this response was inherent to the hall and dated back to its original construction: "When Ouyang Xiu first built this hall, he meant to do no more than use this site in order to take in the view of the mountains of Jiangnan. But as soon as the hall was built, deep emotions were born."[36] In the late seventeenth century, these images of prosperity and destruction had a particular resonance, especially in this city of survivors and migrants.

Sites mentioned within the ancient relics section of the gazetteer were frequently invoked as subjects in poetry of the "embracing the past" genre. Stephen Owen has termed rumination on the past the dominant mode of knowing in Chinese classical literature: "The master figure. . . . is synecdoche, the part that leads to the whole, some enduring fragment from which we try to reconstruct the lost totality . . ."[37] Owen elsewhere explains that "the *huaigu* might indeed contain a few lines of speculation on what the site had been like in the past, but the center of the poem was inevitably the poet's present: what *he* saw, what *he* felt, and (reducing the imaginative act to a mental process) what *he* imagined."[38] The historic past was thus reconfigured as part of personal experience: occupying a significant physical space, the poet juxtaposed his own experience with the events that gave the place meaning. This way of seeing and writing about place became prevalent in late seventeenth-century Yangzhou, only to diminish again in the eighteenth century. Thus, early Qing poets visited famous sites and used those sites to express mournful feelings on dynastic and cultural change.[39] That the poets writing in this nostalgic mode included both Ming *yimin* and Qing officials suggests that these feelings of loss were part of a standard repertoire, a pose grounded in a particular moment and particular sites.

The concentration of sites in the northern suburbs, and the focus on the ancient past, can be seen in the selection of the city's famous views, or prospects. Of the "Eight Views of Weiyang" listed in the Kangxi gazetteer, at least six and probably seven were located in the northern suburbs of Yangzhou. Three were natural landmarks, one was Red Bridge, one a famous temple, and three famous for their association with the Sui emperor and his court.[40] Pingshan Hall is rather conspicuously absent from this list, though people visited the site and composed "embracing the past" poems. The Sui sites no longer existed in their original forms, but their locations were well known from literary and gazetteer accounts. During the late seventeenth century, these sites were particularly popular subjects of nostalgic poetry in the "embracing the past" mode. In this subgenre of poetry, a person tours a site with historical connotations and is inspired to invoke the past, adopting a tone of regret or loss.[41] In the case of these sites, writers paid mournful tribute to a dynast murdered for his decadent proclivities, while reflecting on their own memories of extravagance and political loss.[42] By the Qianlong period, the list of great views had expanded to twenty-four, and the emphasis had shifted away from historical and natural sites in favor of gardens constructed in honor of the imperial tours. Indeed, with its sharply contemporary focus, the Qianlong-period list bears little resemblance to its predecessor. During the mid-eighteenth century, reflection on loss and evanescence faded as literary themes, to be replaced by monumentalism, decadence, and consumption.

Emergent Itineraries

With the reconstruction of Pingshan Hall in 1674, the area north-west of the city wall was given a material and moral focus. Kong Shang-ren, writing in 1688, describes the ambit of the established itinerary in a comment worthy of extensive quotation:

Of the sites in Yangzhou, Pingshan Hall is the greatest. It is said that Red Bridge, Ocean of the Law Temple, and Guanyin Pavilion are all ornaments attached to Pingshan Hall. Red Bridge is relatively close [to the city], and those on enchant-ing excursions to Red Bridge must also stop at the Ocean of the Law Temple. Pingshan Hall is relatively far, so those on harmonious excursions there must rest at Guanyin Pavilion. Moreover, each of these four has its optimal season: in the area around Red Bridge, a confusion of sundry tourists and courtesans shade and shine on each other, so it is best matched to spring. Above the Ocean of the Law Temple, the halls and pavilions thrust upward and lotuses bloom on all four sides, so it is best matched to summer. With its pure and cultivated pine groves, juxta-posed with the distant mountains and river, Pingshan Hall is especially well suited to autumn. If [one seeks] broken grasses and frozen dikes contrasted with the ancient city wall on the heights, there is nothing more suitable for a winter tourist than Guanyin Pavilion. From Red Bridge to Ocean of the Law, from Ocean of the Law to Pingshan Hall and Guanyin Pavilion, there is a progression of scenic sites. From spring to summer, from summer to autumn and winter, the seasons change in compliance with the heavens. It is like a poem: if Pingshan Hall is the central couplet, the poem begins with Red Bridge, continues with Ocean of the Law Temple, and concludes with Guanyin Pavilion. The tourist's selection of sites is also like the selection of poetry; even if one's eyes and hands are very discerning, one certainly cannot split inches and skip over lines of ink.[43]

Kong's comments reveal the position that the reconstructed Pingshan Hall occupied in leisure itineraries. Until the Qianlong period, when a canal was dredged to accommodate the emperor's pleasure boats, this itinerary was divided into water and land components. Tourists exited the city through Zhenhuai (also known as Guangchu) gate, continuing by boat until they reached Ocean of the Law Temple. From there, it was necessary to proceed on foot. Kong's comments also highlight the seasonality and aestheticism of scenic appreciation. Although the sites were clearly part of the same itinerary, each was associated with a particular mood and was best enjoyed in its optimal season. These seasonal moods also highlight supposed class preferences: the association of Red Bridge with spring links the site with sensual pleasures. In contrast, autumn is the proper season for poetic nostalgia and was conventionally the season preferred by members of the lettered classes. Yuan Yao's magnificent painting, "Hanjiang shenglan tu" (The Scenic Sights of Yangzhou), depicts this same itinerary in 1747, with Red Bridge on the lower left, the Ocean of the Law Temple (renamed Lotus Nature Temple during the Kangxi emperor's Southern Tours) featured prominently at the center, and Pingshan Hall and Guanyin Temple on the heights. Meticulously detailed in its representation of architecture and scenery and filled with commercial and touristic vignettes, the painting suggests the longevity and popularity of this tourist route into the eighteenth century.[44]

Kong further articulates the connection between elite tourism and Pingshan Hall in another essay, in which he comments: "Tourists in Yangzhou always go searching for famous sites . . . But the elegant and the base are not at all alike. The elegant person must ascend Pingshan Hall, whereas the base person must look for Hortensia Daoist Temple."[45] According to Kong, even the base tourists had lost interest in the Daoist temple, its decayed buildings and lack of natural charms having little appeal for the ordinary visitor. He then rather playfully overturns this typology by describing an elegant gathering he organized on the grounds of the abandoned temple, a site which "ought to be noisy and was not, and that although near the marketplace remained pure."[46] This inversion only highlights the class associations of the sites, for had such images not existed in the minds of his contemporaries, there would have been little point in his manipulating them.

FIGURE 4.1. *Hanjiang shenglan tu* (The scenic sights of Yangzhou). Handscroll, 1747. Color on silk, 165.2 × 262.8 cm. Courtesy of the Palace Museum, Beijing.

Scenic sites with historical associations like Pingshan Hall enabled visitors to identify with previous visitors by engaging in aesthetic activities that also affirmed their status as members of the contemporary elite. The most appreciated sites in Yangzhou, as indicated by the length of accompanying literary commentary in the early Qing gazetteers, were those originally constructed in the Song dynasty, particularly those associated with Ouyang Xiu (1007–72). This phenomenon parallels one that Craig Clunas describes for Suzhou gardens of the mid-Ming, where the most famous gardens were those associated with the eleventh and twelfth centuries, although by the early Qing, interest in the Song heritage appears to have taken on a new meaning.[47] By identifying with Song culture heroes, Kangxi-era elites looked beyond the disasters of the immediate past to focus on the historical past. This shift signaled the (re)creation of a historically referenced, but ostensibly timeless, cultural realm.

The 1674 Renovation:
Economy, Politics, and the Discerning Tourist

Even in the first decade of Qing rule, officials, merchants, and other local residents began to undertake the individual and collective sponsorship of renovation projects, including temples, gardens, shrines, and the prefectural school. Officials first turned to the reconstruction of elements of the urban landscape that were national in character (in that every city "ought" to have one) like the school, the shrines to particular cultural figures and historical personages, and the city wall. For example, the school was renovated in 1645 (immediately after the massacre), with a commemorative stele added in 1652.[48] During the early Kangxi reign, further renovations of the prefectural school were sponsored by its principal, by the salt censor, and by the local magistrate.[49] Several shrines were restored during this period, including the Shrine of Master Dong.[50] Construction and renovation projects of this type signaled economic and political recovery and, in the case of schools and shrines, symbolized the incorporation of the locale into a nested hierarchy of nationally sanctioned administrative centers. Shrine restoration activities seem to have accelerated during the late Kangxi, Yongzheng, and Qianlong periods, but clearly some projects were initiated even in the immediate aftermath of the conquest, and indeed such projects seem to have been essential to the restoration of a sense of order to the city and a sense of confidence to its elites.

Such projects were often jointly sponsored by wealthy members of the local community working together with prominent officials, indicating that the resources were available for projects given high priority. The case of the pavilion at the Jade Hook Cave provides one example of an "ancient relic" that was reconstructed through this division of labor. The Jade Hook Cave was said to have disappeared into a well located behind the Fanli Daoist Temple (often called the Hortensia Daoist Temple) during the Tang dynasty. Centuries later, a pavilion was built over the well. During the Qing conquest, the military occupiers stabled their horses in the pavilion, thereby causing considerable damage. The censor, Xia Renquan, wished to restore the temple and pavilion, and he invited the participation of the transport commissioner, Wang Weixin; the magistrate, Jin Zhen; and Wang Maolin, who as a Yangzhou native and Hanlin academician was a member of the local and national elite. The four searched for the ancient site together, and once they had found it the censor said: "The temples and boundaries of the prefecture are the responsibility of the magistrate, thus the restoration of the old foundations is the responsibility of Jin Zhen. Organizing laborers and supplies can only be accomplished by the Transport Commissioner. Thus Wang Weixin will raise the funds and gather the workers. The Academician Wang Maolin must take up his pen and record the renovation for posterity."[51] Similarly, according to the magistrate's account, funds and materials to support the renovation of Pingshan Hall were provided by officials, salt censors, and local elites.[52] Wang Maolin made the initial request, but permission for the renovation had to come from the prefectural magistrate.[53] The renovation of Pingshan Hall in 1674 thus provides an excellent example of a project whose symbolic weight attracted the attention of patrons both moneyed and powerful. It also marked a new stage in the economic and spiritual recovery of the city.

Politically, the timing of the renovation seems inopportune, or at least odd. In 1674, two of the three generals empowered by the Qing state to protect and govern the unstable southern and southwestern frontiers revolted against the throne, an act of war that threatened to divide China along north-south lines. In an essay praising the magistrate of Yangzhou, Jin Zhen, Wang Maolin, who was then in mourning for his mother at home in Yangzhou, wrote: "In the spring of the thirteenth year of the current emperor [1674], Fujian and Yunnan erupted in rebellion. The southeast was in a panic. The people of Yangzhou are easily frightened, so false rumors filled the streets, families hid in their homes, friends fled. The city gates were left ajar at night, the streets were clogged with refugees."[54]

Wang's statement that Yangzhou people were susceptible to fear and rumor merits closer attention. The 1810 biography of Jin Zhen also juxtaposes the arrival of the new magistrate in 1674 with the events in the south and southeast, again highlighting the susceptibility of the local people to frightening tales: "In 1674, [Jin Zhen] was sent to fill a vacancy as prefectural magistrate of Yangzhou. Just then, the total revolt of the Three Feudatories troops was rumored all along both sides of the Yangzi River. People were shocking each other with these rumors. Weiyang [Yangzhou] was right in the middle of this. The residents of the city were stricken with fear . . ."[55] The content of the gossip is left ambiguous, perhaps for political reasons. Did fear and rumor in fact refer to official concern over the local people's susceptibility to Ming revivalist rhetoric, a worry that they might feel a certain temptation to turn on the Qing overlords who just nineteen years earlier had set fire to their city? This politicized reading is suggested by a 1685 gazetteer reference to the "poisonous events in Yunnan and Fujian stirring up fear among the people."[56] The rumors also may have expressed widespread fear that change could send newly repaired lives spinning into chaos and bloodshed.

The revolt of the Three Feudatories was to last until 1681, but after the initial shock waves of rumor and panic subsided, these events seem to have affected Yangzhou only tangentially, after some initial plundering by Qing troops stationed in the Zhenjiang area.[57] According to an unabashedly laudatory essay by Wang Maolin and Jin Zhen's biography in the gazetteer, the mood shifted after the arrival of the new magistrate, whose dignity and calm demeanor reassured the panicking masses and whose warnings about bandits in the countryside induced urban dwellers to return to the sheltering walls.[58] Indeed, his success at addressing the damage caused by Qing troops, who had confiscated food, grain, and wine from the local people, earned him the praise of the governor general and promotion to the transport and salt circuit based at Nanjing.[59] The biographical essays in the gazetteers and Wang Maolin's essay honoring Jin Zhen focus almost exclusively on two events: his management of the panic associated with the Three Feudatories Rebellion and the renovation of Pingshan Hall.[60] These juxtaposed events are intended by the gazetteer editors as proof of the moral excellence and administrative skill that this prefectural magistrate showed during his short tenure in Yangzhou.

The first event obviously fulfilled that function. But what of the second, the event whose significance is at the heart of this chapter? An examination of several texts associated with the reconstruction of Pingshan Hall indicates that the renovation was represented as something more significant than a magisterial good deed or an exercise in developing scenic sites for mere touristic enjoyment. Wang Maolin proposed the renovation to Jin Zhen when they met in the capital.[61] On that occasion, he composed a poem reiterating his request, which reads:

> The pavilions and peaks recline at Pingshan.
> When Mr. Ouyang had leisure from governing,
> He gathered a thousand lotuses and brought them here.
> Two rows of officials and singing girls passed back and forth
>   by moonlight.
> Today we again meet an esteemed magistrate,
> Guests on pure excursions want to climb there again.
> But sadly trees and springs are seized by monks,
> The overgrown weeds at Shugang await your trimming.[62]

This poem incorporates three themes: first, it underscores and romanticizes the link between Ouyang Xiu, the hall, and leisure entertainments. Second, it baldly flatters Jin Zhen by proposing in the fifth line a possible connection between him and Ouyang Xiu. Third, it illustrates the sad state of the hall and Wang's desire to restore it as a site for new leisure entertainments, termed "pure" to eliminate possible confusion over who would be doing the climbing. Wang thus draws upon elite identification with the site and its founder in order to influence the man who had the political power to authorize the hall's restoration. Wang alludes to the famous story of how Ouyang Xiu enjoyed his leisure hours at the hall, playing drinking games with his friends amidst lotus blossoms and courtesans.[63] The allusion again suggests an opportunity for the newly appointed prefectural magistrate to model himself on Ouyang Xiu both in moral character and in leisure pursuits with the cultural elite. It also alludes to the romantic, even slightly eroticized image of Yangzhou, city of moonlight and courtesans, before quickly returning to images reiterating the moral qualities of the magistrate, and of the guests desirous of "pure" excursions, by which we can assume he means appropriately exclusive and aesthetic elite gatherings.

According to his own later report, Wang had long wanted to restore the hall, and he and his brother Yaolin unsuccessfully petitioned a previous magistrate for permission to rebuild it in 1661 when it was first taken over by the monks.[64] Evidently, his efforts in Beijing in the autumn of 1673 were more successful, and the new magistrate agreed that the hall ought to be restored. The military events described above intervened, however, and it took several months before the confusion cleared. In the interim, Wang Maolin's mother died and he returned to his home to observe the customary three years of mourning. Construction began during the autumn and was completed by the end of the year. The events surrounding the renovation feature prominently in publications of the period, and subsequently. The gazetteer published in 1675, only a year after the project's completion, covers the renovation extensively and includes many of the poems composed at a banquet convened to celebrate Jin Zhen's role in the renovation.[65] These same poems appear in the Qianlong-era literary guides to Pingshan Hall and the surrounding area.

Five men of diverse (and fluid) political commitments wrote the commemorative essays that were carved into steles to mark the renovation project, suggesting that the re-creation of Pingshan Hall had an appeal that transcended questions of political allegiance.[66] Such commemorative essays are morally prescriptive texts, and not innocent sources of information. Indeed, these essays contradict each other on several points. A close reading of them is thus necessary, providing insights into the values and priorities of the men selected to write them. The essays commemorating the 1674 renovation were written by the magistrate Jin Zhen, Wang Maolin, the famous "loyalists" Wei Xi and Mao Qiling, and a local literatus with an interest in water control named Zong Guan.[67] The diverse political beliefs of these men suggest either that the re-creation of Pingshan Hall had an appeal beyond politics, or that political divisions had already been subsumed within a shared cultural identity. A third possibility is that these authors were *chosen* (or even in some cases hired) to highlight the renovation's political symbolism.

According to Jin Zhen's commemorative essay, "The wood and stone were strong and finely finished, the paint was fresh and bright . . . The view of five hundred years ago was suddenly restored."[68] The magistrate sponsored a huge party to celebrate the reconstruction of the hall, which was attended by more than one hundred famous locals and thousands of onlookers, as well as at least several carefully chosen guests of national reputation.[69] The retired minister of revenue, Cao Rong, led the group in composing poetry, beginning with a fifty-line ode commemorating the event.[70] According to Jin Zhen's account:

The prefectural gentry and scholars and famous individuals from all over the realm all composed poems to harmonize with his, they played on bells and chimes, and the effect was marvelous, revealing the beauty of the hall. Everyone who talked about it said that it was comparable to the times when [the Song masters] Su [Shi], Wang [Anshi], Qin [Guan], and Liu [Chang] gathered here and composed poetry. I only regretted that I was not Ouyang Xiu myself.[71]

The magistrate thus positions himself relative to the pantheon of Song-dynasty culture heroes and the literati identity that they embodied. His principal concern, however, seems to lie elsewhere. After expressing his regret over not being Ouyang Xiu, he comments: "And so the rise and decline of the hall is only a small matter. But what does it mean when the happiness of human feelings seems to depend upon its restoration? Just recently, the southeast has unfortunately encountered many difficulties. The borders of Wu and Yue have had wars increasing the burden on the people, inciting them to sadness that lasts to the end of days."[72] This emphasis on the political situation may accord with the conventional expectations for magisterial writing. It is, as always, hard to tell where the feelings of the author lie, given the highly stylized formulae according to which such texts were produced. Still, Jin clearly sought to capture his sense that history was "at a juncture of myriad difficulties and urgent matters" and to use the restoration as part of a healing process. His reference to the demands of "human feelings" further suggests an appeal to the fundamental, "universal" qualities of (elite) humanity. The term "human feelings" originates in the Liyun chapter of the Book of Rites: "What can be called 'human feelings'? Joy, anger, sorrow, fear, love, hate, and desire. These seven are innate, not learned."[73]

That this project marked an effort to create common ground is evident in the participation of Ming literary figures like Wei Xi.[74] The content of his essay, however, suggests a preoccupation with class distinction and moral education that transcended political commitments. Indeed, written at the express request of the former magistrate Jin Zhen, Wei's essay focuses on the magistrate's role as moral exemplar. His essay also highlights the distinction between the cultured and uncultured of Yangzhou: "[Yangzhou] is a place where powerful officials and the rich and mighty sojourn, so the people are often fond of profits and enjoy parties and tours, seeking songs and pursuing courtesans, wearing fashionable clothes and eating well. Only the very worthiest among them have any interest in things of culture."[75] By contrast, he points out that the presence of prominent visitors and residents drinking wine and reciting poetry at the hall had transformed the city's tawdry and mercantile atmosphere, demonstrating the efficacy of the hall's presence. He writes:

And so, when he repaired and elevated this fallen and dilapidated structure, he and those of prominent local families and visitors gathered to drink wine and write poetry, which caused people that saw and heard this to have a joyful admiration for the landscape and things of culture. As a result, every family was reciting poems, until literature and poetry transformed the atmosphere of money and trading. Moreover, Yangzhou is flat and wet; only this hill is a bit higher and thus suitable for warfare. By building this hall and making it a place for ceremonies, he [Jin] may have intended to pacify its military atmosphere with the presence of literary activities.[76]

He explains that the hall's construction on the heights signaled the triumph of culture over violence and poetry over commerce. This is a metaphor for what Wang Maolin and his associates sought to achieve in the city: a post-conquest political reconciliation and the triumph of transcendent cultural values. Although Wei distinguishes between Yangzhou's cultured and uncultured inhabitants, he suggests the possibility of moral education improving the customs of the entire prefecture, and he represents the hall as simultaneously the prefecture's "most scenic spot" and the locus of moral and cultural improvement. Wei's words and participation testify to the fact that by the 1670s even once-staunch supporters of the Ming cause could join in officially sponsored projects, at least when those projects appealed to shared definitions of elite identity and culture.

In his inscription, Mao Qiling writes: "[Jin]'s great restoration of what is known as Pingshan Hall, can this merely be a place for sightseeing? It also derives from a feeling for the actions of former people, and for prosperity and decline, decline and the restoration of prosperity . . ."[77] Thus he, too, highlights the distinction between the hall's function and ordinary sightseeing, a distinction that lies in a sense of history and identification with past exemplars. He juxtaposes his discussion of Pingshan Hall with a reference to the Orchid Pavilion in his hometown of Shaoxing, perhaps the most conventional symbol of the elite literary gathering, aligning the hall with another site laden with significance to members of his social class.[78] Similarly, the local literatus Zong Guan's essay emphasizes the distinction between ordinary and informed leisure, while highlighting the hall's higher moral and historical functions. He writes: "They say that it is right that the magistrate should have a beautiful place for sightseeing in which to relax on his leisure days. They do not understand the reason that the hall was rebuilt . . ."[79] He explains that he wrote his stele inscription in order to remind those who came to the hall on future excursions that the hall was rebuilt to illustrate the processes of decline and prosperity and the moral legacies of past individuals, and not to provide the magistrate with a sightseeing venue.[80] The restoration of the hall thus here too serves as a metaphor for the return to prosperity and the reconstitution of the elite class.

The local gentleman and national official Wang Maolin was the first to promote the recovery and renovation of the hall.[81] In his commemorative stele, he concerns himself with the use of the hall in elite leisure activities and with the formation of local elite identities. He begins with the statement that "since the Six Dynasties period, Yangzhou has had a vast number of famous Daoist temples, pavilions, ponds, and terraces, which are recorded in the gazetteer. Few of these survive today. The land is lacking in tall mountains and deep valleys suitable for touring and viewing."[82] Wang believed that scenic sites, whether natural or manmade, fostered an identity that was simultaneously local and transregional—by virtue of gazetteer reference and through the literary and epigraphic legacies associated with elite touring activities (and he stated the same in other essays with reference to other counties and prefectures). Furthermore, Ouyang Xiu was a national figure known for his strong connection to Yangzhou, and in local iconography he signified the integration of local identity into a transregional class identity. Wang then states that "in both the past and present, Yangzhou has been hailed as a famous prefecture, officials gather here, visitors and guests arrive daily. If there were no place for them to go to carry out rituals and hold banquets, how shameful it would be."[83] Wang also uses this essay to demonstrate his own leading role in the renovation by itemizing the financial and material details of the project. Indeed, Wang's proprietary interest in the site is further illuminated by the numerous parties that he sponsored there—and the fact that he took up residence in the hall one summer. In order to understand the factors that led to the hall's restoration, we need to trace the personal and class-related considerations that motivated Wang's campaign to save what he saw as his hometown's most important scenic and cultural site.

Wang Maolin: Renovating an Identity

Wang Maolin provided the creative impetus behind the renovation of Pingshan Hall. He lobbied for the project with the new prefectural magistrate and, as we have seen, articulated its meaning in his stele inscription. He also made use of Pingshan Hall in order to bolster his own position, and by extension his family's position, in local society. Thus in order to understand the full significance of the Pingshan Hall renovation, we also need to explore the relationship between that project and the life of its main proponent. Our main source of information on Wang Maolin is his collected works, *The Hundred Foot Wutong Pavilion Literary Collection* (Baichi wutongge shiwenji). Like many such compilations, *The Hundred Foot Wutong Pavilion Literary Collection* was named after its owner's garden residence, manifesting the strong identification between owner, book, and garden, reflecting the strong connection between person, place, and writing that we have seen elsewhere.[84] Located on Dong-guan Avenue in the New City, Wang's home incorporated several named landscape and architectural elements, including the Mountain Viewing Tower and the Twelve Inkstones Studio, the latter named after a dream in which Wang found twelve marvelous antique inkstones.[85] The garden and its constituent buildings provided ample subject matter for the literary efforts of the many friends and visitors who gathered there. In social circles such as Wang's, poetry functioned the way snapshots do today (and poetry writing was fundamentally a *social* activity), and thus the writings included in the poetry collection can be read as a record of his friends and their activities—and of the locations where they gathered. Sifting through the chronologically arranged poems in the *Hundred Foot Wutong Pavilion Poetry Collection,* one can trace Wang's travels—primarily between Yangzhou, Nanjing, Beijing, Suzhou, and Hangzhou—and his interests, friendships, and social activities. Here are those publicly private aspects of a life neglected by the official biographical sources.[86]

Born in 1639, Wang Maolin was a native of Jiangdu County, Yangzhou Prefecture. His ancestral home was in fact Shexian in southern Anhui (Huizhou); however, the family had long had official registration in Yang-zhou.[87] The youngest of five sons (including a half brother by a concubine), Wang Maolin appears to have been born into a privileged family, the reputation of which he thought to be marred by insinuations in historical sources that under the Sui, their distant ancestor had been a bandit.[88] His great-grandfather was a salt merchant in Yangzhou, one of the Huizhou merchants who dominated the salt trade in the region.[89] Members of the Wang clan are mentioned in the biographical sections of the Kangxi edition of the *Lianghuai Salt Monopoly Gazetteer,* which was edited and published by the salt merchants themselves, although the clan's prominence in Yangzhou seems to have been somewhat overshadowed by that of other surnames.[90] His father, Wang Rujiang, although a commoner, apparently also controlled considerable wealth and property as a landlord and owner of a transport business.[91] In his tomb inscription for Wang's father, Shi Runzhang wrote: "To begin with, he was not very poor. He had accumulated so much money in his trunks that he did not count it."[92] However, between the roving bandits of the late Ming and the violence of the Qing conquest, which Wang Maolin refers to as the "terrifying massacre and plunder of the southern crossing," the family property and businesses were severely damaged, and Wang Rujiang's second son and members of the extended family were killed.[93]

Wang Maolin credits his parents with protecting and educating the children, and with restoring the family business and social connections after the disasters of the 1640s. Periodic reference to the sons' childhood interest in horseback riding and archery, as well as their access to a prominent local essayist as tutor, suggests that the family had recovered at least some of their holdings in both money and land.[94] Still, Wang also complains about the difficulties he encountered in Beijing as a drafter in the secretariat with limited resources, difficulties that left his once-wealthy clan dependent on him, and "in truth not at all unlike impoverished and mean families," implying that the family fortunes were reversed again after, or as a result of, his own examination success.[95] The text in which he outlines the rise and fall of his family's fortunes is not an innocent chronology, however, but rather a formal invocation in which he ritually reported events affecting himself and his siblings to his deceased parents. Thus he can be expected to underscore his own role in the family's decline, while praising his parents for their success. That Wang Maolin was reduced to selling his writings in the capital in 1671 does, however, suggest that the family encountered financial difficulties after his examination success, and also highlights the relationship between official elites and the cultural marketplace.[96]

Of the five brothers, Wang Maolin was the most conventionally successful: he passed the provincial examination in 1663 and the metropolitan examination in 1667 and was chosen as a member of the Hanlin Academy in 1670. Apparently his success in this most legitimate of channels elevated the prestige of the family considerably but strained their economic resources. His brothers followed very different career paths, due perhaps to their divergent interests and talents, or perhaps to the intrusion of outside events into their education. No written record survives for the oldest son, Maolin's half brother Qilin, who appears to have been a farmer.[97] The second son, Zhenlin, died during the siege of Yangzhou by Gao Jie in 1644. The third, Zhaolin, was a playboy of sorts, enjoying horseback riding, archery, music, and entertainments with young friends and courtesans.[98] The fourth, Yaolin, was a tribute student, and thus had some small measure of official standing. He was also a poet, and traveled in the same elevated social and academic circles as his more successful younger brother. The explanation for the family's reduced straits may lie here: with the exception of the eldest, none of the sons was productive or particularly frugal. Wang Maolin's success in the examinations placed him in a position of authority and ritual responsibility within the family and clan, despite the fact that he was the youngest son.

Wang Maolin was six years old in 1644 when Qing soldiers entered

Beijing and declared their imperial intentions. Later that same month, troops commanded by Gao Jie, a former bandit who had allied himself with the loyalist Ming court at Nanjing, were assigned to guard Yangzhou on behalf of the loyalist cause. The people of Yangzhou, fearing their new "protectors," refused to grant them entry and resisted for more than a month. During this time, Gao's troops pillaged the surrounding country-side.[99] Evidently, the Wang family holdings were threatened during the assault, and Maolin's father sent his wife, Li, and his two younger sons to the coastal salt-producing region to seek refuge with family friends.[100] As an adult, Wang returned to the area where he had once been a refugee and composed a poem, which reads:

In the jiashen year [1644] in Yangzhou, during the last week of the fourth month, the arrows fell like rain on the city wall and people were murdered at night in the city. At the time I was just seven. I remember it over and over as if it were still real. My father defended the empty city; we were sent to the seaside as refugees. We held our mother's hand to support her; as we traveled we encountered hard-ships. My fourth brother was ten. As always he stumbled as he walked. We sought refuge at Liuzhuangchang. The master was an old friend of father's; he said he owed my father a debt and it was time to repay. They switched rooms to make space for me, brought water for my bath. Two old servants cooked my dinner; they gave me rice and meat. There were two lovely young maids, who flitted about me like birds. These were children's games and not shameful. I often comforted my mother. Middle brother died in the fighting. Fourth brother joined the army. Mother cried constantly, until her mouth was parched and her lips were burning. I was young and didn't understand. I demanded food and was scolded by my mother. After the chaos we started for home . . .[101]

Written twenty-three years after the event, the poem evinces a certain emotional distance, perhaps due to the generic demands of five-character line verse or the youthful sensibility that the author sought to convey. He records the experience as one of both displacement and entitlement, pre-senting his younger self as a pampered refugee from the besieged city who was ignorant of the shortages and suffering that the rapacious soldiers had caused in the countryside and unaware of the demands he was plac-ing on his generous host. When finally he returns to this haven as an adult, the once-wealthy household by the shore has vanished: the family has died or fled and their property is covered with weeds.[102] Circumstances denied Wang the opportunity to express his gratitude in person. Instead, he voices his regret according to the conventions of a nostalgic poem, medi-tating on loss and displacement by focusing on a ruined physical space.

A brief period of quiet followed the first siege of Yangzhou, once the Nanjing government redirected Gao Jie and his troops to Guazhou, the

walled Yangzi River port just south of the prefectural city. The general Shi
Kefa was put in charge of the Ming troops at Yangzhou. During the
twelve-month period between Gao Jie's siege and the Qing onslaught,
Wang Maolin began his formal education. He entered the prefectural primary school to study the classics, and his father taught him to recite Tang
poetry.[103] A mourning poem written after his mother's death suggests that
she was also actively involved in his education, listening to him recite his
lessons at night and rewarding him with sweets when he performed
well.[104] Wang's first year of primary school was interrupted by the Qing
army's assault on Yangzhou. When the Qing soldiers broke through the
city wall in May 1645, a six-day rampage of rape, fire, and killing ensued.
Wang Maolin's mother attempted to commit suicide by jumping in a well,
but she miraculously survived and was rescued two days later. In another
mourning poem written after his mother's death, Wang wrote:

There was chaos in Yangzhou in 1645 / People were murdered round the clock /
Fires set in the city erupted at night / The new ghosts cried out in torment / My
mother aimed to be a martyr / The mud in the well seemed sweet / The water in
the well was one hundred feet deep / That she survived was due to the support of
the gods.[105]

To evade the order to wear the queue, Wang's father Rujiang shaved his
head to impersonate a monk. When the soldiers came into the city, they
rounded up the false monks, and killed all of them except Rujiang. Soon
after, a wealthy acquaintance from the coast (Liuzhuangchang) sent a
boat to look for Rujiang and his wife, and took the family back to the village until the situation in the city settled down.[106]

    Wang Maolin's family experienced the conquest as a tragic and horri-
fying event. Even though Wang aestheticized his family's suffering by rendering it in verse form, we can still sense the degree to which these years
were marked by loss of life, dignity, and property, and the extent to which
survival seemed the outcome of historical accident and extraordinarily
good luck. Despite these formative experiences, Wang himself adapted
remarkably well to Qing rule, and his adult life was marked by remark-
able upward mobility as he moved up the examination ladder from Yangzhou to high positions in Beijing. One can read the act of reconstructing
a building, at least one as closely allied with sources of cultural legitimacy
as Pingshan Hall was, as part of a larger effort to reposition himself and
his family within the new social order.

    His involvement in the unprecedented construction of a clan shrine
honoring his extended family and other Huizhou natives in Yangzhou,
and his performance of annual rites there, bestowed ritual legitimacy on

this sojourning clan, literally inscribing their presence on Yangzhou soil and into the Yangzhou social structure.[107] Likewise, he seems to have viewed the renovation of Pingshan Hall as a vehicle for ensuring his own posterity, that of his family, and that of his community. A year after the initial restoration was completed in 1674, Wang Maolin organized a much more extensive (and expensive) round of renovations, expanding the site by several *mu* (roughly half an acre), in order to better recreate earlier descriptions of the landscape around the hall. He solicited funds from the censor, the transport commissioner, the magistrate, various subordinate officials, members of the examination elite, and salt merchants in order to construct an additional building called the "Tower of True Enjoyment" (Zhenshang lou).[108] The new building enshrined Ouyang Xiu and other Song dynasty officials who had served in this locale. His own commemorative essay, which was later inscribed in stone on the site, states that this second phase of renovation cost 2418.25 taels for material, required 18,560 man-days of labor (e.g., approximately fifty men), and took a full year to complete.[109] Following convention, Wang emphasized the fact that not a penny came from the common people.[110] The second renovation also included extensive changes to the landscaping, including the planting of wutong trees, peaches, pears, plum, bamboo, willows, and apricots, and the expansion of the system of gates and dikes. It also included the construction of a pavilion on which stelae inscriptions by previous visitors were displayed.[111] In a gesture unusual in such commemorative essays, Wang acknowledges the contribution of the commoner responsible for building operations by name, describing him as "indispensable."[112] Wang downplays the grandeur of the result, stating modestly that it is "no more than a few feet in height, and the hall is no more than other buildings, it lacks the marvelous beauty of. . . . sacred mountains, it is really just a place to remember Ouyang Xiu."[113] The renovation was timed to correspond to the former magistrate Jin Zhen's return to Yangzhou on business related to his new appointment as vice-circuit intendant for posts and salt. Despite protestations that all of this would enhance the legacy of the former prefectural magistrate, clearly it was a self-aggrandizing gesture on Wang's part, too.

This shrine contained Confucian ritual instruments and implements, as well as an image of Ouyang Xiu. It also seems to have been associated with a nominal or short-lived academy. According to the *Record of the Painted Pleasure Boats of Yangzhou*, when Wang Maolin built the Tower of True Appreciation, he also built a classroom, with the inscription "Ouyang Wenzhong Academy." In 1736, Wang Yinggeng renovated Pingshan Hall, adding the Luochun Hall and the "Western Garden." He also changed the inscription over the gate so that it read "Pingshan Hall," and the name "Academy" subsequently fell out of use.[114] The descriptions of "lecture halls" and "academies" in the eighteenth-century accounts imply that Wang Maolin intended for there to be an academy dedicated to Ouyang Xiu on the premises. These accounts seem to be based on the content of the inscription, rather than the function of the buildings. This academy does not appear in the section devoted to schools in the Kangxi, Yongzheng, or Jiaqing editions of the prefectural gazetteer. By his own account, Wang Maolin seems to have intended "The Ouyang Wenzhong Academy" as a creative replica of Ouyang Xiu's own lecture hall.[115]

The presence of the so-called academy, the shrine, and the ritual implements lends a thoroughly Neo-Confucian cast to Wang's description of the hall. Indeed, Wang's comments imply an irreconcilable conflict between the Buddhist and Confucian occupants of this space. He writes: "Below the hall was the site where [Ouyang] had lectured, to the left was a bell and to the right a drum. These ritual musical instruments are lofty and grand, thereby reminding later people that they cannot worship the Buddha in this place."[116] According to Wang, the hall, built by Ouyang Xiu, had been the best destination in the prefecture, but unfortunately after five hundred years of imposing grandeur "without declining," it was converted to a Buddhist temple.[117] A poem he wrote on the occasion of a surveying visit to Pingshan Hall prior to the renovation contains several even more explicitly anti-Buddhist lines:

> Who would have thought that ten years later
> Monks would invade our boundaries
> Nuns and Buddhas sit in our hall
> No one remembering Ouyang Xiu?
> Those who did this
> Will receive the calumny of myriad mouths.[118]

His contemporaries Mao Qiling and Zong Guan similarly emphasized this dichotomy in their commemorative stelae. Zong's essay is particularly emphatic in his condemnation of the Buddhists, stating that the hall is "not something that can be taken away by the arts of wicked monks."[119]

Yet, this conflict was by no means inherent to the site. After all, the hall's founder, the Song exemplar Ouyang Xiu, built his retreat on the grounds of a Buddhist temple, as was common practice during the Northern Song period.[120] During the Southern Song, as Neo-Confucianism began to absorb Buddhism's metaphysical agenda, hostility toward Buddhism increased among the literati, who sought to define this new form of Confucianism as a separate and unique philosophy.[121] During the late Ming, efforts to resolve the contradictions among the "three teachings" led to increased gentry patronage of Buddhist temples and monasteries. Furthermore, as Timothy Brook has pointed out, this patronage had a sociopolitical dimension, with temples providing a venue for disaffected literati that was largely beyond the purview of the state. With the rise of the Confucian fundamentalism of the Donglin partisans during the final decades of the Ming, we see the beginning of an intellectual backlash against Buddhism and Buddhist influences on Confucian thought.[122] This was expressed through the resurgence of anti-Buddhist rhetoric, and, according to Kai-wing Chow, renewed attention to Confucian ritual.[123] Chow describes this ritualism as an effort by the gentry to reassert moral control over their local communities—control that had been challenged by growing commercialization and urbanization in the sixteenth century.[124] He also argues that after the Qing conquest, renewed interest in ritualism reflected the gentry's three major concerns—Han cultural identity, Confucian ethics, and social hierarchy—and that the Qing state had a vested interest in supporting these conservative forces in its own pursuit of local control.[125]

Wang Maolin re-constructed Pingshan Hall as a Confucian shrine complete with ritual objects and an academy, thereby demarcating it as a Neo-Confucian space in opposition to the neighboring Buddhist temple. This clear division of space eventually blurred. The shrine to Ouyang Xiu shifted to a new site within the city walls during the eighteenth century, and the academy, if it ever existed in fact, lost even its sign during the 1736 renovation. As early as 1686, Buddhist monks had returned to Pingshan Hall in some capacity, and Kong Shangren paid them for the privilege of planting twenty willow trees on the grounds of the hall.[126] Two years later, Kong presented Daohong, the abbot of Pingshan Hall, with a poem. The presence of Daohong seems to have occasioned some discomfort among Kong's peers. Zong Yuanding comments that "Daohong is the master of Pingshan Hall, and he also oversees the Sui Hunting Park. The magnificence of famous sites always depends on temple monks. How regrettable."[127] In the eighteenth century, too, we see monks living in the hall, and this is no longer a cause for anxiety or particular comment. In the early twentieth century, guidebooks and travelers' tales describe Daming temple under the rubric of Pingshan Hall, with no clear demarcation between the historic temple and Ouyang Xiu's former hall.[128] Clearly the spatial and ideological boundaries of Pingshan Hall were constantly being renegotiated. The renovation project organized by Wang Maolin took place in a very particular social and ideological context and did not represent the expression of immutable values, despite the renovator's claims to the contrary. Through his involvement in the remaking of Pingshan Hall as a Neo-Confucian site, Wang Maolin expressed his identification with the dominant social and intellectual community of his period.

Wang Maolin wrote the couplet that was inscribed in the doorway of the new shrine, again marking in stone his personal association with the hall and its famous founder. He reinforces this connection through a story that appears several times in his collected writings, both in essays and in comments on poems. According to Wang, Su Shi and Ouyang Xiu appeared to him in a dream on the day of the hall's completion and told him to write the couplet, "I climb up to this tower / Ah the grandeur! Oh the view!" This anecdote also appears in the 1810 edition of the Yangzhou gazetteer as part of the entry of Pingshan Hall in the "Ancient Relics" section, publicly affirming the association between Wang and the site, and Wang's position in local society, as well as aligning him with the Song literary heroes.[129] Wang thus used the renovation of the hall to position himself relative to a (retrospectively constructed) genealogical narrative of Confucian legitimacy descended from worthies like Ouyang Xiu. Wang and his friends carried out ritual sacrifices to Ouyang Xiu and other Song worthies at the Tower of True Enjoyment as part of their social outings. For example, on the seventh day of the sixth lunar month in 1677, Wang Maolin and a group of his peers, including Zong Guan, Sun Mo, Sun Zhiwei, Cheng Sui, Deng Hanyi, and Huang Yun, among others, took a boat to Pingshan Hall.[130] While there, they prayed at the wooden tablet of Ouyang Xiu at the Tower of True Enjoyment, and having carried out this ritual, they had a drinking and poetry party there.[131] The poem composed by Sun Zhiwei on this occasion praises the host, Wang Maolin, linking him to the hall and its restoration. It also touches upon issues of re-creation and recreation, literati lineages and status longevity, while also referring to the disastrous events of the recent past and the renovation as a restoration of hallowed views and values:

> When I left for Yuzhang to serve as a teacher,
> The hall was completed, the tower still un-begun.
> Returning I met the worthy Drafter [i.e., Wang Maolin]
> He said the hall could be climbed, the well it did flow.
> The invitation came in a rush ten days ago
> To go rambling after the rain.
> As the lotus flowers bloom, their leaves wither
> Like floating sleeves of singing girls.
> I see this and feel the scorch of disaster

In chaotic times the dragons fought.
On the highlands, suddenly expansive embrace
On two sides of the river, hills green as ever.
Past people rely on the power of their pens
For their names to transcend the separation of time.
Was it here that Yangdi once had his palaces
Where Ouyang seems to walk?
Traces of True Enjoyment remain even now
How can sitting be work when flutes are playing?
The gentlemen's strivings compete for a thousand autumns
As Ouyang followed Han Yu as the model for generations.
The students laugh at themselves like Liu Kun
The sacrifices are prepared, the ritual implements arranged.[132]

Not only did Wang's peers confirm his relationship to the site in their poetry, the next generation did so in a more literal fashion. The local people enshrined Wang Shizhen in the Tower of True Enjoyment later in the Kangxi reign, and during the Yongzheng reign, they began to venerate Magistrate Jin and Wang Maolin at the shrine.[133] Moreover, Wang Maolin's family arranged for him to be buried on the grounds of the building he had restored.

Even before being enshrined there, Wang Maolin enjoyed a period of residence in the hall he reconstructed. During the summer of 1677, he "avoided the heat" at Pingshan Hall. While there, he edited and wrote commentary for a collection of poetry by Du Fu, Han Yu, Su Shi, and Lu You. This project itself adheres to the orthodox poetry canon of Wang's time in its choice of Tang and Song masters. He also entertained friends, including Sun Zhiwei and Zong Guan.[134] It is not clear whether Wang Maolin alone enjoyed the privilege of extended residence in the hall. Kong Shangren seems to have spent at least one night there for moon viewing in the winter of 1686.[135] Still, Wang's summer respite underscored his involvement with this place and highlighted his position in local society. The connection between Wang's family and the hall continued when Cheng Mengxing, Wang's grandson (through his daughter), edited the *Pingshan tang xiaozhi* (Little gazetteer of Pingshan Hall), dated 1752.[136]

Wang Maolin's social circle included some of the most important official and literary figures active in China during the early Qing. Entry into these most restricted social circles stemmed in part from his examination success and in part from his talent as a poet. Recalling his school days, Wang wrote:

After I was fifteen, I devoted myself to the study of the eight legged essay. It was not something that I innately liked. For a time I amused myself with the books I

enjoyed, especially rhymes and poetry. My teacher said that this would interfere
with my study of the eight legged essay and would not permit me to read them.
So I just studied them in secret and refused to stop.[137]

Ironically, it was his facility at composing social poetry and calligraphy
that brought him the attention of the emperor and popularity among the
cultural elite.[138] He indicates his disrespect for the former teacher who
failed to recognize this aspect of the social world of the educated elite by
contrasting the teacher's response with his father's joy in his son's writing. He further recalls that it was his success in the poetry section of the
prefectural examinations that first brought him to the attention of Wang
Shizhen, who was then serving as the judge for Yangzhou prefecture.
From this time onward, Wang Maolin considered himself to be a student
of Wang Shizhen.[139] The two appear together along with Chen Tingjing,
Wang Youdan, and Xu Qianxue, in a garden scene painted by the famous
portraitist, Yangzhou native, and sometime ceremonial usher at the Court
of State Ceremonies in Beijing, Yu Zhiding. The painting, "An Elegant
Gathering at Southside Villa [Chengnan yaji]," depicts a poetry party
hosted by Chen Tingjing in a garden near Beijing, probably in 1682. The
garden, located west of Anding Gate, was also known by the name "Mr.
Zhu's Garden," and was evidently a popular springtime destination for
officials stationed in the capital.[140] The painting testifies to the longevity
and portability of personal networks formed in Yangzhou years earlier, a
network grounded in shared tastes and affinities, especially for poetry.

  Indeed, possession of cultural, particularly poetic, capital seems to
have been the price of admission into the highest circles active in Yangzhou (and elsewhere) during the early Qing. The role of poetry in the formation of social groups during the Qing has been pointed out by Stephen
Owen, who calls poetry a means to establish social prestige. Owen also
highlights the growth of poetry clubs among women, the celebration of
regional, local, and family traditions as a result of an increased (in absolute numbers) reading audience.[141] Membership in the most prominent of
such circles does not seem to have been limited by locale, and indeed, the
same men weave in and out of Wang's chronological biography, socializing with him in Yangzhou, Beijing, Hangzhou, Suzhou, and elsewhere. By
privileging poetry as a means to establish social prestige, men like Wang
Maolin created a nonpolitical realm of engagement and interaction that
reconstituted a social group challenged in the late Ming and during the
conquest. At the same time, these men made active use of great men from
the past as symbols. Ouyang Xiu, to choose the most relevant example,
appears to have been a key node in the formation of elite identity, and, at

FIGURE 4.2. Yu Zhiding, *An Elegant Gathering at Southside Villa* (Chengnan yaji) (detail). Color on silk, 50.8 × 126.5 cm. Courtesy of National Museum, Tokyo.

least in Yangzhou, he functioned as a symbol of national significance with a connection to the locale. In other words, he embodied the integration of the locale into a transregional network of values, imagined as universal, historical, and immediate.

Wang Maolin not only highlighted the link between his hometown and the Song culture hero, he also represented himself as being "like Ouyang Xiu." In one particularly telling instance, he juxtaposes his performance as a ritually filial son with that of Ouyang Xiu in his funeral arrangements for his father.[142] By underscoring the Song official's connection to the city and to himself, Wang positioned himself and his city relative to a national context—a context relevant to a literary elite that transcended local origins, that was, if not national, at least transregional in orientation.

Wang Maolin used the hall not only to link himself publicly to the great men of the past, but also to highlight his connection to the great men of the present, and perhaps thereby also to legitimize his project. Again, the men of the present he chose were those whose reputations had both local and transregional resonance. In particular, he drew upon his connection to Wang Shizhen, a man he considered his teacher and patron. In a letter to Wang Shizhen from the early 1670s, Wang Maolin describes the plan to restore the hall and his role in it; moreover, he invites Wang Shizhen to join the long list of prominent visitors to the site in anticipation of the project's completion. He writes:

Yangzhou was a prosperous area in past, but of the ancient relics, not one in a hundred survives. Pingshan is the piece of land where Ouyang Xiu once toured and entertained . . . The ancient trees were abundant, and even in the sixth month it was not hot. Looking down, with all of the mountains of Jiangnan arrayed below, it was the greatest sight of the whole prefecture. After the fighting [i.e. the conquest], the hall fell into disrepair; common monks converted it into a temple. Some of us despised this but our power was not yet adequate to change it. When I first met you, you were an official in this place, and you shook Yangzhou with your poetry. In your spare time, you and your guests took wine to Red Bridge, beneath Pingshan. Moreover, you rhymed poems with those of Ouyang Xiu . . . These were all recited and it was said by the people of the city that they were not inferior in romantic spirit to those of Ouyang Xiu; moreover, people said it was a pity that you never saw his hall. Since then, five or six years have flown by, and my brother and I, and similar-minded people of the prefecture, have come up with a plan to restore it and have written to notify the four corners. Those who at the time created rhyming lyrics to commemorate the great event have arrived one after another. It may also be worth your coming from the capital to see. Moreover, the old group of elegant poets are as always not far away. Even though the hall is not yet finished, can you be without something to say? Just as all of the gentlemen recited poems while playing the game of passing flowers to the courtesans, we are still waiting for your arrival.[143]

This letter not only contains flattering comparisons between Wang Shizhen and Ouyang Xiu but also highlights Wang Shizhen's role as a central figure in local literary circles. Naturally, he points to Red Bridge, alluding to both the gatherings Wang sponsored there and the site's proximity to Pingshan Hall. He explains the situation, describes the impending renovation, reminds Wang of his lasting connection to Yangzhou's literary elite, and, in essence, invites Wang Shizhen to bestow his favor on the project with the legitimating power of a few of his words. Here again, we see the role played by contemporary personalities in the formation of local identity envisioned within a transregional framework.

In an essay about the magistrate of a county in Jiangxi, Wang Maolin highlights the role of scenic destinations as part of a constellation of features catalogued in the gazetteer that made it possible to visualize an individual county within a nested hierarchy of administrative units, enhancing its reputation and thereby attracting potential visitors. He writes:

All counties must have landscapes, consisting of pavilions and halls, fords and bridges, shrines and temples, and famous people, represented by distinguished officials, upright men, exemplary women, lofty monks, and Daoist priests, and also the hundred things of land and water, such as strange beasts and unusual bugs, lovely flowers and beautiful trees—which all are noted together in the gazetteer. The person who governs the locale must collect the local customs. He who collects local customs and presents them to the whole country thereby adorns the county's reputation for surpassing beauty and shows it to others so that they will all come.[144]

Thus, the locale, through the gazetteer, is fitted into the country as a whole, here described as an administrative unit. Each locale is meant to be distinct in its particular characteristics, but each is also expected to manifest notable characteristics of the sort included in the gazetteer, ranging from virtuous inhabitants to unusual bugs to scenic landscapes. Without these features, presented here as the constituent parts of local identity and local reputation, an individual county would not be a worthy component in the country as a whole, nor would it be a destination worth visiting. Here, Wang clearly conceives of the locale as a node within administrative and status hierarchies. The cultural construction of place, in the form of the creation of worthwhile scenic destinations to record in the gazetteer and to enhance the reputation of the locale, plays an important role in determining the position of a given county in both hierarchies.

The importance that he attaches to outside appreciation of the locale, and the fact that he considers the gazetteer a suitable guide for visitors, comes out in another preface, this one for the new 1675 edition of the Yangzhou gazetteer, which explains, "Moreover, those who come touring look in the gazetteers once they reach their destinations."[145] The use of gazetteers as guidebooks was far from unprecedented. The Ming traveler Xu Xiake hauled along editions of gazetteers in his travels.[146] Significant here is the degree to which Wang links the characteristics of locale, local government, local people, and the existence of scenic sites for touring and places them in a transregional framework. Similarly, in the context of an essay about another county, he describes the good magistrate as one who develops the general characteristics covered in the gazetteer—in particular, scenic beauty, education, and exemplary people. He writes of a county in Jiangxi: "Now again [it] has a famous person to nurture it and elevate it, and so in time free from government work, he must use creativity to perfect and provide scenic sites for viewing and education to develop human knowledge."[147] To Wang and his friends, the re-creation of historic buildings, and recreation in the form of touring scenic sites, played a role in defining their own status identities. At the same time, these activities helped mark local spaces as nodes within the cultural geography of the larger empire. The renovation of Pingshan Hall was part of a process of symbolic reconciliation among a class whose loyalties were divided by the Ming-Qing conflict. By appealing to the pre-Ming elements of elite identity, they elided the disaster of the remembered past and constructed common spaces for shared enjoyment and ritual performance. Soon, however, the symbolic capital of both city and site was appropriated by touring emperors and capitalized on by sponsoring merchants, as we shall see in the next section and, even more explicitly, in the concluding chapter.

Imperial Presents and Imperial Presence

Although the activities involved in leisure touring remained relatively constant, the symbolism invoked by elites to represent both self and site shifted perceptibly in the early eighteenth century, particularly as the Southern Tours of the Kangxi and Qianlong emperors reshaped the ways in which local writers represented their landscape. Writing in 1765, the salt commissioner Zhao Zhibi concluded his preface to the *Illustrated Gazetteer of Pingshan Hall*, an illustrated book about the scenic sites of Yangzhou, with the statement: "People transmit the reputation of a place, and their ability to transmit it depends upon their having made the right contacts. I am lucky to have participated in the magnificence of the imperial procession, and am happy to celebrate the fortune of this hall, which has attracted imperial attention. Thus the duty of editing this book is my responsibility."[148] All of the guidebooks, site gazetteers, and illustrated books on the gardens of Yangzhou were produced during the eighteenth century, the moment of Yangzhou's greatest affluence and scenic glory. These books, and indeed, the sites they describe, all take the Imperial Tourist as their main subject and audience. Writing early in the Qianlong reign, Wang Ying'geng, a wealthy philanthropist who funded countless civic projects including the renovation of Pingshan Hall in 1736, wrote:

In 1684, the Kangxi emperor came on his Southern Tour. The Imperial Chariot graced this spot with its presence. The emperor wrote the two character inscription "Cheerful Feelings" which was hung above the second story of the hall. In 1705, the Imperial Banners came again. The emperor wrote the words "Pingshan Hall" in giant script and the four characters "The Worthies Preserve Pure Customs" which now hang within the hall. And so, using these four characters, the officials are awakening their love and encouraging their loyalty. It is not only the grace of the famous Song minister that enhances and glorifies esteem for this hall. [The emperor's visit] can be called its moment of greatest excellence![149]

Wang continues, stating that having noticed that the roof was beginning to leak and the tiles were falling off, he was inspired to repair the hall

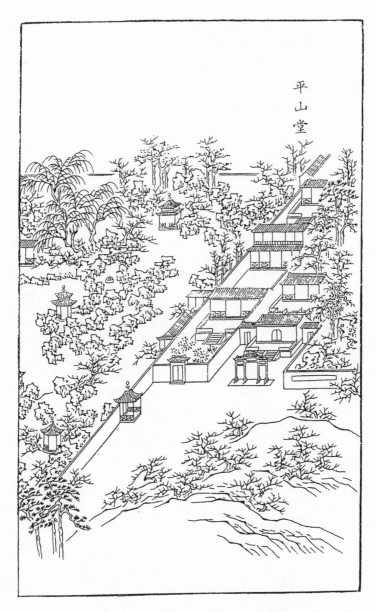

平山堂

FIGURE 4.3. Pingshan Hall. Woodblock illustration. Source: *Guangling ming-sheng tu*, Qianlong period, Court edition.

when he recalled the imperial presence. He then rhapsodically concludes his description of the hall with the following words: "Oh! It has been more than six hundred years since the time of Ouyang Xiu. That this hall reached the pinnacle of its greatness through the glory reflected onto it by the previous emperor, how can it be accidental? How can it be accidental?"[150] The early eighteenth-century guidebooks to Pingshan Hall similarly give priority to the Kangxi emperor's visit. The frequent use of honorific superscript to indicate respect for the emperor in Yin Huiyi's essay commemorating the 1736 renovation provides a striking visual contrast to the 1674 essays, and appears to signal the reorganization of elite identity around the imperial center. As a result of the Southern Tours, the imperial presence was literally inscribed onto the hall through couplets, plaques, and other gifts. These imperial gifts, whether material or literary, alluded to the same symbols invoked by earlier elite visitors.

The focus on the emperor only intensified as the eighteenth century progressed. This should not be surprising given the monumentalist tendencies of the Qianlong emperor.[151] During his reign, the narrow waterway once known as the Baozhang Canal was renamed and reconfigured as "Slender West Lake" (Shouxihu), an extravagant landscape confection offering fabulous views to the touring Qianlong emperor, as well as to local residents and visitors. A water route leading right to Pingshan Hall was dredged in 1757, when the Lotus Dike was opened to form a new canal, and "famous" gardens were constructed on both banks.[152] All of these changes were justified with direct reference to the Southern Tours, though they were certainly also enjoyed by the local populace. The principal focus of Zhao's preface, and of the *Illustrated Gazetteer of Pingshan Hall* as a whole, is the imperial presence, made manifest by the cultural relics produced by the emperor in Yangzhou during his Southern Tours. Even though he mentions Ouyang Xiu as a reason for the site's magnetic appeal, stating that "those who climb up to this hall contemplate and remember old stories about the buildings and cannot leave. If one cannot leave, is it not because of that man [Ouyang]?" the reason that he, like other eighteenth-century writers, gives for the lasting reputation of this site is the imperial presence and imperial attention. This emphasis contrasts sharply with the writings of the 1674 authors, who, as we have seen, were preoccupied with the moral authority and historical significance that Ouyang Xiu conferred upon their activities.

5 The Triumph of Spectacle

TIANNING TEMPLE

Reorienting Yangzhou

This chapter explores a change expressed through the reorientation of Yangzhou's cultural geography—a shift, if you will, from Nanjing-inspired memories to Beijing-inspired advantages. That change signaled the end of the period at the center of this study and the obsolescence of particular ways of seeing and writing about the city of Yangzhou. As the preceding chapters have shown, in the mid-seventeenth century, Yangzhou was imagined within the ambit of Jiangnan, then the source and inspiration for elite culture and its prestige-conferring accouterments. The city's supposed southernness manifested itself in architecture, in place-names, and especially through self-conscious comparisons to, and invocations of, the cities of the Yangzi delta region, to which Yangzhou was linked through transport networks and personal ties. Homages to the local past, inscribed in seventeenth-century poems and tourist itineraries, also marked the city as a southern space and simultaneously situated it in a transregional network of culturally prestigious places that took the cities of Jiangnan as both its ideal and its prototype. By singling out individuals and events from the city's glory days in the Sui and Tang, when it formed part of a distinctly southern imaginary redolent with moonlight, music, and beautiful women, seventeenth-century writers positioned Yangzhou in relation to the prosperous and "cultured" region south of the river. The literary and historical allusions through which the men of the early Qing conceived of Yangzhou and its sites reflected their values and priorities, and indeed responded to their political concerns and personal circumstances.

In the late Ming, the empire's center of gravity was firmly situated in the Yangzi delta, which drew peripheral areas into its cultural orbit through social, political, and literary networks as well as through commercial exchange and fashion.[1] Beijing, with its fratricidal factionalism and indifferent emperors, seemed a distant, even irrelevant, model in this calculus of taste and prestige.[2] Indeed, as Susan Naquin has pointed out, "By the late Ming, even Beijing's nobility aspired to a style of life whose standards were set in the lower Yangzi—Suzhou, Nanjing, and Hangzhou."[3] Banquets prepared by Suzhou chefs were all the rage among those in the capital who could afford them, and Jiangnan influence affected styles in clothing, gardens, architecture, furniture, opera, and art.[4] Similarly, Yangzhou's late Ming gentry and merchant elites modeled their leisure lives and their living spaces, as well as their touring destinations, after those prevailing in cities south of the river. They participated in social and trading networks that implicated them in Jiangnan's culture and economy, and they particularly sought the prestige of public association through things like stele inscriptions and prefaces authored by well-known Jiangnan writers.[5] No surprise, then, that as the chaos of the mid-century collapse and conquest cleared, Jiangnan continued to represent the model of what was seen as universal quality and good taste, and also as a signifier, for some, of what might have been lost in the cataclysm.

As the preceding chapters have shown, the men who rebuilt Yangzhou after 1645 used allusion and architecture to reaffirm their city's southern essence. They capitalized on the city's particular history, and they fitted it, sometimes quite inventively, into a larger paradigm, which they visualized in relation to other places, and with reference to people from the past that they imagined in comfortably familiar terms. They traveled between the cities south of the river and Yangzhou, socializing with the men of the present in ways they supposed the men of the past might have done, forming personal connections through leisure touring and poetry composition at valued sites in those other cities. In so doing, they materially and imaginatively reconstituted the city of Yangzhou in the image of a Jiangnan cultural center. At the same time, they restored the social networks of the pre-conquest period and burnished the image of literati unity and preeminence, despite political differences. The new Qing rulers, too, at times subscribed to, and further validated, this vision of Jiangnan culture and its Yangzhou expression through patronage and imitation, even as their presence in Beijing gradually gave new weight to the capital, and as their heterogeneous tastes conferred prestige on new and "exotic" styles.

Even before Yangzhou's precipitous descent into impoverishment in the late nineteenth century, when it was reconstituted as the undesirable Other to more "modern" coastal cities, Yangzhou's relationship to Jiangnan was transformed through its changing relationship to Beijing. More precisely, the cultural hierarchy of place changed in the eighteenth century, and the relative positions of Beijing and Jiangnan reversed. With the consolidation and centralization of the empire, the political center acquired new cultural weight. This process seems to have intensified with the arrival in the northern capital of a contingent of poets and tastemakers, many of them from Jiangnan, in response to the special boxue hongci examination in 1679, an event accompanied by many well-publicized excursions and literary gatherings. Thus, beginning in the late seventeenth century, and accelerating over the course of the eighteenth century, the capital increasingly became the center of the empire's cultural, as well as political, aspirations. Moreover, intellectual and cultural projects, through imperial patronage and involvement, were organized in relation to the capital, with implications for other urban centers.[6] As Susan Naquin has so amply illustrated, by 1800, Beijing was the "nerve center of the empire and a city of great wealth and glamor," whose status "as a political and cultural center was much less vulnerable to challenge from the Lower Yangzi cities than it had been in the Ming."[7]

By the Qianlong reign, the local arbiters of taste in Yangzhou, increasingly salt merchants and those they patronized, at least in some respects reinvented the city as a southern extension of the capital, rather than a northern outpost of Jiangnan. As we shall see, over the course of the eighteenth century, Beijing became not only a political center but also the source of distinctive styles emulated in other parts of the empire. Other cities in the empire were brought more firmly into Beijing's orbit, but Yangzhou was particularly vulnerable to Beijing influences due to its peculiar economic relationship to the capital, which was articulated through the salt monopoly, and its physical location at the crossroads between north and south. In this context, local sites became meaningful not through poetry and literary reference but through imperial appreciation, and through local efforts to capitalize on imperial appreciation. Moreover, newly constructed sites often responded to imperial tastes, as local craftsmen and patrons elaborated on Beijing-influenced styles.

Yangzhou in the eighteenth century acquired the distinctive characteristics now most closely associated with the city, and it also acquired an enhanced reputation as a trend-setter in its own right. This was the city of fabulous wealth, gardens, theater, jade carvers, Western exotica, renowned academies, and talented artists described by visitors and residents in the late eighteenth and early nineteenth centuries.[8] At the same time, though, the capital was an important part of the local equation, for the city emerged as a place famous for landscape novelties embellished with fashionable northern, or Beijing-style, flourishes that were newly appreciated by local consumers. Yangzhou developed its own distinctive style, in part through local appreciation for, and appropriation of, new styles emanating from the capital, and not simply due to the eclecticism of local commercial tastes. The eighteenth-century city, like its gardens, was said to represent a fusion of "Southern elegance" and "Northern vigor."[9] This hybrid place, toured by Qing emperors and flush with salt money, is the Yangzhou-past that serves as a glamorous reference point for current reimaginings: the Yangzhou of the Qianlong emperor, the Eight Eccentrics, the Painted Pleasure Boats, and the Salt Merchants.

This chapter will explore the processes through which Yangzhou and its sites were transformed over the course of the eighteenth century, as unprecedented wealth underwrote accelerated construction, as the commercial economy flourished and drove changes in local fashion, and as new influences filtered into, and then flooded, the locale. It also will trace an important, parallel shift in the composition of Yangzhou's cultural elite—from a community of literati types in thrall to late Ming literary values to a local society led by salt moguls in thrall to the emperor and to fashion.[10] In this chapter, once again we examine these historical and cultural processes in relation to a particular destination, here, Tianning Temple. The person of the emperor, or rather the Kangxi and Qianlong emperors, will serve as the human, if always larger-than-life, foil for the physical site. In this context, imperial spectacle and Beijing style, salt merchant wealth and material display, overtake and overwhelm the earlier gestures toward the reconstitution of literati networks according to a Jiangnan model. Here, with the temporary triumph of spectacle, this book will find its end.

The Temple's Past

Tianning Temple had been one of the prefecture's largest and most prominent Buddhist institutions even in the seventeenth century. It was listed first in the 1675 gazetteer's section on local temples, with a descriptive entry predictably accompanied by a poem by the prolific Peng Gui entitled "Touring Tianning Temple Again."[11] In the early Qing, as in the late Ming, one presumes, the prominence of this site derived from the temple's ancient origins and its large size and extensive grounds, as well as its suitability for leisure touring and its Chan (Zen) associations.[12] Located outside the walls of the New City, on the other side of the moat just north of Gongchen Gate, the temple evidently had existed in various guises and under various names as early as the Wei-Jin (Six Dynasties) period. With architecture and icons that a later writer described as "Suzhou-style," and historical and imagined ties to Jiangnan history, culture, and social networks, Tianning Temple was one of the many Yangzhou landmarks that symbolically linked the city to the urban centers south of the river.[13]

The prefectural gazetteer explains that, according to local legend, the temple had been a villa belonging to the famous Grand Tutor Xie An (320–85), and that the foreign monk Buddhabhadra had translated the *Huayan sutra* there during the early fifth century.[14] The name "Tianning" was first associated with the site in the early twelfth century during the Northern Song, when the Huizong emperor bestowed the new designation on an existing temple. In the mid-twelfth century, after the loss of North China to the Jurchen and in response to an imperial command, the temple's name plaque was changed to read "Repay Grace and Illuminate Filial Piety Temple" (Bao'en Guangxiao si). Incense was offered to the spirit of the last Northern Song emperor, Huizong. This simultaneously political and religious gesture was not mentioned by the editors of the 1685 edition, however, who may have been constrained by the exigencies of recent, and thus sensitive, events.[15] After repeated name changes and a period of ruin and disuse in the late Yuan, the temple reverted to its Northern Song appellation by the late Ming, and it has continued to be known by that name to the present.[16] During the first decades of the Qing, visitors evidently found these historical associations particularly compelling, as they could experience the landscape in relation to both echoes from the ancient past and more recent events.

During the early Qing, the temple provided a physical space for leisure touring, social gatherings, and religious worship. Beggars clustered outside the gate, in hopes of collecting alms from tourists and worshipers.[17] Monks lived in a dormitory at the rear of the temple complex. Like many Buddhist temples, it also appears to have offered lodgings, and several famous sojourners stayed at Tianning Temple. Poems describing late night gatherings in the temple precinct appear in the literary collections of early Qing visitors to Yangzhou and their local hosts as well as in larger anthologies of contemporary poetry such as Deng Hanyi's *Poetry Survey* (discussed in Chapter 3). Early Qing references to Tianning Temple allude to its place in history and lore while also positioning the temple within the framework of their own touring itineraries. These representations of the temple are sometimes colored by recent experiences of trauma and loss. The description of Tianning Temple found in Tan Qian's travel diary,

A Record of My Journey to the North (Beiyou lu), is typical in this regard: Tan frames his visit to the temple within his larger trip to the capital, as part of a day of sightseeing in Yangzhou, and as a space from which to reflect on the conquest experience.

Tan Qian traveled to Beijing from Zhejiang in the summer of 1653 as part of an official's entourage and recorded his experiences in a diary and a series of poems. He spent six days in the vicinity of Yangzhou city, with the last day devoted to sightseeing in the northern suburbs, then, as his account makes clear, still in a state of disrepair. His account positions the temple in the context of his own sightseeing itinerary and within a more generalized landscape of loss, displacement, history, and memory. He intersperses contemporary description with historical allusion, his emotional response tempered by his rush to complete the sightseeing circuit. He begins his outing by leaving the walled city through the Guangchu Gate in the early afternoon. From there he followed the moat westward toward Plum Blossom Ridge. At this point he and his companions left their boats and followed a row of young elm trees, which lined the path, to the grave of Shi Kefa, the Southern Ming official who died resisting the Qing army.[18] There Tan read the stele installed by Shi's adopted son, contemplated the overgrown grave, and reflected on his own grief and bitterness. He also notes the presence of a shrine to Zeng Xian, a victim of the factional violence of the late Ming, adjacent to Shi's grave. This shrine does not feature prominently in later accounts of visits to Plum Blossom Ridge.

After leaving Plum Blossom Ridge, Tan searched for the entrance to Tianning Temple, which he places in its literary-historical context through references to Xie An and Buddhabhadra. He provides a physical description, writing that "it was grand and magnificent in its construction and was considered the premier Chan [Zen] temple in the region south of the Huai. The gingko trees were also quite old."[19] Tan then asked a temple monk the way to Pingshan Hall, and the monk told him that it was not far. His account continues, as he rushes mournfully back and forth through the other sites centered near Shugang, many of which were still ruins. He writes of the area around Red Bridge, "in truth it was a graveyard."[20] He contrasts the glories of the Six Dynasties and the Tang with the disasters of the recent past, setting up analogies between the fall of the Song and the fall of the Ming. He concludes: "The glory and fame [of this place] were in the [Six Dynasties] Jin and Tang. Today, the west gate is collapsing into ruins. How could Shi Kefa not have been like Li Tingzhi [the famous Southern Song general]? Going and returning we mourned for the past. Indeed it is suited to the mood of the Ruined Citadel."[21] Tan Qian's description of a day spent touring the northwest suburbs suggests that at that time the temple was a node in a landscape defined by grief, inflected by poetry and gazetteer accounts. Several decades later, due to imperial patronage and official presence, it came to be seen as an important point of intersection between the imperial court and the locale.

Awaiting Audience in Tianning Temple

By the late 1680s, the Lianghuai salt monopoly occupied at least one building on the grounds of Tianning Temple. Although the main office of the Lianghuai salt monopoly was in the New City, the salt commissioner also acquired space at the temple for official and ceremonial use. It also seems to have been available as lodgings for visiting bureaucrats, for Kong Shangren lived there in 1689 when he came to Yangzhou as part of his assignment to the River Conservancy project. This physical and administrative link between the Lianghuai salt monopoly and Tianning Temple accounts at least in part for changes in the function and representation of this temple during the age of the Kangxi emperor's Southern Tours, and for its prominence in the Kangxi emperor's tour itinerary. Salt administration officials, after all, played an important role in hosting the emperor during his trips to the south, and responsibility for both the tours and the salt monopoly came under the purview of the imperial household administration. The name of this building, "Awaiting Audience Lodge" (Dailou guan), echoes that of the hall in the Forbidden City where officials prepared for their morning audience with the emperor. It thus suggests a point of intersection between the court and the locale, a nominal analogy between Beijing and Yangzhou. Kong Shangren develops this comparison in an essay about the lodge that was written in 1689, during his period of residence in this building on the temple grounds, after the emperor's first visit to the temple in 1684.[22] In this essay, Kong uses the lodge as a foil for his feelings of isolation and frustration. The building also provides a vehicle for reflections on the relationship between the court and the provinces, and a medium through which to articulate his concern for the future of the River Conservancy project, a preoccupation he shared with the emperor, and the official justification for the emperor's southern tours. Kong's meditation on this Yangzhou temple thus echoes imperial concerns, and, significantly, the tours that brought the emperor into the locale.

In the opening section of his essay, Kong Shangren inquires about the lodge's curious name, asking the caretaker: "Inasmuch as Yangzhou is not the site of the capital and a Buddhist temple is not the place where one awaits court audiences, is it not presumptuous that this lodge is known as 'Awaiting Audience Lodge'?" The caretaker responds that the lodge is operated by the salt and transport commissioner and used for meditation by incoming salt officials on their first night in office. He concludes, "and so, even though the emperor is not close, imperial authority is no more than an inch away, and although the location is physically far [from the capital] there is none among the officials and commoners who dares to be negligent. It was named for this and that is all."[23] Faced with this assertion of official diligence and imperial presence, Kong explores his own feelings of defeat and disappointment. After three years of work, the river project still has not succeeded in alleviating the flooding along the Huai River. He writes,

And in the halls of power, the debate is at an impasse . . . The clerks and runners have absconded, sensing the perilous future. At the same time, my colleagues on this project have either been recalled to court or returned to their hometowns. They have scattered. Or they have died. I count them off on my fingers, and there is not even one of them here. I am alone, solitary, groaning in illness and hunger in this lodge. Leaving me here is useless, and I have no permission to leave. And so, for me, I who resemble the banished exile and wandering official, to see the salt censor, impressive in his embroidered clothes and with his fancy horse, who has come to this place with serious purpose, how can I not feel profoundly ashamed? I have heard that the old Awaiting Audience Lodge [in Beijing] is located outside the court hall, [and] the officials gather there early at the fifth watch of the night, in order to wait for the great gates to open. Those who have memorials to present at this time all bow their heads and consider them . . . All those who plan to debate forthrightly in the palace are among those who wait tremulously in this lodge [in Beijing]. Although it is not that place, this lodge [in Yangzhou] imitates the name. Although I live in this place, I still however cannot claim its truth [i.e., that I am "Awaiting Audience"].[24]

Kong grounds his emotional response in the contrast between the real Awaiting Audience Lodge in Beijing and its counterpart in Yangzhou. He describes the physical setting and the various social groups present. Finally he inscribes his own presence in this space away from the court, and yet somehow close to it, by bestowing a name on the hall of the lodge in which he stayed. The essay concludes as follows:

In the lodge, there is a full complement of gate, chamber, kitchen, and storage. The formal hall is five pillars in size. That is where I dwell. The opening and closing of the doors at dawn and dusk depend on the monks, the coming and going to view and look depend on the tourists, sounds chanted above my seat and the inscriptions left on the walls depend on men of style and elders of the wilderness. The debates on the two rivers, the truth and falseness of inner and outer, with regard to the humble dwellings of the seven counties, and the fate of the myriad people, all depend on the court, and depend on the emperor and mother nature. As for me, one night here is temporary, another night is a long time. Three or four nights, well, then it becomes my usual environment. The sage of old said, "When one is there at court, one worries for his people, and when one is far away among the rivers and lakes, one worries for his emperor." Today, I do not know what is happening at court. As for what is happening amid rivers and lakes, I suddenly hear the melodious sound of an oriole. I am aware of something melancholy and unsettled about it, and thus I have given its name to the hall where I dwell. I have named the hall "Dawn Oriole" (Xiaoying tang), as the name of the lodge is "Awaiting Audience."[25]

With monks, tourists, men of talent, and elderly loyalists wandering the grounds, clearly this is not the lodge in Beijing. And yet, he implies, he himself, and perhaps by extension the site, is somehow closer to the emperor's own objectives than are the squabbling officials at court or the salt commissioner on the eve of his appointment. While emphasizing his own shame relative to the salt censor and the officials "awaiting audience" in Beijing, Kong Shangren's purpose is in fact to demonstrate his own higher loyalty to the emperor and the river project. He does so in part through oblique references to the spurned poet-official Qu Yuan (c. 343–277 B.C.E.). These references are rendered more overt in his friend's comments, which follow the essay:

Service on the river project troubles the heart and wearies the body, and it is still blocked in debate [therefore he was not able to achieve it]. It is not yet clear how [the project] will continue. His concern for the country and for the people, his insomnia and restless heart, can be compared to the solitary official of Xianglei [Qu Yuan]. This inspires sympathy in his readers and makes them sigh repeatedly.[26]

Kong Shangren's essay revolves around several important motifs: the complex political interests at court that stymied the river project; the stylish posturing of the salt monopoly official; Kong's own concern for the people and the emperor, made manifest through the flood control project. The temple figures here as a site of imperial authority "lodged" in the locale, echoing the objectives and experiences of the Kangxi emperor's Southern Tours. Kong surely was aware of the imperial inscription bestowed on the temple by the emperor during the first tour in 1684 and its significance as a marker of imperial patronage. Moreover, he certainly knew of the high priority that the Kangxi emperor placed on water control and the emperor's pursuit of political support beyond the factional conflicts at court—both of which were factors contributing to the Southern Tours. The essay signals an important change in elite engagement with the Yangzhou landscape. The ruined landscape of graveyards and memories seen in Tan Qian's essay has been overwritten. The temple is no longer a site for nostalgic reflection, or even for poetic sociability. Here, it serves as a marker in a political landscape centered on court concerns, rather than on those of an elite community reconstituted on the basis of shared, and ostensibly apolitical, values. The essay thus reflects the temple's position as the beneficiary of imperial patronage and foreshadows its later function as the home of imperially endowed projects and, indeed, as the temporary residence of the Kangxi emperor's grandson, the Qianlong emperor.

An Emperor in a Southern City?

The Kangxi emperor visited Yangzhou six times, in 1684, 1689, 1699, 1703, 1705, and 1707. He experienced a city in transition, for these were the years in which salt merchants and salt monopoly officials began to play an increasingly visible role relative to "regular" administrative officials, literary figures, and examination elites. These diverse and intermingled local groups shaped the emperor's encounter with Yangzhou, as did the emperor's own political agenda. Records of the Kangxi emperor's tours thus describe the city with reference to three dominant images: as a Southern city redolent of moonlight and myth, as a decadent city of merchants bearing expensive gifts, and as an inundated city in need of flood control and tax relief. These images were the product of an interchange between the locale and the court, and they prefigure a more dramatic transformation during the Qianlong period. In this section, I will examine these three images in order to explore the changing social composition and cultural orientation of the city during the period of the Kangxi emperor's Southern Tours.

From the perspective of Beijing, or, indeed, of an emperor on tour, Yangzhou in the mid-Kangxi reign appeared to be part of a constellation of Southern cities, including Suzhou, Hangzhou, and Nanjing, that were famous for luxury products, beautiful women, talented poets, and powerful officials. As we have seen in the preceding chapters, this image was at least in part the product of careful cultivation by men who saw themselves as the conservators of a transdynastic culture expressed through historical reference and poetic allusion. For them, Yangzhou embodied the values and aesthetics of the late Ming urban centers of the Yangzi delta. The emperor, intent on strengthening his position relative to forces at court, looked to Jiangnan for alternative sources of political legitimacy and also, as James Cahill has pointed out, felt a profound attraction for Southern sensuality.[27] At the same time, the official and literati elites also had a growing interest in promoting themselves—and their version of Southern tastes—at court.[28] For example, the artists and patrons who contributed to the painting "The Southern Inspection Tour" *(Nanxun tu)* used the project to praise the emperor and their home provinces, thereby reminding the emperor of the region's cultural and political importance.[29] The emperor in turn appropriated the legitimating features of Southern culture through the representation of the tours in orthodox-style painting, and, indeed, through the tours themselves. Similarly, the Kangxi emperor saw the sights of Yangzhou, produced and packaged by local elites, as part of a larger Southern landscape, associating them with the prestigious, and politically useful, milieu of Jiangnan, and with the decadent pleasures that the south was supposed to offer. Thus the emperor drew upon the symbolic vocabulary that the city's official and literati elites had developed during the decades after the conquest, and he privileged the same destinations that they had favored.

The emperor and his entourage highlighted Yangzhou's Southern character through references to the city's decadence, seductiveness, and sensuality. The version of the South embraced by the Kangxi emperor consisted of elegant scenery, poetry, opera performances, beautiful women, and the local cuisine, as well as encounters with literary and artistic talents, many of whom were at least fancifully associated with late Ming Jiangnan society. The emperor literally invited this "South" into the court, bringing craftsmen, artists, and cooks from Yangzhou to Beijing to serve in imperial workshops, the imperial painting academy, and the palace kitchens.[30] He thus affirmed the image of Yangzhou-as-Jiangnan established by renovators and sightseers in the early Qing, and he completed processes of reconciliation and accommodation formerly enacted at the local level. Practicing calligraphy at the imperial lodge during the fifth tour, in 1705, the emperor affirmed the Southern character of what he had seen, writing, "Every time I visit the South, I am fascinated by the elegance of its scenery and the beauty of its rivers. Although my body resides in the palace, my feeling for excellent mountains and waters is the same as that of ordinary people . . ."[31] In a poem composed on the same occasion, he expresses sympathy for Sui Yangdi, an emperor renowned for debauchery in Yangzhou, writing, "Oh that I would not let my [heart] be driven to follow my lusts and my craving for extravagance."[32] Descriptions of the tours fix Yangzhou, Tianning Temple, and the imperial entourage within a glittering, sensual, and potentially degrading Southern sphere, revealing and subtly transforming a landscape that evoked pre-conquest Jiangnan, as well as the city's own famously decadent past.

The involvement of merchants as donors and hosts during the tours suggests changing social and cultural dynamics at the local level, with the salt merchants playing a more prominent role among the producers of "local" culture, and in mediating the relationship between the locale and the center. The emperor was entertained by a coalition of provincial and prefectural officials, salt monopoly officials, artists, poets, examination elites, and salt merchants. Evidence of merchant involvement is most complete for the fifth tour because of the "Shengzu wuxing Jiangnan quanlu" (A Complete Record of the Kangxi Emperor's Fifth Southern Tour), which Jonathan Spence characterizes as the work of an anonymous "member of the retinue" or "an unusually informed observer."[33] According to the "Complete Record," upon arriving in Yangzhou, the emperor was greeted at canal-side by salt merchants, not officials, all of whom offered an enthusiastic welcome and presented valuable gifts including antiques, paintings, and collectibles to the emperor.[34] The next day, the emperor entered the city proper, where he was greeted by local elites, students, and local elders. He continued by procession to High Bridge, where he attended a huge banquet. The emperor, with an entourage of family members and palace ladies, viewed the lantern boats around Baozhang Lake, toured the sites of Pingshan Hall, and visited Tianning Temple where he saw monks chanting sutras, and conversed extensively with the abbot.[35] That night, the emperor enjoyed a lavish banquet and theatrical performances at an imperial lodge financed and constructed by the Lianghuai salt merchants at Pagoda Bend (also called Sancha he), in the city's southern suburbs. The lodge was illuminated with dragon lanterns, decorated with silk streamers, and filled with antiques and paintings.[36] The emperor reflected on the extravagance of the merchants' expenditures in an essay and a poem he wrote the next day.[37]

On the return trip, the emperor again was entertained by the salt-merchants in the opulent gardens of the imperial villa that they had constructed for him.[38] The following days were filled with opera performances, banquets, and lantern shows. The emperor expressed his pleasure with the arrangements by giving gifts to the assembled officials and by praising the temporary palace with its artificial hill and opulent decorations.[39] The salt merchants were invited to enjoy the surroundings with the imperial entourage as a special privilege, and in return, they again presented gifts. Here, encounters with merchants take place alongside, and even before, encounters with officials. Although artists, poets, and officials also sought exchanges with the emperor, opulence paid for by merchants occupied center stage, at least in this account. By underwriting garden palaces, sponsoring opera performances, and introducing lavish banquets of local cuisine, the merchants produced a quintessentially "Southern" setting for the emperor to enjoy. The merchants' ability to entertain the emperor on so lavish a scale indicates the personal and political power of the Lianghuai salt commissioner, the merchants' new prosperity, and their desire for local and national influence to match their growing wealth. That they chose to emphasize the city's Southern charms not only conformed to imperial expectations (these were after all "Southern" tours) but also followed patterns of representation set in the previous decades of reconstruction and reconciliation.

These images of Southern splendor coexist with references to tax relief and water control, two issues central to the Kangxi emperor's agenda and to the official representation of the Southern Tours. Thus, though records of the tours describe Yangzhou as a luxurious Jiangnan city, they also depict it as part of a devastated landscape in need of imperial relief. Doing so enabled the emperor to represent himself simultaneously as a patron of elite culture and as a nurturing monarch. The emperor thus assumed the legitimacy of a widely recognized "Jiangnan" culture packaged and presented especially by Southern elites, some of whom in turn relied on the emperor to expand their own influence at court. At the same time, his interest in popular welfare and the steps he took to resolve persistent problems such as flooding were consistent with the ideal image of an emperor of China, and thus they further enhanced the emperor's prestige and power. They also had positive implications for the locale. The proclamations issued in the prefecture during the tours, published as a special section in the 1810 gazetteer, deal almost exclusively with the flooding problems faced by the region. An edict from the 1684 tour expresses sympathy for the plight of people in the Yangzhou counties of Baoying and Gaoyou whose homes had been inundated with water from Gaoyou Lake. The emperor concludes that the flooding is due to silting in the Yellow–Huai river system, and that although dredging would help prevent future problems, tax relief is needed to alleviate the suffering of the local population.[40] A second edict from the same tour admonishes local officials to carefully oversee dike maintenance in the counties.[41] Subsequent edicts are quite technical, with detailed discussion of water levels and dike heights, evaluations of the River Conservancy project begun in 1686, and

specific strategies for flood prevention and disaster relief. Although merchants, officials, and writers contrived to produce an archetypal South for
the imperial visit, the emperor's commitment to water control introduced
another perspective, even as the emperor himself deliberately agonized
over the dangerous temptations of this "Southern" city and positioned
himself as a connoisseur of Southern culture. The emperor not only
affirmed the vision of the archetypal South with which he was presented
but also inscribed the landscape with his own image: as patron of culture
and as concerned monarch. Both images embedded the locale in a relationship of obligation and reciprocity with the center that was rooted in
classical ideas about rulership.

The Temple and the Tours, Part 1

During the Kangxi tours, Tianning Temple emerged as one context
for the interchange between Yangzhou and the capital, as it was recast as
an imperially favored destination. Salt monopoly control, and the tight
connection between the salt monopoly and the imperial household, may
account for the attention paid to this temple during the Kangxi emperor's
tours. Although it did not yet house an imperial villa, as is sometimes
assumed, Tianning Temple was among a large assortment of Yangzhou
sites patronized by the Kangxi emperor.[42] Most notably, it was one of the
very few sites visited by the emperor on his first tour in 1684, when he
spent two days in Yangzhou prefecture. It subsequently became an important object of imperial patronage, both physical and literary, as well as a
destination on subsequent tours.[43] According to the 1733 gazetteer, the
temple was a particular favorite of the emperor, who "visited this temple
whenever he came to Yangzhou."[44]

The Kangxi emperor's engagement with local sites, framed by the be-
stowal and reception of gifts, symbolically confirmed Yangzhou's place
in the empire and the emperor's role as a patron of both the city and
the prestigious Jiangnan culture it ostensibly represented. Seventeen of the
twenty-two temples extant in Jiangdu and Ganquan counties during the
early Qing evidently received inscriptions or gifts from the emperor during the tours, and the emperor visited seven of them in person.[45] The emperor was particularly generous in his gifts to Tianning Temple. In fact,
only Gaomin Temple, home of the imperial villa that the salt merchants
built south of the city at Pagoda Bend, received comparable largesse. The
emperor presented Tianning Temple with a range of gifts that included
inscriptions, several items of his own poetry and calligraphy, sutras writ-

ten in the style of famous calligraphers embodying orthodox tastes carved in stone or copied in gold ink, a gold Buddha, a copy of the Kangxi dictionary, a published collection of poems by the emperor, a calligraphy style manual, three inkstones, an incense burner, two enamel vases, purple-gold gauze, a coral (Buddhist) rosary, and two poems about the temple written by the emperor.[46] By composing inscriptions and bestowing gifts at sites of local significance, the Kangxi emperor affirmed the place of the locale and its sites in the imperium and validated existing patterns of elite touring practice. As a giver and receiver of gifts, he became a ritual authority to which the recipient locale submitted. His gifts implied obligation. Through ritually conferred presents, he commanded participation in reciprocal and hierarchical relationships centered around the imperial person.[47]

In 1705, during the fifth tour, the Kangxi emperor ordered his bondservant Cao Yin, then serving as Lianghuai salt commissioner, to establish an imperially sponsored printing office on the grounds of Tianning Temple.[48] Its major task was to be the publication of the *Complete Tang Poems* (Quan Tang shi), the first of several major literary projects undertaken by the Qing court. The project, which included 48,900 poems by 2,200 authors, was completed in the spring of 1707 and represented a major achievement for the dynasty and the salt commissioner.[49] Most likely it was able to hire skilled artisans locally, since Yangzhou had an active official print office and numerous private publishers at least since the start of the dynasty. This project may also have stimulated further developments in publishing, even as it certainly contributed to the city's image as a regional publishing center.

The temple seems to have been chosen for this purpose due to its connection to the salt commissioner's office, which, as we have seen, had controlled the temple's east corridor at least since the late 1680s. Again, this seems to be a case of converging jurisdictions: the salt monopoly offices, the tours, and Cao Yin himself, a banner bondservant, all fell under the authority of the imperial household. The arrival of a group of scholars from the Hanlin academy in Beijing to do the editing for the publishing project marked a growing court presence in the locale and expanded the already extensive personal connections between literary figures in the city and in the capital. Moreover, the establishment of the printing office also paid tribute to the vibrant publishing and poetry circles active in Yangzhou in the late seventeenth century and the city's position as a center of literary culture in both the Tang and the early Qing. At the same time, it validated the literary priorities of the Jiangnan literary elite, who were themselves much enamored of Tang poetry, and it provided added symbolic weight to Qing assertions of continuity with the Tang. Ultimately, though, the publishing project accelerated the dialogue between the court and the locale, expanding the court's cultural influence locally, even as it appropriated local and literary sources of legitimacy.

The legacy of imperial patronage mediated by the salt commissioner and paid for by salt merchants continued at Tianning Temple even after the Southern Tours were over. The emperor ordered the Lianghuai salt commissioner and the Jiangnan textile commissioner to carry out extensive renovations, and they obtained donations from salt merchants totaling more than 14,200 taels to pay for materials and labor.[50] Even though this was significantly more than the amount spent on the renovations of Pingshan Hall three decades earlier, it was still not enough to restore the religious images, according to Li Xu. In a memorial, Li Xu asks for permission to use five hundred taels from the treasury to pay for the restoration of the Buddhist images.[51] He adds, in the formal idiom of court exchange, that to do so would guarantee the eternal memory of the emperor's sagely heart. The contribution would also, of course, symbolically link the emperor to the restoration project, as did the inscription written by the emperor to commemorate its completion.

As was the case with other Yangzhou sites, and as we saw with Pingshan Hall in the preceding chapter, imperial patronage and presence increasingly came to define local significance. Tianning Temple took on new importance in the ranking of local sites during the Kangxi emperor's Southern Tours. The selection of illustrations for the prefectural gazetteer suggests that the imperial presence in the local landscape gave added prestige to several of the prefecture's sites. As time went on, descriptions of Tianning Temple increasingly focused on the imperial visits, rather than the temple's historical or literary heritage. Imperial patronage, and the imperial presence, had the effect of reorganizing the hierarchies of prestige through which sites were viewed, and indeed, to some extent, it reconfigured the relationship between place and meaning. This dynamic became even more pronounced in the Qianlong period, even when applied retrospectively, as the following exchange indicates.

Writing in 1739, the Lianghuai salt control censor Sanbao submitted the following memorial:

Requesting guidance on the following matter. I visited Jinshan temple in Zhenjiang. The peak rising from the river is the best famous sight in the Southeast. Moreover, the temple respectfully hosted the Kangxi emperor during his tour of the South, receiving an imperial plaque, couplets, an imperially composed poem, and a stele inscription. The glories of the imperial handwriting and the scenery will be immortalized together through the generations. Moreover, there was formerly an imperial villa on the west bank of Sancha Canal which had an imperially bestowed name plaque reading "Gaomin Temple" and a stele inscription which also will last forever. It truly was a great sight for a thousand ages. During the more than thirty years that have passed from the time of the Kangxi emperor's tour in 1707 until the present, these two sites have not been repaired. When I went to inspect the waterways on the ninth day of the first month of this year, I visited Jinshan by boat and climbed up to look around. I saw that the imperial plaques and inscriptions and stelae were already old, and that all of the palaces were in ruins . . . If we do not repair them in a timely fashion, they will be completely destroyed. The imperial villa at Sancha Canal is also in poor condition . . . Both of these sites are suitable for restoration. I humbly recall that the Kangxi emperor visited these two sites during his Southern Tours. They cannot be compared with ordinary temples, and instead are in the category of important cultural sites. They thus should be restored and renewed in order to serve as an attractive destination for gentlemen and commoners from every province. I have determined that regular and miscellaneous tax money from the Lianghuai area totaling more than 109,000 taels [from various enumerated sources] is all stored in the transport warehouses and was not entered into the official tally. Can these previously unreported funds be applied to the repairs of the imperial villas or not?. . . .The work will make it possible for the glorious imperial calligraphy and temples to be renewed and to last forever. I humbly await word as to whether we should begin this, and am enclosing drawings for your consideration.

Presumably after looking at the drawings, the Qianlong emperor responded: "Good. Let us do as he asks."[52]

Site and Spectacle

The Kangxi tours were accompanied by only limited construction. With the notable exception of the imperial villa at Gaomin Temple, this consisted primarily of renovation rather than the development of new buildings and scenic sites. Doing so was consistent with the objectives of the tours, which were, after all, primarily about patronizing an existing image of the city and its famous sites—and using them as a backdrop for imperial patronage and benevolence. By contrast, the Southern tours of the Qianlong emperor (in 1751, 1757, 1762, 1765, 1780, and 1784) occasioned the radical reconfiguration of the Yangzhou landscape and a further tightening of connections between the locale and the court. These changes reflected a new, expanded, and more culturally eclectic idea of emperorship. The flurry of construction that these tours inspired culminated in the creation of unprecedented scenic venues, created at least ostensibly in preparation for the imperial tourist, and some of which were built in a new imperial style with roots in Beijing and Central Asia. These new structures included numerous garden scenes, prospects, temples, and pavilions, as well as a new water route to the base of Shugang. This last ostensibly was to ease the passage of the emperor and his entourage but in fact benefited a whole generation of pleasure boaters. Here, as elsewhere, provincial, prefectural, and monopoly officials developed the emperor's itinerary, on the basis of both local and imperial precedent. Beginning after the first tour in 1751, which closely followed the itinerary of the Kangxi tours, officials in Zhejiang and Jiangsu began to propose sites that were "truly in the category of famous districts for imperial sightseeing" and to develop and repair them for the next visit.[53]

The Qianlong reign was a period of monumental construction and the spread of imperially inspired architecture both within and beyond the capital. It was also a period of intentional eclecticism, with Central Asian and Tibetan style temples built in Chengde, and northern-style buildings springing up in Yangzhou.[54] Gardens constructed in honor of the imperial visits reflected stylistic developments associated with the imperial hunting parks and summer palaces. Even though the emperor clearly remained conscious of a style marked "Southern" (for example, he famously imported craftsmen to build a Suzhou-style street in Beijing for his mother's entertainment), many projects carried out in the emperor's name were marked by their monumental invocation of a new and eclectic architectural style.[55] Indeed, the "Beijing style" emulated elsewhere in the empire was the product of a "bicultural city," which spoke Chinese with "Altaicized inflections," ate new Manchu delicacies, and built new Tibetan-style temples.[56]

In a self-consciously multiethnic empire, under a ruler who presented himself as universal emperor, court styles no longer privileged a "Jiangnan" aesthetic, nor were they in thrall to Jiangnan flavors. While the Kangxi emperor introduced a Yangzhou chef to the court, the Qianlong tours were accompanied with hybrid feasts that included local Yangzhou specialties along with dishes of Manchu or Northern provenance. These were known as "Manchu-Han" banquets, and they were served to officials of various ranks.[57] Not all of this cross-pollination responded directly to court orders. The new monumental aesthetic affected the vernacular and commercial architecture of the city as imitators borrowed elements and techniques from imperial models. Bathhouse, brothel, and restaurant architecture were influenced, as well as the fashionably extravagant gardens of wealthy salt merchants.[58] In addition, during the Qianlong period some Yangzhou residents added waterfalls and fountains to their private gardens.[59] These mechanical features do not seem to have been prevalent in Jiangnan, though the western-style gardens at Yuanmingyuan near Beijing featured Jesuit-designed waterworks, and it is possible, especially given the close ties through the imperial household, that there is a connection. Clearly, some among the wealthy and powerful of the city began to look to the capital for inspiration, and those who sought their business did so as well.

The emphasis was on novelty. The new landmarks built in honor of the tours were "named" sites, but not historical ones. They appealed to a taste for the curious and the contemporary.[60] A late eighteenth-century visitor writes: "All this is just a general description of the gardens . . . I happened to be visiting just as the grand ceremonies were being held there during the Emperor's inspection tour of the South. All the works had been completed, and the emperor invited to visit them. Because of this I was able to enjoy a grand spectacle, more magnificent than one can expect to come across in a lifetime."[61] His words highlight the grandeur and pageantry that accompanied this new merchant-built, emperor-centered culture, and the prevailing taste for the novel and spectacular. The gardens around the lake were transformed and combined into a single landscape with multiple vistas. At the same time, some of these private gardens, borrowed for imperial appreciation, were seen and appreciated by visitors and leisure tourists as well. Gardens also could have commercial functions. Some garden owners used the grounds of their villas to raise plants and flowers for sale, and some garden workers made use of pavilions to sell tea and other refreshments. The sites seen in the late eighteenth century were for entertainment—whether the Qianlong emperor's or the merchants'—and the emperor and his entourage were themselves part of the sightseeing spectacle.

The Qianlong emperor inserted himself into the scene through his inscriptions and verse conferred as gifts on salt merchants, who in turn installed them in their gardens.[62] The Qianlong emperor generated far more inscriptions and poems for the famous sites of Yangzhou than his grandfather had done: there are twenty-six double-sided pages in the "Imperial Quill" section of the *Illustrated Gazetteer of Pingshan Hall* (Pingshan tang tuzhi), compared to the Kangxi emperor's two. The Imperial Quill section of the *Illustrated Gazetteer* tells us which gardens received imperial inscriptions and, in many cases, how and where these inscriptions were displayed. The editor also lists gifts of stone carvings, snuff bottles, snuff, jade scepters, embroidered bags, and other small

items. Interestingly, he does not give the personal names of the many officials and merchants who received tokens of the emperor's favor, listing
only gifts related to gardens and pavilions. Thus he privileges the sites and
reinforces the imperial connection to them, at the same time masking the
owners, even though their identities were common knowledge. The Yangzhou landscape thus was rewritten in the imperial hand. Inscriptions and
poetry cemented the relationship between the city, its leading institution
the salt monopoly, and the imperial center.

The Qianlong emperor himself exercised at least some supervision over
the design and construction of sites prepared for the tours, though the merchants provided the inspiration and the cash. In an edict from 1755, the
emperor commanded that drawings for new buildings for the second tour
be submitted for his inspection.[63] Provincial officials submitted memorials reporting on the preparations and sent detailed status reports, price
estimates, models, and illustrations for imperial approval.[64] A likely example of a painting submitted with a memorial reporting on preparations
for the second or third tour is the handscroll "Imperial Villas and Famous
Sights of Yangzhou" (Yangzhou xinggong mingsheng tu), currently held
in the First Historical Archives in Beijing.[65] This blue and green landscape
painting depicts the imperial route with cartouches indicating the names
of the merchants who paid for construction and tabulating the precise
number of structures on each site that each of them funded. In another
example of imperial involvement, the salt commissioner sent samples
of wood being used in the construction of the new villa at Tianning
Temple and the renovation of existing villas at Gaomin Temple, south
of Yangzhou, and Jinshan and Jiaoshan temples near Zhenjiang. He did
so in the name of frugality, while in fact asking for permission to be
extravagant.[66]

The emperor frequently criticized his hosts for excessive spending on
the tours. Although his edicts inveighed against wasteful expenditures
and protested that the merchants should avoid constructing new villas
and lodges, the emperor also explained how such expenditures could be
paid for, citing the enthusiastic participation of the Lianghuai salt merchants. On the one hand, the emperor blamed competition among successive salt censors for the escalating costs of his own entertainment at
Yangzhou, but on the other, at least at first, he repeatedly rewarded those
individuals who helped underwrite the tours with promotions and tax
breaks.[67] The large sums of money that poured into these extravagant
projects generated extraordinary corruption. The cozy relationship between the salt monopoly offices and the emperor became tense, with dis-

astrous consequences for the monopoly officials. The salt commissioner, Lu Jianzeng, who according to Li Dou had been responsible for the construction of the famous twenty-four views, and two other officials, including the salt censor Gao Heng, were arrested and sentenced to death in a huge controversy involving irregularities in the sale and taxation of salt between 1746 and 1767.[68] This crackdown did not put an end to the corruption. A-ke-dang-a, who served as Lianghuai salt commissioner for ten years during Jiaqing and Daoguang periods, was said to have profited greatly from his position, and was known locally as "A, the God of Wealth."[69]

The Qianlong tours as events formed an important part of the larger complex of new sites and cultural markings featured in guidebooks, commemorative publications, and contemporary accounts. First, the emperor's tours were accompanied by public spectacle of unprecedented scale. Second, the emperor's visits affected the ways in which the sites were recorded and seen by other visitors. The much larger imperial entourage of the Qianlong tours consisted of the emperor, high officials, guards, teams of porters, pullers, supervisors, boatloads of horses, imperial guards, stable boys, military personnel, the Grand Secretariat, representatives from the Board of War, an imperial kitchen detail along with sheep or goats, thirty-five milk cows, and three hundred beef cattle, as well as provisions for the livestock.[70] All were carried down the Grand Canal on a flotilla of more than one thousand barges, pulled by a crew of 3,600 men in rotating teams.[71] This created a spectacle for the local people who experienced the emperor's arrival, although in some areas, spectatorship was evidently limited to women who were supervised and organized by soldiers.[72]

When the emperor disembarked at Yangzhou, he followed a route newly paved with patterned bricks and carved stone, which brought the emperor from the dock on the outskirts of town through the streets of the walled city of Yangzhou. All along the route, throngs of onlookers lined the streets and canals. Buildings were decorated with silk streamers, bunting, and decorative fountains. The salt merchants organized theatricals, music performances, and pavilions along the canals to welcome the emperor.[73] Elaborate flower arrangements and auspicious plantings surrounded stages, pavilions, multistoried terraces, and other temporary structures, which consisted of wooden frames covered with multicolored silk decorations and capped with bamboo or enamel tiled roofs. These were furnished and extravagantly decorated with paintings, feathers, real and imitation plants, books, and antiquities; they served as context for performers, both human and mechanical, who were surrounded by swirls of smoke and clouds.[74] "Voluntary" contributions from the Lianghuai salt merchants underwrote the whole production, presumably out of gratitude for tax breaks, promotions, and an increased examination quota for merchant households.

For the 1757 tour alone, the merchants spent 200,000 taels of silver on the construction of garden venues, resting stations, imperial villas, and other destinations.[75] Local efforts and expenditures sometimes reached mythic proportions, even, or especially when, they accorded with imperial tastes or designs. According to local legend, the emperor admired the landscape along the lake at Lotus Nature Temple (formerly Ocean of the Law), commenting that it only lacked a white *dagoba* like the one found in the imperial gardens at Beihai. Eager to impress the emperor, a salt merchant immediately sent to Beijing for the blueprints and paid for the construction of a Mongolian-style structure identical to the one at Beihai; it was built, according to the legend, overnight. The *dagoba* figures prominently in illustrations of Yangzhou's famous sites published during the late Qianlong period. This element, borrowed from a northern landscape and stripped of its original context and religious meaning, seems to signal an intentional architectural convergence between northern capital and local site, extravagantly expressing local allegiance to the imperial center. These elaborate displays can be read as local participation in a culture whose legitimacy derived from proximity to the imperial center.

During the Qianlong period (1736–96), publishers issued guides to the sites of Jiangnan, using the imperial tours and imperial poetry as the principal material. For example, in 1763 the Suzhou native Guo Zhongheng edited and published a pocket-sized edition entitled *Poetry and Illustrations of the Famous Sights of Jiangnan* (Jiangnan mingsheng tuyong), which consisted entirely of the poems written by the Qianlong emperor for presentation to officials and merchants during his first three tours.[76] The cover features a decorative red seal that reads "The Emperor's Writings on the Famous Sights of Jiangsu and Zhejiang Respectfully Recorded from the Third Tour." The book lists or recounts the imperial inscriptions and poetry and also includes descriptions and illustrations of the most important sites. This edition, published only a year after the third tour, seems to assume a popular, or at least a local, audience for imperial compositions, while providing a guide to the sites as they had been imperially seen and inscribed. The table of contents refers to ten Yangzhou sites, at least five of which were newly created for the imperial tours. Two other sites merit illustrations and detailed descriptions due to special imperial

FIGURE 5.1. White Dagoba and Lotus (Five Pavilions) Bridge in 2000. Photo: Ming-Yuen Meyer-Fong.

attention. One of these was Pingshan Hall, and the other, Tianning Temple, the site of a new imperial lodge constructed in honor of the second tour in 1757. These descriptions are accompanied by poems written by the emperor and presented to the "Park Lords," as the emperor rather obliquely referred to his merchant hosts. The imperial sightseer, as well as the sights seen, became part of the spectacle, something that could be marketed to visitors and souvenir seekers.

Other books detailed the imperial route as the new authoritative sightseeing itinerary, and explained in their prefaces that the imperial presence had transformed and given meaning to the local landscape. The Qianlong era tours are, as we have seen, featured extensively in the *Record of the Painted Boats of Yangzhou*, which begins, after all, with the imperial sightseeing route. Yuan Mei and Ruan Yuan, who wrote prefaces for Li Dou, also refer to the imperial visit as a transformative event.[77] Other books detailed the imperial route as the new authoritative sightseeing itinerary, and explained in their prefaces that the imperial presence had transformed and given meaning to the local landscape. The *Illustrated Gazetteer of Pingshan Hall* (Pingshantang tuzhi), compiled by the salt controller Zhao Zhibi, was published locally under official auspices between the fourth and fifth tours of the Qianlong emperor, in 1765. The book covers the imperial tours extensively in the prefaces, the text, and the illustrations and seems in some ways more like a commemorative volume than a guidebook.[78] The first section of the book after the table of contents is a catalogue of imperial calligraphy, poetry, and gifts bestowed on sites (mainly temples and gardens) around the city by the Kangxi and Qianlong emperors, including, where relevant, the locations at which imperial writings were displayed in pavilions. The next section consists of a map and sixty-seven double-pages of illustrations showing the main sightseeing routes in the suburbs west of the city. The longest illustration follows the lake/canal to Pingshan Hall, traces the footpaths around Shu Ridge, and returns to Nine Peaks Garden (Jiufeng yuan) by boat. The remaining two illustrations depict gardens along the east and west bank of the Welcoming Benevolence Canal (Ying'en he). Not simply conventional sightseeing itineraries, these were the very imperial route later described by Li Dou in the first chapter of the *Record of the Painted Boats of Yangzhou*. The remainder of the book is dedicated to brief introductions of the various scenic sights around the lake and Shu Ridge, followed by collected essays and poems about these sights.

The local gazetteer published in 1810 similarly gives pride of place to documents associated with the imperial tours, stating that Yangzhou's fame derived from its position as an imperial destination as well as its important status as both a transport hub and a center of the salt monopoly.[79] Even as local official and commercial outfits produced guides featuring the imperial sightseer, the court publishing house also produced many commemorative publications featuring the sites of the south. In these works, imperial inscriptions and poems appear with the descriptive text.[80] The Qianlong emperor, and his words, became part of the landscape, and Yangzhou, once the ground of historical imagination and literary sociability, was at least rhetorically transformed into a playground of the rich and the royal.

The Temple and the Tours, Part 2

Beginning in 1757, with the second tour, Tianning Temple became the epicenter of imperial influence in the locale, the proximate point from which imperial taste emanated to reshape the local landscape. The spectacle of the Qianlong emperor's later tours unfolds against the backdrop of Tianning Temple and the adjacent imperial lodge, even as the political and economic relationships between city and throne were mediated through the Lianghuai salt merchants whose wealth underwrote the lodge's construction. The lodge itself included decorative, residential, and leisure components: ornamental arches, massive gates, a front hall, a sleeping hall, an inner hall, and a rather large garden complete with pavilions, rockeries, and plantings. Other functional elements of the lodge included a large kitchen, located at the front near the canal, probably for convenient transport of food supplies, and two rows of guardhouses along the east and west sides of the complex. An imperial boating dock was located just in front of the main gate. This evidently facilitated the arrivals and departures of the entourage and its supplies by the convenient water route.

The presence of the emperor and his entourage at Tianning Temple stimulated construction in the neighborhoods closest to the temple, both in the northern district of the New City, and in the neighborhood just north of the city wall. In the *Record of the Painted Boats of Yangzhou,* Li Dou highlights the Northern-style features of several buildings in the neighborhood surrounding Tianning Temple. Li Dou explains that the Buddhist images in Zhongning Temple, built during the age of the Qianlong tours, reflected the methods of the palace workmen, whereas the city's other famous temples (built in an earlier period) were inspired by Suzhou styles. Inscriptions in Tibetan as well as Chinese adorned the walls of Zhongning Temple, alluding to imperial patronage of Tantric Buddhism and the Central Asian influences that were a hallmark of the expansiveness of the Qianlong court.[81] Markets to supply the imperial entourage were set up along the canal between Tianning (Gongchen) Gate and North Gate. These markets were explicitly modeled after neighborhoods in the capital. For example, the residential buildings imitated merchant houses in the Drum Tower neighborhood of Beijing, and other structures resembled the stalls near Qianmen, the famous shopping area in the Han Chinese district of Beijing.[82] Despite its commercial function, this scene was packaged as an imperial sightseeing venue, given the name "Prosperous Markets and Storied Buildings," and featured in illustrated books commemorating the imperial tours. Ten buildings intended to house officials from the imperial entourage were built to resemble the official buildings in the imperial hunting park on the outskirts of Beijing. Because the Southern tours occasioned widespread construction and renovation, Beijing-style architecture permeated certain neighborhoods in Yangzhou in direct response to the aesthetic and practical concerns associated with hosting the emperor and his entourage.

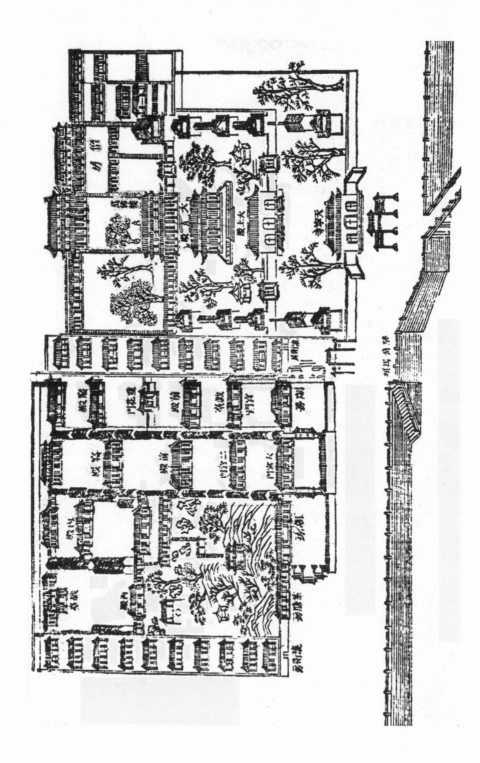

The use of Beijing models affected construction methods as well as style. Armies of convicts participated in the construction of the docks, pavilions, and temples. They were organized into brigades supervised by soldiers, and they wore uniforms identifying them by unit and by garrison. The salt administration (which was itself directly under the Imperial Household administration) provided rations, and the merchants provided money and materials.[83] An edict expressly forbidding local officials and salt merchants from communicating with court eunuchs highlights the close ties, and corrupting influences, which linked the Imperial Household and the local construction projects.[84] Methods used to control workers, artisans, and traders in the Forbidden City were applied to tour-related construction projects. In the Forbidden City, for instance, the Imperial Household Department issued identification cards to temporary employees.[85] In a parallel move in Yangzhou the salt control censor issued identification cards to the merchants, their friends, relatives, servants, cooks, woodcarvers, and actors who had access to the sites. These were to be shown and stamped as they came and went.[86] This parallel highlights the close relationship between the Imperial Household Department and the salt monopoly administration: not only did it oversee the monopoly, but it cooperated closely with the monopoly in organizing the Southern Tours. The use of similar methods and personnel also may indicate that tour-related construction functioned as an extension of the palace and garden building that occurred during the Qianlong period in Beijing and beyond.

The imperial lodge at Tianning Temple remained a symbol of the court's presence as cultural arbiter in the locale even after the last Southern Tour had come to an end. In 1782, the emperor proclaimed that part of the imperially commissioned mega-collectanea, *The Complete Book of the Four Treasuries* (Siku quanshu), had been completed. The emperor commissioned three extra sets of this massive collection to be installed in Yangzhou, Zhenjiang, and Hangzhou, where they could serve the local people's "love of learning and culture." The imperial edict provided specifications for special pavilions to house the books, all of which were to be located in former imperial lodges. The cost of labor and supplies to refit these buildings as libraries was to be covered by donations from the Lianghuai salt merchants and their Hangzhou counterparts. In Yangzhou, the emperor designated a building on the grounds of the imperial flower garden in the Tianning Temple imperial villa, renamed Wenhui ge, as the

FIGURE 5.2. (Opposite) Tianning Temple and Imperial Lodge. Woodblock illustration. Source: Gao Jin et al., *Nanxun shengdian*, 97:12b–13a.

repository for the collection. It was, in a controlled fashion, to be open to local scholars. After all, the edict points out, the books were placed in the locale not for storage but for use in scholarship, and local officials should not be too protective of them. The resulting scholarship, the emperor remarked, would enhance the glory of his reign.[87] The *Siku quanshu* collection itself was a symbol of the monumentalist cultural and intellectual impulses of the Qianlong court—and a symbol of Chinese official and intellectual participation in the court's hegemonizing impulses. The creation of a library for the *Siku quanshu* collection on the grounds of Tianning Temple completed the intrusion of a locally financed court culture into the Yangzhou landscape. By the mid-Qianlong period, the sources of prestige and legitimacy emanated from the court or were generated locally.

But Yangzhou's preeminence was not to last, for the storied wealth of the salt merchants had dissipated by the mid-nineteenth century, and the transformations wrought by the Southern Tours lasted barely past the end of the Qianlong emperor's reign. Writing in the late nineteenth century, Jin Anqing commented that Yangzhou's famous sites had consisted of gardens and pavilions. Even though these were all man-made, they were of extraordinary craftsmanship and each was unique, and moreover, "without the concentrated material wealth and human talents of the sixty year Qianlong reign, none of this would have been easy to achieve." He continues, writing that "during the Jiaqing reign of twenty five years, they had gradually begun to fall into ruin." When Jin visited in 1819, he saw several of the gardens, still gorgeous, but he calculates that only 50 or 60 percent remained of what had been there before. When he returned in 1838, after the restructuring of the Lianghuai salt monopoly, he found that many sights were overgrown with grass.[88] Still, those located beyond Tianning Gate were in good condition, and during the summer months leisure seekers continued to crowd the lake in pursuit of seasonal pleasures. He notes that at that time, Ruan Yuan was still alive. He was quite elderly, but he sometimes toured the hills by palanquin with two or three friends, resting at one of the famous vistas constructed in honor of the Qianlong emperor's Southern Tours. Jin describes Ruan Yuan's activities nostalgically, saying that these old men together were truly "a much told tale of a more peaceful time." He concludes by saying that "the Taiping rebels wreaked havoc here, and destroyed all of the famous sites."[89] Tianning Temple was no exception. A monk at the temple challenged the rebels who occupied the city in 1853. He was killed and the temple was burned. Later, another monk began the process of reconstruction, rebuilding some parts of the temple, including the gate, the meditation hall, the vegetarian kitchens, and a pavilion honoring Guanyin. He added a repository for the scattered bones of people who had died in the recent fighting.[90]

Conclusion

In the mid-seventeenth century, the city of Yangzhou, devastated by war, became the setting for a recovery and reinvention that operated on architectural, cultural, social, and psychic levels. There, a community of elites struggled to reestablish a sense of their social worth and self-esteem—a struggle for dominance—however much it was poetically veneered. Throughout, we have seen how places acquired significance through literary activities and social gatherings, and the ways in which cultural conventions from the past were recycled for new purposes. Values represented by seventeenth-century writers as timeless, universal, and at the same time historically referenced were given physical form in buildings. These sites in turn provided richly imagined settings for the leisure gatherings and literary activities that helped define the elite community. By alluding to a transregional heritage, these sites also served as building blocks in the emerging relationship between the center and the locale. By the middle of the next century, the relationship between the center and locale had changed, and court culture quite literally was inscribed on the Yangzhou landscape. The exquisite gave way to the spectacular as an architecture of historical imagination was replaced by an architecture of cosmopolitan preoccupations. The imperial court appropriated southern taste and imposed courtly spectacle on it. Merchant wealth underwrote this change.

By the middle of the eighteenth century, the quest for imperial recognition combined with the garden building frenzy of wealthy merchants to transform Yangzhou's scenic district. Leisure spaces, once the domain of nostalgic survivors, were reconfigured to reflect the tastes of conspicuously consuming mercantile and imperial patrons. The landscape described in mid-eighteenth century accounts thus feels quite different from the earlier setting, both in its physical elements and in its atmosphere. Spatially, it is the same suburban landscape northwest of the city wall that was described by Kong Shangren and other seventeenth-century men. The main touring itinerary still followed the canal past Red (now Rainbow) Bridge to Baozhang Lake and onward to Pingshan Hall, but many of the intermediate sites had been renamed and embellished to create new effects, and new landscape elements had been added along the way. These are the sites written onto ivory gaming tiles as the twenty-four views of Qianlong-era Yangzhou featured in the *Record of the Painted Boats of Yangzhou* and the *Illustrated Gazetteer of Pingshan Hall*. Each prospect had a glamorous four-character name that advertised its charms: for example, "Rosy Clouds Approach the Waters," "Dazzling Snow at Flat Ridge," and "Spring Flows and Pleasure Boats." In addition, a channel was dredged to create a water route to Pingshan Hall, thereby conveniencing both the Qianlong emperor's imperial barge and ordinary pleasure boats. New boat docks opened at various scenic spots along the narrow lake, facilitating additional boat rentals and boat traffic. Shops selling wine, tea, picnic supplies, and souvenirs opened near the boat landings in order to assist the more perfect excursion.

Merchant money also contributed to the emergence of a complex service economy and elaborate patronage networks. This is the Yangzhou of the *Record of the Painted Boats of Yangzhou* and the commercial economy discussed in much of the current scholarship. Wine shops, bathhouses, restaurants, boat rental operations, inns, haberdasheries, lantern rental stands, teahouses, and shops of every type imaginable proliferated throughout the city, especially at major intersections and along sightseeing routes. Artists flocked to the city in search of patrons and sales. Local drama flourished at established sites around the city. Merchant affluence penetrated many aspects of urban life ranging from community welfare projects to the patronage of famous sites. In this context, even poetry clubs were underwritten by merchants. Certain members of the merchant community assimilated elegantly to literati culture even as their participation redefined that culture. These men assembled poets, gentlemen, and scholars to adorn their garden gatherings.[91] They used money to create a layer of patronage, buying a role for themselves in elite leisure activities. Thus merchants adopted, and thereby changed, the gestures of elite identity creation we saw in the preceding chapters.

As we have seen, during the late seventeenth century a community of highly mobile official and literary elites created a new, historically referenced image for the city, using Yangzhou to reenact their memories of late Ming Jiangnan. In the process, they drew upon a transregional class culture, creating links to local sites. During the eighteenth century, these practices changed in meaning, as merchant patrons inserted themselves into elite social networks and appropriated for themselves many of the sightseeing and renovation practices of the earlier period. In addition, they justified their beautification and construction projects not in terms of a shared historical or literary heritage, but rather in terms of a traveling emperor's interests. Ancient names lost much of their resonance as merchant wealth underwrote the construction of unprecedented sites whose fame derived exclusively from their novelty and glamor. The merchants who built these sites performed elite identity in ways that will seem familiar: they went to similar places, gathered, wrote poetry, drank, and honored many of the same historical figures. And yet, their performances had a different focus, and they were acted out with one eye to the political center and another to the actors' own economic and social advancement.

Glossary

Baimen 白門
Baoqin xi wutong tu 抱琴洗梧桐圖
Baoying 寶應
Baozhang hu 保障湖
Bao Zhao 鮑照
Beihai 北海
Bian Sanyuan 卞三元
Bo Juyi 白居易
Boxue hongci 博學宏詞

Cao Rong 曹溶
Cao Xian 曹憲
Cao Xuequan 曹學佺
Cao Yin 曹寅
Chen Jiru 陳繼儒
Chen Tingjing 陳廷敬
Chen Weisong 陳維崧
Chen Yunheng 陳允衡
Chengde 承德
Cheng Kunlun 程崑崙
Cheng Mengxing 程夢星
Chengnan yaji 城南雅集
Cheng Sui 程邃
Chongcheng he 重城河
ci 詞
Ciren si 慈仁寺
Cui Hua 崔華

Daming si 大明寺
Dailou guan 待漏館
Daohong 道弘
Deng Hanyi 鄧漢儀
Dongguan dajie 東關大街
Donglin 東林
Dong Yining 董以寧

Dong Zhongshu 董仲舒
Dongzi ci 董子祠
Du Jun 杜濬
Du Mu 杜牧

Ershisi qiao 二十四橋

Fahai si 法海寺
Fang Bao 方苞
Fang Yizhi 方以智
Fei Mi 費密
fengliu 風流
Feng Menglong 馮夢龍
fengya 風雅
Fushe 復社

Ganquan 甘泉
Gao Heng 高恆
Gao Jie 高傑
Gaomin si 高旻寺
Gaoyou 高郵
Gongchen men 拱辰門
Gongde yuan 功德院
Gong Dingzi 龔鼎孳
Gu Ling 顧苓
Gu Yanwu 顧炎武
Guazhou 瓜洲
Guanyin ge 觀音閣
Guangchu men 廣儲門
Guangling 廣陵
Guo Zhongheng 郭衷恆

Hanshan si 寒山寺
Hanshang shenglan tu 邗上勝
覽圖

Han Yu 韓愈
Hexia 河下
Hongqiao 紅橋 / 虹橋
huaigu 懷古
huaijiu 懷舊
Huang Yun 黃雲
Hui Dong 惠棟
Huijue 慧覺
Huizhou 徽州
Huizong 徽宗

Jizhao yuan 寂照院
Jiankang 建康
Jiangdu 江都
Jiangnan 江南
Jiangning 江寧
Jiaoshan 焦山
Jin Anqing 金安清
Jinling 金陵
Jinshan 金山
Jin Zhen 金鎮
jing 景
Jingzhong jiaosi 旌忠教寺
Jingzhong miao 旌忠廟
Jiufeng yuan 九峰園
jueju 絕句
jun 君

Kong Shangren 孔尚任

Lanting 蘭亭
Lei Shijun 雷士俊
Li Dou 李斗
Li Shan 李善
Li Songyang 李嵩陽
Li Tingzhi 李庭芝
Li Xu 李煦
Li Yesi 李鄴嗣
Liyun 禮運
Li Zicheng 李自成
Lianxing si 蓮性寺
Lianghuai 兩淮

Lin Gudu 林古度
Liu Chang 劉敞
Liu Kun 劉琨
Liuzhuangchang 劉莊場
Lu Jianzeng 盧見曾
Lu You 陸游
Luochun tang 洛春堂

Mao Danshu 冒丹書
Mao Qiling 毛奇齡
Mao Xiang 冒襄
Meihua ling 梅花嶺
Mei Qing 梅清
Milou 迷樓
mingsheng 名勝

Ouyang Xiu 歐陽修

Peng Gui 彭桂
Peng Sunyu 彭孫遹
Pingshan tang 平山堂

Qianmen 前門
Qian Qianyi 錢謙益
Qin Guan 秦觀
qing 情
Qingming 清明
Qionghua guan 瓊花觀
Qu Yuan 屈原

Rugao 如皋
Ruan Wenda gong yishi shijing
 阮文達公遺事十景
Ruan Yuan 阮元

Sanbao 三保
Sancha he 三岔河
Sang Zhi 桑芝
Shexian 歙縣
Shen Deqian 沈德潛
Shen Gua 沈括
Shenmo tang 慎墨堂

Shi Kefa 史可法
Shi Runzhang 施閏章
Shi Shilun 施世綸
Shouxihu 瘦西湖
Shugang 蜀岡
Siku quanshu 四庫全書
Sima Guang 司馬光
Song Lao 宋犖
Su Shi 蘇軾
Sui Yangdi 隋煬帝
Sun Jinli 孫金礪
Sun Mo 孫默
Sun Zhiwei 孫枝蔚

Taixing 泰興
Taizhou 泰州
Tan Qian 談遷
Tao Yuanming 陶淵明
Tianning si 天寧寺
Tongzhou 通州
tuiguan 推官

Wang Anshi 王安石
Wang Fang 王方
Wang Guan 王觀
Wang Jun 汪鋆
Wang Maolin 汪懋麟
Wang Qilin 汪起麟
Wang Rujiang 汪如江
Wang Shilu 王士祿
Wang Shizhen (1526–1590) 王世貞
Wang Shizhen (1634–1711) 王士禛
Wang Shizhen fangxian tu 王士禛
   放鷴圖
Wang Wan 汪琬
Wang Weixin 王維新
Wang Xizhi 王義之
Wang Xiuchu 王秀楚
Wang Yan 王巖
Wang Yaolin 汪耀麟
Wang Yinggeng 汪應庚
Wang Youdan 王又旦

Wang Youding 王猶定
Wang Zhaolin 汪兆麟
Wang Zhenlin 汪振麟
Wei Jun 魏俊
Wei Xi 魏禧
Weiyang 維揚
Wenchang 文昌
Wenfeng ta 文峰塔
Wenhui ge 文匯閣
Wenxuan 文選
Wenxuan lou 文選樓
Wucheng 蕪城
Wu Qi 吳綺
Wu Sangui 吳三桂
Wu Weiye 吳偉業

Xia Quan 夏荃
Xia Renquan 夏人佺
Xiao Qinhuai 小秦淮
Xiao Tong 蕭統
Xie An 謝安
Xinghua 興化
Xu Chengjia 許承家
Xu Chengxuan 許承宣
Xu Qianxue 徐乾學
Xu Xiake 徐霞客

Yanzi ji 燕子磯
Yangzhou 揚州
Yangzhou xinggong mingsheng tu
   揚州行宮名勝圖
Yaohua ji 瑤華集
Yechun 冶春
Yihong yuan 倚虹園
yimin 遺民
Yizheng 儀徵
Ying'en he 迎恩河
Yingyuan 影園
you 游 / 遊
You Tong 尤侗
Yu Huai 余懷
Yu Zhiding 禹之鼎

Yuyang　漁洋
Yuan Hongdao　袁宏道
Yuan Mei　袁枚
Yuan Yao　袁耀
Yuan Yuling　袁于令
Yue Fei　岳飛
yuefu　樂府

Zeng Xian　曾銑
Zha Jizuo　查繼佐
Zhang Chao　張潮
Zhang Feng　張風
Zhang Wangsun　張網孫
Zhaodai congshu　昭代叢書
Zhao Hongji　趙洪極
Zhaoming taizi　照明太子

Zhao Zhibi　趙之壁
Zhenhuai men　鎮淮門
Zhenjiang　鎮江
Zhenshang lou　真賞樓
Zheng Chenggong　鄭成功
Zheng Xie　鄭燮
Zheng Yuanxun　鄭元勳
Zhongning si　重寧寺
Zhong Xing　鍾惺
Zhou Lianggong　周亮工
Zhuxi ting　竹西亭
Zhu Yizun　朱彝尊
Zong Guan　宗觀
Zong Yuanding　宗元鼎
Zong Yuandu　宗瑗度
Zou Zhimo　鄒祗謨

Notes

1. For an excellent discussion of buildings, writing, elite identity, and ideology, see Katherine Carlitz, "Shrines, Governing-Class Identity, and the Cult of Widow Fidelity in Mid-Ming Jiangnan," *Journal of Asian Studies* 56, no. 3 (August 1997): 612–40.

2. This pairing is a standard motif in Chinese poetry criticism. For a discussion of its importance, see Hans H. Frankel, *The Flowering Plum and the Palace Lady* (New Haven: Yale University Press, 1976), 1.

3. According to Susan Naquin, the term *mingsheng,* meaning famous sights, entered common parlance in the late Ming, through the influence of the literatus Cao Xuequan. See her *Peking: Temples and City Life* (Berkeley: University of California Press, 2000), 254.

4. The poetry that these visitors were inspired to compose is included with the gazetteer entry for each destination. Additional site-centered poems are found in the literary sections, where they are divided by genre. See Jin Zhen, ed., YZFZ, 1675, fanli, 2b.

5. Antonia Finnane, "Prosperity and Decline under the Qing: Yangzhou and Its Hinterland, 1644–1810" (Ph.D. diss., Australian National University, 1987), 100; and Finnane, "Yangzhou: A Central Place in the Qing Empire," in Linda Cooke Johnson, ed., *Cities of Jiangnan in Late Imperial China* (Albany: State University of New York Press, 1993), 122.

6. Qin Guan, "*Yangzhou ji* xu" (Preface to the Yangzhou Collection), in *Huai-hai ji* (Gaoyou: Wangshi kanben, 1837), 17:19b–20b. This essay also appears in the various editions of the Yangzhou gazetteer. See, for example, YZFZ, 1733, 37:14b–15b.

7. The city was also known as Guangling during the Warring States, Han, Six Dynasties, and part of the Tang.

8. See Yudi Yuanming, "Yangzhou cheng de lishi bianqian—Zhongguo gucheng bolan suoying," in Feng Erkang, ed., *Yangzhou yanjiu—Jiangdu Chen Yiqun xiansheng bailing mingdan jinian lunwen ji* (Taipei: Chen Jie xiansheng chuban, 1996), 118 ff.

9. Yudi Yuanming, "Yangzhou cheng de lishi bianqian," 120.

10. The walled area of the early Qing city was approximately two-thirds the size of the Song city. F. W. Mote describes Suzhou as having basically the same form from 1229 to 1945. By comparison, Yangzhou seems morphologically unstable. See Mote's "A Millennium of Chinese Urban History: Form, Time, and Space Concepts in Soochow," *Rice University Studies* 59, no. 4 (fall 1973): 39.

11. Wang Zhenzhong, "Ming-Qing Huishang yu Yangzhou chengshi wenhua de tezheng he diwei," in *Yangzhou yanjiu,* 492. Wang cites the *Ming Taizu shilu,* juan 5, and the Jiajing *Weiyang zhi,* juan 8. For an early Qing reference, see Gu Yanwu, *Tianxia junguo libing shu* (Shanghai: Erlin zhai, 1899), 28:1b.

12. See "Yangzhou fu xinzhu waicheng ji" (Yangzhou prefecture builds a new outer wall), in *YZFZ,* 1733, 5:3a–4a. See also Wang Zhenzhong, "Ming-Qing Lianghuai yanshang yu Yangzhou chengshi de diyu jiegou," *Lishi dili* 10 (1992): 104.

13. *YZFZ,* 1810, 60:3b, citing the Wanli edition of the Jiangdu county gazetteer. The city's spatial layout and functional distribution were retained under the Qing.

14. *YZFZ,* 1810, 60:3b.

15. Antonia Finnane, discussing Yangzhou's role as mediator between North and South China, states that "the emergence of this flourishing town was clearly a function of the unification of North and South China" (Finnane, "Yangzhou: A Central Place," 120–21). Her dissertation offers a detailed account of the city's history, particularly the city's sensitivity to political and economic forces affecting the empire as a whole. See Finnane, "Prosperity and Decline," chap. 1.

16. Perhaps because of this striking duality, Stephen Owen uses the example of Yangzhou to illustrate his discussion of writings about cities in his monumental anthology of Chinese literature. See Owen, *An Anthology of Chinese Literature* (New York: W. W. Norton, 1996), 630–35.

17. Nostalgic poetry about the "Weed-Covered City" fell out of fashion in the eighteenth century. The theme resurfaced in the nineteenth century, after the city was badly damaged during the Taiping War.

18. For a brief biography of Bao Zhao, see William Nienhauser, ed., *Indiana Companion to Traditional Chinese Literature* (Bloomington: Indiana University Press, 1986), 649.

19. See, for example, Wang Shizhen's poem "Yingyuan huaigu" (Embracing the past at Firefly Park), in *YZFZ,* 1810, 31:12b. Note too that in Chinese poetry, ruins are conventionally portrayed as overgrown with vegetation, rather than as collapsing structures.

20. The name "Jiangdu" subsequently was recycled as the name of a county, although the implication of "capital" of course was lost after the Sui.

21. Sima Guang, *Zizhi tongjian* (Comprehensive mirror for aid in government), cited in *YZFZ,* 1810, 65:42a. Translation from Finnane, "Prosperity and Decline," 31.

22. Owen, *Anthology of Chinese Literature,* 631. Owen includes in his anthology translations of five of Du Mu's most famous Yangzhou poems. Note that there are several versions of this poem extant, with variant characters in almost every line. Still, the overall sense of the poem remains consistent and is well represented by the Owen translation. For a line-by-line textual comparison, see Wei Minghua, *Yangzhou wenhua tanpian* (Beijing: Sanlian shudian), 110.

23. For discussion of this literary theme, see Wei Minghua, *Yangzhou wenhua tanpian,* 109–27. A passage from one such work, Yu Ye's (fl. 867) "Yangzhou

meng ji" (Record of a Yangzhou dream), is included as Du Mu's biography in the entry on Yangzhou in the *Fangyu shenglan*, the Song-dynasty guide to the famous sites of the realm. See Zhu Mu, *Songben fangyu shenglan* (Shanghai: Shanghai guji chubanshe, 1991), 504.

24. According to Susan Naquin, the damage to the capital was not extensive. See *Peking*, 289.

25. On the social effects of the Qing conquest in Jiangnan and the formation of militias and bandit gangs, see Kishimoto Mio, "Min-shin kōtaiki no Kōnan sha-kai," *Rekishi to chiri* 483 (November 1995): 4. On gentry-led militias in the Huai River region, see Frederic Wakeman, Jr., *The Great Enterprise* (Berkeley: University of California Press, 1985), 329. On armed conflict between military and civilian groups in the Huai River region, see Lynn Struve, *The Southern Ming, 1644–1666* (New Haven: Yale University Press, 1984), 24–25.

26. Kishimoto Mio, "Min-shin kōtaiki no Kōnan shakai," 5.

27. The four were Liu Zeqing, Liu Liangzuo, Huang Degong, and Gao Jie. See Wakeman, *Great Enterprise*, 327–29, 347–51; *ECCP*, 524–25, 531–32, 348–49, and 410–11.

28. Gao Jie had been a follower of Li Zicheng. The two had a falling-out after Gao ran off with Li's wife in 1635. See *ECCP*, 410.

29. Struve, *Southern Ming*, 25.

30. The Hanlin academician Wang Maolin describes his childhood experiences as a refugee at the seashore in his "Liuzhuang ganjiu" (Remembering the past at Liuzhuang), *Baichi wutongge shiji* (reprint, Shanghai: Shanghai guji chubanshe, 1980), 6:10b–11a.

31. The murdered envoy, Zheng Yuanxun, was a man of considerable stature in the local community. A holder of the jinshi degree and the scion of a wealthy merchant family, he owned "The Garden of Shadows and Reflections," which had been named and inscribed by the renowned art critic Dong Qichang. Zheng also was a member of the Fushe (Restoration Society). On his parley with Gao Jie and his demise, see Dai Mingshi, "Yangzhou chengshou jilue" (A brief account of the defense of Yangzhou), in Chen Henghe, *Yangzhou congke* (1930–34; reprint, Yangzhou: Guangling guji keyinshe, 1995), 2b–3a. See also Wakeman, *Great Enterprise*, 351.

32. For women who committed suicide to avoid rape at the hands of Gao Jie's forces or who died trying to escape, see YZFZ, 1675, 27:34a–34b.

33. Dai Mingshi, "Yangzhou chengshou jilue," 3a.

34. Wakeman, *Great Enterprise*, 547. Note that Wakeman estimates an urban population of more than one million. This seems high—other scholars estimate the population of the city and its surrounding prefecture as one million.

35. See Lynn Struve's translation of Wang Xiuchu's "Yangzhou shiri ji" (Record of ten days at Yangzhou) in her *Voices from the Ming-Qing Cataclysm* (New Haven: Yale University Press, 1993), 33. These hurriedly built gunnery platforms were to prove unstable during the Qing assault: many of the soldiers manning the guns and keeping watch from the walls died when the platforms collapsed.

36. Wakeman, *Great Enterprise*, 549, n. 122. According to Wakeman, the

Qing army led by Dodo included nearly 250,000 Han Chinese troops, many of whom had defected from the guardian generals' armies.

37. For these and comparable examples, see YZFZ, 1675, 25:13a–14a.

38. YZFZ, 1675, 27:24b–41a. For Wang Yan's essay, see YZFZ, 1675, 27:36b–37a.

39. Martino Martini, S.J., "De Bello Tartarico Historia," in Novus Atlas Sinensis (Trento: Museo Tridentino di Scienze Naturali, 1981), originally published in 1655. The "History of the Tartar Wars" was published separately from the atlas, which was published one year later in Amsterdam. Translations soon followed in Italian, German, Dutch, French, and English. By the standards of mid-seventeenth century Europe, "History of the Tartar Wars" was an international bestseller. For Martini's biographical information, see Xu Mingde, "The Outstanding Contribution of the Italian Sinologist Martino Martini to Cultural Exchange between China and the West," in Franco Demarchi and Riccardo Scartezzini, eds., Martino Martini: A Humanist and Scientist in Seventeenth Century China (Trento: University of Trent, 1996), 23–39. I would like to thank Father John Witek, S.J., for helping me translate this passage from the Latin.

40. Wang Maolin, a Qing official from Yangzhou, describes his parents' experience during the conquest in several of his collected poems and essays. See Chapter 4 for a more detailed discussion. The gazetteer provides descriptions of the massacre in several biographies of filial sons and chaste women. See, for example, the biography of Guo Shizhang, who saved his father and six other men, pulling several of them out from under a pile of corpses (YZFZ, 1733, 32:15a–15b).

41. Lucien Mao's translation of the title as "A Memoir of the Ten Days' Massacre at Yangchow" is misleading, though typical of a widespread misconception. The killing lasted for six, not ten, days. Wang Xiuchu, "A Memoir of the Ten Days' Massacre at Yangchow," Lucien Mao, trans., T'ien-hsia Monthly 4, no. 5 (May 1937): 515–37.

42. Wei Minghua, Yangzhou wenhua tanpian, 177.

43. It is featured prominently in Frederic Wakeman's Great Enterprise and in an abridged translation in Struve, Voices from the Ming-Qing Cataclysm (New Haven: Yale University Press, 1984). There is also a French translation: Wang Xiuchu, "Journal d'un bourgeois de Yang-tcheou (1645)," trans. P. Aucourt, Bulletin de l'Ecole Francaise d'Extreme Orient 7 (1907): 297–312.

44. Lucien Mao's translation, however, is more inflammatory in tone than the original, which recognizes the presence of many Han soldiers in the Qing army. For example, where the original reads "da bing" (great or [imperial] soldiers), Mao's translation has "savage soldiers." He also adds the word "Manchu" where it does not appear in the original. For example, his translation, "The report that the Manchu soldiers were to kill everyone in the city" (emphasis added), should actually be read, "The report that the whole city was to be wiped out." See Wang Xiuchu, "Yangzhou shiri ji, Hanying duizhao" (A record of ten days at Yangzhou, Chinese-English bilingual edition), Lucien Mao, trans., in Lin Yutang, ed., Xifeng congshu (Shanghai: Xifengshe, 1930), 14–15, 54–55. Wang Xiuchu identifies soldiers dressed in Manchu-style clothing or speaking Manchu, whom he distin-

guishes from the majority of soldiers, who wear ordinary clothing and speak Chinese. The terms used to describe the behavior of the ordinary soldiers are much more "barbaric" than those used for the Manchu officers. See, for example, Wang Xiuchu, "Yangzhou shiri ji," 57.

45. Wang Xiuchu, "An Account of Ten Days at Yangzhou," in Struve, ed., *Voices from the Ming-Qing Cataclysm*, 36.

46. Wang Xiuchu, "Yangzhou shiri ji," 50–51. (Translation modified based on Chinese text.) See also Struve, *Voices from the Ming-Qing Cataclysm*, 45.

47. Wakeman, *Great Enterprise*, 563.

48. Struve suspects the number and reduces it by a factor of ten, to eighty thousand (*Voices from the Ming-Qing Cataclysm*, 48). Wakeman discusses the debate over the death toll in *Great Enterprise*, 563–64, n. 158.

49. In 1645, six natives of Jiangdu county, Yangzhou prefecture, passed the juren examinations, while twelve natives of Yangzhou prefecture passed the metropolitan (jinshi) examinations in 1647. See Finnane, "Prosperity and Decline," 89.

50. YZFZ, 1733, 13:5b.

51. Towers generally symbolized endurance. More specifically, the building celebrated the immortal cultural legacy of the *Wenxuan*. See Chapter 3 for discussion. See also Frankel, *Flowering Plum*, 115.

52. *Yangzhou fuzhi*, 1733, 18:1a. Note that a shrine honoring Shi Shilun, the transport official Cui Hua, and the salt censor Cao Yin was built in 1718 (*YZFZ*, 1733, 25:30b). For a biography of Shi, who was an incorruptible official and the hero of a popular novel as well as the sometime prefectural magistrate of Yangzhou, see Hummel, *ECCP*, 653–54.

53. Finnane, "Yangzhou: A Central Place," 95.

54. The contrast with the Taiping War (1850–64) is instructive. The administrative buildings, including prefectural and county yamens, the salt and transport administration offices, and the prefectural schools, were all wrecked when the Taipings occupied the city in 1853. The 1874 gazetteer describes the processes through which these buildings were restored during the decade between 1864 and 1874 (*YZFZ*, 1874, juan 3).

55. YZFZ, 1810, 45:1b, cites the Kangxi edition of the gazetteer. See also Finnane, "Prosperity and Decline," 67.

56. See Hongnam Kim, *The Life of a Patron: Zhou Lianggong and the Painters of Seventeenth-Century China* (New York: China Institute in America, 1996), 65, which cites Huang Yuji, "Xingzhuang," in Zhou Lianggong, *Laigu tang ji*, "fulu" (appendix), 1675 edition.

57. For discussion of Zhou Lianggong and his activities in Yangzhou, see Kim, *Life of a Patron*, 65.

58. His Liaodong origins are typical of early Qing administrators, most of whom were northerners, though for the first twenty years after the conquest the majority were Han rather than Manchu. The same was also true of officials in the salt monopoly (Finnane, "Prosperity and Decline," 84).

59. YZFZ, 1733, 27:55b.

60. For the involvement of salt merchants in charitable activities before and after the conquest, see the biographies of merchant-philanthropists in *LHYFZ*, juan 23.

61. *YZFZ*, 1733, 32:20a–b.

62. Tan Qian, *Beiyou lu*, Lidai shiliao biji congkan (1960, reprint, Beijing: Zhonghua shuju, 1997), 13.

63. Kishimoto Mio, *Shindai Chūgoku no bukka to keizai hendō* (Tokyo: Kenbun shuppan, 1997), 239. Kishimoto points out that during this period, prices and incomes were in a state of collapse and poverty was a major preoccupation of intellectuals interested in economic issues.

64. Finnane, "Prosperity and Decline," 130; and *YZFZ*, 1685, 10:54a.

65. *YZFZ*, 1685, 10:61b.

66. Jonathan Spence, *Ts'ao Yin and the K'ang-hsi Emperor: Bond Servant and Master* (New Haven: Yale University Press, 1966), 182. A detailed analysis of the Lianghuai salt monopoly is beyond the scope of this study. For further information on this important institution, see Spence, 166–212 and Ho Ping-ti's still-important article, "The Salt Merchants of Yang-chou: A Study of Commercial Capitalism in Eighteenth-Century China," *Harvard Journal of Asiatic Studies* 17 (1954): 130–68. See also Saeki Tomi, *Shindai ensei no kenkyū* (Kyoto: Tōyōshi kenkyūkai, 1956 and 1962); and Suzuki Tadashi, "Shinsho ryōwai enshō ni kansuru ichikōsatsu," *Shien* 36 (March 1946): 101–134.

67. Spence, *Ts'ao Yin and the K'ang-hsi Emperor*, 183.

68. The merchant representative was Wu Xian, the son of Wu Weiping. This event is recorded in the father's biography in *LHYFZ*, 23:30.

CHAPTER 2

1. Significant portions of this chapter appear also in my article "Making a Place for Meaning in Seventeenth Century Yangzhou," *Late Imperial China* 20, no. 1 (June 1999): 49–84.

2. Dong Yining, "You Chibi ji" (A record of an excursion to Red Cliff), *Dong Wenyou wenxuan*, in *Dong Wenyou quanji*, 1700 ed., juan 15. Dong Yining socialized with Wang Shizhen during Wang's official tenure in Yangzhou. His contemporary You Tong expressed similar sentiments in his preface to Wu Qiushi's *Tianxia mingshan jichao* (Baohan lou, Kangxi period), You preface, 2b.

3. Craig Clunas, *Fruitful Sites* (Durham: Duke University Press, 1996), 31–38.

4. Similar ideas seem to have prevailed in Europe. See Alain Corbin, *The Lure of the Sea: The Discovery of the Seaside in the Western World, 1750–1840*, Jocelyn Phelps, trans. (Berkeley: University of California Press, 1994), 45 ff.

5. See, for example, the commentary on Kong Shangren's "Panghua cun xun mei ji" (Looking for plum blossoms at Panghua Village), in *Huhai ji* (Shanghai: Gudian wenxue chubanshe, 1957), 197. Panghua Village was the name of a wine shop. In his commentary on the sixth lyric of Kong Shangren's "Qingming Hongqiao zhuzhici ershi shou" (Twenty bamboo branch lyrics on Qingming Festival at Red Bridge), Zong Yuanding writes: "Since Mr. Kong invited guests to search for

plum blossoms at Panghua Village, most visitors to Red Bridge stop there on their way home. His literary and drinking parties were praised as the best of the age" (Kong Shangren, *Huhai ji*, 71). In this passage, Zong parallels earlier comments on the effect of Wang Shizhen's parties at Red Bridge on literati touring.

6. Pierre Bourdieu's discussion of the "symbolic production" of a work's value, i.e., the production of "belief in a work," is suggestive on this point. He points out that it is necessary to take into account not only the social conditions behind the production of a work of art but also the social conditions through which a work of art comes to be considered important. The production of symbolic significance for a scenic site, itself partly derived from the importance of cultural works associated with the site, closely parallels the phenomenon described by Bourdieu. See his *The Field of Cultural Production* (New York: Columbia University Press, 1993), 37.

7. Wang Zhenzhong, "Ming Qing Huishang yu Yangzhou chengshi wenhua de tezheng yu diwei," in *Yangzhou yanjiu*, 490 ff.

8. Kong Shangren, "Yu Li Wanpei" (Letter to Li Wanpei), dated 1688, in *Kong Shangren shiwen ji* (Beijing: Zhonghua shuju, 1962), 7:540.

9. Hongnam Kim, *Life of a Patron*, 25–27.

10. Shao Yiping, "Cong *Liechao shiji xiaozhuan* kan wan Ming jingshen de ruogan biaoxian" (Looking at some manifestations of the late-Ming spirit in the *Liechao shiji xiaozhuan*), in Zhang Peiheng, ed., *Mingdai wenxue yanjiu* (Nanchang: Jiangxi renmin chubanshe, 1990), 286 ff. This point can be inferred from quotations that appear in this article in the section on "reckless and romantic behavior" and changing moral attitudes in the late Ming.

11. Jerry Dennerline terms the Fushe (Restoration Society) a "broad coalition of literary societies" that played a major role in the "great factional movement.... in the 1620s and 1630s." See his *The Chia-ting Loyalists* (New Haven: Yale University Press, 1981) 8, 12. For discussion of the Restoration Society's politics, see his pp. 30–42.

12. The contents of the smaller editions of event-associated poetry were later absorbed into the literary collections of individual authors.

13. YZFZ, 1810, 60:2b–3a, cites the Wanli-era *Jiangdu xianzhi*.

14. Shi Kefa's robe and hat were later buried on this same hill, which gave it strong political associations. It was also the site of an important academy, the Plum Blossom Academy, during the eighteenth century.

15. YZFZ, 1810, juan 28. Ten temples were said to have been renovated and one founded during the Hongwu period. Eight temples were founded during the Wanli period, one was restored, and one erected a new stele. While "statistics" generated in this fashion are necessarily suspect, they can be used, I hope, to create a rough overall impression.

16. Wang Zhenzhong, "Ming Qing Huishang yu Yangzhou chengshi wenhua de tezheng he diwei," *Yangzhou yanjiu*, 490–91.

17. Zheng Yuanxun, *zi* Zhaozong, *hao* Huidong. His ancestors came from Shexian (Huizhou), Anhui, but officially his native place was Jiangdu (Yangzhou). He was born into a salt merchant family and had three brothers, each of whom

owned a garden. Discussion of the Zheng brothers and their gardens can be found in the preface to Zheng Qingyou, *Yangzhou Xiuyuan zhi*, Chashi tang, 1773. The Garden of Shadows and Reflections received its name from Dong Qichang, who had visited the garden in the late Ming. For secondary accounts of this gathering, see Zhu Zongzhou, "Hanmo shengxiang de Yangzhou wenren yaji," *Yangzhou shizhi* 32, no. 4 (1994): 87; and Ōki Yasushi, "Kōbotan shikai—Minmatsu Shinsho Kōnan Bunjin Tenbyō," *Tōhōgaku* 99 (January 2000): 33–46. On Zheng's death, see Chapter 1 above.

18. See, for example, Wang Maolin's 1679 poem "Yin moshi jiuyuan kan mudan wan guan nuxi" (Drinking wine in someone's old garden, looking at peonies, and watching a female drama troupe at night), *Baichi wutong ge yigao* (Kangxi edition; reprint, Shanghai: Shanghai guji chubanshe, 1980), 1:3a. See also Wang Ji's poem "Xun Yingyuan jiuzhi" (Looking for the former location of the Garden of Shadows and Reflections), *Huizhai shi*, in *Huizhai ji qizhong*, Kangxi edition, Five-character regulated verse, 4b.

19. Kong Shangren, "Guo Kuangshan *Guangling zengyan* xu" (Preface to Guo Kuangshan's *Guangling zengyan*), in *Huhai ji*, 204.

20. For a detailed discussion of the civil service examinations during the late Ming, see Ōki Yasushi, *Minmatsu no hagure chishiki jin: Fū Bōryū to Soshū bunka* (Tokyo: Kodansha, 1995), 54–92.

21. Herein lies a key difference with Bourdieu's discussion of the relationship between the field of culture and the field of power. Bourdieu describes the field of culture as occupying a dominated position among the dominant classes. However, in the Qing case, cultural and political authority were more closely integrated, and certain highly visible cultural producers were rewarded not simply with prestige, but with political position. Bourdieu, *Field of Cultural Production*, 43.

22. Du Jun, *Bianya tang qianji*, Daoguang reprint, 1:5a. Du describes a visit to Gu's house during which the two old friends knelt before the emperor's calligraphy and wept.

23. On the invention of *"erchen"* during the Qianlong reign, see Andrew Hsieh (Xie Zhengguang), "Gu Yanwu, Cao Rong lunjiao shimo—Ming yimin yu Qingchu dali jiaoyou chutan," *Zhongguo wenhua xuebao* (Hong Kong) n.s. no. 4 (1995): 210. See also Pamela Kyle Crossley, "The Qianlong Retrospect on the Chinese-Martial (hanjun) Banners," *Late Imperial China* 10, no. 1 (June 1989): 93 ff. On the impact of nationalism on the evaluation of the early Qing, see Jiang Yin, "Ming-Qing zhi ji zhishifenzi de mingyun yu xuanze—cong Hou Chaozong de bianjie wenti tanqi," in *Zhongguo zhishifenzi de renwen jingshen* (Henan renmin chubanshe, 1994), 444.

24. Frederic Wakeman, Jr., "Romantics, Stoics, and Martyrs," *Journal of Asian Studies* 43, no. 4 (August 1984): 631–65. Wakeman acknowledges that there was a certain amount of crossover between the categories he outlines. There are striking parallels to the Song case, both in the experience and the hagiography. See also Jennifer Jay, *A Change in Dynasties* (Bellingham: Western Washington University, Center for East Asian Studies, 1991), 245.

25. Andrew Hsieh, "Gu Yanwu, Cao Rong lunjiao shimo," 210.

26. Some such friendships predated the conquest. For example, the "loyalist"

Du Jun's friendship with the "collaborators" Gong Dingzi and Cao Rong dated from his visit to the capital after becoming a juren in 1642. See Du Jun, *Bianya tang quanji*, nianpu (chronological biography), 3a.

27. For a brief history of elite literary and social practice, see Aoki Masaru, "Chūka bunjin no seikatsu," in *Aoki Masaru zenshū*, vol. 7 (Tokyo: Shunju, 1973), 233–38. As part of his broader discussion of the various modes of elite leisure/literary practice, Aoki mentions Wang Shizhen's Red Bridge gatherings as part of a lineage of seasonal gatherings dating back to the Six Dynasties period.

28. You Tong, "Peng Sunyu *Yanlu ci* xu" (Preface to Peng Sunyu's *Yanlu lyrics*), in Sun Mo, *Shiwujia ci* (Sibu beiyao jibu, Shanghai: Zhonghua shuju, 1927–36), 24:1a.

29. In an article aimed at a popular audience, Zhu Zongzhou suggests that Ouyang Xiu made Pingshan Hall a place that every visitor to Yangzhou still must see today, adding that Wang Shizhen did the same for Red Bridge. Zhu Zongzhou, "Wang Shizhen yu Yangzhou," *Zhongguo mingcheng* 32 (March 1995): 48–50.

30. On his social circle in Beijing, see, for example, Song Lao, "Zizheng daifu xingbu shangshu Wang gong Shizhen ji pei Zhang yiren muzhiming" (Tomb inscription for Wang Shizhen, Minister of the Board of Punishments, and his wife nèe Zhang), in Qian Yiji, ed., *Beizhuan ji*, vol. 2 (Beijing: Zhonghua shuju, 1993), 581. Note that Song specifically calls them "the famous gentlemen of the same dynasty."

31. Wang entered the Hanlin Academy by imperial fiat, as a result of his performance during an imperially sponsored poetry competition. He also received numerous gifts from the emperor, notably food and drink. Song Lao, "Zizheng daifu xingbu shangshu Wang gong Shizhen ji pei Zhang yiren muzhiming," 581.

32. The family left their hometown of Xincheng and sought refuge in his mother's hometown of Zouping. An uncle and aunt committed suicide upon learning of the Ming emperor's death; his grandfather retired from office and took the sobriquet "Hidden Gentleman of Ming Farm." Still, the entire family applauded the successes of Wang Shizhen's generation and rewarded their participation in the new government. Wakeman points out that Shandong provided much of the civilian support that staffed the new Qing government in Beijing; he comments that "the sudden prominence of Shandong men in the early Qing was owing in part to the early pacification of their province, and partly to the ready identification of local elites with law and order in rebellious areas." See *Great Enterprise*, 424. For a first-hand account of another family's experiences during the conquest of Shandong, see Timothy Brook, *The Confusions of Pleasure: Commerce and Culture in Ming China* (Berkeley: University of California Press, 1998), 240–44.

33. His grandfather, Wang Xiangqian (d. 1630), was a Ming official who held several important posts, especially in frontier defense. The family produced an impressive ten successful jinshi candidates between 1562 and 1610. See *ECCP*, 820. The eldest brother, Wang Shilu (1626–73), received his jinshi in 1652, and the third brother, Wang Shihu (1633–81), received his in 1670. The second brother, Shixi, was also a poet but never passed the higher level examinations. Wang Shizhen was the most famous of the four.

34. Wang Shizhen, *Wang Shizhen nianpu fu Wang Shilu nianpu* (Beijing: Zhonghua shuju, 1992), 9 (hereafter cited as *WSZNP*). The Zhonghua shuju edition is a modern reprint of the chronological biography that Wang compiled for himself under the title *Yuyang shanren zizhuan nianpu* (Yuyang the recluse's chronological autobiography), along with the biography he compiled for his brother under the title *Wang kaogong nianpu* (Evaluator Wang's chronological biography). Wang completed his autobiography in 1705, when he was seventy-two *sui*. It was published in the Yongzheng period with additional materials by Hui Dong, the grandson of one of Wang's disciples, who edited and published a famous anthology of Wang Shizhen's poetry, *Yuyang shanren jinghua lu xunzuan*.

35. *WSZNP*, 15.

36. For definition of *tuiguan*, see Charles O. Hucker, *A Dictionary of Official Titles in Imperial China* (Stanford: Stanford University Press, 1985), 549.

37. Ciren Temple was a major book market during the early Qing. *ECCP*, 833. Apparently it was a popular meeting place for poets and scholars of this period, for it receives frequent mention in early Qing literary collections. See Zhou Ruchang, *Honglou meng xinzheng* (New studies on the Dream of the Red Chamber) (Shanghai, 1953), cited in Spence, *Ts'ao Yin and the K'ang-hsi Emperor*, 57.

38. Wang Wan was best known as an essayist, and Gong Dingzi, Dong Yining, Zou Zhimo, and Peng Sunyu were all well-known poets and lyric *(ci)* writers.

39. *WSZNP*, 15.

40. Song Lao's epitaph for Wang Shizhen states that "from birth he had unusual gifts. When he first went to the family school, he showed promise at rhymed couplets and could write five- or seven-character line poems. He did not learn this from a teacher. The things he said were a constant surprise to his elders." Song Lao, "Zizheng daifu xingbu shangshu Wang gong Shizhen ji pei Zhang yiren muzhiming," 580.

41. The collection was called the *Luojian tang chugao*. See *WSZNP*, 8.

42. *WSZNP*, 14.

43. Wang's collected works, unlike those of Cao Rong, Gong Dingzi, and other prominent early Qing officials, were saved from the censors by the personal intervention of the Qianlong emperor, who liked Wang's poetry (*ECCP*, 833). For further discussion of the perceived anti-Qing subtext of these poems, and of the "matched rhyme poems" written by others, see Odaira Keiichi, "Yōshū jidai no Ō Gyoyō—Ō Bōrin no sakuhin o te gakari to shite," *Nihon Chūgoku gakkai hō* 38 (1986): 207–208.

44. See, for example, *ECCP*, 832; Hashimoto Shun, "Yōshū ni okeru Ō Gyoyō," *Ritsumeikan bungaku* 245 (November 1965): 46; Zhu Zongzhou, "Wang Shizhen yu Yangzhou," 50.

45. In his later collection of miscellaneous notes, Wang himself wrote that "early in the Kangxi reign [after his return from Yangzhou], those gentlemen who brought their poetry and essays to seek contacts in the capital had to call first upon Gong Dingzi; after that they called on Wang Wan, Liu Tiren, and myself." Wang Shizhen, *Xiangzu biji* (1702; reprint, Shanghai: Shanghai guji chubanshe, 1982), 8:150.

46. Song Lao, "Zizheng daifu xingbu shangshu Wang gong Shizhen ji pei Zhang yiren muzhiming," 581. Note that excerpts from the epitaph quoted in *Yangzhou huafang lu* and *Pingshan tang tuzhi* differ from the *Beizhuan ji* version in their inclusion of a line comparing Wang Shizhen with Bo Juyi and Su Shi. Li Dou does not attribute his quote, but the *Pingshan tang tuzhi* cites the epitaph. YZHFL, 212; and Zhao Zhibi, *Pingshan tang tuzhi* (original preface 1765, Edo edition 1843; reprint, Kyoto: Dōhōsha Shuppansha, 1981), 10:11a.

47. Wang Shizhen, "Baoqin tang ji" (Record of Holding a Zither Pavilion), YZFZ, 1810, 30:17a–17b.

48. Both Du Jun and Yuan Yuling, for example, wrote colophons for this painting, and both participated in the Red Bridge gatherings. Cheng Sui, who attended the second lustration gathering, wrote the title slip for the painting. I am very grateful to Nixi Cura for telling me about these two portraits.

49. The articles by Zhu Zongzhou and Hashimoto Shun cited above are examples of this.

50. While Philip Huang's book *Civil Justice in China* deals primarily with the eighteenth and nineteenth century, his discussion of the normative (or represented) adjudicator is useful here. Although Wang Shizhen was not a magistrate and was principally involved in the adjudication of criminal rather than civil cases, his performance was judged and represented according to the standards outlined by Huang in his discussion of magistrate's handbooks. See Huang, *Civil Justice in China: Representation and Practice in the Qing* (Stanford: Stanford University Press, 1996), 208.

51. On a comparable land tax case from the same period of fiscal crackdown, see Dennerline, "Fiscal Reform and Local Control," in Frederic Wakeman, Jr., and Carolyn Grant, eds., *Conflict and Control in Late Imperial China* (Berkeley: University of California Press, 1975), 111–12.

52. The seventeenth-century sources differ about whether the amount was measured in gold or silver. See "Wang Wenjian gongshi lue, xiong Shilu, Shihu" (Wang Shizhen and his older brothers, Shilu and Shihu), reprinted in WSZNP, 122, uses the word for gold, but the nianpu itself gives the figure in silver (WSZNP, 27). During this period, however, the word for gold *(jin)* was often used as a more elegant way of referring to silver, which was the currency used in most government transactions (Timothy Brook, correspondence, January 1998). Relative to the astronomical figures associated with the Lianghuai salt administration, even during the less prosperous days of the Kangxi period, 20,000 taels seems rather low. For comparison, the 1692 tax quota payable by the Lianghuai salt merchants totaled 290,000 taels (Spence, *Ts'ao Yin and the K'ang-hsi Emperor*, 181). When Cao Yin became salt censor in 1704, he reported a deficit in the salt controller's treasury of 800,000 taels, according to Spence (p. 187). He estimates that Cao Yin's personal debt at the time of his death totaled some 600,000 taels (p. 273). There is no doubt that the salt merchants of the early Kangxi period were less affluent than their successors during the late Kangxi and Qianlong periods, and the relatively depressed market accounted for the much smaller sums.

53. The role of gratitude and honor is emphasized in the most detailed account of this case, which is contained in Li Yuandu, "Wang Wenjian gongshi lue, xiong Shilu, Shihu," *WSZNP*, 122.

54. *WSZNP*, 27. A summary of this case in modern Chinese appears in Zhu Zongzhou, "Wang Shizhen yu Yangzhou," 48. See also Huang Shulin, "Yuyang shanren benzhuan" (Original biography of Yuyang the Hermit), in Wang Shizhen, *Yuyang shanren jinghua lu xunzuan* (Hongdou zhai edition, 1767). This biography is reprinted in an appendix to the *WSZNP*, 112–14; and Li Yuandu, "Wang Wenjian gongshi lue, xiong Shilu, Shihu," *WSZNP*, 121–24.

55. Mao Xiang, quoted in *WSZNP*, 28–29.

56. *WSZNP*, 29.

57. *WSZNP*, 29. Also quoted in *Pingshan tang tuzhi*, 10:12a–12b, which cites Mao Xiang, "Wang Shizhen kaoxu xu."

58. *WSZNP*, 28. A similar juxtaposition can be found in an anecdote in the *Jin shishuo*. See Wang Zhuo, *Jin shishuo*, in Zhou Junfu, ed., *Qingdai zhuanji congkan* (Taipei: Mingwen shuju, 1985), 22.

59. Quoted in *YZHFL*, 212; and *Pingshan tang tuzhi*, 10:11a.

60. *WSZNP*, 23. For an extended comparison of Wang Shizhen and Wang Shilu with Su Shi and his brother, written in 1665 (just after Wang Shizhen left Yangzhou), see Lei Shijun, "Shihu caotang xinjia ji xu" (Preface to Wang Shilu's Shihu studio collection of 1661–64), in *Ailing wenchao* (Xinletang cangban, 1677 ed.), 6:9a–10b.

61. Wang Shizhen, *Xiangzu biji*, 125. See Wang Shunu, *Zhongguo changji shi*, Mingguo congshu (Shanghai: Shanghai shudian, 1992), 261.

62. Wang Shizhen, *Xiangzu biji*, 125.

63. *Ganquan xianzhi*, 1742, 4:7b.

64. *Ganquan xianzhi*, 1742, 4:7b–9a. Note that Zong also had Red Bridge associations. He famously sold flowers at Red Bridge in exchange for wine money and also painted a scene of Red Bridge and sent it to Wang Shizhen in Beijing. See *Zhongguo meishujia renming cidian*, 509.

65. *Ganquan xianzhi*, 1742, 4:9a. See also *YZFZ*, 1685, 7:3b.

66. *Ganquan xianzhi*, 1742, 4:7b. The *Yongzheng huidian* says: "The Board of Rites ritual for welcoming spring was standardized in 1673, so that each province, prefecture, department, and county worshiped and welcomed the Mangshen and earthen buffalo, strictly prohibiting the forcible selection of musicians and prostitutes" (Wang Shunu, *Zhongguo changji shi*, Minguo congshu (Shanghai: Shanghai shudian, 1992), 261). Note that the empire-wide prohibition took place nearly a decade after Wang Shizhen left Yangzhou in 1665.

67. He was involved in several projects designed to raise Wang's profile in Yangzhou. For example, he edited Wang Shizhen's *Yuyang ganjiu ji* (Yuyang's nostalgia collection) and published an annotated edition of his autobiographical chronology.

68. *YZHFL*, 53.

69. *YZFZ*, 1810, 60:8a–8b, cites the 1733 gazetteer. The quote is from the "Local Customs" section of the gazetteer and is included in a subsection on banquets. In his manual for magistrates, the late seventeenth-century official Huang

Liuhong describes the magistrate's obligation to entertain visitors, but he advises his fellow-magistrates to keep their entertaining to a minimum lest it distract them from more important official duties. See Huang Liu-hung, *A Complete Book Concerning Happiness and Benevolence*, trans. Djang Chu (Tucson: University of Arizona Press, 1984), 154–55.

70. Wang Zhuo, *Jin shishuo*, 22.

71. These anthologies included *Guojiang ji* (Crossing the river collection), *Ru Wu ji* (Entering Wu collection), and *Baimen ji* (Nanjing collection).

72. Wang Zhuo, *Jin shishuo*, 68.

73. *WSZNP*, 18.

74. Odaira, "Yōshū jidai no Ō Gyoyō," 209.

75. For example, in 1661, during his trip to Nanjing, he stayed with the commoner *(buyi)* Ding Jizhi, a famous late Ming figure who at that time was seventy-eight *sui*. Ding lived in Qinhuai, and his reputation was closely linked with the pleasure quarters of that district. Wang was evidently most interested in hearing what Ding had to say about the late Ming cultural world. This interest is reflected in the poems Wang wrote to commemorate this occasion. Ding also wrote an opera about Wang Shizhen, and they commissioned a painting album about their visit, for which Chen Weisong wrote an inscription. Hashimoto, "Yōshū ni okeru Ō Gyoyō," 52–53; *WSZNP*, 18.

76. Wang Shizhen, "Luanjiang changhe ji xu" (Preface to the Luanjiang matching-rhyme poem collection), quoted in *WSZNP*, 19. Yizhen is located between Nanjing and Yangzhou; hence the allusions to both suggest that he stands in between and looks in both directions.

77. According to Wu Qi, the bridge had already fallen into ruin by the late Tang. Wu Qi, "*Yangzhou guchui ci* xu" (Prefaces to Yangzhou drum and flute lyrics), in Chen Henghe, *Yangzhou congke* (1930–34; reprint, Yangzhou: Guangling guji keyinshe, 1995), 9a–9b. The images from the Du Mu couplet titled "At Twenty-Four Bridge on a bright moonlit night, where is the jade maiden playing the flute?" are frequently alluded to in Qing poetry about the city. According to Cheng Mengxing, during the Qianlong period Red Peony Bridge (Hongyao qiao), located below Pingshan Hall, was commonly called Twenty-Four Bridge. See Cheng Mengxing, *Pingshan tang xiaozhi* (Wang Family Printers, 1752), 8:32b.

78. Kong Shangren, *Huhai ji*, 197. His statement that the name was changed on account of Wang may be an exaggeration. A modern version of Tan Qian's 1653 diary uses the characters *Hong qiao*, "Red Bridge." In this context, it seems less important that the bridge was actually renamed after Wang Shizhen's parties than that Kong Shangren wanted to mark the parties as a decisive turning point in the bridge's history. Tan Qian, *Beiyou lu*, Lidai shiliao biji congkan (1960; reprint, Beijing: Zhonghua shuju, 1997), 14.

79. Wang Yinggeng, *Pingshan lansheng zhi*, Qianlong period (c. 1742; reprint, Yangzhou: Guangling guji keyinshe, 1988), 1:7a. This privileging of literary text is consistent with the book's structure: each site is matched with works of literature about the site (which confirm the site's importance). In his coverage of Red Bridge, Wang Yinggeng includes the "Seductive Spring" poems, and he also explains who else was present on that occasion.

80. *YZHFL*, 5.

81. *YZHFL*, 10.

82. This lake was also known as "Baozhang Canal," and by the Qianlong period it was increasingly called "Slender West Lake," in reference to the famous West Lake in Hangzhou. A rare reference to this body of water as "Little West Lake" dating from the Kangxi period appears in the entry on "Little Gold Mountain" in Wu Qi, "*Yangzhou guchui ci* xu," 7a. This may suggest a gradual shift in the naming of the place, perhaps from vernacular usage into more widespread literary and official usage.

83. In 1736, a local resident named Huang Lu'ang used his own money to rebuild the bridge, which had fallen into disrepair (*Ganquan xianzhi*, 3:30b). The original wood and lacquer bridge was then replaced with an arched stone bridge; after a pavilion was added to the bridge in 1751, the name "Rainbow Bridge" came into popular usage. This stone bridge appears in the *Pingshan tang tuzhi* and other Qianlong-period illustrations. The current occupant of this site, "Great Rainbow Bridge," was built in 1973. It is both longer and wider than the original bridge, but it imitates the ancient style and purportedly uses cobblestones dating to the Song dynasty. See Zhao Ming, ed., *Yangzhou daguan* (Hefei: Huangshan shushe, 1993), 59. The image of the bridge as "red" evidently became embedded in the literary imagination. The nineteenth-century visitor Linqing states: "The vermilion railings spanning the water, the green trees on the dike, the famous gardens adjacent. . . . were just like the scenery in my fan painting [of Wang Shizhen's gathering at Red Bridge]." This despite the fact that the bridge had long since been reconstructed out of stone. In Linqing, *Hongxue yinyuan tuji*, vol. 1 (reprint, Beijing: Beijing guji chubanshe, 1984), see "Hongqiao tanchun" (Seeking spring at Red Bridge), unpaginated.

84. As seen in the *YZFZ*, 1733; *Ganquan xianzhi*, 1743; and *Jiangdu xianzhi*, 1743. Note that there are some differences in detail between these images. However, the composition is virtually identical.

85. The Ocean of the Law Temple, depicted as a cluster of buildings behind a small stone bridge, occupies the center of the illustration, and Pingshan Hall, Daming Temple, and Guanyin Pavilion occupy the heights.

86. Wu Qi was a native of Jiangdu county, Yangzhou, though his family originally came from Huizhou, Anhui, a likely indication that they engaged in trade. He was chosen as a senior licentiate, and in 1654 he entered the imperial academy. Appointed to positions of increasingly elevated rank, he also wrote operas, one of which attracted imperial attention. He served as prefectural magistrate in Huzhou, Zhejiang, and was discharged from the post in 1669. After spending some time destitute in Suzhou, he moved back to Yangzhou, where he built a garden residence. See *ECCP*, 864.

87. Note that there were two scenic sites in Yangzhou known as "Little Gold Mountain": the one described here, which was located southeast of Baozhang Lake and had its antecedents in the Six Dynasties period, and another dating from the Qianlong period, when dirt from the digging of the channel from the lake to Pingshan Hall was used to construct a new hill. Wu says of Little Gold Mountain

that "when it comes to the touring of scenic sites in Yangzhou, this is the most excellent there is" (*"Yangzhou guchui ci* xu," 7b). He calls Red Bridge the "most beautiful sight in the prefecture" (10b).

88. Wu Qi, "Red Bridge," in *"Yangzhou guchui ci* xu," 10b. The poems written by a group of Wu Qi's friends are no longer extant. Note that Wu Qi and his contemporary Wang Maolin were both members of the Xianxian Poetry Club before they entered government service (*YZFZ,* 1810, 51:25b).

89. Wang Shizhen, "Hongqiao youji" (Record of an excursion to Red Bridge), *WSZNP,* 21.

90. Guo Shijing, *Guangling jiuji shi,* mid-Qing manuscript copy with 1672 preface by Sang Zhi, not paginated.

91. Guo Shijing describes the constant flute music along the canal. According to Li Dou, pleasure boats known as "Lake Touring Boats" *(youhu chuan)* were available in Yangzhou during the Ming. According to the last juan of the *Yangzhou huafanglu,* which focuses on pleasure boats, there were three commercial, multi-storied pleasure boats in Yangzhou. During the Kangxi-Yongzheng period that number increased to five or six. During the early Qianlong period, there were twelve. After 1756, the numbers increased greatly, and by the end of the Qianlong reign, there were 239, associated with twelve docks (*YZHFL,* 403–4). See also Wang Zhenzhong, "Ming-Qing Lianghuai yanshang yu Yangzhou chengshi de diyu jiegou," *Lishi dili* 10 (1992): 120, for these figures and a chart indicating the number of pleasure boats associated with each dock during the Qianlong period. Note that these large pleasure boats were not (as is sometimes assumed) the only recreational craft on Yangzhou waters; there were also numerous private boats, garden boats, temple boats, and official boats. Early Qing accounts describe the area around Red Bridge as bustling with boats, probably of the smaller, private variety.

92. Wang Yinggeng, *Pingshan lansheng zhi,* 1:2b. Zong Yuandu does not appear in any of the standard biographical reference works; thus it is unclear when this passage was written.

93. *YZFZ,* 1664, juan 6. Note that this section of the gazetteer is largely retained from the Wanli edition. According to Li Dou, the name "Little Qinhuai" never entered the gazetteers, suggesting that the name was never official. His discussion only includes post-1645 sources (*YZHFL,* 205–7).

94. Li Dou follows the *Pingshan tang tuzhi* in defining the Little Qinhuai canal as within the city walls at Little East Gate and at the same time showing that during the seventeenth century the name was applied to the canal extending all way to the bridge. Li claims that this nomenclature had fallen out of use, but the *Pingshan lansheng zhi* retains the seventeenth-century usage (*YZHFL,* 205).

95. Nostalgic works portraying the world of the Nanjing pleasure quarters by extension evoked the lost culture of the late Ming in general. The most famous of these include Yu Huai's *Banqiao zaji* (Miscellaneous records of Wooden Bridge), published for the first time in 1697 in the initial installment of the *Zhaodai congshu* (Collectanea for a glorious age), and Kong Shangren's famous drama *The Peach Blossom Fan.* See Lynn A. Struve, "History and *The Peach Blossom Fan,*"

CLEAR 2, no. 1 (January 1980): 55–72, for discussion of nostalgic and historical motifs in the play. Struve correctly emphasizes that these do not reflect a particularly "loyalist" sensibility. Men like Yu Huai, Mao Xiang, You Tong, Du Jun, and Gong Xian moved between the literati communities resident in Nanjing and Yangzhou. For a translation of Yu Huai's *Banqiao zaji*, see Howard Levy, trans., *A Feast of Mist and Flowers* (Yokohama: n.p., 1966).

96. Chen Weisong, "Xiao Qinhuai qu" (Songs of Little Qinhuai), in Wang Yinggeng, *Pingshan lansheng zhi,* 1:5a. Chen Weisong was neither loyalist nor official; rather, he was a frequent candidate for the examinations, which he failed repeatedly from the age of sixteen to fifty-three *sui*. His talent, and his close relationship to Mao Xiang, guaranteed him entrée into official and literary circles. He passed the special Boxue hongci examination in 1679, finally receiving a position in the government as a corrector in the Hanlin academy, and he participated in the Ming history project (*ECCP,* 103).

97. Both Chen and Mao Xiang refer to the recent departure of Wang Shizhen in their song cycles. Wang left his post in Yangzhou in 1665. Wang Yinggeng, *Pingshan lansheng zhi* 1:4a and 5a. In the third line, *jun* should be read as the second person pronoun. Given the nature of their friendship and Mao's presence on this occasion, it seems likely that he is the "you" referred to in the poem. Given the apparent frequency with which Chen and Mao attended the same parties, these poems may well be the product of a single event, though *changhe* poems could be composed by nonattendees after a gathering.

98. Chen Weisong, "Xiao Qinhuai qu," in Wang Yinggeng, *Pingshan lansheng zhi,* 1:4b. The passage "one of Yangzhou's bridges" is translated rather loosely. The original reads "You guo Yangzhou diji qiao," which may be a reference to the famous Twenty-Four Bridge of the Tang. The phrase "ten years" also must be interpreted rather loosely, if the poem in fact was written in 1665. The cities of Yangzhou and Nanjing both fell to the Qing armies in 1645, or twenty years earlier. Mao Xiang, in contrast, refers to experiences thirty years in the past in the first poem in his song cycle. It seems unlikely that these poems would refer to events other than the Qing conquest, given the melancholy tone of the song series and the extent to which these events dominated the poetic imaginations of this circle of men. The span of years, given in round decades, perhaps should be read as formulary numbers—one decade or three—standing for events twenty years in the past. It may also be a double allusion to the Tang poet Du Mu's "ten year Yangzhou dream."

99. Wang Yinggeng, *Pingshan lansheng zhi,* 1:3a. His first poem sets the mood, referring to the enchanting excursions and old events at Qinhuai thirty years earlier, when the scenery was at its best.

100. The archetypical late Ming courtesan Liu Rushi took "Liu," or willow, as her surname when she began her career, and the name is suggestive of her profession. The allusion is also to the Tang concubine Zhang Tailiu, described in the *Taiping Guangji,* and a poem written for her. Her name became the name of a *ci* style popular in the entertainment quarters. Also, the figures of courtesans are frequently compared to willows and willow branches. The allusion is complex, con-

flating women, music, pleasure, and loss. On Liu Rushi, see Dorothy Ko, *Teachers of the Inner Chambers: Women and Culture in Seventeenth-Century China* (Stanford: Stanford University Press, 1994), 276 ff. For discussion of Liu Rushi as courtesan-painter, see Marsha Weidner et al., *Views from Jade Terrace: Chinese Women Artists 1300–1912* (Indianapolis: Indianapolis Museum of Art, 1988), 100–101.

101. Chen Weisong refers to Wang Shizhen as the "greatest spirit of our age," whereas Mao Xiang, clearly senior to Wang in both age and stature, refers to him as "the deeply elegant Student Wang."

102. Wai-yee Li discusses the meaning of pleasure and loss in Chinese literature through the related concepts of enchantment and disenchantment. See her *Enchantment and Disenchantment: Love and Illusion in Chinese Literature* (Princeton: Princeton University Press, 1993), 81–83. Love and the loss of love, pleasure and the loss of pleasure, were invoked as part of a broader complex of personal and political self-representation.

103. For example, the woman Axiu, who attended the gathering at Red Bridge of 1666 described in the *Hongqiao changhe ci* (Red Bridge matched lyrics), appears to have been a courtesan. The participation of courtesans in this event is indicated in Chen Shixiang's second poem (and in Wang Shilu's second poem), which refers to a singing girl performing and pouring wine and to painted boats. Sun Jinli, ed. "Hongqiao changhe diyi ji," in Sun Mo, ed., *Guochao mingjia shiyu* (Xiuning Sunshi Liusong ge, Kangxi period), unpaginated. Poets often associated bridges with the floating world. See Howard Levy, introduction to *A Feast of Mist and Flowers*, 2–3, where he discusses the evolution of a genre of nostalgic records of courtesan districts, from Banqiao (Wooden Bridge) in Nanjing to Yanagibashi (Willow Bridge) in Edo.

104. *YZHFL*, 403. It is not clear whether Li means that there were only three, or whether there were only three that had names, or three that were famous enough to be remembered by the late eighteenth century, or three that were commercially available for rent. He, of course, does not specify. By contrast, in a 1673 poem Wang Ji refers to "pleasure boats as dense as fish scales." Wang Ji, "Shanjian xuji" (In the mountains collection, continued), in *Huizhai ji qizhong*, 28a.

105. Susan Mann, *Precious Records: Women in China's Long Eighteenth Century* (Stanford: Stanford University Press, 1997), 128.

106. For evidence of wine shops in this area during Wang Shizen's tenure in Yangzhou, we need look no further than his 1662 "Hongqiao ji" (Red Bridge record), a frequently anthologized text, which refers to "green [wine shop] banners and white boats." The essay appears in *WSZNP*, 21; Wang Yinggeng, *Pingshan lansheng zhi*, 1:7a–8a; and Gu Yiping and Zhu Zhu, *Yangzhou youji sanwen xuan* (Yangzhou: n.p., 1989). Kong Shangren's essays on Yangzhou contain numerous references to the wine shops of the northwest suburbs.

107. Wang Maolin, *Baichi wutong ge yigao*, 1:2b. Excursions to Red Bridge were an important part of Qingming holiday festivities in Yangzhou during the early Qing, usually attracting large and diverse crowds.

108. *Ganquan xianzhi*, 1743, 3:29b, cites the Yongzheng-era county gazet-

218 NOTES TO CHAPTER 2

teer. This passage is common to the prefectural and county gazetteers beginning at least in the Yongzheng period. It is also cited in the *Yangzhou huafang lu* description of the bridge, which also cites Wu Qi's "*Yangzhou guchui ci* xu" and Wang Shizhen's "Hongqiao youji" (*YZHFL,* 230).

109. Susan Mann, *Precious Records,* 131.

110. Wang Yinggeng, *Pingshan lansheng zhi,* juan 1–3.

111. Wang Shizhen, *Yuyang shihua* (Yuyang's poetry criticism), quoted in the *Ganquan xianzhi,* 3:30a, and in the *Pingshan tang tuzhi,* 10:13a–13b.

112. He attributes the poems composed at the late summer gathering to the earlier spring gathering (*YZHFL,* 211). The same error is replicated in recent works, such as Huang Jingjin's *Wang Yuyang shilun zhi yanjiu* (Taipei: Wenshizhe chubanshe, 1980), 17.

113. Like Li Dou, the editors of the modern compilation *Yangzhou shici* imply a connection between the "Wanshachao" *ci* composed in the summer of 1662 and the spring lustration festival gatherings. Again this suggests the degree to which the image of these spring gatherings has dominated later representations of Wang Shizhen in Yangzhou. See Zhang Shicheng and Xia Yunbi, eds., *Yangzhou shici* (Shanghai: Shanghai guji chubanshe, 1985), 74.

114. Owen, *Anthology of Chinese Literature,* 282. Owen's translation of the "Preface to the Orchid Pavilion Poems" appears on 283–84. For further discussion of the spring lustration ritual, its history, and associated practices, see Ellen Mae Johnston Laing, "Scholars and Sages: A Study in Chinese Figure Painting" (Ph.D. diss., University of Michigan, 1967), 8–14.

115. This is the last in the famous "Seductive Spring" series, written by Wang Shizhen at the 1664 gathering. Quoted in Wang Yinggeng, *Pingshan lansheng zhi,* 1:10b. Wu Qi, writing after the gathering at Red Bridge, describes "Bamboo West Pavilion" as follows: "It is located beside Chanzhi Temple on the north bank of the official canal [Guanhe]. Du Mu's poem reads: 'Who would have known down the Bamboo West Road, the singing and piping that is Yangzhou?' So it was named Bamboo West, and Shang Zigu wrote a flute song about it. It was burned during a fire in the Shaoxing reign, and rebuilt by the magistrate Zhou Zong, and subsequently the old name was restored. Now it again is ruined. The great destination for pleasure trips is now covered with abundant grass. It is like all the twelve towers whose locations cannot be recovered. Alas!" (Wu Qi, "Yangzhou guchui ci xu," 8b). For a translation of the Du Mu poem, see Owen, *Anthology of Chinese Literature,* 632.

116. Kang-I Sun Chang, "Symbolic and Allegorical Meanings in the *Yueh-fu pu-t'i* Poem Series," *Harvard Journal of Asiatic Studies* 46, no. 2 (December 1988): 353, 371. She also notes that the facts of the "incident of the tombs" became well known only in the early Qing, when Wan Sitong (1638–1702) published an anthology of materials related to this incident and Zhu Yizun (1610–95) obtained a manuscript of the *Yuefu buti* poems and had them published. As she points out, these events would have had particular resonance for early Qing readers (p. 381).

117. Kang-I Sun Chang, "Symbolic and Allegorical Meanings in the *Yueh-fu*

pu-t'i Poem Series," 381. It seems likely that interest in the manuscript predated its publication.

118. The essay is reprinted in the annotated nianpu in a format suggesting that it was composed on the occasion of his first spring lustration festival gathering (*WSZNP*, 20–21). For reference to the stele, see Sun Jinli (Jiefu)'s comment on Zong Yuanding's poem "Fulei qianyin huai Wang Ruanting xiansheng" (Repeating the previous rhyme and recalling Mr. Wang Shizhen). Sun Jinli, ed., "Guangling changhe ci," in Sun Mo, ed., *Guochao mingjia shiyu* (Xiuning Sunshi Liusong ge, Kangxi period), "Xiaoxiang ci," 4a.

119. *WSZNP*, 21. See also Wang Yinggeng, *Pingshan lansheng zhi*, 1:7a–8a.

120. Owen, *Anthology of Chinese Literature*, 283–84.

121. This portrait by Yu Zhiding is in the Beijing Palace Museum collection. Xu Zhongling, "Luedu Yu Zhiding de huaxiang," *Gugong Bowuyuan yuankan* 25, no. 3 (1984): 47–48. For one of the thirty-eight colophons by Wang's friends, see Wang Shidan, "Ti Xincheng Wanggong fangxian tu," in Ruan Yuan, *Huaihai yingling ji*, bingji, 1:29a. This image of Wang Shizhen has been reworked in woodblock print form, though stripped of its garden setting and narrative context. The woodblock portrait, complete with the seals of Yu Zhiding, is included in the 1700 edition of his collected poems. For the image, see Lin Ji, ed., Wang Shizhen, *Yuyang shanren jinghua lu*, Houguan Lin Ji xiekeben. For confirmation that the image is the same, see the letters between Wang Shizhen and Lin Ji, in Wang Shizhen, *Wang Yuyang jinghualu jishi*, Li Yufu et al., eds. (Shanghai: Shanghai guji chubanshe, 1999), 1998.

122. For a translation of this inscription, see Richard Vinograd, *Boundaries of the Self: Chinese Portraits, 1600–1900* (Cambridge: Cambridge University Press, 1992), 50–51.

123. Vinograd, *Boundaries of the Self*, 51.

124. Vinograd, *Boundaries of the Self*, 51 and 55.

125. Kondo Haruo, *Chūgoku gakugei daijiten* (China academic encyclopedia) (Tokyo: Daishukan shoten, 1992), 31. See also Zang Lihe et al., eds., *Zhongguo renming dacidian* (Shanghai: Shanghai shudian, 1980), 842.

126. *WSZNP*, 21.

127. Fan Jinmin and Xie Zhengguang (Andrew Hsieh), eds., *Ming yimin lu huiji* (Nanjing: Nanjing University Press, 1995), 745. See also the preface to his poetry collection by Shi Runzhang, "Chen Boji shixu" (Preface to Chen Boji's poetry), *Shi Yushan ji*, vol. 1, Anhui guji congshu (Hefei: Huangshan shushe, 1992), 117.

128. Fang Bao (Wangxi), "Du Chacun xiansheng mujie" (Epitaph for Du Jun), in Du Jun, *Bianyatang yiji* (Huanggang: Shen Zhijian, 1894), fulu (appendix), 1a–1b.

129. *Huangzhou fuzhi*, quoted in full in *Bianyatang yiji*, fulu, 2b–3a.

130. See Du Jun, *Bianyatang quanji*, tici, and *Bianyatang yiji*, Guangxu edition, fulu. In one version, Zhou Lianggong sponsors the contest and in another, Gong Dingzi sponsored it. In a third version, Gong Dingzi organized the party and Zhou Lianggong donated the prize money. In the fourth version, an unnamed

rich man filled a boat with treasure and left a sign saying that whoever composed the best poem would live a long time. Du Jun wrote a poem, submitted it, and left for Nanjing without asking who the sponsor was or receiving the prize.

131. A late nineteenth-century edition of Du Jun's collected works published in his hometown features a woodblock portrait of the poet that is clearly a copy of this seventeenth-century portrait. Du Jun, *Bianya tang yiji*, frontispiece.

132. Wang Shizhen, *Yuyang shihua*, cited in the *Bianyatang yiji*, fulu, 35a–35b.

133. It is not clear whether this collection is still extant as a separate volume; I have not been able to locate it. A similar collection with the same title, but edited by Wang Shizhen's brother Wang Shilu, describes a gathering held at a garden in the suburbs on the occasion of the Little Spring Festival in the tenth month. Zong Yuanding attended the gathering and of course composed a poem to mark the occasion. Cao Erkan's commentary on this poem provides information on the gathering and those who attended. See Zong Yuanding, *Xinliu tang wenji* (New Willow Hall literary collection), 1680, 3:8a.

134. These are reprinted in Wang Yinggeng, *Pingshan lansheng zhi*, 3:1a–a. They contain seasonal imagery appropriate to a late summer outing, and, given Wang Shizhen's account above, it seems quite clear that they were composed on the same occasion as the essay. Wang's comments in the *nianpu* suggest that the poems he published as the *Hongqiao changhe ji* were those composed at the earlier gathering, on the third day of the third month (*WSZNP*, 20–21).

135. To the extent that a group of Yangzhou artists and intellectuals formed a new poetry club in the 1980s and called it the "Green Willow Poetry Club" in reference to this line.

136. *WSZNP*, 20–21.

137. *WSZNP*, 23. This passage was written by Wang Shizhen, and it lists Du Jun as a participant. Note that while biographies of Lin, Du, and Sun are included in juan 10 of the *YZHFL*, Zhang Wangsun is omitted. Du Jun is the subject of one of the twenty poems on the theme "Seductive Spring" composed by Wang Shizhen on the occasion of this gathering, but an annotation (and the poem itself) implies that he was invited but could not in fact attend. This makes the mention of him even more striking. Clearly Wang Shizhen wanted to emphasize his connection to the older man. Wang Yinggeng, *Pingshan lansheng zhi*, 1:10a.

138. See Wang Yinggeng, *Pingshan lansheng zhi*, 1:8b–10b, which is further supported by a poem by Sun Zhiwei entitled "On Qingming, Wang Ruanting invited Lin Maozhi, Zhang Zuwang, Cheng Muqian, Xu Lichen, [Xu] Shiliu, and [my relative] Moyan to take a boat to Red Bridge, [and] while we drank wine, we composed 'Seductive Spring.'" Note his use of style names here to refer to Wang Shizhen, Lin Gudu, Zhang Wangsun, Cheng Sui, Xu Chengxuan, Xu Chengjia, and Sun Mo. Wang Yinggeng, *Pingshan lansheng zhi*, 1:12a. Also, see Li Dou, *YZHFL*, 211.

139. Wang Yu, in *Jiangsu shizheng*, quotes "Meng Oushu bitan." Cited in Qian Zhonglian, ed., *Qingshi jishi*, vol. 1 (Nanjing: Jiangsu guji chubanshe, 1989), 7.

140. Three years after his death, Zhou Lianggong paid for his funeral and arranged for him to be buried on Bell Mountain, Nanjing. Wang Shizhen edited his writings and arranged for their publication.

141. Wang Shizhen, *Yuyang shihua,* quoted in Qian Zhonglian, ed., *Qingshi jishi,* 1:7.

142. Wang Yinggeng, *Pingshan lansheng zhi,* 1:9b.

143. Zhou Lianggong, *Chidu xinchao* (Letters newly published), quoted in Qian Zhonglian, ed., *Qingshi jishi,* 1:6–7.

144. Fan and Xie, *Ming yimin lu huiji,* 669.

145. Later Sun took and failed the Boxue hongci examination, but he was rewarded with a position on account of his seniority. Subsequently, he has been categorized as a "Kangxi" period poet. See, for example, Qian Zhonglian, ed., *Qingshi jishi,* 5:2863–69.

146. *ECCP,* 675; *YZFZ,* 1733, "Sojourners," 33:15a. For the most detailed account, see Chen Weisong's preface to Sun Zhiwei, *Gaitang qianji* (Kangxi edition; reprint, Shanghai: Shanghai guji chubanshe, 1979), 1b.

147. At this time, he moved his household into the New City, where they took up residence next to the Dongxiang Shrine. His residence was called Gaitang, hence the name of his literary collection (Chen preface, 2a–2b).

148. Quoted Qian Zhonglian, ed., *Qingshi jishi,* 1:497.

149. Wang Yinggeng, *Pingshan lansheng zhi,* 1:8b.

150. Wang Yinggeng, *Pingshan lansheng zhi,* 1:9b.

151. And evidently in landscape painting as well. In his memoirs, the nineteenth-century official and traveler Linqing mentions having been given a fan painting of Wang Shizhen's gathering at Red Bridge. Upon seeing the painting, a friend inscribed it with two poems, one by Chen Weisong and one by Zong Yuanding. Linqing, "Hongqiao tanchun" (Seeking spring at Red Bridge), *Hongxue yinyuan tuji,* vol. 1, unpaginated.

152. *YZHFL,* 25.

153. *YZHFL,* 228. For another building named after a Wang Shizhen poem, see *YZHFL,* 229.

154. Zhao Ming, *Yangzhou daguan,* 69.

155. *YZHFL,* 219.

156. *YZHFL,* 209.

157. The identity of the man known as Wu Ershi remains obscure; the name is a style name but does not appear in the standard index of style names. Lei Shijun, *Ailing Wenchao* (Xinletang Cangban, 1677), 8:23a–23b.

158. Lei Shijun, "Song Wang Ruanting xiansheng" (Seeing off Mr. Wang Ruanting), *Ailing tang wenchao,* 4:11a. Note also that Wang Shizhen's self-proclaimed disciple Wang Maolin, who is featured in Chapter 4, praised Lei Shijun's literary collection. This fits with Wang Maolin's general agenda of promoting his hometown and local talents. Lei Shijun was a close friend of Wang Maolin's former tutor Wang Yan, who wrote Lei's epitaph. In addition, Sun Zhiwei and Lei Shijun were related by marriage. Sun's daughter married Lei Shijun's son.

159. Richard Strassberg, *The World of K'ung Shang-jen* (New York: Columbia University Press, 1983), 134.

160. Like Wang, Kong had friends who had made their literary reputations in the late Ming. He socialized with Gong Xian, Du Jun, Mao Xiang, and others—exchanging poetry and letters as well as attending parties. In a letter to Mao Xiang, Kong writes that visiting with him is "like facing classic works by ancient writers, or looking at bronze vessels from a previous dynasty." Kong Shangren, *Kong Shangren shiwen ji,* 7:506.

161. Kong Shangren, *Huhai ji,* 3. The willows and oriole songs mentioned in lines five and six clearly refer to courtesans. Line seven refers to Bao Zhao, the author of the "Wucheng fu" (Rhapsody on the weed-covered city), and line eight refers to Li Bai's poem "Huanghe lou songbie Meng Haoran zhi Yangzhou" (Seeing Meng Haoran off to Yangzhou at Yellow Crane Tower). I have drawn upon Strassberg's translation of this poem, with some emendations. Strassberg, *The World of K'ung Shang-jen,* 134.

162. For example, the author of Kong Shangren's "modern" biography and old-fashioned *nianpu,* Chen Wannai, makes the same comparison. See Chen Wannai, *Kong Shangren,* Gufeng congshu, vol. 11 (Taipei: Heluo tushu chubanshe, 1978), 20.

163. Kong Shangren, *Huhai ji,* 3.

164. Kong Shangren, *Huhai ji,* 3.

165. Kong Shangren, *Huhai ji,* 3. Huang Yun, Deng Hanyi, and Zong Yuanding were all good friends of Kong Shangren. Huang and Zong never served the Qing state and therefore have occasionally been portrayed as "loyalists." Such a portrayal is inaccurate, considering for example that Zong tried several times to pass the civil service examinations and failed. Thus it is more accurate to describe them as poets and romantics according to the late Ming model who happened to live in the early Qing. All three men were natives of counties administered under Yangzhou prefecture, were known to Wang Shizhen, and were considered leading figures in local poetry circles. In addition, Huang Yun's son was married to Zong Yuanding's daughter. See Zong Yuanding, *Xinliu tang wenji,* 3:31a.

166. For an explicit example linking the writings of Kong, Wang, Ouyang, and Su to the reputation of Pingshan Hall, see Kong Shangren, *Huhai ji,* 2.

167. A list of those in attendance appears in Ruan Yuan, *Guangling shishi* (Poems and events in Guangling), juan 7, which is cited and discussed in Aoki Masaru, "Yōshū ni arishi hi no Kō Shōjin," *Aoki Masaru zenshū,* vol. 2, 482.

168. Kong Shangren, *Huhai ji,* 200. Unlike the poetry chapters, in which each comment is accompanied by the name of the commentator, in the prose chapters the comments are anonymous, though evidently they were composed by Wu Qi, Zong Yuanyu (brother of Zong Yuanding), and Du Jie (brother of Du Jun).

169. That this poem should be considered an interpretation of the "Seductive Spring" theme is indicated in Huang Yun's commentary, which reads: "The poets who have written on the theme of 'Seductive Spring' at Red Bridge are numerous. Kong was able to use a deep sense of melancholy to distinguish his version. We only sense its age, and not its beauty." Kong Shangren, *Huhai ji,* 3.

170. Kong Shangren, *Huhai ji,* 3.

171. *YZHFL,* 218–19. There may be problems with Li Dou's dating, as Lu retired from his position in Yangzhou in 1762 (*ECCP,* 542). Indeed, in a letter to Ruan Yuan about the *Record of the Painted Boats of Yangzhou,* Ling Tingkan complains about the book's many mistakes. Ling, *Jiaoli tang wenji* (Beijing: Zhonghua shuju, 1998): 206–7.

CHAPTER 3

1. Eric Hobsbawm and Terence Ranger, "Introduction: Inventing Traditions," in Hobsbawm and Ranger, ed., *The Invention of Tradition* (Cambridge: Cambridge University Press, 1984), 1–14.

2. The gazetteer here refers to the proliferation of sites spuriously linked to Xiao Tong and the *Wenxuan,* not just to the one at Yangzhou. The determination that Xiao Tong could not have visited Yangzhou and the rhetorical question cited in the 1664 gazetteer both appear in the Wanli-era gazetteer, where they are attributed to an even earlier Jiangdu county gazetteer. However, I have not encountered Ming-dynasty references to a tower actually standing on the site. *YZFZ,* 1664, 21:6a; *YZFZ,* 1605, 21:6a.

3. See, for example, Zhang Shicheng and Xia Yunbi, eds., *Yangzhou shici* (Shanghai: Shanghai guji chubanshe, 1985); and Jiang Yangren, ed., *Yangzhou mingsheng shixuan* (Nanjing: Jiangsu guji chubanshe, 1990). Also, see Zhao Ming ed., *Yangzhou daguan* (Hefei: Huangshan shushe, 1993).

4. There is some indication of revived interest in the tower during the late nineteenth century. See for example Guo Xiangqu, ed., *Yangzhou lansheng fu chao* (Yinshan tang, 1879). Nearly every site and anecdote *ever* associated with the prefecture is mentioned somewhere in this multi-volume set, though most of the poems appear to be from the Qing. Three poems on the tower were included in the first collection. It is also mentioned in the undated manuscript *Guangling huaigu sanshi shou* (Thirty huaigu poems on Guangling), in Pan Gao, *Guangling huaigu sanshi shou fu Pingshan tang zalu sanshi shou,* Qing manuscript.

5. For a brief biography of Xiao Tong and discussion of the literary salons that flourished around the Liang imperial court at Jiankang, see David Knechtges' introduction to Xiao Tong, ed., *Wenxuan or Selections of Refined Literature,* vol. 1: Rhapsodies on Metropolises and Capitals, trans. David R. Knechtges (Princeton: Princeton University Press, 1982). Part of the Yangzhou-Jianye (Nanjing) confusion might arise from the fact that several of the Southern dynasties administered the Nanjing region under the name "Yangzhou," though this was not the case during the Liang.

6. There is a tradition that the *Wenxuan* was compiled at Xiangyang, Hubei. However, Qing *Wenxuan* scholars demonstrated that even though Xiao Tong was born at Xiangyang he never lived there as an adult, and instead lived in the Eastern Palace at Jiankang. The literary group associated with Xiangyang in fact was patronized by his brother. Knechtges, in Xiao Tong, *Wenxuan,* 10.

7. The prefectural gazetteer attributes this line of reasoning to the *Jiangdu xianzhi* (Jiangdu county gazetteer), certainly a late Ming edition since the same

passage appears in the Wanli edition of the Yangzhou fuzhi (YZFZ, 1664, 21:6a; YZFZ, 1605, 21:6a). The later Kangxi era gazetteers do not include this passage. The prince died as a result of injuries sustained in an accident that occurred while he was out picking lotuses with palace ladies. Knechtges, in Xiao Tong, Wenxuan, 7.

8. Knechtges, in Xiao Tong, Wenxuan, 10.

9. Indeed, interest in the Wenxuan remained high during the eighteenth century, as it became the object of evidential scholarship and philological research. Knechtges, in Xiao Tong, Wenxuan, 58.

10. See, for example, Zhang Chao, Yuchu xinzhi (Kangxi period; reprint, Beijing: Wenxue guji kanxing she, 1954), fanli (editorial principles), 2.

11. YZFZ, 1685, 18:4a. The 1733 gazetteer entry begins with the same quote (YZFZ, 1733, 23:13a). Both gazetteers attribute this quote to the Daye shiyi ji, a collection of miscellaneous materials about the Sui compiled by Yan Shigu during the Tang. It was included in at least one late Ming compendium (congshu). Indeed, the same quote appears in the Jiajing Weiyang zhi, 7:21a; and in YZFZ, 1605, 21:5b.

12. YZFZ, 1733, 23:13a. The 1685 gazetteer contains substantively the same information using slightly different wording (YZFZ, 1685, 18:4a). Wang Guan was a native of either Gaoyou or Rugao. He served in the Hanlin Academy and was well known for his poetry. He also served as the magistrate of Jiangdu (Zang et al., eds., Zhongguo renming dacidian, 162). He wrote the Yangzhou shaoyao pu (A handbook on the peonies of Yangzhou), which continues to be published in collections of writings on local subjects today.

13. The three gazetteers from this period use the same wording to describe the tower's location, except that the 1664 and 1685 editions refer to the bridge as "Taizi (Crown Prince's) Bridge," indicating either the retention of a misprinted character or a change in the name during the late Kangxi reign. The change from "Crown Prince" to "Great Peace" is ideologically consistent with changes that occurred in the empire during and after the emperor's Southern Tours. (YZFZ, 1664, 21:5b; YZFZ, 1685, 18:4a; YZFZ, 1733, 23:13a.)

14. See Zhu Mu, Songben fangyu shenglan (Shanghai: Shanghai guji chubanshe, 1991), 401–2. The author quotes the Wang Guan passage and then states, "the Tujing [gazetteer] says that this was located in Wenlou Lane. It is said that Sui Yangdi visited here."

15. Zhu Mu, Songben Fangyu shenglan, 403–4. The Ciyuan describes this book in 70 juan as a record of the famous sites of the realm, defined by the Southern Song borders, organized by administrative unit, and beginning with the Southern Song capital of Lin'an (Hangzhou). Much of the material is literary rather than administrative or geographical in nature. See Ciyuan (Beijing: Shangwu yinshudian, 1991), 750.

16. Stephen Owen, "Meditation on the Past at Chin-ling," Harvard Journal of Asiatic Studies 50 (December 1990): 420.

17. YZFZ, 1685, 18:4a.

18. YZFZ, 1685, 18:4a; YZFZ, 1733, 23:13a; YZFZ, 1664, 21:5a–6a.

19. The 1810 gazetteer mistakenly gives the name of the monk as Juejian. YZFZ, 1810, 28:14a.

20. YZFZ, 1664, 21:5b–6a. Li Songyang was a native of Fengqiu, Henan. He had passed the provincial-level examinations, and in 1647 was appointed to serve as the Lianghuai salt censor. When he arrived in Yangzhou, the city was still in a state of distress and had not yet recovered. He played an active role in encouraging the old merchants to return to work and in attracting new merchants to the city. YZFZ, 1733, 27:56a–56b.

21. YZFZ, 1664, 21:5b–6a; YZFZ, 1685, 18:4a. The 1685 account makes no reference to the stele by Li Songyang, though it does mention that the tower served as a shrine.

22. Wang Youding was a native of Nanchang, Jiangxi. He was a tribute student under the Ming. In his later life, he lived in a monastery at West Lake and also resided in Yangzhou after the fall of the Ming. He was good at poetry and ancient style prose and was famous in his time for his calligraphy. He died while visiting West Lake in Hangzhou. See *Zhongguo renming dacidian*, 134; and Yu Jianhua, *Zhongguo meishu jia renming cidian* (Shanghai: Shanghai renmin meishu chubanshe, 1981), 115.

23. A commentary in later editions of this work describes the original contents and notes that they have been cut. Du Dengchun, "Sheshi shimo" (Affairs of the club from start to finish), in Wu Shenglan, *Yihai zhuchen ge ji* (Nanhui Wushi Tingyi tang keben, Qianlong period), 2a.

24. For the paradoxical notion that "eternal" and "transcendent" cultural values were dynamic and ever-shifting, see Peter Bol, *This Culture of Ours: Intellectual Transitions in T'ang and Sung China* (Stanford: Stanford University Press, 1992), introduction.

25. On Wu Qi, see Chapter 2. Wei Xi, Du Jun, and Chen Weisong contributed prefaces to his literary collection. Wang Shizhen, Kong Shangren, Deng Hanyi, Mao Xiang, and Jin Zhen (the prefectural magistrate discussed in Chapter 4) were all among those credited with having read the collection prior to its publication. Their names appear in the long (thirteen double-sided pages) list that follows the table of contents, a veritable who's who of the early Qing literary world (Wu Qi, *Linhui tang quanji*, 1700).

26. Wu Qi, "*Yangzhou guchui ci xu*," 1b.

27. Indeed, towers, like mountains, conventionally symbolized endurance. Frankel, *The Flowering Plum and the Palace Lady*, 115.

28. For excerpts from some of these anthologies, see Xie Zhengguang (Andrew Hsieh) and She Rufeng, eds., *Qingchu ren xuan Qingchu shi huikao* (Nanjing: Nanjing University Press, 1998) (hereafter cited as *Qingchu ren*).

29. YZFZ, 1675, fanli, 2b.

30. YZFZ, 1675, 18:4a–4b. Note that the page number is identical in the 1685 gazetteer, with which there is considerable overlap. Xu Weiping, *Yangzhou difang zhi yanjiu* (Hefei: Huangshan shushe, 1993), 61–62. It should be noted that Peng Gui was one of the three literary consultants who worked on this edition. The others were Sun Zhiwei and He Jiayan. Peng was incredibly prolific, and an

impressive number of his poems are included in the gazetteer. For further evidence of Peng Gui's social contact with Deng Hanyi, Cheng Sui, Sun Mo, Zong Guan, and Fan Guolu, see Deng Hanyi, ed., *Shiguan erji* (Nanyang Dengshi Shenmotang keben, 1678), 3:65a.

31. YZFZ, 1685. The five were Deng Hanyi, Sun Zhiwei, Huang Yun, Wang Fangqi, and Mao Danshu. Their names appear on page 2b of the list of project participants, following the names of the supervisory local officials.

32. YZFZ, 1685, 18:4a–4b. A similar poem appears in the "ancient traces" section of the 1810 gazetteer—under the title "Yingyuan huaigu" (Embracing the past at Firefly Park). The park was a site closely associated with the Sui emperor Yangdi. This poem contains four of the five allusions to the *Wenxuan* or to Prince Xiao Tong. Oddly, it includes no reference to Firefly Park or to the Sui emperor. YZFZ, 1810, 31:12b.

33. For a gazetteer biography of Zong Guan, see YZFZ, 1733, 31:25b.

34. Zhang Huijian, *Ming Qing Jiangsu wenren nianbiao* (Shanghai: Shanghai guji chubanshe, 1986), 834. According to Antonia Finnane, the gazetteer was actually published in 1687. See her "Yangzhou: A Central Place," 122.

35. Zhang Huijian, *Ming Qing Jiangsu wenren nianbiao*, 834. Deng Hanyi and Huang Yun appear to have been particularly close friends as well as fellow Taizhou natives. Their names are frequently mentioned together.

36. On his service in Guichi, see Zhang Huijian, *Ming Qing Jiangsu wenren nianbiao*, 853. See also YZFZ, 1733, 31:25a.

37. YZFZ, 1733, 31:25a.

38. YZFZ, 1685, 18:4b.

39. *Liyang xianzhi*, interpolated into Deng Hanyi, ed., *Shenmotang mingjia shipin*, Kangxi edition. An incomplete copy is housed in the Beijing Library Rare Books Reading Room. The interpolation is unpaginated. Peng Gui served as a secretary to several officials, including Jin Zhen. Evidently, the two met when Jin served as Yangzhou magistrate. Peng Gui became Jin's secretary when Jin moved to a new position in Nanjing. Peng wanted to live near his mother's home in Liyang, which is not far from Nanjing.

40. YZFZ, 1685, 18:4b.

41. The exception being Zou Zhimo's poem titled "Embracing the past at Wenxuan Tower using the same rhyme as Wang Shizhen," YZFZ, 1685, 33:30b.

42. YZFZ, 1685, 33:70a–70b.

43. See YZFZ, 1685, 32:41b, 33:30b, 33:61a–61b, 33:67b, and 33:70a–70b.

44. Timothy Brook, *Praying for Power: Buddhism and the Formation of Gentry Society in Late-Ming China*, Harvard Yenching Monograph Series, 38 (Cambridge: Harvard University Press, 1993), introduction.

45. Hellmut Wilhelm, "From Myth to Myth: The Case of Yueh Fei's Biography," in Denis Twitchett and Arthur Wright, eds., *Confucian Personalities* (Stanford: Stanford University Press, 1962), 146.

46. The story of these two generals appears in the biography of Liu Qi in the Song history, *Songshi* (Zhonghua shuju edition), 11:399 ff, 33:366.

47. YZFZ, 1810, 28:14a.

48. Brook, *Praying for Power,* 29.

49. This information appears in Sang Zhi's commemorative essay (*YZFZ*, 1810, 28:13b). He also mentions an inscription by the famous Tang calligrapher Yan Zhenqing (709–84).

50. Brook, *Praying for Power*, 182. In Yangzhou, at least, there seems to have been a lapse in temple restoration activities during the years immediately preceding and following the conquest (beginning after the Wanli reign), and a marked upsurge during the long reign of the Kangxi emperor, with significant renovation and construction activities continuing in the Qianlong period. See *YZFZ*, 1810, juan 28. However, as we shall see below, gazetteer accounts of renovation activities are often incomplete, and thus unreliable.

51. Brook, *Praying for Power*, 30.

52. Although many of the salt merchants residing in Yangzhou were natives of Huizhou prefecture in Anhui province, they actively underwrote local projects in both their native place and in their city of residence. For numerous examples, see Xie Kaichong, *Lianghuai yanfa zhi*, Kangxi edition, in Wu Xiangxiang, *Zhongguo shixue congshu* (Taipei: Xuesheng shuju, 1966), juan 23.

53. *YZFZ*, 1733, 31:26b–27a.

54. Ruan Yuan, *Guangling shishi*, in *Congshu jicheng*, vol. 7, no. 584 (Shanghai: Commercial Press, 1959), 39. A brief biography of Sang Zhi also appears in Ruan Yuan, *Huaihai yingling ji* (Ruanshi xiaolanghuan xianguan, 1798), jiaji, 1:27a, along with one of his poems.

55. *Zhongguo meishujia renming cidian*, 733.

56. Aoki Masaru, "Yōshū ni arishi hi no Kō Shōjin," 482. See also Ruan Yuan, *Guangling shishi*, 107.

57. See for example Ruan Yuan, *Guangling shishi*, 107, which contains the following entry: "When Kong Shangren of Qufu served in Yangzhou, he often held literary and drinking parties. Once, with Deng Hanyi, Wu Qi, Jiang Yi, Zong Yuanding, and Sang Zhi, he climbed Plum Blossom Ridge and composed poetry. Chen Yi of Changzhou wrote a poem about this."

58. For comparison, see the commemorative essays on the reconstruction of Pingshan Hall in 1674 discussed in Chapter 4. This project also took place in 1674.

59. Zhao Shiling, "Shaanxi fenshou Liangzhuangdao canzheng Cui gong Hua muzhiming," Qian Yiji, ed., *Beizhuan ji*, vol. 7, 2289–92. According to this detailed biography, Cui Hua, a native of Zhili, passed the provincial examinations in 1660. He was nominated for the Boxue hongci examination in 1679 but died before he could take it. Wang Shizhen admired his poetry and referred to him as "my disciple" in *Chibei outan* (Incidental conversations north of the pond). He was also known for his paintings in the bird and flower genre. (*Zhongguo meishujia renming cidian*, 798.)

60. Joanna Handlin Smith, "Social Hierarchy and Merchant Philanthropy as Perceived in Several Late-Ming and Early Qing Texts," *Journal of the Economic and Social History of the Orient* 41, no. 3 (1998): 434–41. Liang Qizi (Angela Leung), "Mingmo Qingchu minjian cishan huodong de xingqi," *Shihuo yuekan* 15, no. 7 (1986): 316. Antonia Finnane provided the reference that enabled me to identify these men.

61. Smith, "Social Hierarchy and Merchant Philanthropy," 437–38. See also Liang Qizi (Angela Leung), "Mingmo Qingchu minjian cishan huodong de xingqi," 310.

62. YZFZ, 1810, 28:13b.

63. YZFZ, 1665, 23:1b; James T. C. Liu. "Yueh Fei (1103–41) and China's Heritage of Loyalty," Journal of Asian Studies 31, no. 2 (February 1972): 294. For a brief biography of Yue Fei, see Hellmut Wilhelm, "From Myth to Myth: The Case of Yueh Fei's Biography," in Denis Twitchett and Arthur F. Wright, eds., Confucian Personalities (Stanford: Stanford University Press, 1962), 146–61.

64. YZFZ, 1733, 14:19b.

65. Jonathan Hay, "Ming Palace and Tomb in Early Qing Jiangling," Late Imperial China 20, no 1 (June 1999): 30.

66. For further discussion of the Ming founder's tomb and its symbolic significance with regard to Qing legitimacy, see Hay, "Ming Palace and Tomb," especially pp. 28–31.

67. On the relationship between Zhu Yizun and Cao Yin, and Zhu's role in the Yangzhou publishing office, see Spence, Ts'ao Yin and the K'ang-hsi Emperor, 51, 163.

68. On Cao Yin's philanthropic activities in Nanjing, see Spence, Ts'ao Yin and the K'ang-hsi Emperor, 157.

69. YZFZ, 1733, 14:20a.

70. Ruan Yuan hired laborers and restored the shrine-temple, inviting friends who shared his interests to carry out rituals honoring the Song generals. Ruan Yuan, Yanjing shi ji (reprint, Beijing: Zhonghua shuju, 1993), 626–27. Ruan involved himself in the restoration of many Yangzhou sites. Moreover, he seems to have been particularly interested in Zhu Yizun, for he restored Zhu's residence in Hangzhou and was involved in the compilation of a gazetteer of that site when he served as an official in Zhejiang. Ruan Yuan et al., Zhucha xiaozhi (Qilu shuge keben, 1798).

71. Wang Zhenzhong, "Ming-Qing Lianghuai yanshang yu Yangzhou chengshi de diyu jiegou," 112. The author states that beginning in the late Ming, the neighborhood around Little East Gate Street was inhabited by many gentry families.

72. Finnane, "Yangzhou: A Central Place," 132. Finnane refers to markets in the southeastern part of the Old City. It is not clear from her account whether these were in operation during the early Kangxi period.

73. Finnane, "Yangzhou: A Central Place," 131. See also Wang Zhenzhong, "Ming-Qing Lianghuai yanshang yu Yangzhou chengshi de diyu jiegou," 105. Wang points out that the New City was relatively wet to begin with; thus the spatial layout of roads and alleys was partly determined by creeks, streams, canals, and marshes.

74. Deng Zhicheng, Qingshi jishi chubian (Hong Kong: Zhonghua shuju, 1974), vol. 1, 364.

75. Wang Shizhen, Juyi lu, cited in WSZNP, 22.

76. Wang Shizhen, "Preface" of Chen Yunheng, ed., Guoya chuji, reprinted in Xie and She, Qingchu ren, 88.

77. On Wang's role in the development and decline of another literary trend, see Jiang Yin, "Wang Yuyang yu Qingchu Songshi feng zhi xingti," 82–97.

78. See Yu Zhou's Preface to *Guoya chuji*, reprinted in Xie and She, *Qingchu ren*, 89.

79. Deng Hanyi, "Preface," in Sun Mo, ed., *Shiwu jia ci*, Sibu beiyao jibu (Shanghai: Zhonghua shuju), 1a.

80. The two men met in 1686, and they visited each other frequently in both Yangzhou and Taizhou while Kong Shangren worked on an imperially sponsored river conservancy project. This project kept Kong in the Yangzhou area for three years, during which time he produced the poetry and essays included in his literary collection, the *Huhai ji* (Lakes and seas collection). Deng Hanyi was one of several of Kong's local friends who wrote commentary for this collection. (Zhang Huijian, *Ming Qing Jiangsu wenren nianbiao*, 850; Aoki Masaru, "Yōshū ni arishi hi no Kō Shōjin," 478–90.)

81. Kong Shangren, *Huhai ji*, 166.

82. Kong Shangren, *Huhai ji*, 11. Note that Kong himself was a Shandong native.

83. Li Yesi, "Da Deng Xiaowei [Hanyi] xiansheng shu" (A letter in response to Mr. Deng Hanyi), *Gaotang shiwen ji* (reprint, Hangzhou: Zhejiang guji chubanshe, 1988), 652. I am grateful to Jonathan Hay for this reference.

84. YZFZ, 1733, 14:12a.

85. YZFZ, 1733, 14:12a. For a description of 'Dong's Well,' the site of the original Dong Zhongshu shrine, see Wu Qi, "*Yangzhou guchui ci xu*," 2b–3a.

86. Chen Weisong, "Gaitang qianji xu" (Preface to the Gaitang collection), in Sun Zhiwei, *Gaitang qianji*, 1b–2a. After abandoning the life of a merchant, Sun rented a house next to the Shrine of Master Dong and embarked on a life of study and poetry composition. He named his rented home Gaitang, alluding to a line in the *Book of Songs (Shijing)* and also to his native province of Shaanxi. Sun composed poems on moving in next door to the Shrine of Master Dong (4:18b) and on choosing a name for his new residence (4:18b–19a). See also Ruan Yuan, *Guangling shishi*, 44–45.

87. Deng Hanyi, *Shiguan chuji*, Nanyang Dengshi Shenmotang keben, 1672, Preface, 1a. This collection is sometimes catalogued under the title *Tianxia mingjia shiguan*.

88. Xia Quan, preface (1828), Deng Hanyi, *Shenmo biji* (Taizhou: manuscript edition), 3a.

89. Wakeman, *Great Enterprise*, 99.

90. His name does not appear, for example, on Ono Kazuko's index of Fushe members. See Ono, *Fukusha seishi sakuin* (Kyoto: Jinbun kagaku kenkyūjo, 1995).

91. Zhang Huijian, *Ming Qing Jiangsu wenren nianbiao*, 564. Du Dengchun indicates that this gathering was in fact the last yearly meeting of the Restoration Society. Du Dengchun, "Sheshi shimo," 10a–10b.

92. A list of those in attendance appears in Du Dengchun, "Sheshi shimo," 10a–10b.

93. Deng Hanyi, *Shiguan chuji*, "Preface," 5a.

94. Chen Zuoming, 1657, reprinted in Xie and She, *Qingchu ren*, 45.

95. Zhang Huijian, *Ming Qing Jiangsu wenren nianbiao*, 632. For a biography of Zha Jizuo, see *ECCP*, 18–19.

96. Gong Dingzi was a Fushe partisan and high-ranking official, now infamous for having served three regimes during his tumultuous political career (*ECCP*, 431). Deng and Gong met in Suzhou, and both attended the Fushe party in 1642. They had many friends in common, and their names appear together in various locales during the period immediately after the conquest. On the trip to Guangdong, see Zhang Huijian, *Ming Qing Jiangsu wenren nianbiao*, 672. Deng Hanyi describes his vocation as a "hired pen" to high officials in the preface to the *Shiguan sanji* (1689; reprint, Zhong Zhizong, Rugao: Shenliu dushu tang, 1750), 5b.

97. Du Jun, "Song Sun Wuyan gui Huangshan xu" (Preface to send Sun Mo off on his return to his hometown at Huangshan), in Du Jun, *Bianya tang wenlu*, Li Zitao, ed., Guochao wenlu xubian, n.d., 1:12a–13a. Note that when Sun Mo declared his intention to return to his hometown at Huangshan, all of his friends wrote essays and poems indicating their responses to his decision. These responses reflected various attitudes toward urban life vs. hometown life and the experience of sojourning. These materials on Sun Mo's proposed return to Huangshan are described by contemporaries as an important literary "event of the age." Both Du Jun and Sun Mo socialized with Deng Hanyi in Yangzhou.

98. Deng Hanyi, *Shiguan chuji*, "Preface," 5a.

99. See for example Deng Hanyi's preface to Sun Mo, *Shiwujia ci* (Lyrics by fifteen gentlemen), 1a–1b. In this collection, Sun Mo (a Huizhou native residing in Yangzhou) assembled the writings of famous national figures, many of whom had local ties.

100. On late-Ming interest in lyric poetry, see Kang-I Sun Chang, *The Late-Ming Poet Ch'en Tzu-lung: Crises of Love and Loyalism* (New Haven: Yale University Press, 1991).

101. You Tong, "Peng Sunyu *Yanlu ci* xu," (Preface to Peng Sunyu's *Yanlu Lyrics*), in Sun Mo, *Shiwujia ci,* 24:1a. In this essay, You Tong matches famous sites in Yangzhou with appropriate lines of verse and sentiments. For example, he writes, "when you mourn for the Sui Hunting Park, it is suitable to rhapsodize about the 'golden lock and heavy gates'; when you pass through the Jade Hook Path, it is appropriate to rhapsodize on 'dawn stars, brightness extinguished.'" Naturally, Pingshan Hall and Wenxuan Tower appear in his litany of sites and poetic lines.

102. R. Kent Guy, *The Emperor's Four Treasuries* (Cambridge: Harvard University Press, 1987), 18; and Lynn Struve, "The Hsu Brothers and Semiofficial Patronage of Scholars in the K'ang-hsi Period," *Harvard Journal of Asiatic Studies* 42 (1982): 259.

103. Sun Jinli, "Guangling changhe ci," 1666, preface.

104. For a publishing project that in many ways paralleled the *Poetry Survey,* see Ellen Widmer's discussion of *Modern Letters* (Chidu xinyu) in her article, "The Huanduzhai of Hangzhou and Suzhou: A Study in Seventeenth-Century

Publishing," *Harvard Journal of Asiatic Studies* 56, no. 1 (June 1996): 82–90. The editor, Wang Qi, in many ways seems to occupy a position, and to make use of a persona, quite similar to Deng Hanyi's.

105. YZFZ, 1733, juan 35.

106. Li Yesi, *Gaotang shiwen ji,* 652. Zhang Chao, who finished editing the third volume of the *Poetry Survey* after Deng Hanyi's death, describes the collection as a "surprise hit around the empire." See Zhang Chao, "Preface," in Deng Hanyi, ed., *Shiguan sanji,* 1a, 4b.

107. Ōki Yasushi, "Sanjin Chin Keiju to sono shuppan katsudō," in *Yamane Yukio kyōju taikyū kinen: Mindai shi ronsō* (Tokyo: Kyuko Shoin, 1990), 1248–49.

108. In all, 585 poets from Zhejiang and Jiangnan appear in the first collection, with 190 poets from the remaining fourteen provinces of the empire.

109. YZFZ, 1675, fanli, 2B.

110. Deng Hanyi, *Shiguan chuji,* fanli, 2a.

111. Fu Lisun, *Hezheng lu,* Yangjia laowu kanben, 1810, 3:2b.

112. Ruan Yuan, *Liangzhe youxuan lu,* quoted in Qian Zhonglian, ed., *Qingshi jishi,* vol. 5, 2815.

113. Ruan Yuan, *Guangling shishi,* 44. This may describe a different, possibly incomplete edition of the *Shiguan,* evidently the same version held in the imperial collection. The *Siku quanshu zongmu tiyao* lists a version of the *Shiguan* with 14 juan, and a *bieji* of 2 juan. It also states that this book was in the imperial collection *(neifu cangben).* See Yongrong, ed., *Siku quanshu zongmu tiyao* (reprint, Taipei: Shangwu yinshu guan, 1978), 39:4:707.

114. Shen Deqian, *Guochao shi bie cai ji,* quoted in Qian Zhonglian, ed., *Qingshi jishi,* vol. 5, 2815.

115. Xia Quan, "Preface," *Shenmo tang biji,* 2a.

116. Yongrong, ed., *Siku quanshu zongmu tiyao,* 4:77, and the *Jinshu zongmu* attached to this edition of the *Siku quanshu zongmu tiyao,* 169. See also the subsection of the *Qingdai jinhui shumu* entitled "List of Books to Be Surrendered" (Shanghai: Commercial Press, 1957), 153. The *Shiguan* is not, however, unique in this regard. For example, the *Bai mingjia shixuan,* edited by Wei Xian, appears both in the *Siku quanshu zongmu tiyao* and among the books banned for including poetry by Qian Qianyi. See Xie and She, *Qingchu ren,* 133.

117. L. Carrington Goodrich, *The Literary Inquisition of Ch'ien-lung* (New York: Paragon Reprints, 1966), 147. The two writers named in the edict became symbolic of those writers who needed to be suppressed, as did Jin Bao, whose name appears in the call for the suppression of the *Shiguan.* Qian Qianyi (1582–1664) was one of the great Ming-Qing scholar-poets, and served as an official under both dynasties. His writings contained anti-Manchu remarks, however, and subsequently were banned by the Qianlong emperor. See *ECCP,* 148–50. See also Goodrich, 100–107. Jin Bao (1614–80) was a Ming official who fought for the loyalist cause until 1650, when factional conflicts led to his torture and near death at the hands of his erstwhile allies. He then became a Buddhist monk. *ECCP,* 166. Qu Dajun (1630–96) was a poet who began his

examination career as a senior licentiate during the early Qing. When his teacher died as a loyal martyr, he stopped preparing for the examinations and dedicated himself to the Ming cause. In 1650, he became a monk. Later, he met and became a close friend of Zhu Yizun, and through Zhu, he greatly widened his social circle. Eventually, he returned to lay life, married, and continued to support the Ming cause while socializing with Qing officials. Some of his writings were found to be subversive during the Yongzheng period, and were investigated and banned again in 1774 for their anti-Manchu content. *ECCP*, 201–2; and Goodrich, 112–37.

118. *Jinshu zongmu*, 169. Note that the figure of "five hundred" poets is based on the abridged version in the imperial collection, which contained only fourteen juan. The indices of banned books published as appendices to later reprint editions of the *Siku quanshu zongmu tiyao* were compiled in the late nineteenth and early twentieth century, though they appear to have been based on primary documents from the late eighteenth century. See Guy, *Emperor's Four Treasuries*, 248–49, n. 94.

119. Goodrich, *Literary Inquisition of Ch'ien-lung*, 217.

120. Ruan Yuan, *Huaihai yingling ji*, quoted in Qian Zhonglian, ed., *Qingshi jishi*, vol. 5, 2816.

121. Guy, *Emperor's Four Treasuries*, 167.

122. Guy, *Emperor's Four Treasuries*, 170.

123. Philip Kuhn, *Soulstealers: The Chinese Sorcery Scare of 1768* (Cambridge: Harvard University Press, 1990), chap. 6.

124. Kanda Kiichirō, "Shinshi no sōshū ni tsuite," 460. Like many scholars, including many of the great eighteenth- and nineteenth-century bibliophiles such as Shen Deqian and Ruan Yuan, Kanda mistakenly believed that the *Shiguan* originally had four volumes, rather than three. See Xie and She, *Qingchu ren*, 153.

125. The copy in the Nanjing Library is patched together from at least two separate editions, with elements from an eighteenth-century edition combined with the original, Kangxi-era, set. The Library of Congress and the Columbia University Library have only the first part. The Library of Congress copy is missing the chapter containing women's poetry.

126. YZFZ, 1810, A-ke-dang-a preface, 2a–2b.

127. Li Dou was part of Ruan Yuan's social circle, and he participated in the compilation of the *Lianghuai yingling ji*. He also attended several parties in honor of Ruan Yuan between 1799 and 1805. In a letter to Ruan Yuan, Ling Tingkan identifies Ruan as the publisher of an edition of Li Dou's book and suggests a broad range of potential improvements. Ling Tingkan, *Jiaoli tang wenji* (reprint, Beijing: Zhonghua shuju, 1998), 206–11. Interestingly, Ling suggests that among other things, Li Dou ought to have included more information on different kinds of Western goods available in Yangzhou, a category also explored by Lin Sumen. I am grateful to Hu Minghui for providing this reference. The author of the *Hanjiang sanbaiyin*, Lin Sumen was Ruan Yuan's mother's kinsman, and traveled as part of Ruan Yuan's official entourage. He lived in the Sui Wenxuan Tower when Ruan Yuan returned to Yangzhou to observe mourning for his father. His

collection of more than three hundred rhymes about Yangzhou includes brief descriptions of local fashions, products, books, and operas, as well as documenting recent imports. Lin Sumen, *Hanjiang sanbaiyin* (Yangzhou: Guangling guji keyinshe photo reprint, 1988), author's preface (1808).

128. He shared a birthday with the great Tang poet Bo Juyi, and both served in Hangzhou. This was duly noted by Jiao Xun, a friend and relative of Ruan, in his essay honoring Ruan Yuan's fortieth birthday. See Zhang Jian et al., eds., *Ruan Yuan nianpu* (original title *Leitang'anzhu dizi ji*), Nianpu congkan (reprint, Beijing: Zhonghua shuju, 1995), 2–3.

129. Wang Zhangtao, *Ruan Yuan zhuan* (Hefei: Huangshan shushe, 1994), 9.

130. Zhang Jian, *Ruan Yuan nianpu*, 3.

131. *ECCP*, 399.

132. Ruan Yuan, "Yangzhou Ruanshi jiamiao bei (Stele for the family temple of the Ruans of Yangzhou," *Yanjing shi ji*, 386–87.

133. Wu Han, *Jiang-Zhe Cangshujia shilue* (Beijing: Zhonghua shuju, 1981), 151.

134. Ruan Yuan, *Yanjingshi ji*, 665.

135. Ruan Yuan, *Wenxuanlou shicun*, Jiaqing edition; *ECCP*, 403.

136. Ruan Yuan, *Yanjingshi ji*, 746.

137. See, for example, the essay titled "Wenxuan lou," in Liang Zhangju, *Guitian suoji*, Qingdai shiliao biji (Beijing: Zhonghua shuju, 1981), 4. Here, in addition to establishing the tower's connection to Wenxuan scholarship (and not to the prince of Liang), the author describes a gathering hosted by Ruan Yuan for several of his elderly peers on the eve of the Opium War.

138. Ruan Yuan, "Xiu Sui Yangdi ling ji" (A record of the restoration of Sui Yangdi's tomb), *Yanjing shi ji*, 624. The magistrate, Yi Bingshou, was well known for his clerical script calligraphy (*RMDZD*, 227). He also wrote an inscription on the grounds of the Sui Wenxuan Tower, according to the inscription on Wang Jun's album leaf. See discussion below.

139. Ruan Yuan, *Yanjing shi sanji*, 692; and *YZHFL*, 6.

140. William T. Rowe, *Saving the World: Cheng Hongmou and Elite Consciousness in Eighteenth Century China* (Stanford: Stanford University Press, 2001), 268–70.

141. Ruan Yuan, *Huaihai yingling ji*, "Preface," 1b.

142. Ruan Yuan, *Huaihai yingling ji*, fanli, 1a.

143. Ruan Yuan, *Huaihai yingling ji*, fanli, 1b.

144. Ruan Yuan, *Huaihai yingling ji*, fanli, 1b.

145. *YZHFL*, 7–8.

146. *YZFZ*, 1874, 5:22a.

147. *YZFZ*, 1874, 11:20a–23a.

148. "Yangzhou huafang jiyou tu" (A map for recalling outings in the painted boats of Yangzhou). This board game is in the Nanjing Library. The explanatory materials suggest that the game depicts sights that can no longer be seen.

149. Wang Jun's name is sometimes transliterated "Wang Yun." However,

according to the authoritative *Hanyu dacidian* (vol. 11, p. 1286), the character is properly pronounced "Jun."

150. *Zhongguo meishujia renming cidian,* 459. The "Yangzhou huayuan lu" is included in the *Yangzhou congke.*

151. See, for example, Jin Anqing, *Shuichuang chunyi* (Beijing: Zhonghua shuju, 1997), 46.

152. The tower fell into disrepair in the nineteenth century and was reconstructed in the Republican period. Its former site in the Manifest Loyalty Temple is currently occupied by a building for storing scriptures (Cangjing lou). The temple was the headquarters of the local Buddhist association during the Republican period, as it is today. Interestingly, the old story about the Wenxuan Tower recently has begun to reappear in guidebooks. It is not one of the city's major attractions today, though it is one of the few reconstructed temples that is at least theoretically open to the public. See, for example, Zhao Ming, *Yangzhou daguan,* 83–84; and Hua Kangsen, *Zizhu luyou shouce: Yangzhou* (Beijing: Zhongguo luyou chubanshe, 1999), 94.

153. See Philip Kuhn, *Rebellion and Its Enemies in Late Imperial China, 1796–1864* (Cambridge: Harvard University Press, 1980); and Mary Backus Rankin, *Elite Activism and Political Transformation in China: Zhejiang Province, 1865–1911* (Stanford: Stanford University Press, 1986).

154. Frederic Wakeman, Jr., "Localism and Loyalism during the Ch'ing Conquest of Kiangnan: The Tragedy of Chiang-yin," in Frederic Wakeman, Jr., and Carolyn Grant, eds., *Conflict and Control in Late Imperial China* (Berkeley: University of California Press, 1975), 84. Jiangyin, Jiading, and Yangzhou have often been cited together by patriotic twentieth-century historians as examples of the brutality of Manchu rulership. Wakeman makes a more subtle point, revealing the fluid nature of the term "loyalism" as it shifts from primarily dynastic to local to national/racial in its orientation.

CHAPTER 4

1. Wang Yinggeng, *Pingshan lansheng zhi,* 4:1a. The line about the eaves is frequently quoted in reference to the name of the hall. The locus classicus is the *Taiping huanyu ji,* a Song-dynasty work by Yue Shi.

2. Shen Gua, "Chongxiu Pingshan tang ji" (A record of the renovation of Pingshan Hall), in Wang Yinggeng, *Pingshan lansheng zhi,* 4:4a–4b.

3. Zhao Hongji, "Chongxiu Pingshan tang ji" (A record of the renovation of Pingshan Hall), in Wang Yinggeng, *Pingshan lansheng zhi,* 4:8a. Also, in the *YZHFL* Li Dou states that "the decline and repair of the Mountain Hall during the Yuan and Ming cannot be clearly analyzed [here he cites three poems from the Yuan that describe the hall as converted to other purposes or in ruins] . . . The poems of the early Ming do not much mention it" (*YZHFL,* 359).

4. Cheng Mengxing, *Pingshan tang xiaozhi,* 1:3a.

5. Zhao Hongji, "Chongxiu Pingshan tang ji," 4:8a–9b. Note also that by the Wanli era, all that survived of Daming Temple, which was adjacent to Pingshan

Hall, was the foundation, and that it too was repaired for the first time in centuries under the administration of Wu Xiu (*YZFZ*, 1810, 28:14b). Frederic Wakeman refers to a resurgence of interest in the literary styles favored by Ouyang Xiu during the 1620s (Wakeman, *Great Enterprise*, 102).

6. Brook, *Praying for Power*, 3.

7. For example, according to a seventeenth-century annotation to a poem in Kong Shangren's *Huhai ji*, Plum Blossom Ridge itself was built by the prefectural magistrate Wu Xiu (*hao*, Pingshan), who also had plums planted there. (Kong Shangren, *Huhai ji*, 169.) Such ridges and ornamental hills were often byproducts of canal dredging projects: earth removed from the canals was used to build hills, which became scenic destinations or garden elements.

8. Wei Xi, "Chongxiu Pingshan tang ji," in Wang Yinggeng, *Pingshan lansheng zhi*, 4:11b. An excellent translation of this essay also appears in Owen, *Anthology of Chinese Literature*, 634. Wei refers to frequent military disasters affecting Yangzhou and alludes to their impact on the hall. This suggests that military disaster caused the most recent decline. The 1673 earthquake might also have been a contributing factor, though the sources are silent on this.

9. Zhu Yizun, "Zhenshanglou ji" (A record of the Tower of True Enjoyment), in Wang Yinggeng, *Pingshan lansheng zhi*, 4:20a.

10. See, for example, Cheng Mengxing, *Pingshan tang xiaozhi*, 1:3b.

11. *YZFZ*, 1664, 21:19a.

12. Brook, *Praying for Power*, 28.

13. Zong Guan, "Chongxiu Pingshan tang ji" (A record of the renovation of Pingshan Hall), in Wang Yinggeng, *Pingshan lansheng zhi*, 4:16b. The phrase seems either to have been or to have become a set phrase, for Shen Deqian begins his preface to *Pingshan tang xiaozhi* (A small gazetteer of Pingshan Hall) with the same words (Cheng Mengxing, *Pingshan tang xiaozhi*, Wangshi keben, 1752, Shen preface, 1a). Note that according to the *Pingshan lansheng zhi*, the decision to renovate was made in the autumn of Kangxi 12 (1673) (Wang Yinggeng, *Pingshan lansheng zhi*, 4:2a). However, the renovations were not completed until the seventh month of the following year, i.e., Kangxi 13 (1674), as stated in Wang Maolin's essay commemorating the renovation. See Wang Maolin, "Chongjian Pingshan tang ji," in Wang Yinggeng, 4:15a. Thus, Chen Congzhou and other authors are incorrect in placing the renovation in 1673. See, for example, Chen Congzhou, "Yangzhou Daming si," *Wenwu* 9 (1963): 21.

14. For a sustained point by point comparison of Pingshan Hall and Tiger Hill, see Wang Yingquan's preface to Wang Yinggeng, *Pingshan lansheng zhi*, 2a–3a.

15. *YZHFL*, 345. Identical sources are also cited in Wang Yinggeng, *Pingshan lansheng zhi*, 3:30a. Li Dou cites Zhu Mu's (Song-dynasty) *Fangyu shenglan*, Zhu Xi's (Song-dynasty) *Zhuzi leibian*, and Lu Shen's (Ming-dynasty) *Zhiming lu*, all of which claim Sichuan origins for this ridge; Shu is the ancient name for the Sichuan region. Alternatively, the *Taiping Huanyu ji* says that because the tea grown on Shugang resembles that of a place in Shu, the ridge was called Shugang; yet another account argues that the spring water here tastes like the water of the

Shu river, hence the name. Alternative names for the ridge include Kunlun and Guangling, or Broad Ridge (a name also used to refer to the city). Li and Wang also present the competing claim made by Yao Lu in the *Lu shu*, which states that the ancient dictionary *Erya* uses the character *shu* (Sichuan) for *du* (solitary); hence the name "Shu Ridge" refers to the fact that the mountain stands alone. Wang Yinggeng comments: "Today there are some people who point out that the mountain resembles Sichuan, whereas others say that the formation comes from Sichuan. They have not yet read the *Erya*."

16. Zhu Maowei, "Yangzhou lishi renwen zongji," in Feng Erkang, ed., *Yangzhou yanjiu*, 390.

17. On the site's function as a cemetery, see for example Ruan Yuan, *Huaihai yingling ji*, jiaji, 2:18b, and bingji, 3:14b.

18. An album leaf by Wu Bin (active 1591–1643), "A record of yearly observances—ascending the heights," is one example. The album leaf is in the National Palace Museum, Taipei (Lina Lin, ed., *Special Exhibition of Autumn Landscapes* (Taipei: National Palace Museum, 1989), 48–49.

19. YZFZ, 1685, 7:4a. According to the gazetteer, women dressed up in stylish clothing and makeup for these excursions.

20. Jonathan Hay, "The Leisure Zone: Depictions of the Sub-urban Landscapes of Seventeenth Century Jiangnan" (unpublished paper, cited by permission), 3. Similarly, the northwest suburbs of Beijing also constituted a leisure zone; see Naquin, *Peking*, 102–4.

21. See for example Kong Shangren, "Yu Chenhu xuanshi xiaoyin" (A brief introduction to Yu Chenhu's poetry selection), *Huhai ji*, 207.

22. The name "Slender West Lake" came into common use during the late eighteenth century. However, it seems to have been coined somewhat earlier.

23. Anonymous, *Yangzhoufu tushuo*, Wanli-era manuscript edition. For reference, see also Wang Chung-min, *A Descriptive Catalogue of Rare Chinese Books in the Library of Congress* (Washington, D.C.: Library of Congress, 1957), vol. 1, 31.

24. Chen Weisong, "Yiyuan Youji" (Record of an excursion at Yi Garden), in *Chen Weisong xuanji*, ed. Zhou Shaojiu (Shanghai: Shanghai guji chubanshe, 1994), 377–79. Also quoted in full in Ruan Yuan, *Guangling shishi*, 95.

25. YZFZ, 1685, 19:6a. On the second restoration, see Wei Xi, "Chongxiu Fahai si ji" (Record of the renovation of the Ocean of the Law Temple), 38:49b–51a. Wei states that the temple had been ruined in the conquest, and describes how a man was inspired to restore the temple due to a dream. He does not mention the Shunzhi-period restoration. Chanzhi Temple was also partially restored during the Shunzhi reign (YZFZ, 1685, 19:3b).

26. Hay, "Leisure Zone," 3, 5.

27. Kong Shangren, "Pingshan tang yajishi xu" (Preface to poems written at an elegant gathering at Pingshan Hall), *Huhai ji*, 219–20.

28. Yüan Hung-tao, *Pilgrim of the Clouds: Poems and Essays from Ming China*, trans. Jonathan Chaves (New York: Weatherhill, 1978), 93.

29. Timothy Brook, *Geographical Sources of Ming-Qing History* (Ann Arbor: Center for Chinese Studies, 1988). The publication of "gazetteers" for Tiger

Hill began in the fifteenth century and continued with at least one per century through the twentieth (pp. 95–96). There were three gazetteers for Pingshan Hall in the eighteenth century (pp. 87–88). Also note that though Tiger Hill is included in late Ming books on the famous mountains of the realm, Pingshan Hall is not.

30. Many of the sites mentioned in the gazetteer no longer survived in fact, but only in textual memory. See, for example, YZFZ, 1810, juan 31.

31. Brook, *Praying for Power*, 162.

32. The essay reads in part: "In 1063, Mr. Diao of Danyang came from his position as director of the Board of Works to take care of some matters in the prefecture. This was only seventeen years after the time of Ouyang Xiu, but what was left of Pingshan Hall was already decayed and collapsed, and could no longer be propped up. After one year, Mr. Diao had it completely taken down and rebuilt." Shen Gua, "Chongxiu Pingshan tang ji," in Wang Yinggeng, *Pingshan lansheng zhi*, 4:4a–4b.

33. Examples can be found in the renovation essays published together in Wang Yinggeng, *Pingshan lansheng zhi*, 4:1a–17b. For an example from Ouyang Xiu's lifetime, see the essay by Shen Gua in Wang Yinggeng, *Pingshan lansheng zhi*, 4:3b–5a.

34. Naquin, *Peking*, 62.

35. He writes: "Those who visit take the character of the place and make it their own character. That is always the same. How is this? Jinshan makes people feel broad and strong. Huishan makes people feel mournful. Tiger Hill and West Lake make people feel fascinated and captivated. The only one that can make people feel deep emotion is Pingshan Hall" (Kong Shangren, "*Pingshan tang yaji shi* xu," *Huhai ji*, 219).

36. Kong Shangren, "*Pingshan tang yaji shi* xu," *Huhai ji*, 219.

37. Stephen Owen, *Remembrances: The Experience of the Past in Classical Chinese Literature* (Cambridge: Harvard University Press, 1986), 3.

38. Stephen Owen, *The Great Age of Chinese Poetry* (New Haven: Yale University Press, 1991), 122.

39. The prominent position of Sui and Six Dynasties sites in Kangxi-era poetry and tourist itineraries can be seen in Wu Qi, "*Yangzhou guchui ci* xu"; and Kong Shangren's poetry cycle on the scenic sites of Yangzhou, written in 1689, *Huhai ji*, 165 ff.

40. YZFZ, 1810, 31:63a. One of the three Kangxi-period editions of the *Yangzhou fuzhi* is listed as the source for information on the Eight Views; however, the particular edition is not specified.

41. Philip Kafalas, "Nostalgia and the Reading of the Late Ming Essay: Zhang Dai's *Tao'an Mengyi*" (Ph.D. diss., Stanford University, 1995), 34. Kafalas points out that this sub-genre has its roots in the rhapsody tradition of the late Han, with many examples of such works in the *Wenxuan*, the important sixth-century literary anthology. He also points out that *huaijiu* and *huaigu* are closely linked terms with overlapping meanings, but that *gu* generally suggests antiquity and old times, whereas *jiu* often implies old friends. Wang Shizhen defined *huaigu* as follows: "*Huaigu* is thinking about the people in the past. Living in a different time, think-

ing of each other across distant generations. Beyond a thousand miles, after one hundred generations, it is as if they were in the same room, or even more as if they were living in the same village." (Wang Shizhen, *Yuyang shanren jinghua lu xunzuan* [Hongdou zhai keben, 1767], 1:25a).

42. A collection of poems by three authors resident in Yangzhou during this period titled *Guangling yonggu shi* (Poems celebrating the ancient sites of Guangling) provides a brief introduction to each site, followed by linked verse poems on each. Many of the sites existed only in imagination, and the poems still reflect on vitality and destruction. These reflections seem more conventionalized than in the earlier *huaigu* poems. The section on Pingshan Hall reads: "At Daming Temple northwest of the city wall. Later occupied by monks. In this dynasty, the magistrate Jin Zhen renovated it." Two of the three poems refer to Ouyang Xiu, and one asks if Jin Zhen can be compared to his predecessor. The other refers to the site's literary legacy. (Mei Geng et al. *Guangling yonggu shi*, 1696.)

43. Kong Shangren, "Yu Chenhu xuanshi xiaoyin," 207. Note that the contrast between "enchanting" and "harmonious" implies a contrast between indulgence with courtesans at Red Bridge and the more refined entertainments associated with Pingshan Hall. This is further reinforced by the seasonal symbolism.

44. Yuan Yao's "Hanjiang shenglan tu" is a horizontal scroll now in the Beijing Palace Museum collection. Painted in 1747, its huge size, 165.2 cm 262.8 cm, suggests that it may once have been mounted as a screen or in an entrance hall.

45. Kong Shangren, "Qionghua guan kanyue xu" (Viewing the moon at Hortensia Daoist Temple), *Huhai ji*, 193.

46. Kong Shangren, "Qionghua guan kanyue xu," *Huhai ji*, 193.

47. Clunas, *Fruitful Sites*, 19.

48. YZFZ, 1733, 19:19b. On shrines, see YZFZ, 1733, 25:19b–20a. Interestingly enough, the term *chongxiu* meaning "to renovate" is used to describe the "re-editing" of local gazetteers. Gazetteers, like schools, shrines, and temples, were an important component in the construction of local administrative identity.

49. YZFZ, 1733, 19:19b.

50. YZFZ, 1733, 25:19b–20a.

51. Wang Maolin, "Yugou dongtian ji" (Record of Jade-Hook Cave), *Baichi wutongge wenji*, 3:8a–8b.

52. Jin Zhen, "Chongxiu Pingshantang ji," in Wang Yinggeng, *Pingshan lansheng zhi*, 4:10a.

53. Wang Maolin, "Yugou dongtian ji," *Baichi wutongge wenji*, 3:8b.

54. Wang Maolin, "Zeng Yangzhou zhifu Jin gong xu" (Preface presented to the Yangzhou prefectural magistrate Mr. Jin), *Baichi wutongge wenji*, 2:77a.

55. YZFZ, 1810, 45:8b.

56. YZFZ, 1685, 22:71b. The term *gu*, translated as "poisonous," is often used to describe situations of political unrest. The 1733 edition of the YZFZ makes the political nature of these rumors quite explicit (27:60a).

57. The *Shilu* is filled with references to the Three Feudatories Uprising; indeed the fighting was clearly the emperor's principal concern. Chapter 2 of Jonathan Spence's *Emperor of China* suggests the emperor's preoccupation with the war

(Spence, *Emperor of China: Self Portrait of K'ang-hsi* (New York: Vintage Books, 1974). There were troop movements in the Yangzhou vicinity during this period because major garrisons were located in Nanjing and Zhenjiang (immediately across the river from Yangzhou). However, the only direct references to Yangzhou and its subsidiary counties from 1674 to 1676 regarded tax forgiveness due to drought or flooding.

58. Wang Maolin, *Baichi wutongge wenji*, 2:77a.

59. Wang Maolin, *Baichi wutongge wenji*, 2:77b.

60. The 1685 gazetteer notes that upon his departure the people begged him to stay on in Yangzhou despite his promotion and that they wanted to built a shrine for him but were unable to obtain permission. The populace begging a departing official to stay is a conventional image. (*YZFZ*, 1685, 22:71b.)

61. This meeting seems to be of the type described in Huang Liuhong's manual for magistrates, which was written during the 1670s. Huang wrote: "After a magistrate designate receives his appointment certificate, some of the local gentry living in the capital may wish to get acquainted with him . . . If they present their visiting cards and ask for private interviews, he should receive them graciously and ask their advice with humility. If there are men of prominence from the assigned district living in the capital, he should pay visits to them as a matter of courtesy. . . . to get on friendly terms with them and also to let them assess the personality and appearance of the new magistrate" (Huang Liu-hung, *Complete Book Concerning Happiness and Benevolence*, 78).

62. Wang Maolin, *Baichi wutongge ji*, 11:15b.

63. This story, from the "Record of Avoiding Heat" by Ye Meng of the Song dynasty, also appears in the eighteenth-century literary guides to Pingshan Hall and its environs. It was the most prevalent image of Ouyang Xiu enjoying himself with his friends at the hall.

64. Wang Maolin, "Pingshan tang ji," *Baichi wutongge wenji*, 3:6b. See also Wang Yinggeng, *Pingshan lansheng zhi*, 4:14b–16b.

65. *YZFZ*, 1675. For the poems, see 34:2b–27b; for the commemorative essays, see 39:67a–72b.

66. These essays appear to have been written some time after the project was completed, as they mention the second phase of the renovation, which was completed the following year. The essays were collected in Wang Yinggeng, *Pingshan lansheng zhi*, juan 4.

67. For further information on Zong Guan, see Chapter 3. Several of his essays on local subjects appear in the 1685 gazetteer, including works on the subject of irrigation and coastal management (*YZFZ*, 1685, 4:19b and 4:22a). For a brief account of the ways in which the hall's completion was commemorated, see Ruan Yuan, *Guangling shishi*, 103.

68. Jin Zhen, "Chongjian Pingshan tang ji" (Record of the rebuilding of Pingshan Hall), in Wang Yinggeng, *Pingshan lansheng zhi*, 4:10a.

69. Jin Zhen's account states that more than one thousand people were in attendance, and Zhu Yizun's essay commemorating the construction of the "Hall of True Enjoyment" the following year includes a statement reading: "I heard that

on the day the hall was completed, more one hundred gentlemen of national reputation gathered there" (Zhu Yizun, "Zhenshang lou ji," in Wang Yinggeng, *Pingshan lansheng zhi,* 4:19b). In Cheng Mengxing's 1752 work *Pingshantang xiaozhi,* the author refers to the several thousand who "came to watch" (1:3b) and the more than one hundred people from the prefecture's "renowned class" who all participated in the writing of poetry (1:4a).

70. Poems composed on this occasion can be found in Wang Yinggeng, *Pingshan lansheng zhi,* juan 5. The authors include Wang Maolin, Wang Yaolin, Deng Hanyi, Wang Ji, Peng Gui, Gong Xian, Zong Guan, Xu Chengjia, Zhou Zaijun (eldest son of Zhou Lianggong), and several others. For Cao Rong's poem, see 5:38b–40a. This juan also includes the poems composed by Wang Maolin and Jin Zhen when they visited the site and decided to restore the hall. Such poems were also included in the individual literary collections of their authors; see, for example, Wang Ji, "Junbo Jin gong fujian Pingshan tang zhaotong zhujun yanji" (Prefectural magistrate Jin restored Pingshan Hall and invited the gentlemen for a banquet), in *Shanjian xuji* (Among the mountains collection, continued), Huaizhai ji qizhong, 19a ff; and Wang Maolin, "Zhongdong Pingshan tang luocheng taishou Jin gong zhaotong zhujun yanji" (In mid-winter, Pingshan Hall was complete and prefectural magistrate Jin invited all the gentlemen for a banquet), *Baichi wutongge ji,* 12:11a.

71. Jin Zhen, "Chongjian Pingshan tang ji," in Wang Yinggeng, *Pingshan lansheng zhi,* 4:10b. Note that the reference to bells and chimes strongly suggests that they enacted a Confucian ritual, thereby treating the hall as a shrine.

72. Jin Zhen, "Chongjian Pingshan tang ji," in Wang Yinggeng, *Pingshan lansheng zhi,* 4:10b.

73. *Liji,* "Liyun," 2:19. This is my own translation. See also James Legge, *Li Chi: The Book of Rites,* vol. 1 (New Hyde Park, N.Y.: University Books, 1967), 379.

74. Two other commemorative essays by Wei Xi appear in the literary section of the 1685 gazetteer. One is entitled "Yangzhou Tianfei gong beiji" (Stele record for the Heavenly Consort Temple), and the other, "Chongxiu Fahai si ji" (A record of the renovation of Ocean of the Law Temple), YZFZ, 1685, 38:47a–49b and 38:49b–51a. This seems to indicate that Wei either actively participated in the commemoration of Yangzhou's reconstruction—or that his was a much-sought-after (and readily available) commemorative voice.

75. Wei Xi, "Chongjian Pingshan tang ji," in Wang Yinggeng, *Pingshan lansheng zhi,* 4:12a–12b. See also Owen, *Anthology,* 634–5.

76. Wei Xi, "Chongjian Pingshan tang ji," 4:12b.

77. Mao Qiling, "Fuxiu Pingshan tang ji," in Wang Yinggeng, *Pingshan lansheng zhi,* 4:14a.

78. Mao Qiling, "Fuxiu Pingshan tang ji," in Wang Yinggeng, *Pingshan lansheng zhi,* 4:14a. For Mao Qiling's experiences during the Qing conquest, see R. Keith Schoppa, *Xiang Lake* (New Haven: Yale University Press, 1989), 96–98. For his activities as a chronicler of Xiang Lake, and his reentry into government service in the 1680s, see Schoppa, 103–105.

79. Zong Guan, "Fuxiu Pingshan tang ji," in Wang Yinggeng, *Pingshan lansheng zhi*, 4:17b.

80. Zong Guan, "Fuxiu Pingshan tang ji," in Wang Yinggeng, *Pingshan lansheng zhi*, 4:17b.

81. There is some confusion over Wang's year of birth. Even within his own literary collection, he gives dates ranging from 1638 to 1640. His tomb inscription, written by Xu Qianxue, says that he was born in 1640, which is the date given in the publisher's preface to the 1980 photo-reprint edition of his literary collection. However, according to the Japanese scholar Odaira Keiichi, the tomb inscription contains many inaccuracies. Odaira cites Wang Shizhen's biography of Wang Maolin as the most accurate source, which gives 1639 as the year of Wang's birth. Odaira Keiichi, "Ō Kōmon Bōrin nempu shōkō," *Tōhō Gakuhō* 59 (March 1987): 360.

82. Wang Maolin, "Pingshan tang ji," *Baichi wutongge ji*, 3:6a.

83. Wang Maolin, "Pingshan tang ji," *Baichi wutongge ji*, 3:6a.

84. The major source for this section is Wang's literary collection, the *Baichi wutongge ji*. The 1980 Shanghai reprint edition of Wang's collected works includes his poetry collection, prose collection, surviving works, and the *Jinpi ci* (Brocade lute lyrics). The poetry collection consists of sixteen chronologically ordered chapters containing poems written during the years 1662–78. This poetry collection was first published by Wang himself in 1678 and represents approximately 45 percent of his total poetic output. His prose collection is organized by genre and was published posthumously by his nephew Wang Quan in 1715. In addition, his nephew published a selection of his later poems, again in chronological order, under the title *Surviving Works of the Hundred Foot Wutong Pavilion* (Baichi wutongge yiji), which was also published in a photo-reprint edition by Shanghai guji chubanshe in 1980.

85. Liang Zhangju, *Langji congtan, Qingdai shiliao biji congkan* (Beijing: Zhonghua shuju, 1981), 21; and YZFZ, 1810, 31:22a–22b. According to Liang, Wang's garden was named after the ancient wutong tree housed in it. The New City location bespeaks Wang's merchant ties, as does his Huizhou ancestry.

86. Odaira Keiichi has produced a systematic chronology of Wang's life based on the poetry and prose collections as part of a collective research project titled "Kōnan bunjin no kenkyū" (Research on the Jiangnan literati), led by Arai Ken. See Odaira, "Ō Kōmon Bōrin nempu shōkō." Note that Odaira cites texts only by chapter (juan) and not by page. For Wang Maolin's literary collection, I cite both Odaira's article and the photo-reprint edition, giving both chapter and page. I have cross-referenced other sources where possible. Odaira's chronological biography is invaluable. He has identified all individuals by personal name, provided basic biographical information, presented descriptions of sites and gardens from local gazetteers, given punctuated extracts from essays, and brought together poetry from particular events by various authors.

87. Although he resided in Yangzhou most of his life (except when he was in Beijing or traveling), his social circle included many other officials of Huizhou origin whose families had moved elsewhere. He was responsible for the construction

of a shrine to his own clan and Huizhou worthies in Yangzhou. See Wang Shi-zhen's biography, "Bibu Wang Jiaomen zhuan" (Biography of the official Wang Jiaomen), in Wang Maolin, *Baichi wutongge yigao* (Shanghai: Shanghai guji chu-banshe, 1980), 3b. Wang Maolin also traveled in southern Anhui for several months after his first attempt to pass the metropolitan examination in Beijing in 1664 (Odaira, "Ō Kōmon Bōrin nempu shōkō," 364).

88. The position of the family's two daughters in the birth order is unclear. Shi Runzhang, "Wang Juefei [Rujiang] xiansheng muzhiming" (Epitaph for Mr. Wang Juefei), *Shi Yushan ji* (Hefei: Huangshan shushe, 1992), vol. 1, 415. On the ancestor, see "Gaozu wen" (Essay on my ancestors), *Baichi wutongge wenji*, 7:23a.

89. Ho Ping-ti's famous article deals primarily with the eighteenth century, but is relevant here for reference. Ho Ping-ti, "The Salt Merchants of Yang-chou: A Study of Commercial Capitalism in Eighteenth Century China," *Harvard Journal of Asiatic Studies* 17 (1954): 130–68; see especially pp. 143–44 for a brief dis-cussion of the late Ming period.

90. *LHYFZ*, Kangxi edition. See especially juan 20–24, "Renwu."

91. On his father's commoner status, see Shi Runzhang, "Wang Juefei xian-sheng muzhiming," *Shi Yushan ji*, 415.

92. Shi Runzhang, "Wang Juefei Xiansheng muzhiming," 415.

93. Wang Maolin, "Gao xian kaowen" (Report to my deceased parents), *Bai-chi wutongge wenji*, 7:25b.

94. Odaira, "Ō Kōmon Bōrin nempu shōkō," 359. On Wang Yan, the tutor from whom Wang Maolin and his elder brother Wang Yaolin studied the classics, see Ruan Yuan, *Guangling shishi*, 38–39; and Wang Shizhen, "Bibu Wang Jiao-men zhuan," *Baichi wutongge yigao*, 2a. Wang Yan was friendly with Lei Shijun and participated in the outing to Red Bridge described by Lei in Chapter 2.

95. For "no different from impoverished and mean families," see "Gao xian kaowen," *Baichi wutongge wenji*, 7:26a. Perhaps the economic turmoil of the early Kangxi period offers a better explanation for the family's financial straits.

96. Odaira, "Ō Kōmon Bōrin nempu shōkō," 396.

97. Odaira, "Ō Kōmon Bōrin nempu shōkō," 359; "Gao xian kaowen," *Bai-chi wutongge wenji*, 7:27a.

98. Odaira, "Ō Kōmon Bōrin nempu shōkō," 359; "Wang xiong Wang Gong-zhi muzhiming," *Baichi wutongge wenji*, 5:34a. He died in 1672 at the age of forty sui. Wang Maolin attributes Zhaolin's death to an illness he contracted while horseback riding and entertaining himself with courtesans, during a trip to visit his brother, who was serving in the capital (5:34b).

99. Odaira, "Ō Kōmon Bōrin nempu shōkō," 360; *ECCP*, 410–11.

100. Odaira, "Ō Kōmon Bōrin nempu shōkō," 360. Note that the boundaries of Yangzhou prefecture extended to the coast until the Yongzheng period. Liu-zhuangchang was a sea-salt producing area located in the northeast corner of Xinghua county, Yangzhou prefecture (*Zhongguo gujin diming dacidian*, 1148). That Wang's father sent his wife and children to a salt-producing area is a further indication of his connection to the salt trade.

101. Odaira, "Ō Kōmon Bōrin nempu shōkō," 360; Wang Maolin, Liuzhuang ganjiu" (Remembering the past at Liuzhuang), *Baichi wutongge ji,* 6:10b–11a. Note that in Chinese, this is a rhymed poem in five-character lines. My translation is meant to convey the events recalled, rather than the poetic style. This passage provides another example of the confusion surrounding Wang's age. According to Wang, he was just seven at the time of the siege. However, calculating from the birth year cited in Wang Shizhen's biography followed by Odaira, his age would have been six *sui.*

102. In other words, a ruin. "Liuzhuang ganjiu," *Baichi wutongge ji,* 6:11a.

103. Odaira, "Ō Kōmon Bōrin nempu shōkō," 360.

104. "Aishi" (Grieving poem), a poem written in 1673 while Wang Maolin was in mourning for his recently deceased mother, is part of a series of ten poems praising his mother for her contributions to the family and for her virtuous behavior. See *Baichi wutongge ji,* 11:19a.

105. "Aishi," *Baichi wutongge ji,* 11:19b.

106. Odaira, "Ō Kōmon Bōrin nempu shōkō," 361; Shi Runzhang, "Wang Feijue xiansheng muzhiming," *Shi Yushan ji,* vol. 1, 415.

107. Wang Shizhen's biography of Wang Maolin, "Bibu Wang Jiaomen zhuan," in *Baichi wutongge yigao,* 3b.

108. The name of this building is itself taken from Ouyang Xiu's "Poem in Response to Liu Yuanfu (Chang)'s 'Pingshan Hall.'" See Zhang Shicheng and Xia Yunbi, eds., *Yangzhou shici* (Poems and lyrics of Yangzhou), in *Zhongguo Mingsheng guji shici congshu* (A collectanea of poems and lyrics on China's famous sites and ancient traces) (Shanghai: Shanghai guji chubanshe, 1985), 37. The poem reads: "Though Yangzhou's glory has long diminished / Even now we can clamber up the ridge / The mountains lie beyond the vast expanse / Flowers bloom among overgrown ponds and terraces / In every household ancient flute songs persist / Raising a toast to the scene, I am among you / I think of your *true enjoyment* from afar / And I regret that I cannot relax in your midst."

109. "Pingshan tang ji," *Baichi wutongge wenji,* 2:7a. At first the figure 18,560 might seem to represent the number of workers, but it also appears to be outrageously high. Timothy Brook suggests that the number refers to man-days rather than to individual men (correspondence, October 1997). See also Martin Heijdra, "The Socio-Economic Development of Ming Rural China," (Ph.D. diss., Princeton University, 1994), p. 355. The fact that *ren* (man) is not used as a measure word for *gong* (labor) in this context further supports this interpretation.

110. Wang mentions this fact in both his essay commemorating the renovation and his essay honoring the prefectural magistrate. The phrase "He did not levy a single coin or impress a single laborer" used in the second essay is a set phrase for describing construction and renovation projects. Wang Maolin, "Zeng Yangzhou zhifu Jin gong xu," *Baichi wutongge wenji,* 2:78a.

111. Wang Maolin, "Pingshan tang ji," *Baichi wutongge wenji,* 2:6b.

112. Wang Maolin, "Pingshan tang ji," *Baichi wutongge wenji,* 2:7a.

113. Wang Maolin, "Pingshan tang ji," *Baichi wutongge wenji,* 2:7a.

114. YZHFL, 358.

115. In discussion of the second round of renovations led by Wang Maolin, Zhao Zhibi cites Cheng Mengxing's *Pingshantang xiaozhi,* stating that Wang Maolin had expanded the hall to include the Tower of True Enjoyment as a shrine to the Song worthies above, with classrooms added below (Zhao Zhibi, *Pingshantang tuzhi,* 1:3b).

116. Wang Maolin, "Pingshan tang ji," *Baichi wutongge wenji,* 3:6b.

117. He is clearly being disingenuous about the five centuries without decline.

118. Odaira, "Ō Kōmon Bōrin nempu shōkō," 411; Wang Maolin, "Tong zhuzi yao Changzhen taishou fanzhou you Pingshan yinyi xiufu fende tangzi" (I and the various gentlemen invite prefectural magistrate Jin Zhen [zi Changzhen] to tour Pingshan by boat having decided to restore it; I am assigned the rhyming character *tang* [hall]), *Baichi wutongge ji,* 12:9a.

119. Zong Guan, "Chongxiu Pingshan tang ji," in Wang Yinggeng, 4:17b.

120. According to the *Huanyu ji* quote cited in most guides to the hall, Ouyang Xiu originally built the hall in the southwest corner of the Daming Temple precincts. See, for example, Li Dou, *YZHFL,* 355–56. The same comments appear verbatim but unattributed in Wang Yinggeng, *Pingshan lansheng zhi,* 4:1a; and also in Zhao Zhibi, *Pingshan tang tuzhi,* 1:2b.

121. Brook, *Praying for Power,* 16.

122. Patricia Ebrey, *Confucianism and Family Ritual in Imperial China* (Princeton: Princeton University Press, 1991), 188–89.

123. Kai-wing Chow, *Confucian Ritualism in Late Imperial China* (Stanford: Stanford University Press, 1994), 1.

124. Kai-wing Chow, *Confucian Ritualism,* 1.

125. Kai-wing Chow, *Confucian Ritualism,* 44.

126. Zong Yuanding mentions this transaction in his comments on Kong's poem "Buzhong Pingshan tang yangliu" (Adding willows at Pingshan Hall), in Kong Shangren, *Huhai ji,* 10. Ouyang Xiu himself was famous for planting willows at the hall, and Kong quite literally emulates his worthy predecessor. Zong points out the then well-known association between Ouyang and the willows in his commentary. For another anecdote on the subject, see *YZFZ,* 1810, 72:4a.

127. Kong Shangren, "Zeng Pingshan Daohong shangren" (Presented to Daohong, Abbot of Pingshan), *Huhai ji,* 66.

128. Yang Zeyou, *Yangzhou youlan zhinan* (Yangzhou: Yangzhou zhi cheng yinshuguan, 1916). See also Wang Tongling, *Jiangzhe luxing ji* (Cixiang congkan, Republican period, c. 1925).

129. *YZFZ,* 1810, juan 31.

130. All of these men were local residents and visitors of literary reputation. Note that these ritual activities preceded the official enshrinement of Ouyang Xiu on this site by Jin Zhen, the former magistrate, who was in town on business. The enshrinement ceremony took place on September 9, 1677 (the thirteenth day of the eighth month), and was followed by a banquet and drinking party. Among others, the following guests attended: Wang Maolin, Cheng Sui, Du Jun, Sheng Fusheng, Deng Hanyi, Fang Hengxuan, Xu Qianxue, Zong Guan, Hua Gun, Xu

Chengjia, Huang Yun, Wang Yaolin, Sun Mo, and Sun Zhiwei. See Odaira, "Ō Kōmon Bōrin nempu shōkō," 425.

131. Odaira, "Ō Kōmon Bōrin nempu shōkō," 424.

132. Sun Zhiwei, *Gaitang xuji* (reprint, Shanghai: Shanghai guji chubanshe, 1979), 6:13a–13b.

133. *YZHFL*, 362.

134. Odaira, "Ō Kōmon Bōrin nempu shōkō," 424.

135. Kong Shangren, *Huhai ji*, 19.

136. Evidence of this family connection can be found in his poem "Shu waizu Jiaomen xiansheng *Baichi wutongge shiji* hou" (Written at the end of my maternal grandfather's *Hundred Foot Wutong Pavilion Poetry Collection*). Cheng was born into a wealthy salt merchant family in 1679, became a jinshi in 1712, served as compiler in the Hanlin Academy, and returned home to Yangzhou after a relatively brief official career. On the connection to Wang Maolin, see Cheng Mengxing, *Jinyou tang quanji*, Jiangfeng ji, 16a. On the Cheng family and their fortune, see Ho Ping-ti, "The Salt Merchants of Yang-chou," 158–59. Publication of the *Pingshan tang xiaozhi* was sponsored by the Wang family. This could either be the Wang clan of Wang Maolin, or the clan of Wang Yinggeng, the 1736 renovator. These two may in fact have been members of the same extended family, for they shared a surname and connections to the salt trade.

137. Odaira, "Ō Kōmon Bōrin nempu shōkō," 361; Wang Maolin, "Jianshan lou shiji xu" (Preface to mountain viewing building poetry collection), *Baichi wutongge wenji*, 2:47a.

138. Wang Shizhen's biography of Wang Maolin includes the following anecdote: "The emperor also knew of him. One day, in the Forbidden City, one hundred pieces of fine paper were prepared, and the emperor ordered all the officials in the Hanlin Academy and others to present their calligraphy, and he chose the twenty-four best examples to mount on screens. Wang Maolin's calligraphy was among those selected" (Wang Shizhen, "Bibu Wang Jiaomen zhuan," *Baichi wutongge yigao*, 2b–3a).

139. Odaira, "Ō Kōmon Bōrin nempu shōkō," 361; Wang Maolin, "Jianshanlou shiji xu," *Baichi wutongge wenji*, 2:47a.

140. Wang Shizhen, *Yuyang shanren jinghua lu jishi*, vol. 3, 1514.

141. Owen, *Anthology of Chinese Literature*, 1128.

142. Wang Maolin, "Gao xian kaowen," *Baichi wutongge wenji*, 7:27a.

143. Yang Bin, ed., *Chidu xinbian jiaji, yiji, bingji, dingji, waiji* (A new compilation of letters, vols. 1–5) (Qing manuscript, Beijing library microfilm), dingji, juan 3, n.p.

144. Wang Maolin, "Song Liu Cishan xu" (Preface on sending off Liu Cishan), *Baichi wutongge wenji*, 2:64a.

145. Wang Maolin, "Chongxiu *Yangzhou fuzhi* xu" (Preface to the revised edition of the Yangzhou prefectural gazetteer), *Baichi wutongge wenji*, 2:52a.

146. Zheng Zu'an, "Xu Xiake luxing yanjiu erti," *Shilin* 28, no. 4 (1992): 13.

147. Wang Maolin, "Song Liu Cishan xu," *Baichi wutongge wenji*, 2:64a.

148. Zhao Zhibi, *Pingshan tang tuzhi*, author's preface.

149. Wang Yinggeng, *Pingshan lansheng zhi*, 4:2b–3a. Wang Yinggeng's extraordinarily extensive philanthropic activities included refurbishing schools, providing land to support schools, and donating ritual vessels and instruments. See *YZFZ*, 1810, 19:5b–6a.

150. Wang Yinggeng, *Pingshan lansheng zhi*, 4:3a.

151. Harold L. Kahn, "A Matter of Taste: The Monumental and Exotic in the Qianlong Reign," in Ju-hsi Chou and Claudia Brown, eds., *The Elegant Brush: Chinese Painting under the Qianlong Emperor* (Phoenix: Phoenix Art Museum, 1985), 291, 297.

152. *YZHFL*, 309.

CHAPTER 5

1. On Suzhou's primacy as a model for fashion and consumption, see Brook, *Confusions of Pleasure*, 221.

2. The Chongzhen emperor was evidently an exception to this generalization. Jerry Dennerline describes him as "extremely active in state affairs and even-handed in his approach to factional intrigue." This characterization does not, however, affect the argument made here regarding cultural influence. See Dennerline, "Fiscal Reform and Local Control: The Gentry-Bureaucratic Alliance Survives the Conquest," in Frederic Wakeman, Jr., and Carolyn Grant, eds., *Conflict and Control in Late Imperial China* (Berkeley: University of California Press, 1975), 101.

3. Susan Naquin, *Peking*, 187. (I have changed her spellings of these place-names to Pinyin romanization for the sake of consistency.) See also her pp. 280–81 for comparison of Beijing and Suzhou, and Beijing and Nanjing.

4. On the fashion for Suzhou chefs, see Deng Yunxiang, *Honglou fengsu tan* (Beijing: Zhonghua shuju, 1987), 465. On other influences, see p. 463.

5. For example, Zheng Yuanxun, scion of a prominent local family discussed in earlier chapters, asked the famous art theorist Dong Qichang to name and inscribe his garden, the Yingyuan (Garden of shadows and reflections). The magistrate responsible for the construction of the Wenfeng Pagoda in the sixteenth century asked a famous Suzhou official and art patron to compose the stele inscription for the new landmark.

6. On Beijing's emergence as a major intellectual center, alongside Suzhou, Hangzhou, and Yangzhou, see Guy, *Emperor's Four Treasuries*, 47–48.

7. Naquin, *Peking*, 451 and 469.

8. On jade cutters and Western exotica, as well as other distinctive local products, practices, and personages, see Ling Tingkan, *Jiaoli tang wenji*, 206–11. On gardens, theater, artists, academies, and temples, see *YZHFL*. On clothing, shoes, hats, Western exotica, theater, pleasure boats, artists, luxury products, and food in the early nineteenth century, see Lin Sumen, *Yangzhou sanbaiyin*. Note that Ling Tingkan wrote one of the prefaces to Lin Sumen's book.

9. Chen Congzhou, "Yangzhou Daming si," 9, 10; Zhu Jiang, *Yangzhou yuan-lin pinshang lu* (Shanghai: Shanghai wenhua chubanshe, 1990), 179.

10. Ho Ping-ti's article on the salt merchants deals extensively with their taste for the extravagant, as well as the institutions that made their wealth possible. He also discusses their social mobility, both upward and downward. Ho Ping-ti, "The Salt Merchants of Yang-chou," 130–68; see especially 154–68.

11. *YZFZ*, 1675, 19:1a.

12. Awareness of Chan-literati connections in the past and the presence of temples in scenic areas are cited by Timothy Brook as important sources of late Ming gentry interest in Buddhism. See Brook, *Praying for Power,* 316–17.

13. On Tianning Temple's Suzhou-style icons, see *YZHFL,* 92.

14. *YZFZ*, 1810, 28:17a–17b. In 1733 the local magistrate Yin Huiyi inscribed a stone stele that stated that "the Buddhist monk Buddhabhadra Zunzhe translated the Huayan sutra here" (*YZHFL,* 79).

15. *YZFZ*, 1733, 25:11b; and *YZFZ*, 1685, 19:1a.

16. *YZFZ*, 1733, 25:11b. On destruction in the late Yuan, see *YZFZ*, 1685, 19:1a. Tianning Temple today houses the Yangzhou City Museum and a flea market dealing in antiques, curios, stamps, and phone cards.

17. In a letter, Kong Shangren notes the presence of beggars (*Kong Shangren shiwen ji,* 7:520).

18. Tan Qian, *Beiyou lu,* Lidai shiliao biji congkan (Beijing: Zhonghua shuju, 1997), 13.

19. Tan Qian, *Beiyou lu,* 14.

20. Tan Qian, *Beiyou lu,* 14. The term he uses, "Beimang," is the name of a hill near Luoyang, Henan, which functions as a metaphor for graveyards and tombs.

21. Tan Qian, *Beiyou lu,* 14. The Southern Song loyalist Li Tingzhi led the defense of Yangzhou against the Mongols and fled the city to continue the resistance before his arrest and execution at Yangzhou in 1276. Jennifer Jay describes Li's relationship to the city as ambivalent; the local population had suffered hardship due to his commitment to the beleaguered Song ruling house and his tendency to favor his soldiers over local civilians. See Jay, *A Change in Dynasties* (Bellingham: Western Washington University, Center for East Asian Studies, 1991), 118–19. Here, Tan seems to imply that the two men, Li and Shi, were heroes of a similar type, and thus equally deserving of veneration.

22. Kong Shangren, *Huhai ji,* 201–2.

23. Kong Shangren, *Huhai ji,* 201.

24. Kong Shangren, *Huhai ji,* 201–2.

25. Kong Shangren, *Huhai ji,* 202.

26. Kong Shangren, *Huhai ji,* 202.

27. James Cahill, "The Emperor's Erotica," *Kaikodo Journal* 11 (spring 1999): 24. On the "Southern literati" as an alternative to "Northern" court factionalism, and the role of the Southern Tours in this dynamic, see Silas Wu, *Passage to Power: K'ang-hsi and His Heir Apparent* (Cambridge: Harvard University Press, 1979), chap. 4.

28. On early Qing factional politics, see Robert Oxnam, *Ruling from Horseback: The Politics of the Oboi Regency* (Chicago: University of Chicago Press,

1976); and Lawrence D. Kessler, *K'ang-hsi and the Consolidation of Ch'ing Rule* (Chicago: University of Chicago Press, 1976).

29. Maxwell Hearn, "The Kangxi Southern Inspection Tour: A Narrative Program by Wang Hui" (Ph.D. diss., Princeton University, 1990), 59. Unfortunately, the scroll depicting the Yangzhou portion of the tour is missing or no longer extant. Hearn hypothesizes that the missing scroll most likely focused on three principal elements: tax forgiveness for Jiangnan province, the visit to Yangzhou, and the change in mode of transportation from horses to boats (p. 108).

30. On painters brought to Beijing from Yangzhou during the Kangxi period as representative of a "romantic and erotic" Jiangnan urban culture, see Cahill, "Emperor's Erotica," 24–25; and Cahill, "The Three Zhangs, Yangzhou Beauties and the Manchu Court," *Orientations* 27, no. 9 (1996): 59. The chef of the Jiangnan provincial military commander was brought on board at Yangzhou to teach the imperial cooks how to prepare local delicacies. Anon., "Shengzu wuxing Jiangnan quanlu," in Wang Kangnian, ed., *Zhenqi tang congshu* (Beijing: Qiantang Wangshi paiyinben, 1910), 45b–46a.

31. Anon., "Shengzu wuxing Jiangnan quanlu," 7b–8a. For a slightly different translation, see Silas Wu, *Passage to Power,* 90.

32. Cahill, "Emperor's Erotica," 24; Silas Wu, *Passage to Power,* 90. For more on Yangzhou and the "cultural tension" between North and South, see Chapter 1. Wu's discussion is marred by overwrought adjectives, reliance on regional stereotypes, and melodramatic narrative. Still, his work is suggestive in positioning Yangzhou as the archetypal "Southern" city during the age of the Kangxi emperor's Southern Tours.

33. Spence, *Ts'ao Yin and the K'ang-hsi Emperor,* 141.

34. Spence, *Ts'ao Yin and the K'ang-hsi Emperor,* 144; and Anon., "Shengzu wuxing Jiangnan quanlu," 7a.

35. Anon., "Shengzu wuxing Jiangnan quanlu," 7b.

36. Anon., "Shengzu wuxing Jiangnan quanlu," 7b.

37. Anon., "Shengzu wuxing Jiangnan quanlu," 7b. The essay and poem express concern about decadence and decay and at the same time reveal the emperor's interest in "Southern" sensuality. For a thoughtful discussion of these events, see Jonathan Hay, *Shitao: Painting and Modernity in Early Qing China* (Cambridge: Cambridge University Press, 2001), 74–77.

38. Spence, *Ts'ao Yin and the K'ang-hsi Emperor,* 149. Spence implies that the merchants built more than one villa. In fact, there seems to have been one villa, which is referred to by the names of an adjacent temple and several nearby landmarks. See the stele composed by the Kangxi emperor, quoted in *YZFZ,* 1733, 25:4a.

39. Anon., "Shengzu wuxing Jiangnan quanlu," 44b.

40. *YZFZ,* 1810, 1:2a.

41. *YZFZ,* 1810, 1:2b.

42. Spence in *Ts'ao Yin and the K'ang-hsi Emperor,* citing Qianlong-era sources on the Qianlong tours, makes this assumption, as do many local historians, boosters, and guidebook writers (p. 159). However, there is no Kangxi-era evidence indicating that the temple was used as an imperial villa.

43. In *Ts'ao Yin and the K'ang-hsi Emperor,* Spence, relying on the *Shilu,* makes the oft-cited statement that Kangxi avoided Yangzhou for political reasons on his first tour (p. 127). In fact, the *Qiju zhu* (which was not available to Spence) indicates that the emperor spent two days inspecting flood control projects in the area, visiting Pingshan Hall and Tianning Temple, and bestowing gifts of imperial inscriptions on the two sites. See *Qiju zhu,* 1243–44; and Hearn, "Kangxi Southern Inspection Tour," 19.

44. YZFZ, 1733, 25:11b.

45. Ganquan and Jiangdu both had their county seats in the walled city of Yangzhou. Note that Ganquan was carved out of Jiangdu during the Yongzheng reign, so what is called "Ganquan and Jiangdu" in the 1733 gazetteer would have just been Jiangdu during the Kangxi reign. The statistics are based on YZFZ, 1733, juan 25.

46. YZFZ, 1733, 25:11b.

47. I am grateful to Michael Chang for this insight, based on the work of Marcel Mauss's *The Gift;* Chang elaborates it in an unpublished seminar paper entitled "Diaries of a Moving Monarch: Some Southern Tours as Seen from the Imperial Diaries (*Qiju zhu*)" (UCSD, June 1996).

48. On Cao Yin's role in the publishing project, see Spence, *Ts'ao Yin and the K'ang-hsi Emperor,* 157–65.

49. Spence, *Ts'ao Yin and the K'ang-hsi Emperor,* 162.

50. Gongcheng 1-1: "Li Xu zouwei zhongxiu Yangzhou Tianning si foxiang zhe," Kangxi period, roll 1, frame 7 on microfilm. This memorial is undated. However, Spence uses another memorial, which describes the renovation of Tianning Temple and cites a comparable sum of salt merchant funds. The memorial he discusses is dated Kangxi 59 (1720) and was submitted by Cao Fu. The actions by Cao Fu described in the Gongcheng memorial submitted by Li Xu correspond to those in the memorial submitted by Cao Fu himself, cited by Spence in *Ts'ao Yin and the K'ang-hsi Emperor,* 275–76.

51. For more on the renovation of Tianning Temple by Li Xu and Cao Fu (Cao Yin's adoptive son), see Spence, *Ts'ao Yin and the K'ang-hsi Emperor,* 275–76. He cites the Cao Fu Archives, no. 2852, dated 59/6/10.

52. 18 Jianzhu 4-20: "Lianghuai xunyanyushi Sanbao zou qing xiuli Jinshan si ji Yangzhou xinggong zou" (A memorial submitted by the Lianghuai salt control censor Sangao asking to repair Jinshan Temple and the Yanzhou imperial villa), 3/2/6, roll 1, frames 431–33.

53. 67 Jianzhu 14-34: "Liangjiang Zongdu chen Huang Tinggui deng zou wei xiuji Qingliangshan mingqu zou" (A memorial submitted by the governor general of Liangjiang, Huang Tinggui, et al., on the renovation of the Qingliangshan famous [scenic] area), 15/10/21, roll 1, frames 1745–46.

54. Jiangnan-style gardens were also built at Chengde during the reigns of the Kangxi and Qianlong emperors. On these gardens as an expression of "implicit political claims of suzerainty," see Philippe Foret, *Mapping Chengde* (Honolulu: University of Hawaii Press, 2000), 19. On the significance of the Tibetan and Central Asian–style outer temples built in Chengde (Jehol) after 1755, see, for example, Foret's pp. 15, 20–22, 25, 49–53, and 67.

55. Harold L. Kahn, "A Matter of Taste: The Monumental and Exotic in the Qianlong Reign," in Ju-hsi Chou and Claudia Brown, eds., *The Elegant Brush: Chinese Painting under the Qianlong Emperor* (Phoenix: Phoenix Art Museum, 1985), 291, 297.

56. Mark Elliott, *The Manchu Way: The Eight Banners and Ethnic Identity in Late Imperial China* (Stanford: Stanford University Press, 2001), 101.

57. YZHFL, 102.

58. Chen Congzhou, *Yangzhou yuanlin* (Shanghai: Kexue jishu chubanshe, 1983), 4 and 8.

59. Zhu Jiang, *Yangzhou yuanlin pinshang lu,* 129–31.

60. Such sites resembled the new centers for leisure and relaxation that developed in Edo (present-day Tokyo) after it became the shogun's new capital. Far from the ancient heartland of Japanese literary culture, these sites lacked ancient poetic resonances; instead, they often housed teahouses, theaters, and "other institutions catering to leisure enjoyment." See Henry D. Smith II, *Hiroshige: One Hundred Famous Views of Edo* (New York: George Braziller, 1986), 10–11.

61. Shen Fu, *Six Records of a Floating Life* (New York: Penguin, 1988), 110–11; and *Fusheng liuji,* in *Ming Qing xiaopin xuankan* (Changsha: Yueli shushe, 1991), 119.

62. Zhao Zhibi, *Pingshan tang tuzhi,* "Imperial Quill," 15a.

63. YZFZ, 1810, 1:15b.

64. On the submission of drawings for a site in Nanjing, see 67 Jianzhu 14-34: "Liangjiang Zongdu chen Huang Tinggui deng zou wei xiuji Qingliangshan mingqu zou," 15/10/21, roll 1, frames 1745–46. For a progress report on preparations in the Hangzhou area, see 65 Jianzhu 14-2: "Minzhe zongdu Ke-er-ji-shan zou bao Zhejiang sheng banli xinggong deng xiang chaiwu shizai qingxing zou" (A memorial submitted by the governor general of Minzhe, Ke-er-ji-shan, reporting on the true status of the imperial villas and other projects), 15/8/1, roll 1, frame 1723.

65. This extraordinary painting, categorized as a map, is no longer available for viewing at the archives. I am extremely grateful to Stephen Shutt for allowing me to see his detailed notes about it. A poor black-and-white reproduction of a detail can be found in Fu Chonglan, *Zhongguo yunhe chengshi fazhanshi,* between pp. 342 and 343. The catalogue title of the painting is "Jiangsu Yangzhou xinggong gongdian louge jianlou quan tu."

66. 88 Jianzhu 20-13: "Lianghuai yanzheng Gao Heng zou wei jiejiao xiujian Tianning dengchu xinggong jiesheng muzhi ji yunxing zou" (Memorial submitted by the Lianghuai salt commissioner Gao Heng about economizing on wood for the imperial villas at Tianning and elsewhere, and on wood shipments), 27/7/29, roll 1, frame 2204.

67. YZFZ, 1810, 1:19a.

68. *ECCP,* 542. Lu died in prison, and Gao Heng and another official involved were beheaded.

69. Jin Anqing, "A Caishen" (A, the God of Wealth), in Ouyang Zhaoxiong and Jin Anqing, eds., *Shuichuang chunyi,* Qingdai shiliao biji (1877; reprint,

Beijing: Zhonghua shuju, 1997), 63. The essay enumerates A-ke-dang-a's expenditures on items including banquets, operas, flowers, paintings, books, calligraphy, and clothing.

70. *YZHFL*, 2. Li bases his discussion of the tours on the *Nanxun Shengdian*, the official imperial account commissioned to commemorate the tours.

71. Zhu Zongzhou, "Qianlong nanxun yu Yangzhou," *Yangzhou shiyuan xuebao (shehui kexue)* 77, no. 4 (December 1989): 136.

72. *YZHFL*, 2.

73. Qian Yong (1759–1844) observed that the performance of operas in Yangzhou reached its zenith during the Southern Tours of the Qianlong emperor, and the Lianghuai salt merchants were also prominent patrons (Qian Yong, *Luyuan conghua* [1838; reprint, Beijing: Zhonghua shuju, 1979], 332).

74. For the specifics, see *YZHFL*, 19–20. The hyperbole of this description is consistent with Li Dou's discussion of other activities of the salt merchants and may reflect his negative assessment of their tastes. Here and elsewhere in Li's account, they are shown to favor garish spectacle—and (oddly enough) mechanical amusements.

75. Fu Chonglan, *Zhongguo yunhe chengshi fazhan shi* (Chengdu: Sichuan renmin chubanshe, 1985), 342.

76. Guo Zhongheng, ed., *Jiangnan mingsheng tuyong* (Suzhou: Yuanfen tang, 1763). The small size and coarse paper suggest that the edition was a relatively inexpensive one. On the inside of the front cover, there is a decorative red seal indicating that the book contains imperial poetry on the famous sites of the Jiangnan region.

77. Ruan Yuan, *Yanjing shi sanji*, 691; also *YZHFL*, 6; Yuan Mei preface, *YZHFL*, 7.

78. See, for example, Zhao Zhibi, *Pingshan tang tuzhi*.

79. See both the preface by Deqing, pp. 1a–1b, and the "Principles of Inclusion," *YZFZ*, 1810.

80. *Yangzhou mingsheng tu*, Palace edition, Qianlong period. The somewhat later *Tianning si tu* (Illustrations of Tianning Temple) in the Tōyōbunko collection contains similar illustrations and text, although in a different order. See also Walter Fuchs, *Die Bilderalben fur de Sudreisen des Kaisers Kienlung im 18 Jahrhundert* (Weisbaden: Steiner, 1976), which contains forty-eight fine color reproductions of some of these illustrations.

81. *YZHFL*, 92–95.

82. *YZHFL*, 100.

83. *YZHFL*, 101.

84. *YZFZ*, 1810, 1:24b. The same edict refers to officials sent by the court to inspect local arrangements.

85. Evelyn Rawski, *The Last Emperors: A Social History of Qing Imperial Institutions* (Berkeley: University of California Press, 1998), 84.

86. *YZHFL*, 101.

87. *YZFZ*, 1810, 1:26b–27a.

88. The position of Lianghuai salt censor was abolished by Tao Zhu in 1831.

This action may have improved the management of salt revenue; however, it marked the beginning of the end of Yangzhou's prosperity. *ECCP,* 710–11. Jin Anqing's account of Yangzhou's decline during this period is consistent with the more famous postfaces to the *Yangzhou huafanglu* written by Ruan Yuan in 1834 and 1839. *YZHFL,* 7–8.

89. Jin Anqing, "Guangling mingsheng" (The famous sights of Yangzhou), in Ouyang Zhaoxiong and Jin Anqing, eds., *Shuichuang chunyi,* 46–47.

90. *YZFZ,* 1874, 5:22a.

91. On the most famous merchant-patrons, Ma Yueguan (1688–1755) and Ma Yuelu (1697–after 1766), see Ginger Cheng-chi Hsu, *A Bushel of Pearls: Painting for Sale in Eighteenth-Century Yangzhou* (Stanford: Stanford University Press, 2001), chap. 2.

Bibliography

A-ke-dang-a 阿克當阿 and Yao Wentian 姚文田, eds. *Yangzhou fuzhi* 揚州府志 (Yangzhou prefectural gazetteer). 1810. Reprint, Taipei: Chengwen, 1974.

Anonymous. "Shengzu wuxing Jiangnan quanlu" 聖祖五行江南全錄 (A complete record of the Kangxi emperor's fifth tour of Jiangnan). In Wang Kangnian, ed. 汪康年. *Zhenqi tang congshu* 振綺堂叢書. Beijing: Qiantang Wangshi paiyin ben, 1910. Library of Congress.

———— *Yangzhou fu tushuo* 揚州府圖說 (Illustrations and explanations of Yang-zhou prefecture). Wanli period edition. Library of Congress.

———— *Yangzhou mingsheng tu* 揚州名勝圖 (Illustrations of the famous sights of Yangzhou). Palace edition, Qianlong period. Tokyo Metropolitan Library.

Aoki Masaru 青木正児. "Chūka bunjin no seikatsu" 中華文人の生活 (The lives of the Chinese literati). *Aoki Masaru zenshū* 青木正児全集 (Complete works of Aoki Masaru), vol. 7. Tokyo: Shunjū, 1973, 218–38.

———— "Yōshū ni arishi hi no Kō Shōjin" 揚州に在りし日の孔尚任 (The Kong Shangren of Yangzhou days). *Aoki Masaru zenshū*, vol. 2. Tokyo: Shunjū, 1973, 478–90.

Atwell, William. "From Education to Politics: The Fu She." In William T. de Bary, ed., *The Unfolding of Neo-Confucianism*. New York: Columbia University Press, 1975, 333–67.

Bol, Peter. *This Culture of Ours: Intellectual Transitions in T'ang and Sung China*. Stanford: Stanford University Press, 1992.

Bourdieu, Pierre. *The Field of Cultural Production*. Trans. Randal Johnson. New York: Columbia University Press, 1993.

Brook, Timothy. *The Confusions of Pleasure: Commerce and Culture in Ming China*. Berkeley: University of California Press, 1998.

———— *Geographical Sources of Ming-Qing History*. Ann Arbor, Mich.: Center for Chinese Studies, 1988.

———— *Praying for Power: Buddhism and the Formation of Gentry Society in Late-Ming China*. Harvard Yenching Monograph Series, 38. Cambridge: Har-vard University Press, 1993.

Cahill, James. "The Emperor's Erotica." *Kaikodo Journal* 11 (spring 1999): 24–43.

———— "Huangshan Paintings as Pilgrimage Pictures." In Susan Naquin and Ch'un-fang Yu, eds., *Pilgrimage and Sacred Sites in China*. Berkeley: University of California Press, 1992, 246–92.

———— "The Three Zhangs, Yangzhou Beauties, and the Manchu Court." *Orien-tations* 27, no. 9 (October 1996): 59–68.

Carlitz, Katherine. "Shrines, Governing Class Identity, and the Cult of Widow Chastity in Mid-Ming Jiangnan." *Journal of Asian Studies* 56, no. 3 (August 1997): 612–40.

Chang, Kang-I Sun. "A Guide to Ming-Ch'ing Anthologies of Female Poetry and Their Selection Strategies." *The Gest Library Journal* 5, no. 2 (winter 1992): 119–60.

———— *The Late-Ming Poet Ch'en Tzu-lung: Crises of Love and Loyalism.* New Haven: Yale University Press, 1991.

———— "Symbolic and Allegorical Meanings in the Yueh-fu pu-t'i Poem Series." *Harvard Journal of Asiatic Studies* 46, no. 2 (December 1988): 353–86.

Chang, Michael. "Diary of a Moving Monarch: Some Southern Tours as Seen from the Imperial Diaries (Qiju zhu)." Unpublished paper, 1996.

Chen Congzhou 陳從周. "Yangzhou Daming si" 揚州大明寺 (Daming Temple, Yangzhou). *Wenwu* 文物 9 (1963): 21–23.

———— *Yangzhou yuanlin* 揚州園林 (Yangzhou Gardens). Shanghai: Kexue jishu chubanshe, 1983.

Chen Wannai 陳萬鼐. *Kong Shangren* 孔尚任. In Gufeng congshu 古風叢書, vol. 11. Taipei: Heluo tushu chubanshe, 1978.

———— *Kong Shangren nianpu* 孔尚任年譜. Taipei: Commercial Press, 1973.

Chen Weisong 陳維崧. *Chen Weisong xuanji* 陳維崧選集 (Selected works of Chen Weisong). Ed. Zhou Shaojiu 周韶九. Shanghai: Shanghai guji chubanshe, 1994.

Cheng Mengxing 程夢星. *Jinyou tang quanji* 今有堂全集 (Complete works of Cheng Mengxing). Qing xiekeben. Yangzhou Library.

———— *Pingshan tang xiaozhi* 平山堂小志 (Small gazetteer of Pingshan Hall). Wang Family Printers, 1752. Library of Congress.

Chow, Kai-wing. *The Rise of Confucian Ritualism in Late Imperial China.* Stanford: Stanford University Press, 1994.

Ciyuan 辭源. Beijing: Shangwu yinshudian, 1991.

Clunas, Craig. *Fruitful Sites.* Durham, N.C.: Duke University Press, 1996.

Corbin, Alain. *The Lure of the Sea: The Discovery of the Seaside in the Western World.* Trans. Jocelyn Phelps. Berkeley: University of California Press, 1994.

Crossley, Pamela Kyle. "The Qianlong Retrospect on the Chinese-Martial (hanjun) Banners." *Late Imperial China* 10, no. 1 (June 1989): 63–107.

Dai Mingshi 戴名世. "Yangzhou chengshou jilue" 揚州城守紀略 (An Account of the defense of Yangzhou). Comp. Chen Henghe 陳恆和. *Yangzhou congke* 揚州叢刻 (Yangzhou collectanea). 1930–34. Reprint, Yangzhou: Guangling guji keyinshe, 1995.

Daqing Shengzu Ren Huangdi shilu 大清聖祖仁皇帝實錄 (The veritable records of the Kangxi emperor's reign). Taipei: Hualian chubanshe, 1964.

Deng Hanyi 鄧漢儀. *Guanmei ji* 官梅集. Original preface, 1647. Manuscript copy, Taizhou: Gujiu shudian, 1980. Nanjing Library.

———— *Shiguan chuji* 詩觀初集 (Poetry survey, first collection). Nanyang Dengshi Shenmotang keben, 1672. Library of Congress.

———— *Shiguan erji* 詩觀二集 (Poetry survey, second collection). Nanyang Dengshi Shenmotang keben, 1678. Nanjing Library.

——— *Shiguan sanji* 詩觀三集 (Poetry survey, third collection). Nanyang Dengshi Shenmotang keben, 1689. Reprint, Zhong Zhizong, Rugao: Shenliu dushutang, 1750. Nanjing Library.

——— *Shenmo biji* 慎墨筆記 (Random jottings from Careful-with-Ink Studio). Comp. Xia Quan 夏荃. Preface, 1828, Taizhou: manuscript edition. Yangzhou Library.

——— *Shenmotang mingjia shipin* 慎墨堂名家詩品 (Poetry by famous people from Careful-with-Ink Studio). Kangxi edition, incomplete copy, Beijing Library, Rare Book Room.

Deng Yunxiang 鄧雲鄉. *Honglou fengsu tan* 紅樓風俗談 (A conversation on customs in [Dream of the] Red Chamber). Beijing: Zhonghua shuju, 1987.

Deng Zhicheng 鄧之誠. *Qingshi jishi chubian* 清詩紀事初編 (Qing poems on events, preliminary edition). Hong Kong: Zhonghua shuju, 1974.

Dennerline, Jerry. *The Chia-ting Loyalists: Confucian Leadership and Social Change in Seventeenth-Century China*. New Haven: Yale University Press, 1981.

——— "Fiscal Reform and Local Control: The Gentry-Bureaucratic Alliance Survives the Conquest." In Frederic Wakeman, Jr., and Carolyn Grant, eds., *Conflict and Control in Late Imperial China*. Berkeley: University of California Press, 1975, 87–120.

Dong Yining 董以寧. *Dong Wenyou quanji* 董文友全集 (The complete works of Dong Yining). Shulin lansun tang, 1700, Shanghai Library, Changle Road branch.

Du Dengchun 杜登春. "Sheshi shimo" 社事始末 (Affairs of the club from start to finish). Wu Shenglan 吳省蘭, ed., *Yihai zhuchen geji* 藝海珠塵革集. Nanhui Wushi Tingyi tang kanben. Qianlong period. Library of Congress.

Du Jun 杜濬. *Bianya tang quanji* 變雅堂全集 (The complete works of Du Jun). Daoguang edition. Nanjing Library.

——— *Bianya tang wenlu* 變雅堂文錄 (Prose writings of Du Jun). Ed. Li Zutao 李祖陶. Guochao wenlu xubian 國朝文錄續編. Shanghai: Saoye shanfang, 1900.

——— *Bianya tang yiji* 變雅堂遺集 (Surviving collection of Du Jun). Huanggang: Shen Zhijian, 1894. Nanjing Library.

Ebrey, Patricia. *Confucianism and Family Rituals in Imperial China*. Princeton: Princeton University Press, 1991.

Elliott, Mark. *The Manchu Way: The Eight Banners and Ethnic Identity in Late Imperial China*. Stanford: Stanford University Press, 2001.

Fan Jinmin 范金民 and Xie Zhengguang 謝正光 (Andrew Hsieh), eds. *Ming yimin lu huiji* 明遺民錄彙輯 (A compilation of records of the Ming *yimin*). Nanjing: Nanjing daxue chubanshe, 1995.

Fei Mi 費密. *Feishi yishu sanzhong* 費氏遺書三種 (Three surviving works by Mr. Fei). Chengdu: Daguan Tangshi Yilan tang, 1908. Nanjing Library.

Fenlizhai xingzhe 芬利齋行者. (Pseud.). "Zhuxi huashi xiaolu" 竹西花事小錄 (A short record of matters related to Zhuxi [Yangzhou] courtesans). In *Xiangyan congshu* 香艷叢書, vol. 6. 1914. Reprint, Shanghai: Shanghai shudian, 1991, 427–46.

Finnane, Antonia." Prosperity and Decline under the Qing: Yangzhou and Its
    Hinterland, 1644–1810." Ph.D. diss., Australian National University, 1987.
——— "Yangzhou: A Central Place in the Qing Empire." In Linda Cooke John-
    son, ed., *Cities of Jiangnan in Late Imperial China*. Albany: State University
    of New York Press, 1993, 117–49.
Foret, Philippe. *Mapping Chengde: The Qing Landscape Enterprise*. Honolulu:
    University of Hawaii Press, 2000.
Frankel, Hans. *The Flowering Plum and the Palace Lady*. New Haven: Yale Uni-
    versity Press, 1976.
Fu Chonglan 傅崇蘭. *Zhongguo yunhe chengshi fazhan shi* 中國運河城市發展史
    (A history of the development of China's Grand Canal cities). Chengdu: Si-
    chuan renmin chubanshe, 1985.
Fuchs, Walter. *Die Bilderalben fur die Sudreisen des Kaisers Kienlung im 18
    Jahrhundert*. Wiesbaden: Steiner, 1976.
Fujitani, Takashi. *Splendid Monarchy: Power and Pageantry in Modern Japan*.
    Berkeley: University of California Press, 1996.
Ganza, Kenneth. "The Artist as Traveler: The Origin and Development of Travel
    as a Theme in Chinese Landscape Painting of the 14th–17th Centuries." Ph.D.
    diss., Indiana University, 1990.
Gao Jin 高晉 et al. *Nanxun shengdian* 南巡盛典 (Great canon of the Southern
    Tours). 1771 Preface. Reprint, Shanghai: n.p., 1882.
Goodrich, L. Carrington. *The Literary Inquisition of Ch'ien-lung*. New York: Par-
    agon Book Reprint Company, 1966.
Gu Yanwu 顧炎武. *Tianxia junguo libing shu* 天下郡國利病書 (The strengths and
    weaknesses of the administrative regions of the empire). Shanghai: Erlin zhai
    tushuchengju, 1899.
Gu Yiping 顧一平 and Zhu Zhu 祝竹. *Yangzhou youji sanwen xuan* 揚州遊記散
    文選 (A selection of excursion records and essays about Yangzhou). Yangzhou:
    n.p., 1989.
Guangling mingsheng tu 廣陵名勝圖 (Illustrations of the famous sights of Guang-
    ling [Yangzhou]). Qianlong court edition, Incomplete copy. Tokyo Municipal
    Library.
Guo Shijing 郭士璟. *Guangling jiuji shi* 廣陵舊跡詩 (Poems on the Old Relics of
    Guangling [Yangzhou]). Preface, 1672. Manuscript copy by Jiao Xun 焦循
    (1763–1820). Beijing Library, Rare Books Room.
Guo Xiangqu 郭湘渠, ed. *Yangzhou lansheng fuchao* 揚州攬勝賦鈔 (Rhapsodies
    on all the sights of Yangzhou). Yinshan tang, 1879.
Guo Zhongheng 郭衷恆, ed. *Jiangnan mingsheng tuyong* 江南名勝圖詠 (Illus-
    trations and poems on the famous sights of Jiangnan). Suzhou: Yuanfen tang,
    1763. Naikaku Bunko.
Guy, R. Kent. *The Emperor's Four Treasuries: Scholars and the State in the Late
    Ch'ien-lung Period*. Cambridge: Harvard University Press, 1987.
Hashimoto Shun 橋本循. "Yōshū ni okeru Ō Gyoyō" 揚州における王漁洋 (Wang
    Shizhen in Yangzhou). *Ritsumeikan Bungaku* 立命館文学 245 (November
    1965): 45–65.

Hay, Jonathan. "The Leisure Zone: Depictions of the Sub-urban Landscapes of Seventeenth-Century Jiangnan." Unpublished paper.

——— "Ming Palace and Tomb in Early Qing Jiangning." *Late Imperial China* 20, no. 1 (June 1999): 1–48.

——— "Shitao's Late Work (1697–1707): A Thematic Map." Ph.D. diss., Yale University, 1989.

——— *Shitao: Painting and Modernity in Early Qing China.* Cambridge: Cambridge University Press, 2001.

He Tang 何鏜. *Mingshan gaisheng ji* 名山概勝記 (Records of all the sights of famous mountains). Late Ming edition. Tōyōbunko, Tokyo Metropolitan Library, Naikaku Bunko.

Hearn, Maxwell K. "The Kangxi Southern Inspection Tour: A Narrative Program by Wang Hui." Ph.D. diss., Princeton University, 1990.

Heijdra, Martinus Johannes. "The Socio-Economic Development of Ming Rural China (1368–1644): An Interpretation." Ph.D. diss., Princeton University, 1994.

Ho Ping-ti. "The Salt Merchants of Yang-chou: A Study of Commercial Capitalism in Eighteenth-Century China." *Harvard Journal of Asiatic Studies* 17 (1954):130–68.

Hobsbawm, Eric, and Ranger, Terence. "Introduction: Inventing Traditions." In Hobsbawm and Ranger, eds., *The Invention of Tradition.* Cambridge: Cambridge University Press, 1984, 1–14.

Honig, Emily. *Creating Chinese Ethnicity: Subei People in Shanghai, 1850–1980.* New Haven: Yale University Press, 1992.

Hsieh, Andrew. "Gu Yanwu, Cao Rong lunjiao shimo—Ming yimin yu Qingchu dali jiaoyou chutan" 顧炎武, 曹溶論交始末—明遺民與清初大吏交友初談 (Ming yimin and the collaborators: The case of Gu Yanwu and Cao Rong). *Journal of Chinese Studies* (Hong Kong) n.s. 4 (1995): 205–22.

Hsu, Ginger Cheng-chi. *A Bushel of Pearls: Painting for Sale in Eighteenth-Century Yangzhou.* Stanford: Stanford University Press, 2001.

——— "Patronage and the Economic Life of the Artist." Ph.D. diss., University of California, Berkeley, 1987.

Hua Kangsen 華康森. *Zizhu luyou shouce: Yangzhou* 自助旅游手冊：揚州 (A self-service travel handbook: Yangzhou). Beijing: Zhongguo luyou chubanshe, 1999.

Huang Bian 黃汴. *Tianxia shuilu lucheng* 天下水陸路程 (A guide to the waterways and roads of the empire). 1570. Reprint, 1635. Reprint, Taiyuan: Shanxi renmin chubanshe, 1992.

Huang Jingjin 黃景近. *Wang Yuyang shilun zhi yanjiu* 王漁洋詩論之研究 (Research on Wang Shizhen's poetry theory). Taipei: Wenshizhe chubanshe, 1980.

Huang Liu-hung. *A Complete Book Concerning Happiness and Benevolence: A Manual for Local Magistrates in Seventeenth Century China.* Trans. Chu Djang. Tucson: University of Arizona Press, 1984.

Huang, Martin. *Literati Self-Re/Presentation: Autobiographical Sensibility in the Eighteenth-Century Chinese Novel.* Stanford: Stanford University Press, 1995.

Huang, Philip C. C. *Civil Justice in China: Representation and Practice in the Qing.* Stanford: Stanford University Press, 1996.

Huang Xiang 黃湘. *Jiangdu xianzhi* 江都縣志 (Jiangdu county gazetteer). 1743. Library of Congress.

Huang Yun 黃雲. *Tongyin lou shi* 桐引樓詩 (Poems from Tongyin Tower). Unpaginated manuscript. Yangzhou Library.

Hucker, Charles O. *A Dictionary of Official Titles in Imperial China.* Stanford: Stanford University Press, 1985.

Hummel, Arthur W. *Eminent Chinese of the Ch'ing Period.* Washington: U. S. Government Printing Office, 1943. Reprint, Taipei: Southern Materials Center, 1991.

Jay, Jennifer W. *A Change in Dynasties.* Bellingham: Western Washington University, Center for East Asian Studies, 1991.

Jiang Yangren 江揚仁, ed. *Yangzhou mingsheng shixuan* 揚州名勝詩選 (A selection of poems on the famous sights of Yangzhou). Nanjing: Jiangsu guji chubanshe, 1990.

Jiang Yin 蔣寅. "Ming-Qing zhi ji zhishifenzi de mingyun yu xuanze—cong Hou Chaozong de bianjie wenti tanqi" 明清之際知識分子的命運與選擇 - 從侯朝宗的變節問題談起 (The fate and choices of intellectuals during the Ming-Qing transition: the problem of Hou Fangyu's apostasy). In *Zhongguo zhishifenzi de renwen jingshen* 中國知識分子的人文精神 (The humanistic spirit of Chinese intellectuals). Henan renmin chubanshe, 1994, 443–56.

———. "Wang Yuyang yu Qingci zhi faren" 王漁洋與清詞之發軔 (Wang Shizhen and the origins of Qing lyric poetry). *Wenxue yichan* 文學遺產 no. 2 (1996): 91–99.

———. "Wang Yuyang yu Qingchu Song shifeng zhi xingti" 王漁洋與清初宋詩風之興替 (Wang Shizhen and the rise and fall of the early-Qing fad for Song poetry). *Wenxue yichan* no. 3 (1999): 82–97.

Jin Zhen 金鎮. *Yangzhou fuzhi* 揚州府志 (Yangzhou Prefectural Gazetteer). 1675. Nanjing Library.

Kafalas, Philip. "Nostalgia and the Reading of the Late Ming Essay: Zhang Dai's *Tao'an Mengyi.*" Ph.D. diss., Stanford University, 1995.

Kahn, Harold L. "A Matter of Taste: The Monumental and Exotic in the Qianlong Reign." In Ju-hsi Chou and Claudia Brown, eds., *The Elegant Brush: Chinese Painting Under the Qianlong Emperor.* Phoenix: Phoenix Art Museum, 1985, 288–302.

Kanda, Kiichirō 神田喜一良. "Shinshi no sōshū ni tsuite" 清詩の総集について (On Qing poetry anthologies). *Shinagaku* 支那學 2, no. 6 (February 1922): 73–76, and 2, no. 8 (April 1922): 71–77. Reprint, Tokyo: Kobundo shobo, 1969, II, 469–73, 631–37.

Kangxi chao qijuzhuce 康熙朝起居注冊 (Court diaries of the Kangxi reign). Beijing: Zhonghua shuju, 1983.

Kessler, Lawrence D. *K'ang-hsi and the Consolidation of Ch'ing Rule.* Chicago: University of Chicago Press. 1976.

Kim, Hongnam. *The Life of a Patron: Zhou Lianggong and the Painters of Seventeenth-Century China.* New York: China Institute in America, 1996.

Kishimoto Mio 岸本美緒. "Min-shin kōtaiki no Kōnan shakai" 明清交替期の江南社会 (Jiangnan society during the Ming-Qing transition). *Rekishi to chiri* 歴史と地理 483 (November 1995): 1–10.

—— *Shindai Chūgoku no bukka to keizai hendō* 清代中国の物価と経済変動 (Prices and economic change in Qing China). Tokyo: Kenbun shuppan, 1997.

Ko, Dorothy. *Teachers of the Inner Chambers: Women and Culture in Seventeenth-Century China.* Stanford: Stanford University Press, 1994.

Kong Shangren 孔尚任. *Huhai ji* 湖海集 (Lakes and seas collection). Shanghai: Gudian wenxue chubanshe, 1957.

—— *Kong Shangren shiwen ji* 孔尚任詩文集 (A collection of Kong Shangren's poetry and prose). Beijing: Zhonghua shuju, 1962.

Kuhn, Philip. *Rebellion and Its Enemies in Late Imperial China, 1796–1864.* Cambridge: Harvard University Press, 1980.

—— *Soulstealers: The Chinese Sorcery Scare of 1768.* Cambridge: Harvard University Press, 1990.

Laing, Ellen Mae Johnston. "Scholars and Sages: A Study in Chinese Figure Painting." Ph.D. diss., University of Michigan, 1967.

Legge, James. *Li Chi: The Book of Rites.* 2 vols. New Hyde Park, N.Y.: University Books, 1967.

Lei Shijun 雷士俊. *Ailing wenchao* 艾陵文鈔. Xinletang cangban, 1677. Nanjing Library.

Lei Yingyuan 雷應元, ed. *Yangzhou fuzhi* 揚州府志 (Yangzhou Prefectural Gazetteer). 1664. *Xijian Zhongguo difangzhi huikan* 稀見中國地方志彙刊 (A collection of rarely seen Chinese local gazetteers), vol. 13. Beijing: Zhongguo shudian, 1992.

Levy, Howard. *A Feast of Mist and Flowers.* Yokohama: n.p., 1966.

Li Dou 李斗. *Yangzhou huafang lu* 揚州畫舫錄 (Record of the painted boats of Yangzhou). Reprint, Yangzhou: Guangling guji keyinshe, 1984.

Li Fusun 李富孫. *Hezheng lu* 鶴徵錄. Yangjia laowu kanben, 1810.

Li Shuhuan 李叔還 ed. *Daojiao dacidian* 道教大辭典 (Dictionary of Daoism). Taipei: Juliu tushu gongsi, 1979.

Li, Wai-yee. *Enchantment and Disenchantment: Love and Illusion in Chinese Literature.* Princeton: Princeton University Press, 1993.

Li Yesi 李鄴嗣. *Gaotang shiwen ji* 杲堂文集. Reprint, Hangzhou: Zhejiang guji chubanshe, 1988.

Liang Qizi 梁其姿 (Angela Leung). "Mingmo Qingchu minjian cishan huodong de xingqi—yi Jiangzhe diqu wei li" 明末清初民間慈善活動的興起—以江浙地區為例 (The rise of philanthropic activities in the late Ming and early Qing—using the Jiangsu and Zhejiang region as an example). *Shihuo yuekan* 食貨月刊 15, no. 7 (1986): 52–79.

Liang Zhangju 梁章鉅. *Langji congtan* 浪跡叢談. *Qingdai shiliao biji congkan* 清代史料筆記叢刊 (A collection of Qing dynasty random jottings for use as historical materials). Beijing: Zhonghua shuju, 1981.

———— *Guitian suoji* 歸田瑣記. *Qingdai shiliao biji congkan.* Beijing: Zhonghua shuju, 1981.

Lin, Lina, ed. *A Special Exhibition of Autumn Landscapes.* Taipei: National Palace Museum, 1989.

Lin Sumen 林蘇門. *Hanjiang sanbaiyin* 邗江三百吟 (Three hundred rhymes of Hanjiang [Yangzhou]). 1808. Reprint, Yangzhou: Guangling guji keyinshe, 1988.

Ling Tingkan 凌庭堪. *Jiaoli tang wenji* 校禮堂文集. Beijing: Zhonghua shuju, 1998.

Linqing 麟慶. *Hongxue yinyuan tuji* 鴻雪因緣圖記 (A pictorial record of my travels and contacts). Reprint, Beijing: Beijing guji chubanshe, 1984.

Liu, James T. C. "Yueh Fei (1103–41) and China's Heritage of Loyalty." *Journal of Asian Studies* 31, no. 2(February 1972): 291–97.

Ma Yueguan 馬曰琯. *Hanjiang yaji* 邗江雅集 (Elegant gatherings of the Hanjiang Poetry Club). Xiaolinglong shanguan, Qianlong period. Yangzhou Library.

———— *Linwu changchou lu* 林屋唱酬錄 (A record of matched rhymes at Linwu Cave). In Yan Yiping 嚴一萍, ed., *Baibu congshu jicheng* 百部叢書集成 (One hundred collectanea gathered together). Shanghai, Yiwen yinshu guan, n.d.

Mann, Susan. *Precious Records: Women in China's Long Eighteenth Century.* Stanford: Stanford University Press, 1997.

Mao Xiang 冒襄. "Nianpu" 年譜 (Chronological biography). In Mao Guangsheng 冒廣生, ed., *Rugao Maoshi congshu* 如皋冒氏叢書 (A collectanea of [works by] the Mao family of Rugao). Rugao: Maoshi kanben, Guangxu era.

Martini, Martino, S.J. "De Bello Tartarico Historia." (History of the Tartar wars), in *Novus Atlas Sinensis.* 1655. Reprint, Trento: Museo Tridentino di Scienze Naturali, 1981.

———— *Novus Atlas Sinensis.* 1655. Reprint, Trento: Museo Tridentino di Scienze Naturali, 1981.

McDermott, Joseph. "The Making of a Chinese Mountain, Huangshan: Politics of Wealth in Chinese Art." *Asian Cultural Studies* 17 (March 1989): 145–76.

Mei Geng 梅庚 et al. *Guangling yonggu shi* 廣陵詠古詩 (Poems invoking the past at Guangling [Yangzhou]). 1696. Nanjing Library.

Meyer-Fong, Tobie. "Making a Place for Meaning in Seventeenth Century Yangzhou." *Late Imperial China* 20, no. 1 (June 1999): 49–84.

Mote, F. W. "A Millennium of Chinese Urban History: Form, Time, and Space Concepts in Soochow." In Robert Kapp, ed., *Four Views of China. Rice University Studies* 59, no. 4 (fall 1973): 35–65.

Naquin, Susan. *Peking: Temples and City Life, 1400–1900.* Berkeley: University of California Press, 2000.

Nienhauser, William, ed. *Indiana Companion to Traditional Chinese Literature.* Bloomington: Indiana University Press, 1986.

Odaira, Keiichi 小平桂一. "Yōshū jidai no Ō Gyoyō—Ō Bōrin no sakuhin o tegakari toshite" 揚州時代の王漁洋—汪懋麟の作品を手がかりとして (Wang Shizhen during his tenure in Yangzhou—with reference to the works of Wang Maolin). *Nihon Chūgoku gakkai ho* 日本中国学会報 38 (1986): 202–16.

———— "Ō Kōmon Bōrin nempu shōkō" 汪蛟門懋麟年譜小稿 (A brief draft chronological biography of Wang Maolin). *Tōhō Gakuhō* 東方学報 59 (March 1987): 359–461.

Okamoto Sae 岡本さえ. "Shindai kinsho" 清代禁書 (Book banning in the Qing). *Tōyō bunka kenkyūjo kiyō* 東洋文化研究所紀要 73 (March 1977): 45–116.

———— "Kenryu kinsho" 乾隆禁書 (Book banning in the Qianlong reign). *Tōyō bunka kenkyūjo kiyō* 東洋文化研究所紀要 115 (March 1991): 1–60.

Ōki Yasushi 大木康. "Kōbotan shikai—Minmatsu Shinsho Kōnan bunjin tenbyō 黄牡丹詩会―明末清初江南文人点描 (The yellow peony poetry party—a sketch of late-Ming and early-Qing Jiangnan literati). *Tōhōgaku* 東方学 99 (January 2000): 33–46.

———— *Minmatsu no hagure chishiki jin: Fū Bōryū to Soshū bunka* 明末のはぐれ知識人―馬夢龍と蘇州文化 (A deviant intellectual of the late Ming: Feng Meng-long and Suzhou culture). Tokyo: Kōdansha, 1995.

———— "Sanjin Chin Keiju to sono shuppan katsudō" 山人陳継儒とその出版活動 (The hermit Chen Jiru and his publishing activities). In *Yamane Yukio kyōju taikyū kinen: Mindai shi ronsō* 山根幸夫教授退休記念: 明代史論叢 (A collection of essays on Ming history in honor of the retirement of Professor Yamane Yu-kio). Tokyo: Kyuko Shoin, 1990, 1230–51.

Ono Kazuko 小野和子. *Fukusha seishi sakuin* 復社姓氏索引 (An index of people in the Restoration Society). Kyoto: Jinbun kagaku kenkyūjo, 1995.

Ouyang Zhaoxiong 歐陽兆熊 and Jin Anqing 金安清. *Shuichuang chunyi* 水窗春囈. 1877. Reprint, *Qingdai shiliao biji congkan*. Beijing: Zhonghua shuju, 1997.

Owen, Stephen. *An Anthology of Chinese Literature*. New York: W. W. Norton, 1996.

———— *The Great Age of Chinese Poetry*. New Haven: Yale University Press, 1981.

———— "Place: Meditation on the Past at Chin-ling." *Harvard Journal of Asiatic Studies* 49, no. 2 (December 1990): 417–57.

———— *Remembrances: The Experience of the Past in Classical Chinese Literature*. Cambridge: Harvard University Press, 1986.

Oxnam, Robert. *Ruling from Horseback: The Politics of the Oboi Regency*. Chicago: University of Chicago Press, 1976.

Pan Gao 潘鎬. *Guangling huaigu sanshi shou fu Pingshan tang zayong sanshi shou* 廣陵懷古三十首附平山堂雜詠三十首 (Thirty poems reflecting on the past at Yangzhou with thirty miscellaneous rhymes on Pingshan Hall). Manuscript edition. Shanghai Library.

Pfister, Louis. *Notices Biographiques et Bibliographiquessur Les Jesuites de L'ancienne Mission de Chine*. San Francisco: Chinese Materials Center, 1976.

Qian Yiji 錢儀吉. *Beizhuan ji* 碑傳集 (A collection of stele biographies). Beijing: Zhonghua shuju, 1993.

Qian Zhonglian 錢仲聯, ed. *Qingshi jishi* 清詩紀事 (Qing poems on events). Nan-jing: Jiangsu guji chubanshe, 1989.

Qin Guan 秦觀. *Huaihai ji* 淮海集. Reprint, Gaoyou Wangshi kanben, 1837.

Qin Ying 秦瀛. *Jiwei cike lu* 己未詞科錄. Shi'en tang ben, 1807.

Ralston, David. "Formal Aspects of Fiction Criticism and Commentary in

China." In David Ralston, ed., *How to Read the Chinese Novel*. Princeton: Princeton University Press, 1990, 42–74.

Rankin, Mary Backus. *Elite Activism and Political Transformation in China: Zhejiang Province, 1865–1911*. Stanford: Stanford University Press, 1986.

Rawski, Evelyn. *The Last Emperors: A Social History of Qing Imperial Institutions*. Berkeley: University of California Press, 1998.

Rowe, William T. *Hankow: Commerce and Society in a Chinese City, 1796–1889*. Stanford: Stanford University Press, 1984.

——— *Hankow: Conflict and Community in a Chinese City, 1796–1885*. Stanford: Stanford University Press, 1989.

——— *Saving the World: Chen Hongmou and Elite Consciousness in Eighteenth-Century China*. Stanford: Stanford University Press, 2001.

Ruan Yuan 阮元. *Guangling shishi* 廣陵詩事 (Poems and events of Guangling [Yangzhou]). *Congshu jicheng* 叢書集成, vol. 7, no. 584, Shanghai: Commercial Press, 1959.

——— *Huaihai yingling ji* 淮海英靈集 (The heroic spirits of the Huaihai region). Ruanshi Xiaolanghuan xian'guan, 1798.

——— *Wenxuanlou shicun* 文選樓詩存 (Poems from the Tower of Literary Selection). Jiaqing edition. Nanjing Library.

——— *Yanjing shi ji* 揅經室集. Reprint, Beijing: Zhonghua shuju, 1993.

——— and Yang Pan 楊蟠. *Zhucha xiaozhi* 竹垞小志 (A small gazetteer of Bamboo Knoll). Qilu shuge keben, 1798. Nanjing Library.

Saeki Tomi 佐伯富. *Shindai ensei no kenkyū* 清代塩製の研究 (Research on the Qing dynasty salt administration). Kyoto: Tōyōshi kenkyūkai, 1956 and 1962.

Schoppa, R. Keith. *Xiang Lake: Nine Centuries of Chinese Life*. New Haven: Yale University Press, 1989.

Shao Yiping 邵毅平. "Cong *Liechao shiji xiaozhuan* kan wan Ming jingshen de ruogan biaoxian" 從列朝詩集小傳看晚明精神的若干表現 (Looking at some manifestations of the late-Ming spirit in the *Liechao shiji xiaozhuan*). In Zhang Peiheng 張培恆, ed., *Mingdai wenxue yanjiu* 明代文學研究 (Research on Ming dynasty literature). Nanchang: Jiangxi renmin chubanshe, 1990, 277–95.

Shen Fu 沈復. "Fusheng liuji" 浮生六記 (Six records of a floating life). *Ming-Qing xiaopin xuankan* 明清小品選刊 (A selection of short works from the Ming and Qing). Changsha: Yueli shushe, 1991, 67–222.

——— *Six Records of a Floating Life*. Trans. Leonard Pratt and Su-hui Chiang. New York: Penguin, 1988.

Shen Meng 慎蒙. *Mingshan zhusheng yilan* 名山諸勝一覽 (All the sights of famous mountains at a glance). Wu Yushen shi, 1576. Tōyōbunko.

Sheng Yi 盛儀. *Jiajing Weiyang zhi* 嘉靖維揚志 (Gazetteer of the Weiyang region from the Jiajing reign). 1542. Manuscript edition. Microfilm, Library of Congress.

Shi Runzhang 施閏章. *Shi Yushan ji* 施愚山集. In *Anhui guji congshu* 安徽古籍叢書. Hefei: Huangshan shushe, 1992.

Smith, Henry D., II. *Hiroshige: One Hundred Famous Views of Edo*. New York: George Braziller, 1986.

Smith, Joanna Handlin. "Social Hierarchy and Merchant Philanthropy as Perceived in Several Late-Ming and Early Qing Texts." *Journal of the Economic and Social History of the Orient* 41, no. 3 (1998): 417–51.

Spence, Jonathan D. *Emperor of China: Self Portrait of K'ang-hsi.* New York: Vintage Books, 1974.

——— *Ts'ao Yin and the K'ang-hsi Emperor, Bondservant and Master.* New Haven: Yale University Press, 1966.

Strassberg, Richard E. *The World of K'ung Shang-jen: A Man of Letters in Early Ch'ing China.* New York: Columbia University Press, 1983.

Struve, Lynn A. "History and *The Peach Blossom Fan.*" *CLEAR* 2, no. 1 (January 1980): 55–72.

——— "The Hsu Brothers and Semiofficial Patronage of Scholars in the K'ang-hsi Period." *Harvard Journal of Asiatic Studies* 42 (1982): 231–66.

——— *The Southern Ming, 1644–1662.* New Haven: Yale University Press, 1984.

——— *Voices from the Ming-Qing Cataclysm.* New Haven: Yale University Press, 1993.

Sun Jinli 孫金礪, ed. "Guangling changhe ci" 廣陵唱和詞 (Matched rhyme lyrics of Guangling [Yangzhou]). In Sun Mo 孫默, ed., *Guochao mingjia shiyu* 國朝名家詩餘 (Lyrics by famous men of our dynasty). Xiuning Sunshi Liusong ge, Kangxi period. Nanjing Library.

——— "Hongqiao changhe diyi ji" 紅橋唱和第一集 (First collection of matched rhyme lyrics at Red Bridge). Sun Mo, ed., *Guochao mingjia shiyu.* Xiuning Sunshi Liusong ge, Kangxi period. Nanjing Library.

Sun Mo 孫默. *Shiwujia ci* 十五家詞 (Lyrics by fifteen poets). *Sibubeiyao jibu.* Shanghai: Zhonghua shuju, 1927–36.

Sun Zhiwei 孫枝蔚. *Gaitang ji* 溉堂集. Kangxi edition. Reprint, Shanghai: Shanghai guji chubanshe, 1979.

Suzuki Tadashi 鈴木正. "Shinsho ryōwai enshō ni kansuru ichikōsatsu" 清初兩淮塩商に関する一考察 (An inquiry into the Lianghuai salt administration in the early Qing). *Shien* 史苑 36 (March 1946): 101–34.

Tan Qian 談遷. *Beiyou lu* 北游錄 (Journey to the north). Reprint, *Qingdai shiliao biji congkan.* Beijing: Zhonghua shuju, 1997.

Twitchett, Denis. "Problems of Chinese Biography." In Arthur Wright, ed. *Confucian Personalities.* Stanford: Stanford University Press, 1962, 24–39.

Vinograd, Richard. *Boundaries of the Self: Chinese Portraits, 1600–1900.* Cambridge: Cambridge University Press, 1992.

Wakeman, Frederic, Jr. *The Great Enterprise: The Manchu Reconstruction of Imperial Order in Seventeenth-Century China.* Berkeley: University of California Press, 1985.

——— "Localism and Loyalism During the Ch'ing Conquest of Kiangnan: The Tragedy of Chiang-yin." In Frederic Wakeman and Carolyn Grant, eds., *Conflict and Control in Late Imperial China.* Berkeley: University of California Press, 1975, 43–86.

——— "Romantics, Stoics, and Martyrs." *Journal of Asian Studies* 43, no. 4 (August 1984): 631–65.

Wang Chung-min, *A Descriptive Catalogue of Rare Chinese Books in the Library of Congress*. Washington, D.C.: Library of Congress, 1957.

Wang Ji 汪輯. *Huizhai ji qizhong* 悔齋集七種 (Seven collections from the Studio of Regrets). Kangxi edition. Shanghai Library.

Wang Jun 汪鋆. "Yangzhou huayuan lu" 揚州畫苑錄 (A record of the painters of Yangzhou). In Chen Henghe, comp. *Yangzhou congke*. 1930–34. Reprint, Yangzhou: Guangling guji keyinshe, 1995.

Wang, Liping. "Tourism and Spatial Change in Hangzhou, 1911–1927." In Joseph Esherick, ed., *Remaking the Chinese City: Modernity and National Identity, 1900–1950*. Honolulu: University of Hawaii Press, 2000, 107–20.

Wang Maolin 汪懋麟. *Baichi wutongge ji* 百尺梧桐閣集 (The Hundred-foot Wutong Tree Pavilion collection). Kangxi edition. Reprint, Shanghai: Shanghai guji chubanshe, 1980.

——— *Baichi wutong ge yigao* 百尺梧桐閣遺稿 (Surviving works from the Hundred-foot Wutong Tree Pavilion). Kangxi edition. Reprint, Shanghai: Shanghai guji chubanshe, 1980.

Wang Shizhen 王士禎. *Chibei outan* 池北偶談 (Incidental conversations north of the pond). *Qingdai shiliao biji congkan*. Beijing: Zhonghua shuju, 1997.

——— *Wang Shizhen nianpu fu Wang Shilu nianpu* 王士禎年譜附王士祿年譜 (A chronological biography of Wang Shizhen with a chronological biography of Wang Shilu). Beijing: Zhonghua shuju, 1992.

——— *Xiangzu biji* 香祖筆記 (Orchid notes). Shanghai: Shanghai guji chubanshe, 1982.

——— *Yuyang shanren jinghua lu* 漁洋山人精華錄 (Masterpieces by Yuyang the Hermit). Ed. Lin Ji 林佶. Houguan Lin Ji xiekeben. Library of Congress.

——— *Yuyang shanren jinghua lu jishi* 漁洋山人精華錄集釋 (Masterpieces by Yuyang the Hermit compiled and explained). Ed. Li Yufu 李毓夫 et al. Shanghai: Shanghai guji chubanshe, 1999.

——— *Yuyang shanren jinghua lu xunzuan* 漁洋山人精華錄訓纂 (Masterpieces by Yuyang the Hermit explained and compiled). Hongdou zhai. Library of Congress.

Wang Shunu 王書奴. *Zhongguo changji shi* 中國娼妓史 (A history of Chinese prostitutes). 1934. Reprint, *Minguo congshu* 民國叢書 (Collectanea of works from the Republican period). Shanghai: Shanghai shudian, 1992.

Wang Tongling 王桐齡. *Jiangzhe luxing ji* 江浙旅行記 (A record of travels in Jiangsu and Zhejiang). Cixiang congkan 慈祥叢刊. Republican period (c. 1925). Tōyōbunko.

Wang Xiuchu 王秀楚. "Yangzhou shiri ji, Hanying duizhao" 揚州十日記, 漢英對照 (A record of ten days at Yangzhou, Chinese-English bilingual edition). Trans. Lucien Mao. In Lin Yutang 林語堂, ed., *Xifengcongshu* 西風叢書. Shanghai: Xifengshe, 1930.

——— "A Memoir of the Ten Days' Massacre at Yangchow." Trans. Lucien Mao. *Tien-hsia Monthly* 4, no. 5 (May 1937): 515–37.

——— "Journal d'un bourgeouis de Yang-tcheou (1645)." Trans. P. Aucourt. *Bulletin de l'Ecole Francaise d'Extreme Orient* 7 (1907): 297–312.

Wang Yinggeng 汪應庚. *Pingshan lansheng zhi* 平山攬勝志 (A gazetteer of all the sights at Pingshan Hall). Preface, 1742. Reprint, Yangzhou: Guangling guji ke-yinshe, 1988.

Wang Zhangtao 王章濤. *Ruan Yuan zhuan* 阮元傳 (Biography of Ruan Yuan). Hefei: Huangshan shushe, 1994.

Wang Zhenzhong 王振忠. "Ming-Qing Huishang yu Yangzhou chengshi wenhua de tezheng he diwei" 明清徽商與揚州城市文化的特徵和地位 (The Lianghuai salt merchants of the Ming-Qing period and the special characteristics and status of Yangzhou urban culture). In Feng Erkang 馮爾康, ed., *Yangzhou yanjiu—Jiangdu Chen Yiqun xiansheng bailing mingdan jinian lunwenji* 揚州研究—江都陳軼群先生百齡冥誕紀念論文集. Taipei: Chen Jie Xiansheng chuban, 1996, 489–509.

——— "Ming Qing Lianghuai yanshang yu Yangzhou chengshi de diyu jiegou" 明清兩淮鹽商與揚州城市的地域結構 (Lianghuai salt merchants and the re-gional structure of Yangzhou city during the Ming and Qing). *Lishi dili* 歷史地理 10 (1992): 102–16.

——— "Ming Qing Yangzhou yanshang shequ wenhua ji qi yingxiang" 明清揚州鹽商社區文化及其影響 (The culture and influence of the Yangzhou salt mer-chants' district during the Ming and Qing). *Zhongguo shi yanjiu* 中國史研究 2 (May, 1992): 104–16.

Wang Zhuo 王晫. *Jin shishuo* 今世説 (Tales of the world for today). In Zhou Junfu 周駿富. *Qingdai zhuanji congkan* 清代傳記叢刊 (A collectanea of Qing biog-raphies). Taipei: Mingwen shuju, 1985.

——— and Zhang Chao 張潮, eds. *Tanji congshu* 檀几叢書 (The sandalwood bench collection). Reprint, Shanghai: Shanghai guji chubanshe, 1992.

Wei Minghua 韋明鏵. *Yangzhou wenhua tanpian* 揚州文化談片 (Conversational essays on Yangzhou culture). Beijing, Sanlian shudian, 1994.

Wei Xian 魏憲. *Huang Qing bai mingjia shixuan* 皇清百名家詩選 (A selection of poems by one hundred famous writers of the imperial Qing). Fuqing: Weishi Zhenjiang tang kanben, Kangxi period.

Weidner, Marsha, et al. *Views from Jade Terrace: Chinese Women Artists 1300–1912*. Indianapolis: Indianapolis Museum of Art, 1988.

Widmer, Ellen. "The Huanduzhai of Hangzhou and Suzhou: A Study in Seventeenth-Century Publishing." *Harvard Journal of Asiatic Studies* 56, no. 1 (June 1996): 77–122.

Wilhelm, Hellmut. "From Myth to Myth: The Case of Yueh Fei's Biography." In Denis Twitchett and Arthur F. Wright, eds., *Confucian Personalities*. Stanford: Stanford University Press, 1962, 146–61.

——— "The Po-hsueh Hung-ju Examination of 1679." *Journal of the American Oriental Society* 71, no. 1 (March 1951): 60–66.

Wu Ezhi 吳鶚峙. *Ganquan xianzhi* 甘泉縣志 (Ganquan county gazetteer). 1743. Library of Congress.

Wu Han 吳含. *Jiang-zhe cangshujia shilue* 江浙藏書家史略 (A brief history of book collectors in Jiangsu and Zhejiang). Beijing: Zhonghua shuju, 1981.

Wu Qi 吳綺. *Linhui tang quanji* 林蕙堂全集 (Complete works of Wu Qi). 1700. Library of Congress.

——— "Yangzhou guchui ci" 揚州鼓吹詞 (Prefaces to drum and flute lyrics of

Yangzhou). In Chen Henghe, comp., *Yangzhou congke*. 1930–34. Reprint, Yangzhou: Guangling guji keyinshe, 1995.

Wu Qiushi 吳秋士. *Tianxia mingshan jichao* 天下名山記鈔 (Essays on the famous mountains of the realm). Baohan lou, Kangxi period. Tōyōbunko.

Wu, Silas. *Passage to Power: K'ang-hsi and His Heir Apparent*. Cambridge: Harvard University Press, 1979.

Xiao Tong. *Wenxuan, or Selections of Refined Literature*. Vol. 1, Metropolises and Capitals. Trans. David R. Knechtges. Princeton: Princeton University Press, 1982.

Xie Kaichong 謝閣寵. *Lianghuai yanfa zhi* 兩淮鹽法志 (Gazetteer of the Lianghuai salt administration). Kangxi edition. Reprint, Wu Xiangxiang 吳相湘. *Zhongguo shixue congshu* 中國史學叢書. Taipei: Xuesheng shuju, 1966.

Xie Zhengguang 謝正光 (Andrew Hsieh) and She Rufeng 佘汝豐, eds. *Qingchu ren xuan Qingchu shi huikao* 清初人選清初詩彙考 (Early Qing poets select early Qing poetry). Nanjing: Nanjing University Press, 1998.

Xu Mingde, "The Outstanding Contribution of the Italian Sinologist Martino Martini to Cultural Exchange between China and the West." In Franco Demarchi and Riccardo Scartezzini, eds., *Martino Martini: A Humanist and Scientist in Seventeenth Century China*. Proceedings of the International Symposium on Martino Martini and Cultural Exchanges Between China and the West. Trento: University of Trento, 1996, 23–39.

Xu Weiping 許衛平. *Yangzhou difangzhi yanjiu* 揚州地方志研究 (Research on Yangzhou gazetteers). Hefei: Huangshan shushe, 1993.

Xu Yinong. *The Chinese City in Space and Time: The Development of Urban Form in Suzhou*. Honolulu: University of Hawaii Press, 2000.

Xu Zhongling 許忠陵. "Luedu Yu Zhiding de huaxiang" 略讀禹之鼎的畫像 (A brief reading of Yu Zhiding's portraits). *Gugong bowuyuan yuankan* 故宮博物院院刊 (Beijing) 25, no. 3 (1984): 46–49.

Yang Bin 楊賓, ed. *Chidu xinbian jiaji, yiji, bingji, dingji, waiji* 尺牘新編甲集, 乙集, 丙集, 丁集, 外集 (A new edition of letters, collections 1–5). Qing manuscript, Beijing Library microfilm.

Yang Jialuo 楊家駱, ed. *Sanshisanzhong Qingdai zhuanji zonghe yinde* 三十三種清代傳記綜合引得 (Index to thirty-three Qing dynasty biographies). Reprint: Taipei: Dingwen shuju, 1973.

Yang Xun 楊洵, ed. *Yangzhou fuzhi* 揚州府志 (Yangzhou prefectural gazetteer). 1605. Microfilm, Library of Congress.

Yang Zeyou 揚則友. *Yangzhou youlan zhinan* 揚州遊覽指南 (A guide to touring Yangzhou). Yangzhou: Yangzhou zhi cheng yinshuguan, 1916.

Yao Jinyuan 姚覲元. *Qingdai jinhui shumu* 清代禁燬書目 (A list of books banned during the Qing) and *Qingdai jinshu zhijian lu* 清代禁書知見錄. Shanghai: Commercial Press, 1957.

Yin Huiyi 尹會一, ed. *Yangzhou fuzhi* 揚州府志 (Yangzhou prefectural gazetteer). 1733. Library of Congress.

Yingjie 英傑, ed. *Xu Yangzhou fuzhi* 續揚州府志 (Yangzhou prefectural gazetteer, continued). 1874. Library of Congress.

Yongrong 永瑢, ed. *Siku quanshu zongmu tiyao* 四庫全書總目提要 (An annotated full list of the complete library of the four treasuries). Taipei: Shangwu yinshu guan, 1978.

Yu Jianhua 俞劍華. *Zhongguo meishujia renming cidian* 中國美術家人名辭典 (A biographical dictionary of Chinese artists). Shanghai: Shanghai renmin meishu chubanshe, 1981.

Yu Huai 余懷. Banqiao zaji 板橋雜記 (Miscellaneous essays on the Nanjing pleasure quarters). Reprint, Nanjing: Jiangsu wenyi chubanshe, 1987.

Yu, Pauline. "Song Lyrics and the Canon: A Look at Anthologies of Tz'u." In Pauline Yu, ed., *Voices of the Song Lyric in China*. Berkeley: University of California Press, 1994, 70–103.

Yuan Hung-tao. *Pilgrim of the Clouds: Poems and Essays from Ming China.* Trans. Jonathan Chaves. New York: Weatherhill, 1978.

Yudi Yuanming 余棣元明. "Yangzhou cheng de lishibianqian—Zhongguo gucheng bolan suoying" 揚州城的歷史變遷—中國古城博覽縮影 (Historical changes in the Yangzhou city wall—a concise overview of an ancient Chinese city wall). In Feng Erkang, ed., *Yangzhou yanjiu—Jiangdu Chen Yiqun xiansheng bailing mingdan jinian lunwen ji.* Taipei: Chen Jie Xiansheng chuban, 1996, 105–38.

Zang Lihe 臧勵龢. *Zhongguo gujin diming dacidian* 古今地名大辭典 (Dictionary of Chinese place names past and present). 1931. Reprint, Shanghai: Commercial Press, 1982.

——— *Zhongguo renming dacidian* 中國人名大辭典 (Dictionary of Chinese biographies). 1921. Reprint, Shanghai: Shanghai shudian, 1980.

Zeitlin, Judith. *Historian of the Strange: Pu Songling and the Chinese Classical Tale.* Stanford: Stanford University Press, 1993.

——— "Ruined Verses: Writings on Walls and Anxieties of Loss in Late Imperial China." Unpublished paper presented at the Symposium on Ruins in Chinese Visual Culture, University of Chicago, May 17, 1998.

Zhang Chao 張潮. *Yousheng ji* 友聲集 (Friends' voices collection). Kangxi edition. Beijing Library, Beihai Branch.

——— *Yuchu xinzhi* 虞初新志. Reprint, Beijing: Wenxue guji kanxing she, 1954.

Zhang Huijian 張慧劍, ed. *Ming Qing Jiangsu wenren nianbiao* 明清江蘇文人年表 (A chronological table of Jiangsu literati during the Ming and Qing). Shanghai: Shanghai guji chubanshe, 1986.

Zhang Jian 張鑑, et al., eds. *Ruan Yuan nianpu* 阮元年譜 (original title: *Leitang'anzhu dizi ji* 雷塘庵主弟子記). Nianpu congkan 年譜叢刊. Beijing: Zhonghua shuju, 1995.

Zhang Shicheng 張石承 and Xia Yunbi 夏雲璧, eds. *Yangzhou shici* 揚州詩詞 (Poems and lyrics of Yangzhou). Shanghai: Shanghai guji chubanshe, 1985.

Zhang Wanshou 張萬壽, ed. *Yangzhou fuzhi* 揚州府志 (Yangzhou prefectural gazetteer). 1685. Library of Congress.

Zhao Ersun 趙爾巽, ed. *Qingshi gao* 清史稿 (Draft history of the Qing). Beijing: Lianhe shudian, 1942.

Zhao Ming 趙明, ed. *Yangzhou daguan* 揚州大觀 (An overview of Yangzhou). Hefei: Huangshan shushe, 1993.

Zhao Zhibi 趙之壁. *Pingshan tang tuzhi* 平山堂圖志 (Illustrated gazetteer of

Pingshan Hall). 1765. Edo, 1843. Reprint, Kyoto: Dōhōsha shuppansha, 1981.

Zheng Qingyou 鄭慶祐. *Yangzhou Xiuyuan zhi* 揚州休園志 (Gazetteer of Xiu Garden, Yangzhou). Chashi tang. Author's preface, 1773. Tōyōbunko.

Zheng Zu'an 鄭祖恩. "Xu Xiake luxing yanjiu erti" 徐霞客旅行研究二題 (Two themes from research on Xu Xiake's travels). *Shilin* 史林 28, no. 4 (1992): 9–14, 25.

Zhou Sheng 周生. "Yangzhou meng" 揚州夢 (Yangzhou dream). Zhu Jianmang 朱劍芒, ed. *Meihua wenxue mingzhu congkan* 美化文學名著叢刊. Shanghai: Shijie shuju, 1982.

Zhu Jiang 朱江. *Yangzhou yuanlin pinshang lu* 揚州園林品賞錄 (A record of evaluating and appreciating Yangzhou gardens). Shanghai: Shanghai wenhua chubanshe, 1990.

Zhu Maowei 朱懋偉. "Yangzhou lishi renwen zongji" 揚州歷史人文蹤跡 (Historical and biographical traces in Yangzhou). Feng Erkang, ed. *Yangzhou yanjiu— Jiangdu Chen Yiqun xiansheng bailing mingdan jinian lunwenji.* Taipei: Chen Jie xiansheng chuban, 1996, 389–418.

Zhu Mu 朱穆. *Songben Fangyu shenglan* 宋本方域勝覽 (A Song edition of the topography book for visiting spots of scenic beauty). Reprint, Shanghai: Shanghai guji chubanshe, 1991.

Zhu Zongzhou 朱宗宙. "Hanmo shengxiang de Yangzhou wenren yaji" 翰墨生香的揚州文人雅集 (Elegant literati gatherings in Yangzhou). *Yangzhou shizhi* 揚州史志 32, no. 4 (1994): 87–88.

——— "Wang Shizhen yu Yangzhou" 王士禎與揚州 (Wang Shizhen and Yangzhou). *Zhongguo mingcheng* 中國名城 32. (March 1995): 48–50.

Zong Yuanding 宗元鼎. *Xinliu tang wenji* 新柳堂文集 (Prose works from New Willow Studio). Preface, 1680. Nanjing Library.

Index